Education and the Commercial Mindset

Education and the Commercial Mindset

SAMUEL E. ABRAMS

Harvard University Press

Cambridge, Massachusetts, and London, England ■ 2016

First printing

Library of Congress Cataloging-in-Publication Data

Names: Abrams, Samuel E., 1964– author.
Title: Education and the commercial mindset / Samuel E. Abrams.
Description: Cambridge, Massachusetts : Harvard University Press, 2016. |
    Includes bibliographical references and index.
Identifiers: LCCN 2015042042 | ISBN 9780674049178 (hardcover : alk. paper)
Subjects: LCSH: Privatization in education. | Education and state. | School management
    and organization. | Educational accountability. | School improvement programs.
Classification: LCC LB2806.36 .A36 2016 | DDC 379.1—dc23
LC record available at http://lccn.loc.gov/2015042042

To the memory of

Dorothy Bach (1921–2009)

and

Walter Clarkson (1932–2005),

model teachers

CONTENTS

Est modus in rebus.

[There is a middle ground for all things.]

Horace, *Satires,* I.i.106 (ca. 35 B.C.)

PROLOGUE

The market needs a place, and the market needs to be kept in place.

Arthur M. Okun, *Equality and Efficiency: The Big Tradeoff* (1975)

■ AT THE END of a long day in May 2001, I sat at my desk facing a wall in the far corner of Room 205 at the Beacon School, a public high school on Manhattan's West Side, slowly working my way through a pile of American history papers, nodding at sharp observations, shaking my head at muddy paragraphs, jotting comments in the margins, occasionally looking to my left out the window at the trees in a neighboring housing project taking in the setting sun.

Staying late had been my habit since I started teaching in 1989. My commute home was always easier, I found, with a set of papers graded and the next day carefully planned. Moreover, there was something sublime about an empty classroom, swept, straightened out, and silent, perfect for reflection and concentration.

Steve Stoll, the school's codirector, knocked on my open door and walked in. Stoll also stayed late and often stopped by to ask how my classes were going or to discuss an article in the *Economist* or the *New Yorker* that he was sure I too had read. But the purpose of his visit this time was clearly different. He looked burdened, took a seat, and explained that he had learned a few hours earlier that the school's programmer, a colleague in the history department named Brian Alm, would be leaving for a position as an assistant principal at a high school in Rockland County.

I knew this meant trouble. The programmer is the person responsible for constructing the master schedule, figuring out who teaches and takes what courses, when, and where, and then defending those decisions at the beginning of each semester against complaints from teachers, students, and parents alike. At Beacon, as at many urban public schools across the country, a fixed number of classrooms for a growing number of students heightened this challenge. Furthermore, enrollment could unpredictably spike in September. Before the application process in New York was overhauled in 2004, all high schools—except a small number of selective schools granted the right to admit students by scores on a citywide exam or other specific criteria—had to program everyone sent at the beginning of the academic year by the Board of Education from its pool of several thousand unassigned students.[1] Under such pressure and amid such turmoil, Alm was a study in composure. He was also the school's third programmer in as many years to leave the position and the only one to succeed in streamlining a complicated process.

Playing up my affection for detail and order as well as my interest in educational policy, Stoll suggested that I take over. "Plus," he said, "you'll teach two classes instead of four and you can decide which classes."

"But I don't know anything about computers," I said.

"You'll learn," Stoll replied with the authority of someone who had taught in the New York City school system for twenty-four years, cofounded Beacon in 1993, and codirected the school since then through funding crises, staffing imbroglios, and curriculum battles.

After a few days of mulling, I agreed to take the job and thus began a journey that forced me to grapple anew with questions at the heart of the educational debate about bureaucracy, teacher tenure, standardized testing, privatization, and accountability. The classroom provided one crucial vantage point, the programming office another. The two together form the foundation for this study of the expanding role of commercial firms and concepts in school management.

■

The first thing I learned in my new position as Beacon's programmer was that I indeed knew nothing about computers. The second was that knowing nothing about computers didn't mean I didn't know enough about basic organizational procedure to realize that the computer system used by the Board of Education for scheduling, report cards, and transcripts was archaic. Worse, I learned that there was little if any assistance available from the department at the City University of New York that managed this obsolete system for the Board of Education. Telephone calls for help to this department, the University Application Processing Center, or UAPC to everyone who did programming, typically went unanswered. In the rare event I reached someone, I got hit with a torrent of mysterious acronyms and codes.

Fortunately, at Beacon we didn't depend entirely on UAPC for our scheduling needs. Alm had rigged Microsoft Access, a database management system, to enroll students, list courses, and create rosters. With the help of the school's technology coordinator, Chris Lehmann, a talented coder who knew his way around the city's complex school system, Alm had also devised a way to export all this information to someone at UAPC. Over the summer, I learned enough about Microsoft Access to allay my fears that I had made a mistake in taking on this role.

It was nevertheless obvious after a tense September of programming more than sixty students sent by the Board of Education from its pool of unassigned newcomers and of reprogramming countless students who had petitioned to add or drop courses that Microsoft Access was a Band-Aid, not a solution. A bumpy transition into the second semester confirmed this conclusion. It was also obvious that UAPC, barely updated since its development in the early 1970s, though costing the Board of Education $5 million to $6 million a year, stood to remain nothing more than an expensive citywide data warehouse that scheduled students according to a rigid algorithm and generated cryptic report cards and transcripts, the latter of which provoked regular phone calls to the school's guidance counselor from puzzled college admissions officers.[2]

For regulatory reasons, we couldn't do anything about report cards and transcripts. Those had to come from the Board of Education, which would be renamed the Department of Education in 2002 under Mayor Michael Bloomberg. But we had some autonomy with respect to scheduling. And going forward, it was clear we would need conventional academic scheduling software. The enrollment at Beacon had climbed to 917 by October 2001, up from 783 the preceding spring.[3] In addition, the school's many electives—ranging from art, drama, computer programming, creative writing, and dance to photography, digital film, computer animation, and music theory—called for an intricate schedule meshing such minor courses meeting two days a week with academic courses meeting four.

With Microsoft Access, we had to manually place students in specific course sections and toggle between several windows of information before reprogramming a student. With conventional academic scheduling software, we could let the computer sort students into sections according to their course preferences (and repeat this process over and over until we had a balanced program); we could also view a variety of data on one screen that made programming and reprogramming students something akin to playing a video game, albeit a monotonous one.

The industry standard for academic scheduling software at that time was SASI, an acronym for Schools Administrative Student Information. But SASI, a product of education giant Pearson School Systems, cost about $10,000 and involved an annual user fee. I knew Beacon didn't have that kind of money and in February 2002 sought advice from a friend who was the technology coordinator at a private school in Potomac, Maryland. I suspected that this friend, Geoff Wagg, would have an answer. He did: PCR Educator, a small company in neighboring Bethesda that produced and serviced scheduling software for private schools, including Wagg's school.

Wagg put me in touch with PCR Educator's founder, president, and chief engineer, Tom deBettencourt, who took the train up to New York four days after a phone call to do a two-hour demo. It was precisely what we needed. And the price was right: $3,000 for the package, negotiated down from the standard cost of $5,000, plus an annual service charge of $800. Stoll consulted Ruth Lacey, his partner in codirecting as well as cofounding the school. Equally tired of the stress and confusion that marred the beginning of each semester, Lacey agreed that $3,800 was a wise investment. Stoll wrote a check and thus put the school on the path to a smoother future.

■

Over the ensuing weeks, I devoted my after-school hours to mastering PCR Educator and intermittently began to wonder if the advocates of educational privatization weren't after all right. The system suffered, as many had long argued, from glaring inefficiencies. With the assistance of the Economic Development Council in the 1970s, the Board of Education made some headway in improving payroll, inventory, storage, construction, and auditing protocols, but cumbersome methods and procedures persisted.[4] Hiring and purchasing also remained convoluted.[5] And with UAPC, New York was spending millions on a data management system that was outdated two decades ago. Meanwhile, an outside provider like PCR Educator sold a state-of-the-art product for a fraction of the cost. Moreover, PCR Educator's annual service charge yielded patient assistance over the phone from 8 a.m. to 7 p.m. and later if you needed to reach deBettencourt at home, as I did several times with questions about such technical matters as coding course preferences for students, segmenting the loading process of student choices by particular cohorts, and creating what-if scenarios to test the feasibility of different master schedules.

As the school's programmer, I was also forced to wrestle with the pervasive contention among critics of tenure that underperforming teachers are overprotected. The complaints from students who wanted to switch out of classes led by particular teachers were too numerous and consistent to be unreliable. Yet I knew the problem was not as simple as many critics had contended. Setting aside that some teachers were unpopular because they were demanding, not because they were incompetent, it was and remains clear that teachers need the protection of due process from capricious administrators, and schools need a secure, stable workforce to evolve as solid, healthy institutions. In addition, the daily grind of teaching as many as five classes with up to thirty-four students in each class can cause even the hardiest veteran a bad year or two, especially in a system with plenty of troubled students and without much support for struggling teachers. Such qualifications, however, don't suffice for the parent of a student who isn't being challenged, the taxpayer who reads in the newspaper about the mountain of documentation necessary for a principal to commence termination proceedings, or the teacher whose classes grow with transfers from classes taught by a floundering colleague.[6]

As a teacher of economics as well as history, I knew that Friedrich von Hayek, Milton Friedman, George Stigler, and their disciples at the University of Chicago and elsewhere had been arguing for decades that private markets, unrestrained by organized labor, would provide better service than government agencies in nearly every domain, from mass transit, road maintenance, postal delivery, waste collection, utilities, and air traffic control to law enforcement, corrections, pension funding, health care, and education.[7]

The call for privatizing education, I came to learn from a course on the subject I was taking one afternoon a week at the time—taught by Henry Levin at Teachers College, Columbia University—may be dated back to 1955, when Friedman made his initial case for vouchers to amplify school choice. Friedman stipulated that vouchers be accepted at schools run as businesses as well as at conventional schools. "Governments could require a minimum level of schooling financed by giving parents vouchers redeemable for a specified maximum sum per child per year if spent on 'approved' educational services," Friedman wrote in an essay entitled "The Role of Government in Education." "Parents would then be free to spend this sum and any additional sum they themselves provided on purchasing educational services from an 'approved' institution of their own choice. The educational services could be rendered by private enterprises operated for profit, or by non-profit institutions. The role of government would be limited to assuring that the schools met certain minimum standards such as the inclusion of minimum common content in their programs, much as it now inspects restaurants to assure that they maintain minimum sanitary standards."[8]

To Levin, Friedman's proposal stood at once to undermine social cohesion and sidestep the challenges handicapping the underprivileged students vouchers were primarily intended to help. Levin had cautioned in an article in the *Urban Review* in 1968 that the competition generated by vouchers between schools for students could have a splintering rather than a catalytic effect and urged infrastructural reforms instead to coordinate schools with an array of support services, from health care to recreation.[9]

While Friedman's proposal for vouchers failed to gain traction, it repeatedly took the diluted form of legislation on Capitol Hill for tuition tax credits for parents of children in private elementary and secondary schools. Such legislation passed in the Senate in 1969, 1970, 1971, 1976, 1977, 1978, 1982, 1983, and 1984 yet died each time in the House of Representatives.[10] On the heels of such failure, a bipartisan commission appointed by President Ronald

Reagan to study how privatization could lead to "more effective government" issued a report in 1988 recommending federal support of a school choice system that included private schools, with the exception of religiously affiliated schools.[11]

Friedman's endorsement of competition from for-profit institutions was not advanced in that report, but it was echoed in two books at that time by Myron Lieberman: *Beyond Public Education,* published in 1986, and *Privatization and Educational Choice,* published in 1989. In the latter, Lieberman wrote: "The only ways to improve American education are to (1) foster private schools that compete with public schools and among themselves and/or (2) foster for-profit competition among service providers within the public school system. . . . There is no public policy reason why school districts that can contract with ServiceMaster for custodial and maintenance services, or ARA for food services, or Burns International for security services, or ETS for testing services, or for dozens of other non-instructional services should not have the same right to contract for instructional services."[12]

Paul Hill, Lawrence Pierce, and James Guthrie fleshed out this argument in 1997 in their book *Reinventing Public Education: How Contracting Can Transform America's Schools.* Beyond hiring companies like Sylvan Learning Systems for remedial intervention or Dialogos International for foreign-language instruction, they wrote, municipalities and townships should outsource school management.[13] The National Center on Education and the Economy echoed this recommendation in 2007 in a widely publicized report entitled *Tough Choices or Tough Times.*[14]

In the early 1970s, more than 150 school districts had, in fact, negotiated performance contracts with private firms to provide instructional services in math and reading. Lieberman, among other scholars, wrote in detail about this brief chapter in American educational history.[15] If students exhibited gains on exams, the firms retained their contracts and received bonuses; if not, the firms would owe school districts a refund.[16] Yet discouraging results brought a swift end to performance contracting. In Lieberman's opinion, contractors should have been permitted more latitude and time.[17]

The new approach first suffered a black eye in 1970 with news that an Oklahoma-based company called Dorsett Educational Systems had allowed students in its remediation program at a school in Texarkana, Arkansas, to preview exam questions.[18] Dorsett, it was discovered, wasn't merely teaching to the test. The company was teaching the test itself—on the grounds that it had been assigned, according to a company administrator, too many low-functioning students.[19] Soon after, the Office of Economic Opportunity (OEO), run at the time by Donald Rumsfeld, concluded that a $5.6 million one-year experiment in performance contracting exhibited no benefits. The OEO initiative involved six randomly selected companies providing supplementary instruction in reading and math to 13,000 disadvantaged children in eighteen school districts across the country.[20] In a program assessment published in 1972, the OEO found that children in schools receiving additional instruction from performance contractors did no better than children in ordinary schools.[21]

The one company in the country that had a performance contract to run every aspect of a school also failed to deliver. Behavioral Research Laboratories (BRL) of Palo Alto, California, saw a three-year contract negotiated in 1970 to manage an elementary school in Gary, Indiana, terminated a year early because of low scores in both reading and math as well as declining attendance.[22] The harsh response to BRL from teachers and community leaders didn't help. BRL's prepackaged curriculum and emphasis on drill and practice alienated teachers who valued autonomy. And BRL's very management of a school angered citizens who prized local involvement in developing educational policy.[23]

Despite BRL's ominous lessons, twenty years later, Educational Alternatives Inc. (EAI) ventured into the field of for-profit management of public schools. EAI, based in Minneapolis, provided curriculum guidance and professional development to one school in Miami from 1991 to 1995, managed nine schools in Baltimore from 1992 to 1996, and ran the central office of the school system of Hartford, Connecticut, along with five of the city's schools from 1994 to 1996. Disappointing results and persistent conflict with teachers and community leaders had again spelled an early end to outsourced school management.[24]

Much as Lieberman argued that contractors didn't get the flexibility or time they needed in the early 1970s, Hill, Pierce, and Guthrie contended that EAI never obtained from Baltimore or Hartford the control over resources and staff necessary to achieve its goals.[25] In EAI's wake, another Minnesota company entered the business of school district management but exited soon after. From 1993 to 1997, the Public Strategies Group Inc., based in St. Paul, served as the superintendent of the Minneapolis Public Schools. Amid news of disappointing results for Minneapolis students on statewide exams, the school board terminated its contract with the company.[26]

By 2001, however, educational privatization was no longer an academic or experimental matter. Edison Schools Inc., headquartered on the fifteenth floor of a Manhattan office tower on the northeast corner of Fifth Avenue and Forty-Third Street, was running a network of 114 schools with 74,000 students across twenty-three states; a little over half of these schools were district schools, while the remainder were charter schools, an alternative introduced in Minnesota in 1992 and financed with public money but privately managed. When Edison began operations in 1995, it started with four schools (three district schools and one charter school) with 2,250 students across four states.[27]

Friedman's ideas had taken hold. While Friedman's endorsement of vouchers had not gained wide support,[28] his recommendation that for-profit operators run public schools had gained significant ground. Edison was big, growing, and not alone. Among Edison's competitors at that time were the Leona Group of East Lansing, Michigan, with thirty-three schools in two states; Mosaica Education of New York, with twenty-two schools in eleven states; and National Heritage Academies of Grand Rapids, Michigan, with twenty-eight schools in three states.[29] These companies together quickly came to be known as educational management organizations, or EMOs. They were education's answer to health maintenance organizations, or HMOs, likewise dedicated to improving service, containing costs, and, in many cases, making a profit.

The rise of EMOs nevertheless generated for me more questions than answers. I had always seen education and business as belonging to separate spheres, much like public radio and commercials. The two were not supposed to mix. Yet the same was long ago said about lending money and charging interest, barred in Europe until the sixteenth century and later by usury laws deriving from passages in Exodus, Leviticus, Deuteronomy, Psalms, and Ezekiel.[30] Selling life insurance policies and annuities was also at the outset judged unethical for putting a price on longevity but in time became main-stream practice.[31]

Clearly, the New York City school system was hobbled by just the kind of inefficiencies that commercial enterprises are built to expose and extirpate. On the other hand, the OEO experiment's poor results, BRL's failure, and EAI's demise indicated that commercial management of schools is fraught with difficulties. Going outside the system to a company in Maryland for scheduling software and support constitutes one level of change. The purchased good and service are both subject to straightforward assessment and thus simple contract enforcement. Turning over public schools to for-profit operators means something far more involved. Day-to-day education is a notoriously opaque process. The immediate consumer is, after all, a child or adolescent who can know only so much about how material should be covered. And the parent, taxpayer, and policy maker are at a necessary distance.

More fundamentally, educators, like doctors, do not have as much control over outcomes as businessmen because, in technical terms, the production function in education, as in health care, is by nature more complex. The traditional production function for industry comprises capital investment, labor, and technological innovation. In education, facilities and supplies constitute capital investment; administrators, teachers, and support staff equal labor; and pedagogical strategy takes the form of technological innovation. However, in education, the students themselves amount to a fourth input.[32]

EMOs have in large part won contracts to turn around schools in low-income communities; middle- and upper-income communities have rarely needed such intervention.[33] As abundant research has made clear, students in low-income communities do not come to school as equipped to flourish as their counterparts in middle- and upper-income communities.[34] Accordingly, much as doctors struggle in caring for patients raised in communities impaired by lead poisoning, drug abuse, teenage pregnancy, poor air quality, inadequate recreational opportunities, and substandard grocery stores (lacking fresh produce basic to balanced diets), educators struggle in running classrooms in these communities. For educators, the struggle is, in fact, compounded by substantial peer group effects, with troubled students causing trouble for classmates.[35] With such exogenous factors unaddressed and without much if any additional funding per pupil, EMOs have thus faced a steep challenge no matter how impressive their building renovations, how sharp their personnel, how innovative their curricula, and how sophisticated their data systems.

■

While EMOs have been constrained by these inherent difficulties, the businessperson's emphasis on efficiency and results has nevertheless won extensive support among legislators and educational policy makers. The rise of EMOs and the growth of this emphasis on efficiency and results belong to the same narrative.

Nomenclature is one sign of this metamorphosis. The superintendents of several school districts—including Baltimore, Chicago, Cleveland, Gwinnett County, Georgia, Minneapolis, and Prince George's County, Maryland—are now called chief executive officers. Their staff members are likewise titled chief operating officers, chief financial officers, and chief information or technology officers.

No Child Left Behind (NCLB), passed by Congress in 2001 and signed into law by President George W. Bush in 2002, is a more fundamental illustration. With the noble goal of identifying and closing "the achievement gaps between minority and nonminority students, and between disadvantaged children and their more advantaged peers," NCLB mandated, first, that at all schools receiving federal funding, students in grades three through eight and at one year at the secondary level be tested in reading and math;[36] and, second, that schools exhibit Adequate Yearly Progress (AYP), meaning annual improvement on these exams at each grade level and for each subgroup (defined by race, ethnicity, income bracket, disability, and degree of English proficiency).[37]

If schools fail to achieve AYP for two consecutive years, they are identified for "school improvement" and must permit students to transfer to a better school within the district; if schools fail to achieve AYP for three consecutive years, local district officials must use a portion of their Title I money, allocated by the federal government to assist disadvantaged students, to contract with outside organizations, for-profit or nonprofit, to provide "supplementary educational services" (SES) in the form of after-school and summer tutoring;[38] if such failure happens the next year, schools get targeted for "corrective action" and may be reorganized and restaffed like any underperforming division of a corporation; if such failure ensues for a fifth consecutive year, schools are slated for "restructuring" and may be turned over to a for-profit company like Edison, a nonprofit charter operator, or the state.[39] In addition, NCLB stipulated that states "include sanctions and rewards, such as bonuses and recognition, . . . to hold local educational agencies and public elementary and secondary schools accountable for student achievement" and, moreover, create, or aid local educational agencies in creating, "merit-based performance systems."[40]

Race to the Top (RTTT), crafted by the Obama administration and passed by Congress in 2009 as part of the American Recovery and Reinvestment Act, built on NCLB. Under RTTT, states have been awarded additional federal funds for tying teacher assessments and pay to student performance on these exams.[41] With the Common Core State Standards, conceived by the National Governors Association in 2009 and rolled out in 2013 to unify expectations across the country, the focus on testing and data promises to intensify.

The concentration on testing and data is already heavy. With superintendents, principals, and teachers held accountable for exam results, the pressure to teach to those exams has become burdensome if not oppressive. A stadium effect has set in. Much as successive rows of spectators at a baseball, football, or soccer game must rise to their feet to view a big play on the field, superintendents, principals, and teachers must devote themselves to test preparation when their colleagues across the state are doing so.

The pressure is acute even if state exams are not graded on a curve. Proficiency levels on criterion-referenced tests, constructed to gauge mastery of material, derive from degrees of competence defined by earlier tests. Criterion-referenced tests, as opposed to norm-referenced tests, thus have a built-in curve. And if criterion-referenced tests prove too easy one year or the next, with more students achieving proficiency than expected, teachers, schools, and districts nevertheless get measured against each other. The proficiency rates of students of one teacher, school, or district are compared to the proficiency rates of students of other teachers, schools, and districts.

Schools in this environment forfeit vitality. Students in grades three through eight typically spend part of each day drilling in math and reading in preparation for annual exams and, to the same end, take monthly benchmark assessments. Science, social studies, and physical education as well as recess, art, music, and drama get minimized.[42] Faculty meetings center on test preparation and data analysis, not curriculum enrichment.[43] Even Secretary of Education Arne Duncan conceded in his August 2014 back-to-school message to school leaders and teachers that testing is "sucking the oxygen out of the room in a lot of schools."[44] Principals in many schools across the country, in fact, have come to call their offices dedicated to analysis of test data their war rooms.[45] A year after Duncan's concession, the Obama administration acknowledged it had put too much emphasis on testing and urged Congress to "reduce over-testing" in revising NCLB.[46]

■

This transformation has by no means happened overnight. Half a century ago, the historian Raymond Callahan described the widespread influence of commerce on American schooling and traced it back to a convergence in the early 1900s of the embrace of Frederick Winslow Taylor's theory of scientific management and the domination of local school boards by businessmen.[47] The historian Richard Hofstadter at the same time maintained that a mercantile spirit basic to the nation's identity had left its stamp on schools.[48] Yet fifty years ago, the nomenclature of business didn't apply to the titles of school district leaders and their staff members; there was little if any talk of tying teacher pay to student performance; cities did not outsource school management or launch school turnaround efforts; nobody spoke of schools as belonging to regional portfolios of academic options to be periodically rebalanced according to exam results; charter schools did not exist; history and science did not take a back seat to reading and math in the name of test prep in core subjects; and, apart from the OEO experiment in the 1970s, the federal government played no role in devising and funding performance-based incentive programs.[49]

The rise of nonprofit charter school networks, in particular, illustrates the corporate influence on education. Significant supplementary funding comes from corporate foundations. Captains of industry, commerce, and finance steer the boards of these networks, from the Knowledge Is Power Program (KIPP), Achievement First, Uncommon Schools, and Mastery Charter Schools to Success Academy, Rocketship Education, and YES Prep. The leaders of these networks bear the same executive titles as their counterparts in the corporate world and earn much more than their peers in district offices. Staff work without union protection. And the focus of these networks on exam results sets the national standard.

With the number of charter schools as a whole—from solo operations to network members—growing from 2 in Minnesota in 1992 to 6,440 across forty-two states and the District of Columbia by 2013,[50] the appeal and force of educational outsourcing cannot be questioned. At the helm of this movement, New Orleans became a predominantly charter school district in the wake of Hurricane Katrina,[51] the Los Angeles Board of Education decided in 2009 to turn over 250 of the city's 750 schools to outside operators,[52] and Mayor Michael Bloomberg vowed in 2009 to double the number of New York's charter schools from 100 to 200 during his third term.[53] In these three cities and many more, the proportion of public school students attending charter schools grew significantly. By 2014, 93 percent of public school students in New Orleans attended charter schools; 53 percent did so in Detroit; 44 percent in Washington, D.C.; 33 percent in Philadelphia; 30 percent in San Antonio; 23 percent in Los Angeles; 14 percent in Chicago; and 8 percent in New York.[54]

Edison's evolution is one subject of this book, covered in Chapters 1 through 7, as an illustration of the forces for and against commercial educational management. The applicability of business methods to education is another subject, covered in Chapter 8. A third subject is the rise of two nonprofit charter networks, KIPP, a national organization, and Mastery Charter Schools, confined to Philadelphia and nearby Camden, New Jersey. The story of KIPP and Mastery as nonprofit versions of Edison is covered in Chapters 9 and 10.

A fourth subject of this book is the impact of the commercial mindset on education abroad and what we may learn from its diverse manifestations. The United States is not alone in applying business principles to education. In 1981, Chile became a laboratory for Milton Friedman's case for educational privatization. In adopting a full-fledged voucher system, the Chilean government gave parents the option to send their children to state schools or for-profit or nonprofit independent schools. By 1990, 18 percent of the nation's 2.7 million schoolchildren used vouchers to attend 1,592 schools operated by for-profit entities. By 2008, 31 percent of the nation's 3.5 million schoolchildren used vouchers to attend 3,118 such schools.[55] Meanwhile, thousands of low-fee commercially run primary and secondary schools have opened over the past decade without government support across sub-Saharan Africa and Asia. Dissatisfied with public options, parents are sending their children to such schools in cities as different as Lagos, Harare, and Hyderabad.[56]

In Chile's path, Sweden implemented a voucher system in 1992 that made government money available to operators of for-profit as well as nonprofit independent schools. While growth of this sector in Sweden, which I explore in Chapter 11, has not matched that of Chile, it has been substantial and has defied the image of Sweden as a nation guided by state institutions alone. As of 2013, 13 percent of Sweden's 1.3 million schoolchildren used vouchers to attend 942 schools operated by for-profit organizations.[57] Impressed with the freedom and choice conferred in Sweden, the conservative government in Norway proposed in its legislative agenda in 2013 implementing a variation on its neighbor's model.[58]

Conservatives in England have likewise since advocated following in Sweden's path in outsourcing the management of schools to for-profit firms.[59] Conversely, Finland, whose school system I explore in Chapter 12, has to great effect gone in the opposite direction. The Finns have rejected privatization, standardized testing, and data-driven management yet employed their own mix of business strategies to construct a system achieving international renown. While much has been written about the paradox of excellent schooling in Finland without strict accountability measures, this unlikely alignment with core business strategies has gone largely unexplored.[60]

Some business practices clearly serve schools well. As I learned in my first year as the programmer at the Beacon School in 2001–2002 and continued to learn over six subsequent years in the same capacity, schools can and should adopt some practices from the business world. Because of sophisticated scheduling software from an outside provider, Beacon's enrollment continued to grow without causing much logistical difficulty.[61] We were also spared the endless troubles experienced in 2004–2005 by high schools throughout the city without stand-alone scheduling software. When the

New York City Department of Education finally acknowledged the limitations of UAPC and rolled out a Web-based replacement in 2004 called High School Scheduling and Transcripts (HSST), it failed to sufficiently test all functions in advance, purchase enough servers to handle traffic, or provide adequate training for programmers, despite spending $5.1 million in developing the new system. The result over the first year, as *New York Times* education columnist Samuel Freedman documented in two stories, was glacial service; periodic crashes; lost data; delayed rosters, report cards, and transcripts; botched attendance records; and overwhelmed HSST supervisors who couldn't keep up with distress calls.[62]

In time, however, HSST became a solid scheduling platform, and the Department of Education under Joel Klein, Mayor Bloomberg's schools chancellor from 2002 to 2011, became a markedly more efficient, albeit controversial, central office. The department's interactive Web site, its data-tracking system (developed in collaboration with IBM), and its reporting structure improved transparency. With his Open Market Transfer Plan, Klein sealed a deal with the United Federation of Teachers in 2005 to abolish the right of senior teachers in the system to vacancies in choice schools and thus both empowered principals to make their own staffing decisions and shielded competent junior teachers from sudden displacement.[63] Yet the department's focus on test scores raised serious questions about the metrics it used for determining academic progress; and its vigorous support of charter schools provoked equally serious questions about the effects of schools competing for students.

This makeover of the New York City Department of Education, the evolution of Edison, KIPP, and Mastery, the effects of NCLB and RTTT, and the course of educational reform in countries as different as Chile, Sweden, and Finland indicate that some business practices translate well and some don't. Distinguishing which do from which do not is critical. As with the economy in general, so with education in particular, Arthur M. Okun's dictum applies: "The market needs a place, and the market needs to be kept in place."[64] This book is about defining that place.

1

FUNDAMENTAL CHANGE

If schools need fundamental change, not just tinkering, then an entirely new, profit-based alternative such as the Edison Project offers the best hope, perhaps the only hope, for providing new models of education.

Benno Schmidt, President and CEO, Edison Project, "Educational Innovation for Profit," *Wall Street Journal*, June 5, 1992

■ IN 1990, *Vanity Fair* ran a long story about Chris Whittle, his burgeoning media empire based in Knoxville, Tennessee, called Whittle Communications, and the launch of Channel One TV, the company's daily twelve-minute cable news program with two minutes of commercials beamed to classrooms in middle and high schools across the country. On the first page of the article, Whittle is pictured at the kitchen table in his apartment in New York's fabled Dakota with two books and a pile of papers before him. One of the books is a paperback edition of Myron Lieberman's *Privatization and Educational Choice*, endorsing, as noted in the Prologue, for-profit management of schools.[1]

When asked in an interview fifteen years later about the influence of Lieberman on his conception of the Edison Project, as his company was initially titled, Whittle said Lieberman's thinking was significant and added: "Right after the announcement [of the Edison Project], Myron was a big supporter of our separate system of private schools. But he would probably say we made a mistake in running public schools without full managerial freedom. That may have been too much of a compromise for him."[2]

Though the Edison Project—which would be renamed Edison Schools in 1999 and EdisonLearning in 2008—evolved into a subcontractor working with public school districts without such autonomy, it was conceived as something quite different. In unveiling the Edison Project at a news conference at the National Press Club in Washington, D.C., on May 16, 1991, Whittle described an enterprise that appeared to comport with the recommendations of Lieberman as well as Milton Friedman: an independent for-profit chain of schools that would break the mold of traditional education and outperform public schools across the country. Whittle said tuition would be just under the per-pupil expenditure of neighboring public schools. To contain costs, the Edison Project, Whittle said, would "harness student power" by putting students to work as tutors, office aides, and cafeteria workers.[3]

To be wired with the latest technology and open eight hours a day and eleven months a year, Whittle's schools were slated to serve elementary, middle, and high school students as well as children as young as one in day-care programs.[4] With this model, Whittle forecasted dramatic growth: 200 schools with 150,000 students by 1996 and 1,000 schools with 2 million students by 2010.[5] Whittle said he would need $2.5 billion to $3 billion to open the first 200 schools and would raise the money from private investors.[6]

To justify such bold expectations, Whittle built on an argument made by Friedman in 1975 for "highly capitalized chain schools, like supermarkets."[7] Whittle would claim repeatedly that much as locally owned restaurants, hardware stores, clothiers, groceries, and banks had been replaced by national brands like McDonald's, the Home Depot, Gap, Safeway, and Bank of America, schools, too, could and should be run by major corporations.[8] "In each case," Whittle contended, "customers decided to go to these new establishments because they liked what was offered there. Such a trade has not been made in schools, though, because no options have been offered there."[9]

To Whittle, the community involvement in local affairs that Alexis de Tocqueville and many social analysts since had hailed as basic to the vitality of American society served an antiquated purpose.[10] And yet the concept of chain schools represented a brazen challenge to a fundamental aspect of everyday American life. The concept of an outside company running even one school represented such a challenge, as evidenced by the aforementioned pushback from community leaders in Gary, Indiana, to Behavioral Research Labs in the early 1970s.[11] Whittle was nevertheless certain his idea would be embraced in view of his dismay at the quality of leadership, instruction, and facilities he observed in visiting schools across the country in selling Channel One.[12]

Naming his company after the legendary inventor Thomas Alva Edison, Whittle maintained that just as Edison did not fiddle with candles to create the lightbulb but rather devised an utterly different approach to achieve a better and more cost-effective form of lighting, American educators had to break with past practices to develop a new way to teach children.[13] This new way, the implication was clear, would be as superior to current methods as a lightbulb to a candle.[14] "These won't look like schools you know," Whittle said at the company's inaugural news conference.[15]

What Whittle left out in introducing the Edison Project was vouchers. Vouchers were basic to the recommendations of Friedman and Lieberman. Whittle's case about options for consumers between local and national brands, the scope of his ambitions, the national stage on which he announced his plans, and the estimated price of tuition falling below the per-pupil expenditure of neighboring public schools all suggested that the Edison Project was never intended to be an independent chain of schools—or certainly not for long.[16] The Edison Project, as Whittle depicted it, made sense only as an expensive gambit. If Whittle got the infrastructure in place early and if vouchers won political approval, the Edison Project stood to be the front-runner in a booming market.

Whittle had good reason to believe vouchers would soon become a reality. George H. W. Bush was in the White House. His secretary of education, Whittle's fellow Tennessean Lamar Alexander, was an ardent advocate of vouchers. And Whittle knew Alexander well. Alexander was both a former stakeholder in Whittle Communications and a member of Channel One's advisory board.[17]

At base, Whittle's new way called for imposing the rigor of business—its timelines, quality standards, costing methods, and accountability measures—on education. Whittle, for instance, routinely argued that if Federal Express can tell customers exactly when a package shipped and where it was in transit, schools must be able to pinpoint for parents their children's levels of proficiency in reading and math throughout the year; this argument later appeared in a series of full-page advertorials for the company in *Education Week*.[18] Exhibiting no doubts about whether learning could or should be monitored in such a precise manner, Whittle conveyed conviction that schooling differed little from package delivery or any commercial enterprise. "The biggest contribution business can make to education," he said, "is to make education a business."[19]

Whittle was far from alone in calling for a corporate makeover of American education. Others long before Whittle and concurrently saw schools as being in desperate need of business solutions. As early as 1912, the education scholar and administrator James Phinney Munroe employed the language of scientific management made popular by the industrial efficiency expert Frederick Winslow Taylor in calling for greater accountability. In opening his book *New Demands in Education,* Munroe wrote: "The fundamental demand in education, as in everything else, is for efficiency—physical efficiency, mental efficiency, moral efficiency." Munroe continued: "The potential economic worth of each school pupil, to say nothing of his moral value as a householder and as a citizen, is enormous, provided he be so educated, by his family, by his environment, and by his schools, as to become an efficient member of society."[20]

While Munroe prescribed a genuinely progressive curriculum, with as much emphasis on the arts and athletics as on academics,[21] and while he specified that the authority of school boards be limited to "matters non-educational,"[22] his tone was managerial. "We need 'educational engineers' to study the huge business of preparing youth for life," he contended, "to find out where it is good, where it is wasteful, where it is out of touch with modern requirements, where and why its output fails; and to make report in such form and with such weight of evidence that the most conventional teacher and the most indifferent citizen must pay heed."[23]

In this same spirit, one month before Whittle rolled out the Edison Project, President George H. W. Bush proclaimed the formation of the New American Schools Development Corporation (NASDC) as a central component of his America 2000 education strategy and announced Alcoa CEO Paul O'Neill as the organization's chairman. Defining the NASDC as "a private-sector research and development fund of at least $150 million to generate innovation in education," Bush pledged to follow up on its recommendations by urging Congress to commit "$1 million in start-up funds for each of . . .

535 New American schools—at least one in every congressional district—and have them up and running by 1996."[24]

O'Neill was soon after replaced by Thomas Kean, president of Drew University and former Republican governor of New Jersey. Kean's fifteen fellow board members comprised some of most powerful people in American business, including Louis Gerstner, chairman and CEO of RJR Nabisco; Frank Shrontz, chairman of Boeing; Lee Raymond, president of Exxon; James R. Jones, chairman and CEO of the American Stock Exchange; John Ong, chairman of BF Goodrich; and Paul Tagliabue, commissioner of the National Football League. Their mission was to lead the way in breaking the mold of conventional schooling.[25] And their language was no less bold or ambitious than Whittle's.

"The R&D teams," stated the NASDC declaration of purpose, ". . . can be expected to set aside all traditional assumptions about schooling and all the constraints that conventional schools work under. . . . Time, space, staffing and other resources in these new schools may be used in ways yet to be imagined. Some schools may make extensive use of computers, distance learning, interactive video-discs and other modern tools. Some may radically alter the customary modes of teaching and learning and redesign the human relationships and organizational structures of the school. Whatever their approach, all New American Schools will be expected to produce extraordinary gains in student learning."[26]

This ambition to realize significant improvement in student achievement, echoed by Whittle in his vision for the Edison Project, drew, in turn, on the widespread sentiment that America's schools were in decline and accordingly posed a grave threat to national prosperity. No document captured this sense of crisis more than the 1983 report *A Nation at Risk: The Imperative for Educational Reform*. Issued by President Ronald Reagan's National Commission on Excellence in Education (NCEE), the report alleged, "Our once unchallenged preeminence in commerce, industry, science, and technological innovation is being overtaken by competitors throughout the world." The authors of the report—an array of educators, researchers, and public officials ranging from school principals and university presidents to a former governor of Minnesota—contended that Americans could take pride in their schools of the past, but "a rising tide of mediocrity" was overtaking today's schools.[27]

As specific evidence, the NCEE authors made the following claims: "The College Board's Scholastic Aptitude Tests (SAT) demonstrate a virtually unbroken decline from 1963 to 1980. Average verbal scores fell over 50 points and average mathematics scores dropped nearly 40 points. College Board achievement tests also reveal consistent declines in recent years in such subjects as physics and English. Both the number and proportion of students demonstrating superior achievement on the SATs (i.e., those with scores of 650 or higher) have also dramatically declined."[28]

In its most ominous words, the report affirmed, "If an unfriendly foreign power had attempted to impose on America the mediocre educational performance that exists today, we might well have viewed it as an act of war."[29] Declaring history unkind to idlers,[30] the NCEE recommended a longer school day and year; more academic rigor; more homework; "a nationwide (but not Federal) system of state and local standardized tests"; performance-based pay for teachers; and a new tier of master teachers to develop teacher education programs and mentor junior colleagues.[31]

■

The relationship between knowledge and prosperity was not in dispute. The economic consequences of a skilled workforce were well established. The economist Robert Solow famously gave mathematical expression to the role of knowledge in economic growth with his reformulation of the production function in 1956. In adding technological change as a variable to be multiplied by capital investment and labor, Solow laid the foundation for a new understanding of national output. Long since called "Solow's residual," this variable elucidated the extraordinary impact of know-how, explaining, Solow wrote a year later in a follow-up article, approximately 88 percent of the increase in U.S. productivity from 1909 to 1949.[32]

The evidence cited by the NCEE for a decline in the effectiveness of schools, however, was in dispute. In examining College Board test data a decade after the publication of *A Nation at Risk*, several statisticians determined that the NCEE had substantially overstated the decline in scores and thus called into question the premise for the call to arms. The statisticians concluded that because year after year more disadvantaged students were applying to college and, therefore, taking the required SAT and achievement tests, the mean scores necessarily dropped. Some of the statisticians argued that this "composition effect," whereby the performance of the whole does not reflect the performance of its subgroups, meant that there was no real drop in scores and that, accordingly, the alleged educational crisis was confined to underfunded schools in poor inner-city minority communities. Other statisticians contended the decline was real but only half as bad as the NCEE had made it out to be.[33]

To the historian Lawrence Cremin, the case of the NCEE was from the start brittle. Writing in between the publication of *A Nation at Risk* and the statistical reassessments, Cremin argued that the country's schools were yet again being blamed for a loss of U.S. economic competitiveness when competitiveness is "to a considerable degree a function of monetary, trade, and industrial policy" decided in Washington, DC. "To contend that problems of international competitiveness can be solved by educational reform," Cremin wrote, "especially educational reform defined solely as school reform, is not merely Utopian and millennialist, it is at best foolish and at worst a crass effort to direct attention away from those truly responsible for doing something about competitiveness and to lay the burden on the schools."[34]

Amid the sense of urgency, however, Cremin's critique and the statisticians' qualifications gained little attention. The plight of students in poor districts, rural as well as urban, was, after all, conspicuous.[35] In addition, the naysayers were battling a movement of international scope. The year before Cremin leveled his refutation, British prime minister Margaret Thatcher had won Parliament's approval of a sweeping overhaul of schooling that mandated a variation on nearly each recommendation made in *A Nation at Risk* and went several steps beyond. Devised to reverse an alleged decline in academic achievement, Britain's Education Reform Act of 1988 created a national curriculum with "attainment targets" and a corresponding system of standardized exams to be taken by students aged seven, eleven, and fourteen; facilitated the development of league tables by ordering the publication of exam results by school; sanctioned performance-based pay of teachers; and originated a market for school competition by authorizing "grant-maintained schools."[36]

With overlapping tactics and the same mission, both the NASDC and Whittle picked up where the NCEE as well as Britain's Parliament had left off. With the assistance of the RAND Corporation's Institute on Education and Training along with an independent panel of senior educators, the NASDC reviewed 686 proposals in its initial year and in July 1992 settled on grants to eleven design teams. Three designs placed technology at the core of curricula and teachers on the periphery. Two implemented the methods of corporate organization: Modern Red Schoolhouse, based in Indianapolis and headed by William Bennett, secretary of education under President Ronald Reagan; and National Alliance for Restructuring Education (now America's Choice), run by the National Center for Education and the Economy in Rochester and dedicated to the widely popular production principles of Total Quality Management.[37] Nine more design teams were funded in 1993 and another seven in 1995.[38] While Congress never followed up with the funding Bush had envisioned for 535 New American schools, new models were in place in approximately 1,500 schools by 1999. Yet the "extraordinary gains in student learning" expected by the NASDC never materialized. A study published that year by the American Institutes for Research concluded that it was unclear any gains had been achieved.[39]

■

Like Gerstner, Shrontz, Raymond, Jones, Ong, Tagliabue, and all other members of the NASDC board but Kean, Whittle did not have a background in education. Whittle majored in American studies at the University of Tennessee and exhibited a flair and passion for both politics and business. He helped run a program called Youth in Government devised by Tennessee Republican senator Howard Baker that took top high school seniors from across the state to the nation's capital to learn about legislative, judicial, and foreign affairs through visits to Congress, the Supreme Court, and the State Department.[40] As a senior, he served as a popular president of the university's Student Government Association and cofounded with several friends a small publishing company in Knoxville called Collegiate Enterprises.[41]

After earning his bachelor's degree in 1969, Whittle enrolled at Columbia Law School but found the study of law too dry and dropped out after a semester.[42] He subsequently took a position as a staffer on the campaign of

Wally Barnes for the Republican nomination for governor of Connecticut and quickly rose to become the campaign manager.[43] After Barnes lost, Whittle nearly embarked on a career in education. He committed to a position as a history teacher at a now-defunct alternative private high school in Connecticut called Westledge, whose head he had met while working for Barnes, but he backed out at the last minute to rejoin his friends from college in running Collegiate Enterprises. The prospect of making a fortune was too good to turn down, Whittle later said.[44]

Collegiate Enterprises sold textbook and lecture summaries called *Time Savers*. Whittle came up with the idea as a college senior after hearing about *Cliff's Notes* study guides, begun at the University of Nebraska in 1958. Collegiate Enterprises also published free ad-filled local consumer guides for college campuses, starting with the University of Tennessee in 1969 and spreading to one hundred schools across the country within five years.[45] Renamed the 13–30 Corporation in 1971, the company targeted that age group with niche magazines sponsored by single advertisers,[46] such as *Student Traveler*, filled with ads exclusively for Nissan.[47]

As 13–30's national sales director, Whittle went on to make the fortune he had sought. After selling a 50 percent stake in the company for $3.2 million in 1977 to the Bonnier Group, a media conglomerate based in Stockholm intent on establishing an American beachhead, Whittle and several partners bought financially troubled *Esquire* magazine at a steep discount and moved to New York to turn the magazine around. As *Esquire*'s publisher, Whittle steered the magazine back to profitability. He sold his share in *Esquire* in 1986, took charge of 13–30, and renamed the company Whittle Communications.[48] With the debut in 1988 of *Special Report*, Whittle stunned Madison Avenue. A quarterly issued in six versions (devoted to either family, health, sports, lifestyle, personalities, or fiction), *Special Report* was aimed at patients sitting in the waiting rooms of doctors' offices and distributed for free. The magazines were arrayed in a dedicated oak display case Whittle Communications provided each medical practice. In no time, Whittle set a record for ad revenue in the initial year of a publication, selling $41 million of ad space to Procter & Gamble, General Foods, and twelve other major corporations; the previous record for ad revenue in the initial year of a publication was $8 million, set in 1974 by *People*.[49] One month after the appearance of the first issue of *Special Report,* Time Inc. paid $185 million for a 50 percent stake in Whittle Communications, $40 million of which went to Whittle himself.[50]

By 1990, Whittle Communications had 1,000 employees, $220 million in annual revenue,[51] and a new red-brick headquarters resembling a New England college campus under construction in the center of Knoxville. Designed by the celebrity architect Peter Marino, the headquarters would cost $56 million.[52] Among senior executives were Hamilton Jordan, White House chief of staff during the Carter administration; William S. Rukeyser, former managing editor of *Fortune;* and Gerry Hogan, former chief operating officer of the Turner Broadcasting System.[53] In addition to magazines like *Student Traveler* and *Special Report,* Whittle's portfolio by 1993 included the Big Picture, a monthly series of wall posters mixing educational content with ads and displayed in hallways and lunchrooms in 11,000 elementary schools;[54] as a complement to *Special Report,* a single-advertiser TV news program by the same name for waiting rooms in 30,000 doctors' offices;[55] Medical News Network, an interactive news and information service sponsored by drug companies and relayed by satellite to 5,000 doctors' offices;[56] the Larger Agenda, a series of short topical hardcover books by such noted authors as James Atlas, John Kenneth Galbraith, William Greider, Arthur Schlesinger Jr., and Michael Lewis punctuated with ads for Federal Express and sent free every two months to 150,000 corporate executives and government officials;[57] and, of course, Channel One, viewed every morning of the academic year by approximately 8 million students in 11,861 middle and high schools across the country within four years of its introduction in 1989.[58]

■

Soon after his announcement of the Edison Project in 1991, Whittle assembled a seven-member school design team at his new headquarters in Knoxville.[59] With the nation's dominant companies in medical care, overnight package delivery, and prison management, Tennessee had led the way in challenging the public sector with for-profit operations. The same state that became home to Hospital Corporation of America in 1968, Federal Express in 1973, and Corrections Corporation of America in 1983 was now home to the nation's boldest effort at educational privatization.

Whittle introduced his design team with a group photo in identical full-page ads on the same day in March 1992 in the *New York Times* and the *Wall Street Journal*; the same full-page ad ran two days later in *Education Week*. Below the photo and above brief biographies of the seven members of the design team ran the following declaration: "They're starting school all over again."[60]

For two years, this team convened monthly for three or four days of collaboration, either in Knoxville, New York, or Washington, DC. Only one of the seven members, Sylvia Peters, had been a K–12 educator. Peters had earned a national reputation as an elementary school principal who had led parents and community activists to create a safe haven for her students amid a crime-ridden neighborhood in Chicago. The remaining members comprised Chester Finn, a professor of educational policy at Vanderbilt University in Nashville, a former assistant secretary of education under President Reagan, and an architect of President Bush's America 2000 education strategy; John Chubb, a senior fellow at the Brookings Institution and coauthor with Terry Moe of a highly regarded book advocating vouchers called *Politics, Markets, and America's Schools;* Dominique Browning, an assistant managing editor at *Newsweek* and a former editor at *Esquire;* Lee Eisenberg, the editor in chief of *Esquire* when Whittle was the magazine's publisher; Nancy Hechinger, the founder and head of Hands-On Media, a producer of interactive reference material; and Daniel Biederman, president of the Grand Central and Thirty-Fourth Street Partnerships and a leader in the field of managing public services with private resources.[61] This group, in turn, brought aboard another forty researchers to help them design the Edison program.[62]

The most prominent member of Whittle's team would be the Edison Project's CEO and president. In a coup that made the front page of the *New York Times* on May 26, 1992, Whittle lured Benno Schmidt from the presidency of Yale University and thereby brought the Edison Project national attention and clout overnight. Two days later, identical full-page ads for the Edison Project again appeared in the *New York Times* and the *Wall Street Journal,* this time featuring a picture of Schmidt in a professorial pose above an announcement of his move, headlined by the following quote: "America's schools need fundamental, structural change. Not tinkering around the edges."[63]

Though Schmidt was struggling in his sixth year as president of Yale, his departure came as a surprise. Many students criticized him as remote. Some wore "Where's Benno?" T-shirts to protest his frequent absence from campus. And many professors found him imperious for having bypassed a search committee in naming a friend as the dean of the School of Organization and Management and for having urged major cuts without much faculty input. Yet Schmidt didn't appear to be leaving. And he certainly didn't appear to be someone who would leave to run a school-management company with no track record, no less a company founded by someone as controversial as Whittle.[64]

Moreover, like Whittle, Schmidt had no background in K–12 education. Though a career educator, Schmidt's experience was confined to the university level and, at that, the rarefied realm of Ivy League teaching, scholarship, and administration. Before becoming president of Yale in 1986, Schmidt had been the dean of Columbia Law School for two years. Prior to that, he had been a professor of constitutional law at Columbia since 1969 and previously a clerk directly out of Yale Law School for Chief Justice Earl Warren. Schmidt nevertheless embraced this unlikely challenge.[65] And he brought with him Yale's chief financial and administrative officer, Michael Finnerty, to become Edison's chief financial officer.[66]

Despite this lack of experience in K–12 education, Schmidt, along with Whittle, spoke with conviction about what ailed it and what should be done. They contended that no cause in the United States was as pressing as K–12 education and no remedy as promising as for-profit management. In the front-page article in the *New York Times* announcing Schmidt's decision to leave Yale to lead Edison, Schmidt and Whittle forecasted that Edison could have a revolutionary impact. Whittle placed the company's mission in the context of the Cold War and employed the language of historical inevitability: "You have to have a West Berlin for East Berlin to fall, and what we're really doing here is building West Berlin." Schmidt added: "The reason this hasn't been done before is that this thing is a matter of D-Day dimensions. Only someone with a high tolerance for risk would even be willing to contemplate it." Schmidt predicted, "If this venture succeeds, there's nothing, there's nothing, that could be done, aside from changing human nature, that could be more constructive for our society."[67]

Elaborating two weeks later in a *Wall Street Journal* op-ed, Schmidt wrote: "If schools need fundamental change, not just tinkering, then an entirely new, profit-based alternative such as the Edison Project offers the best hope, perhaps the only hope, for providing new models of education. What other approach can overcome the fragmentation, inertia, political and bureaucratic constraints and vested interests that make it so hard to innovate in our current educational system?" Schmidt continued: "The world has been revolutionized in recent years by the demand for freedom and choice. . . . Competition, freedom of opportunity, and diversity serve the causes of progress and human dignity. These lessons have a profound bearing on American education, if we will but heed them."[68]

To Schmidt, a central problem was inefficient spending. Elaborating on claims made by the authors of *A Nation at Risk* and on arguments made by the education economist Eric Hanushek, Schmidt attacked the mismatch of growing expenditures and declining results.[69] While per-pupil spending had approximately doubled in real dollars since 1965, Schmidt wrote, scores in math, science, reading, and writing on the National Assessment of Educational Progress (NAEP) had not improved since 1970, and scores on the SAT had dropped.[70]

As with the NCEE's claims about College Board scores a decade earlier, Schmidt's charges, too, required qualification. While per-pupil spending had climbed considerably since 1965, much of that spending went to new services. As Richard Rothstein explained a year later in a combative rebuttal entitled "The Myth of Public School Failure," about 30 percent of the additional funding went to programs in special education mandated by the federal government since 1975 to help children with cognitive, emotional, and physical handicaps; about 10 percent went to free or subsidized breakfasts and lunches for a growing population of children from low-income homes; about 5 percent went to expanded busing of students to meet integration orders; and about 3 percent went to initiatives focused on keeping students from dropping out.[71] Moreover, with health-care expenditures in the United States climbing from 5.6 percent of GDP in 1965 to 13.1 percent of GDP in 1992, a significant portion of the additional spending on education went to covering escalating medical insurance costs for staff.[72]

This last qualification points to a more fundamental explanation for the rising cost of education, whether it be primary, secondary, or tertiary: the costs for all labor-intensive sectors—from health care to carpentry, masonry, musical performance, and education—climbed considerably over this time period for the simple reason that the costs of services that cannot be significantly improved by technological innovation are intrinsically inflationary. Termed "the cost disease" by the economist William J. Baumol, this phenomenon plagues labor-intensive sectors indiscriminately. Only sectors benefiting substantially from technological innovation—such as automobile, TV, or laptop manufacture—have succeeded in cutting costs and thus boosting productivity.[73] And yet no chorus emerged to criticize carpenters, masons, and musicians for underperformance. To counteract what has come to be called Baumol's Law, customers have merely substituted recorded music for the work of live musicians and prefabricated units for the work of carpenters and masons. Doing something similar in education—and advocates of online learning to this end have indeed been hard at work—has proved much more difficult because of the importance of personal interaction between teacher and student. For similar reasons, barbers, too, have been safe and stand to remain so, a point well made by Kurt Vonnegut in *Player Piano,* his 1952 novel about a futuristic society where machines have displaced nearly all workers.[74]

Schmidt was, however, justified in depicting "political and bureaucratic constraints and vested interests" as obstacles to better schooling. Some of the most ardent advocates of public education, after all, had conceded that many mandated pedagogical policies, hiring practices, and work rules conflicted with effective instruction. This was especially true in big cities like New York. No less established a champion of public education than Deborah Meier, founder and leader of the progressive Central Park East schools in Harlem and winner of a MacArthur Foundation "genius" grant in 1987, recounted in detail her frustration with the city's educational bureaucracy in an essay in *The Nation* in 1991 advocating school self-governance and choice; four years later Meier fleshed out her case in a frequently indignant book, *The Power of Their Ideas: Lessons for America from a Small School in Harlem.*[75] Seymour Fliegel, a former teacher and principal and Meier's onetime regional supervisor, conveyed even greater frustration in his 1993 book, *Miracle in*

East Harlem: The Fight for Choice in Public Education, telling the transformational story of one school district's unlikely triumph over centralized authority and urban politics.[76]

Whether such school self-governance and choice would improve systems at large was another matter. That was certainly the hope of Fliegel, Meier, and like-minded reformers.[77] In the opinion of the political scientist Jeffrey Henig, by contrast, the school choice movement stood to hurt public education through further segregation by race, class, and academic achievement. Echoing Henry Levin's case against vouchers three decades earlier, Henig contended in his book *Rethinking School Choice: Limits of the Market Metaphor,* published in 1994, that school choice ultimately derived from a failure of collective will to support all schools appropriately and, accordingly, dodged a pressing challenge rather than tackle it.[78] With charter schools taking off in 1992 and multiplying year after year, Henig's concerns found expression in more and more countervailing voices.[79]

There was nevertheless no denying in 1992 that many political and bureaucratic forces got in the way of good schooling. The weight and divisiveness of such forces, in turn, testified to the failure of collective will that Henig identified as fundamental to the nation's educational woes. Nor was this problem new.

In his comprehensive study of the New York City Board of Education, *110 Livingston Street,* published in 1968, the sociologist David Rogers described the city's school system as "typical of what social scientists call a 'sick' bureaucracy—a term for organizations whose traditions, structure, and operations subvert their stated missions and prevent any flexible accommodation to changing client demands."[80] In a follow-up study fifteen years later, *110 Livingston Street Revisited,* Rogers and his coauthor, Norman Chung, acknowledged some progress since the system was decentralized in 1970, and much authority, as a result, deputized to thirty-two community school boards. However, Rogers and Chung observed that decentralization did nothing to address the problem of struggling principals and teachers, while generating a tangle of new problems: many community school boards overstepped bounds in administrative and pedagogical matters; resorted to patronage in making hires and furnishing contracts; and failed to coordinate operations effectively with headquarters, and vice versa.[81] The dysfunctionality

Bel Kaufman had satirically depicted in her classic 1965 novel, *Up the Down Staircase,* was not merely grounded in the author's experience as a veteran New York City teacher but also confirmed and reconfirmed by social science. The novel's nonsensical memos, convoluted procedures, and dizzying regulations were but one step from reality.[82]

Outside New York, Ted Sizer, a professor of education at Brown University and the founder of a consortium of progressive public schools, made arguments similar to Meier's and Fliegel's in his books *Horace's Compromise,* published in 1984, and *Horace's School,* published in 1992: district officials should confer on principals and teachers more autonomy to do their jobs and grant students more freedom to choose their schools.[83] Even Albert Shanker, the long-standing leader of the American Federation of Teachers and the very personification of teacher unionism, criticized the rigidity of educational authorities and advocated giving teachers the right to create and manage their own schools as the proper remedy. Issuing this proposal in a 1988 address at the National Press Club, Shanker thus helped lay the foundation for charter schools.[84]

■

In calling for for-profit school management, however, Schmidt, along with Whittle, was taking frustration with educational bureaucracy to a new level. Choice within the public system for schools managed by veteran district educators such as Meier constituted a second way of educational organization; the Beacon School, where this book began, was founded as part of this movement. Choice outside—or within—the public system for schools managed by for-profit operators amounted to a third way. Friedman and Lieberman had endorsed it. The Office of Economic Opportunity had given it a brief trial and deemed it a failure. The leaders of Educational Alternatives Inc. (EAI) and Edison saw no alternative.

Whittle's pick as chief educational officer, John Chubb, never mentioned for-profit management in the seminal book on school choice he had two years earlier coauthored with Terry Moe, *Politics, Markets, and America's Schools.* The core concerns of Chubb and Moe were the freedom of parents and children to choose schools and the freedom of school administrators to run their schools without meddling from school boards. This second freedom, Chubb and Moe wrote, was of paramount importance. "Autonomy has the strongest influence on the overall quality of school organization of any factor that we examined," they concluded.[85]

With the autonomy of a private school system, the Edison Project would be free from school board interference and union opposition. With such freedom, Whittle and Schmidt promised significant pedagogical reform and envisioned great progress. The program constructed by their design team called for lengthening the school day by two hours and the school year by thirty days (to match the Japanese academic calendar of 210 days); providing every student with a home computer to facilitate parent-teacher communication as well as independent student inquiry; dividing schools into "academies," in turn separated into "houses," to promote a greater sense of belonging for teachers as well as students; appointing master teachers to supervise and inspire junior colleagues; instituting a student dress code of collared shirts or blouses in solid colors and khaki slacks or skirts; scheduling an hour a day of music or art for all students; starting all students with instruction in Spanish in preschool, with the expectation that they be conversant in the language upon completion of eighth grade; requiring the study of Latin from sixth grade through eighth; and keeping all students on pace in math to complete courses in calculus or probability and statistics before graduation from high school.[86]

Edison's academic curriculum, in particular, was based on standardized outcomes and vetted by two former U.S. assistant secretaries of education, the policy analyst Bruno Manno and the historian Diane Ravitch, both proponents at the time of market-based reforms and standardization; two decades later Ravitch would become a leading opponent.[87]

In sync with the NASDC and its goal of "extraordinary gains in student learning," the Edison Project set its bar high. Schmidt wrote in his introduction to the Edison design team's 110-page book laying out this new educational program that Edison aimed to bring about "quantum gains in students' academic performance and in the quality of their lives," all at "the same amount per student as the average school district now spends."[88] Tuition was accordingly projected to be about $5,500.[89]

Atop Whittle's initial positioning of the company in 1991 as a solution to the country's educational malaise, all these widely publicized claims about spending no more than the average school district, "fundamental change," and "starting school all over again" made clear that the Edison Project was never meant to be an independent for-profit network of schools funded by tuition. Vouchers were implicit. The business plan otherwise did not add up.

It was, in fact, reported in the *New York Times* in connection with Schmidt's announcement to join the Edison Project that the company put "great stock" in Education Secretary Lamar Alexander's plan to implement a national system of vouchers. Whittle was quoted in that *Times* article as saying: "If vouchers existed, we couldn't build schools fast enough. But we're assuming no vouchers to start."[90]

With Bill Clinton's defeat of Bush in November 1992, Whittle's assumption that the Edison Project would succeed with or without vouchers was put to the test in the investment community. Whittle had said in 1991 that he would need $2.5 billion to $3 billion to open the company's first 200 schools by 1996 and would raise the money from private investors. His three major partners in Whittle Communications had agreed in 1992 to commit amounts proportionate to their stakes in the media company. Time Warner, which that year scaled back the 50 percent stake in Whittle Communications it had taken in 1988 as Time Inc. to 37.5 percent, invested $22.5 million. Philips Electronics of Holland, which bought a 25 percent stake in the company in 1992 for $175 million, invested $15 million. Associated Newspapers of Britain, holding a 24 percent stake in the company, contributed $14.4 million. Whittle himself, who along with a small group of investors controlled the remaining 13.5 percent of the company, added $8.1 million.[91]

Though Whittle claimed in July 1992 that investors would be lining up to fund the launch of the Edison Project,[92] he had no more takers. Whittle approached the Walt Disney Company, Apple Computer, Paramount Communications, AT&T, McDonald's, Cox Enterprises, and PepsiCo. All declined to invest. As late as September 1993, Whittle had managed to raise no more than $60 million. His goal of $2.5 billion to $3 billion was out of sight.[93]

Without vouchers to make tuition free or at least more affordable and without the capital to build a new network of schools, Whittle shifted course and became, as Lieberman had recommended as an alternate path to reforming schools, a for-profit entity "within the public school system," yet not necessarily with the control over staff that Lieberman had described as indispensable.[94] In running charter schools, Edison would have the freedom to hire and fire staff, but that would not be the case in running conventional district schools. In the latter case, Edison would be bound by the union regulations Lieberman had decried as ruinous.

According to Whittle, he had been advised at the winter meeting of the National Governors Association in Washington, D.C., in 1993 by Governor Roy Romer of Colorado, Governor Bill Weld of Massachusetts, and Governor John Engler of Michigan to get out of the brick-and-mortar business and remodel Edison as a subcontractor managing public schools.[95] From the beginning, Whittle had said he hoped Edison would eventually branch out to run public schools as a subcontractor.[96] And Chubb later wrote that Edison's design team had concluded by December 1992 that working with public school districts should be part of the company's business plan.[97] While such an undertaking was decidedly secondary, circumstances quickly made it primary. In September 1993, Edison officials announced that the company would put on hold its plans to build its own schools and enter the business of subcontracting.[98] In shifting course, Whittle conceded what John Golle had three years earlier. Golle, the founder and CEO of EAI, had also initially intended to manage an independent network of private schools but found the start-up costs too high and refashioned his company as a subcontractor.[99]

In its new form, Edison was forced to scale back the curriculum advanced by its design team. Although Edison did divide its schools into academies and houses, institute a neat student dress code, create cohorts of master teachers, and provide home computers for every student, it could afford to lengthen the school day by only one hour, not two, and the school year by only eighteen days, not thirty. Nor could Edison provide the resources necessary to achieve its art, music, or foreign-language ambitions.[100]

With this modified program—anchored by the Success for All reading program, developed at Johns Hopkins University, and by Everyday Mathematics, developed at the University of Chicago—Edison took over four elementary schools in 1995 with 2,250 students: a charter school in Boston; a district school in Mount Clemens, Michigan; another district school in Sherman, Texas; and a third district school in Wichita, Kansas. From there, the company grew significantly, eclipsing EAI, which in 1996 would see one contract for running nine schools in Baltimore terminated after three-and-a-half contentious years and another contract for managing all of Hartford's schools cut to five and then nullified after two equally difficult years.[101] By 1998, Edison was running forty-three schools with 23,900 students across twelve states; by 1999, the company was running sixty-one schools with 37,500 students across seventeen states.[102]

■

With Edison's impressive growth, the company gained confidence from investors. With $12 million from Donaldson, Lufkin & Jenrette, $20 million from J.P. Morgan Capital Corp., $20 million from a Swedish fund called Investor Growth Capital, and $30 million from Microsoft cofounder Paul Allen's Vulcan Ventures on top of earlier investments by Time Warner, Philips Electronics, Associated Newspapers, and other investors, Edison had raised $232 million in total by the summer of 1999.[103] But the company needed far more money even in its reinvented role as a subcontractor: start-up costs in taking over district schools involved renovating buildings as well as purchasing new computers for both the classroom and each student's home; start-up costs in partnering with charter school boards typically involved leasing or buying property as well.[104]

Earlier in the year, Edison had turned to Merrill Lynch to go public. Much as managing public schools as a subcontractor was not central to Whittle's initial strategy, going public did not appear to be either. But here again, Whittle had little choice. His media empire in Knoxville had collapsed in 1994. Only Channel One was posting a profit. His other properties—in particular, the single-advertiser magazines, Special Report TV, Medical News Network, and the Larger Agenda book series—were hemorrhaging money. K-III Communications (renamed Primedia in 1997), a conglomerate in New York controlled by the venerable private equity group Kohlberg Kravis & Roberts, now known as KKR, paid $240 million for Channel One.[105] The rest of Whittle Communications, valued as a whole in 1992 at more than $750 million, was dissolved.[106] Time Warner and Philips Electronics wrote off their respective investments in Whittle Communications of $185 million and $175 million and were forced to come up with an additional $60 million to meet the company's payroll. Whittle Communications had turned out to be a shimmering house of cards constructed from blind ambition and aggressive accounting.[107] Reginald K. Brack Jr., chairman of Time Inc., called the six-year partnership with Whittle Communications the company's Vietnam.[108]

The brand-new stately company headquarters would be purchased by the federal government for under half its cost and transformed into the Howard H. Baker Jr. U.S. Courthouse.[109] Whatever plans Whittle may have had to use Whittle Communications to subsidize the Edison Project were buried.

That Whittle went on to raise the aforementioned money from Donaldson, Lufkin & Jenrette, J.P. Morgan, Investor Capital Growth, and Paul Allen testified to his legendary skills as a salesman. That Whittle won over Merrill Lynch and a range of Wall Street voices further testified to such prowess. Typical of bullish analysts and commentators were Michael T. Moe, the director of growth equity research at Merrill Lynch, and James K. Glassman, a financial columnist for the *Washington Post*.[110]

In a widely circulated 192-page report entitled *The Book of Knowledge: Investing in the Growing Education and Training Industry,* published by Merrill Lynch seven months before it took Edison public in November 1999, Moe praised Edison in a one-page sidebar as the nation's leading EMO and trumpeted the company's potential. In assessing the market for educational privatization in general, Moe wrote, "It is our prediction that 10% of the publicly-funded [*sic*] K–12 school market will be privately managed ten years from now, implying a market of over $30 billion in today's dollars."[111] In assessing Edison's future in particular, Moe declared a year later in a *BusinessWeek* article that by 2005, Edison would be running 423 schools with 260,000 students and generating $1.8 billion in revenue. Echoing Moe, Scott Soffen, an analyst at Legg Mason, said in the same article, "In the near term, you're going to see growth not unlike the Internet."[112]

While Moe's report may not be considered a work of disinterested analysis, given that Merrill Lynch was Edison's lead underwriter and stood to make—and did make—millions of dollars in fees for taking Edison public, Glassman's assessment requires no such qualification.[113] As early as 1995, Glassman, in a column entitled "It's Elementary: Buy Education Stocks Now," cited Edison as a company to watch and suggested that in ten years private firms might be running 20 percent of the nation's K–12 public schools and generating

$100 billion in revenues.[114] Joining Moe, Soffen, and Glassman in lauding Edison and forecasting dramatic growth for EMOs in general were Howard M. Block of Banc of America Securities, Jeff Silber of Gerard Klauer Mattison, and Greg Cappelli and Brandon Dobell of Credit Suisse First Boston.[115] Banc of America Securities and Credit Suisse First Boston, along with Donaldson, Lufkin & Jenrette and J.P. Morgan Securities, assisted Merrill Lynch in underwriting Edison's initial public offering.[116] If Moe, Soffen, Glassman, Block, Cappelli, and Dobell were right, Edison would become, as Whittle had envisioned, the Gap, McDonald's, or Safeway of education.

2

MARKET DISCIPLINE

Schools must meet the test any high-performance organization must meet: results. And results are not achieved by bureaucratic regulation. They are achieved by meeting customer requirements by rewards for success and penalties for failure. Market discipline is the key, the ultimate form of accountability.

Louis Gerstner, *Reinventing Education: Entrepreneurship in America's Public Schools* (1994)

■ WITH EDISON'S INITIAL PUBLIC OFFERING in November 1999, the company netted $109 million from the sale of 6.8 million shares at $18 apiece,[1] and in the process underscored the permanence of its place in the educational world by changing its name from the Edison Project to Edison Schools.[2] The company raised more money through two secondary offerings: one in August 2000, netting $71 million from the sale of 3.35 million shares at $22.88 apiece; and another in March 2001, netting $81 million from the sale of 3.53 million shares at $24.56 apiece.[3]

This scale of investment in an education company was new, but not the method or, as time would tell, the fate. White, Weld & Co. of Boston, along with Hambrecht & Quist of San Francisco, among other underwriters, took Behavioral Research Laboratories (BRL) public in February 1971 at $15 a share and quickly sold 424,000 shares to raise more than $6 million for the Palo Alto–based education company.[4] BRL at the time was managing an elementary school in Gary, Indiana, as well as preschools, foreign-language academies, and reading centers across the country; BRL also developed and implemented math and reading programs for school districts nation-wide.[5] BRL peaked at $17 a share the following month and then began an inexorable slide on repeated news of disappointing earnings.[6] By 1974, the company was trading for pennies and soon after suffered the shame of delisting.[7]

Two investment banks in Minneapolis—John G. Kinnard & Co. and Dain Bosworth Inc.—likewise raised $6 million for Educational Alternatives Inc. (EAI) in April 1991 by taking the company public at $4 a share.[8] Michael T. Moe, who, as noted earlier, vigorously endorsed Edison as Merrill Lynch's director of growth equity research, worked at the time as a financial analyst for Dain Bosworth. Moe claimed that EAI was "in the right place, at the right time, with the right service" and forecasted dramatic expansion.[9] EAI climbed to $48.75 in November 1993 and then commenced its own inexorable slide on repeated news of disappointing earnings as well as accounting irregularities and misrepresentations of test data. By 1996, EAI was trading under its initial offering price of $4. By 2000, EAI too was trading for pennies and soon after was delisted.[10]

Also new was the scale of potential return for the leaders of a school management company. Whittle and Schmidt stood to benefit enormously if Edison became what they had envisioned. With 11.3 million shares (or nearly 25 percent of the company's total) when Edison went public, Whittle held a stake worth $203.4 million at the outset, a stake that would be worth much more, of course, if the stock went up, as it would, climbing to $38.75 per share in 2001. Schmidt, in turn, held 929,000 shares when the company went public, making his portion worth $16.7 million. In both form and degree, such compensation was unheard of in the world of K–12 education, let alone education in general but for the evolving for-profit postsecondary sector defined by the likes of DeVry and the University of Phoenix.[11]

■

While taking Edison public may never have been part of Whittle's original plan, the move comported with his pursuit of growth and accountability as well as substantial profit. If Edison was going to be like any other major business, it should have access to capital markets, compete for the favor of investors, and stand up to the scrutiny of Wall Street analysts. What applied to the schools it ran should apply to the company itself.

Competition defined Edison, as it defined those who contended that schools should be run like businesses. Louis Gerstner, in amplifying the message he helped broadcast as a founding board member of the New American Schools Development Corporation (NASDC), made clear in his book *Rein-*

venting Education, published in 1994, that schools must vie with each other like any service provider in the marketplace: "From a business perspective, . . . the central problem for American public schools is that they have not been forced to continuously adapt themselves to the changes in their students and the demands of society and the economy."[12]

For Gerstner, who had recently moved from the helm of RJR Nabisco to that of IBM, the crucible of competition among schools would lead to progress: "Schools must meet the test any high-performance organization must meet: results. And results are not achieved by bureaucratic regulation. They are achieved by meeting customer requirements by rewards for success and penalties for failure. Market discipline is the key, the ultimate form of accountability."[13]

To Whittle and his team launching Edison, the reward for results for school operators should be no different from the reward rendered the likes of R.J.R. Nabisco and IBM. If the company succeeded in its goal of providing a "world-class education" to disadvantaged students at the same cost as public schools, Edison officials maintained, profits should follow.[14] While tension certainly existed between reinvesting money in its schools and returning it to investors, explained John Chubb soon after the company opened its first schools, such tension was healthy: "The pressure to make profits has forced the Edison Project to improve the service it offers communities, not compromise it."[15]

Whittle and his team exuded the same conviction as Gerstner. Some of this conviction seemed rooted in the customary regard businesspeople accord competition. Much of Whittle's conviction, however, derived from the success of Channel One. Despite harsh criticism from students, parents, educators, and consumer rights groups alike, Channel One profited immensely as a business collaborating closely with school districts. In defending Edison as a for-profit enterprise, Whittle repeatedly cited Channel One's battle. Whittle did so before Edison opened its first school in 1995. And he made the same argument as late as 2005 when Edison was retrenching in the face of public opposition rather than growing as he and Wall Street forecasters had predicted.[16]

If not Whittle's most unconventional venue for advertising, Channel One was certainly his most controversial. In exchange for wiring schools and equipping them with satellite dishes, twenty-five-inch televisions, and videocassette recorders, Channel One obtained a commitment from school administrators to show students every morning a twelve-minute news program incorporating four thirty-second commercials.[17] Among advertisers would be Wrigley's Chewing Gum, Snickers, Fritos, Pepsi, Mountain Dew, Nintendo, Xbox, Clearasil, Stridex, Head & Shoulders Shampoo, Nike, Converse, Levi's Jeans, Pizza Hut, McDonald's, and the U.S. Army. The cost to Channel One for installation was approximately $50,000 per school with a minimum of 5,000 schools to start, meaning an initial outlay of $250 million.[18] The revenue potential with each thirty-second commercial costing $150,000 was $600,000 a day, or approximately $100 million a year.[19]

As educational programming, Channel One differed little in principle from *Schoolhouse Rock!,* the widely acclaimed series of brief animated musical segments that aired on ABC between Saturday morning cartoons from 1973 to 1985 and was revived in the 1990s. Sponsored by General Mills, Kellogg's, and McDonald's, among others, *Schoolhouse Rock!* brought to millions of children mini-lessons in math, grammar, civics, and science with such episodes as "Three Is a Magic Number," "Conjunction Junction," "I'm Just a Bill," and "Interplanet Janet."[20] Yet *Schoolhouse Rock!* was viewed at home at parental discretion. Channel One was viewed during homeroom as a mandatory part of the school day.

Before beginning a five-week pilot of Channel One at six schools across the country in March 1989, Whittle published an op-ed in the *New York Times* to win over critics of commercials in the classroom. Whittle wrote that while students can benefit immensely from modern video technology and specifically from a daily news program, only 3 percent of the country's schools had satellite dishes and only 10 percent of classrooms had televisions. "Were this a perfect world," Whittle argued, "we would agree that Government, not commercials, should provide this technology and programming. . . . But in today's world of $20 textbook budgets and tough fiscal constraints, two minutes of appropriate advertising is not a bad solution."[21]

To buttress his case, Whittle ran seven full-page ads in March in the *New York Times* during the launch of the pilot and another seven in June to report the results of studies of the program's popularity and its academic impact.[22] In the first of the fourteen ads, appearing the same day as his op-ed and on the final page of the paper's business section, a simple exclamation in white ran across a black background: "Dinner's ready!" Occupying the bottom quarter of the page was commentary, with the following heading: "For too many students, this is the 6:00 news." The ad continued: "Teenagers have more on their minds than world news. And it shows. In a recent television special, high school students reported that Chernobyl was Cher's full name. That the Ayatollah Khomeini was a Russian gymnast. And that the District of Columbia was a country in Latin America. It's not fair to ask the overburdened teachers in our underfunded schools to solve this problem alone. Obviously a news program that teenagers will watch would help."[23]

The next day, Whittle ran another attention-grabbing ad, this one appearing on the final page of the paper's front section. Taking up the top three-quarters of the page were three columns of blank spaces, numbered from one to fifty-seven. Commentary again ran below, this time with the following heading: "Here's a list of everyone willing to donate $250,000,000 to schools." The ad continued: "No one can afford it. Including us. And it's becoming apparent that government can no longer equip schools on its own. . . . It seems obvious to us that it's time to explore new, innovative approaches to the funding of education. And that's what we believe we've done with Channel One."[24] The five remaining ads of this initial blitz appeared over the ensuing two weeks, carried similar messages, and generated enough buzz to warrant an article in the *New York Times* about the advertising firm behind the campaign.[25] Of the seven follow-up ads in June, three appeared with a picture of fireworks and claimed underneath that "an overwhelming majority" of polled viewers wanted Channel One in their schools, that the same held for polled parents of school-age children, and that students who had watched Channel One did significantly better on current events assessments than those who had not.[26]

Whittle's efforts paid off. A year after the pilot, Channel One was in 3,600 schools across thirty-eight states.[27] In its second year, Channel One was in 8,216 schools and every state but Alaska, Hawaii, and Nevada.[28] Though public schools in California, New York, and Rhode Island were barred by state education authorities from contracting with Channel One, private schools in those states were, of course, free to make their own decisions. Catholic schools had signed up in disproportionate numbers. Of the country's Catholic high schools, 65 percent (or 844) were wired with Channel One.[29] In 1992 educational authorities in Rhode Island and California backed down.[30] In 1995 educational authorities in New York did the same.[31] Channel One appeared to be on its way to fulfilling Whittle's prediction in 1989 that the program would someday be viewed in 20,000 of the country's schools.[32] By 1999, Channel One had a daily audience of 8 million students in more than 12,000 schools, and the cost of the network's thirty-second commercial spots had climbed to $200,000.[33]

Whittle's full-court press to disarm his opponents didn't end with his fourteen full-page ads in the *New York Times*. He also spent a significant sum on lobbying legislators in Albany, Sacramento, and other state capitals to get Channel One into schools.[34] In addition, much as he and his successors would in leading Edison, Whittle worked hard to bring aboard prominent people from many corners. With the inauguration of Channel One, Whittle succeeded in appointing to the program's advisory board none other than Albert Shanker.[35] Whittle moreover created a noncommercial program for teachers about best pedagogical practices. Called the Educators Channel, it was moderated by Judy Woodruff, Washington correspondent for the *MacNeil/Lehrer Newshour* on PBS and beamed for free by Whittle Communications to any school with a satellite dish. Though Shanker stepped down from the Channel One advisory board a year later, saying that he feared his association as president of the American Federation of Teachers was being used as an endorsement of the program, he agreed to sit on the advisory board of the Educators Channel. The chair of this latter board was the progressive scholar Linda Darling-Hammond, at the time the codirector of the Center for School Reform at Teachers College, Columbia University.[36]

◼

While Whittle was right in claiming many years later that Channel One overcame resistance from opponents to commercials in the classroom to become a profitable operation, he was wrong, according to academic studies, that Channel One would accomplish its purpose of significantly improving student awareness of current events, and he was wrong that Channel One would continue to keep its critics at bay and grow. Whether or not these studies proved to be decisive in determining the future of Channel One, the opponents of commercials in the classroom ultimately prevailed, and advertisers drifted away.

In a review of Channel One during its pilot stage, *Wall Street Journal* media critic Robert Goldberg described the program as "MTV meets CNN," with smart graphics, seductive music, breathless movement from one story to the next, and seamless integration of commercials. "By the end of the first three shows," Goldberg wrote, "I was exhausted. And what sank in? Not much—that Eastern [Airlines] was on strike, and that there are teens in the U.S.S.R. and they're just like us, except different." Moreover, Goldberg wrote, "at a certain point in this slick, fast-paced show, I had a strange feeling—a feeling that the news and the ads were actually starting to merge. Chatty, upbeat, full of flash and pizzazz, they became impossible to tell apart."[37]

Goldberg's concern that Channel One lacked depth was soon confirmed by a series of studies building on the preliminary studies conducted after the pilot in 1989. Much as the Ford Foundation concluded in the 1960s after spending $20 million on classroom televisions and educational programs— transmitted to schools in six midwestern states in that presatellite era by circling aircraft—that television fared poorly as an instructional device,[38] the researchers studying Channel One found little if any pedagogical value to the daily news program.

The first study was carried out by the Institute for Social Research at the University of Michigan and commissioned by Whittle himself. In administering multiple-choice current events tests from 1990 to 1992 to students at forty-six schools, half of which showed Channel One and half of which did not, the University of Michigan researchers found that students at Channel One schools exhibited only a 3 percent advantage. While the same researchers documented advantages of 5 percent for high school students and 8 percent for middle school students in a third year of their study, these gains applied only to five schools where teachers actively integrated stories from the Channel One broadcasts into their curricula.[39] Sowing further doubt among skeptics were subsequent studies by other researchers that concluded that Channel One was found disproportionately in high-poverty schools, delivered only teaspoons of substance amid a banquet of rich images and sounds, and conveyed ad content with considerably more effectiveness than news.[40]

This last determination—reported in a peer-reviewed article in 2006 in the medical journal *Pediatrics* detailing how much better middle school students recalled commercials from Channel One than news stories—got to the heart of the program's problem. Much as Goldberg worried after watching three episodes of the pilot in 1989 that Channel One was, in essence, a subtle vehicle for advertisers to nurture brand loyalty among young consumers, critics from across the political spectrum described Channel One as guilty of trespassing. Bill Honig, California's superintendent of public instruction, piped up in opposition just as the pilot wrapped up. "We are given these kids in trust," Honig said. "We can't sell access to them."[41] Thomas Sobol, New York's commissioner of education, echoed Honig, decrying Channel One as an "intrusion of materialism and commercialism."[42] When Whittle tried in 1993 to add a fifth commercial to the twelve-minute broadcast, he added fuel to the fire. "Right from the beginning, we have described this as a classic example of a slippery slope," responded William L. Rukeyser, special adviser to Honig (and, ironically, a third cousin of Whittle Communications senior executive William S. Rukeyser). "This is akin to allowing a multinational company to strip mine in a national park. Naturally, the company is going to try to get a few extra tons of coal a day."[43]

Though Whittle failed to get his fifth commercial, opposition to Channel One nevertheless continued. Groups as different as Action for Children's Television, Consumers Union, Ralph Nader's Commercial Alert, the Christian parents' organization Citizens for Excellence in Education, and Phyllis Schlafly's Eagle Forum relentlessly beat the same drum.[44] Nader and Schlafly, in fact, appeared before the same Senate committee on May 20, 1999, to testify against Channel One. The hearing had been convened at the urging of Alabama Republican Richard C. Shelby, yet another Channel One critic. Schlafly called the program "a devious device to enable advertisers to circumvent parents." Nader called it "the most brazen marketing ploy in the history of the United States."[45]

Reflecting two decades later on his battle with Channel One, William L. Rukeyser said that had Whittle forgone California and New York, he may well never have generated such wide-ranging criticism. "Whittle's mistake may have been his impatience," the retired California official said. "He went where he wasn't wanted and pushed and pushed, and though he won permission for his program, he in the process engendered so much negative publicity he would have otherwise been spared."[46]

By the time *Pediatrics* published its clinically dry assessment in 2006, Channel One was a hobbled giant. Though still viewed in approximately 12,000 schools across the country, Channel One was losing advertisers and failing to attract new ones. Kraft Foods and Kellogg's, for example, had stopped running commercials on Channel One because of growing criticism of such companies as being partially responsible for the rising incidence of childhood and adolescent obesity. From 2002 to 2005, ad revenue dropped 31 percent, from $99 million to $68 million.[47] From 2005 to 2006, ad revenue fell another 31 percent, plummeting to $49 million.[48]

In April 2007, Primedia, which had paid Whittle Communications $240 million in October 1994 for Channel One, sold the cable program to Alloy Inc., a publicly traded New York–based media and marketing firm best known for developing such TV series as *Gossip Girl, The Vampire Diaries,* and *Pretty Little Liars.* The price represented nothing more than assumption of liabilities.[49] Given that the purpose of sophisticated private equity groups like Kohlberg Kravis & Roberts (KKR), the majority owner of Primedia, is to beat the market, the irony of such a loss is profound. While KKR may have retained sizable earnings during its early ownership of Channel One, the private equity group had nothing to show for its investment over the long term. Had KKR instead placed $240 million in a simple S&P 500 index fund in September 1994, it would have seen that investment grow by April 2007 to more than $840 million.[50]

Under Alloy Inc., Channel One saw its audience dwindle and ad revenue slide. By March 2010, Channel One was down to 8,000 schools,[51] and many of its commercials were merely program promotions for TV shows on CBS, with whose news division Channel One had partnered to produce stories.[52] Though reports by Alloy Inc. to the Securities and Exchange Commission do not break out revenue according to specific subsidiaries, it is clear from its annual filings that Channel One was generating no more than $29 million a year and probably much less.[53] In June 2010, Alloy was itself purchased by the private equity firm ZelnickMedia.[54]

■

If public opposition scuttled Channel One within fifteen years, it stood to do the same in much less time to an educational management organization (EMO) set on the controversial course of making a profit running public schools. Once Channel One had taken care of the fixed costs of wiring schools and purchasing and installing satellite dishes, televisions, and videocassette recorders, it had only the variable costs of production to worry about. With more client schools and thus more ad revenue, those variable costs of producing the program dropped in relative terms and brought down average total costs. Channel One could achieve economies of scale and did. More schools meant a lot more money.

For an EMO, more schools necessitate more personnel. There is a linear relationship between expansion and more teachers, education's units of production. All labor-intensive sectors are, in this regard, as previously noted, constrained by Baumol's Law.[55] Yet Baumol's Law hits education especially hard. In such labor-intensive sectors as law, consulting, and insurance, competition indeed forces firms to contain budgets but not to the degree of taxpayer and school board vigilance. Because of the collective nature and purpose of public education, pay for top school officials, as will be discussed in Chapter 8, pales in comparison to that of leaders of law firms, consultancies, and insurance companies. The same holds for military officers, police chiefs, judges, civil servants, and legislators. Moreover, because children and adolescents are the immediate consumers in schools and, as such, not in much of a position to judge the quality of service rendered, any and all apparent incentives for providers to cut corners must be curbed. This makes the EMO business particularly tough. Making it tougher still is that teachers and staff in traditional district schools are usually protected by strict union contracts; and while teachers and staff in charter schools are rarely unionized, managing charter schools often calls for considerable funding to lease or buy property.

Salaries and benefits for teachers in school districts across the country, according to the National Center for Education Statistics, have been stubbornly consistent year after year: in 1990–1991, they amounted to 56 percent of annual spending; in 1995–1996, 57 percent; in 2000–2001, 56 percent again; and in 2005–2006, 55 percent. If salaries and benefits for support staff—from guidance counselors and attendance secretaries to librarians and speech pathologists—are included, the percentages jump to 63, 64, 63, and 63 again, respectively. If salaries and benefits for custodians, bus drivers, and cafeteria workers are added, the percentages climb to 73, 74, 72, and 72 again, respectively. What remains are salaries and benefits for school and central administrators, ranging over these four sample years from 5 percent to 6 percent; the cost of supplies and purchased services, ranging from 15 percent to 18 percent; and tuition and other costs, consistently amounting to 2 percent (see Table 2.1).[56]

Under these circumstances, an EMO is hard pressed to achieve economies of scale. While supplies and services might be more efficiently bought through bulk purchasing, and while school and central administration might be rationalized through careful regional coordination, the potential for significant savings is limited. In fact, expansion in education can result in diseconomies of scale, researchers have found, because of additional administrative layers necessary for larger operations. "Cost function results indicate potentially sizeable cost savings up to district enrollment levels between 2,000 and 4,000 students," concluded three scholars in a 2002 study, "and that sizeable diseconomies of size may begin to emerge for districts above 15,000 students."[57] This stood to be all the more true for an EMO with schools spread across the country rather than concentrated in one region.

As with nearly all commercial enterprises, marketing costs constituted another burden. To make its case, Edison invested heavily in marketing. In addition to running full-page ads at the outset in *Education Week,* the *New York Times,* and the *Wall Street Journal,* Edison ran 121 full-page ads in *Education Week* from 2004 through 2007, of which more than half appeared as advertorials on the second page of the magazine.[58] Edison also sponsored several annual two-day retreats for prospective clients at the luxurious Broadmoor Hotel and Resort in Colorado Springs and paid substantial salaries to marketing executives to pitch the company.[59] As many as twelve company vice presidents, called developers, crisscrossed the country studying the needs of school districts, cold-calling superintendents, meeting with

Table 2.1　Total expenditures by percentage for U.S. public elementary and secondary schools by function and subfunction

Budget item	1990–91	1995–96	2000–01	2005–06
Teacher salaries	44.9	44.9	44.4	41.6
Teacher benefits	11.1	11.9	11.4	13.1
Support staff salaries	6.0	6.0	6.3	6.4
Support staff benefits	1.5	1.6	1.6	2.0
Maintenance salaries	4.4	4.1	3.9	3.6
Maintenance benefits	1.3	1.2	1.1	1.3
Transportation salaries	1.6	1.5	1.6	1.5
Transportation benefits	0.4	0.5	0.5	0.6
Cafeteria salaries	n/a	1.5	1.4	1.3
Cafeteria benefits	n/a	0.4	0.4	0.5
School admin. salaries	4.4	4.4	4.3	4.1
School admin. benefits	1.1	1.2	1.1	1.3
District support salaries	1.3	1.4	1.6	1.5
District support benefits	0.5	0.5	0.5	0.6
District admin. salaries	1.3	1.1	1.0	0.9
District admin. benefits	0.4	0.3	0.3	0.3
Purchased services	8.1	8.5	9.1	9.6
Supplies	7.3	7.4	8.1	8.2
Tuition	0.6	0.6	0.7	0.9
Other	1.5	1.0	1.0	1.0

Data source: National Center for Education Statistics, *Digest of Education Statistics,* 2009, table 180, 1990–1991 through 2006–2007, http://nces.ed.gov/programs/digest/d09/tables/dt09_180.asp.

school officials, and negotiating contracts. These developers, according to Richard O'Neill, senior vice president and general manager of Edison's Partnership Division from 1997 to 2005, earned $150,000 to $175,000 a year and incurred approximately $75,000 a year in expenses.[60]

Developers, O'Neill said, on average pitched Edison to at least fifty school districts for every contract they won. Moreover, on account of pressure from headquarters to add schools and increase gross revenue, many developers closed deals that were not financially viable. This was the heaviest marketing cost, O'Neill said. It was not the retreats at the Broadmoor or the salaries and expenses of developers that cost Edison so much, he said, but the losses deliberately absorbed to boost market share. "Every school in California was and remains under water," O'Neill said in 2006. "The contracts for the two schools in Macon, Georgia, were under water. And the deal to run nine schools in Chester, Pennsylvania, was so poorly structured, it cost Edison maybe $34 million over four years."[61]

More fundamentally, Edison's marketing problem was the lack of evidence that the company was putting theory into practice in fulfilling its purpose of bringing about academic gains. While Edison's schools may have struck observers as orderly, modern, and vibrant, there was no independent confirmation as of 2000 that their students were learning more than students in neighboring schools in the same districts. In a 300-page study of achievement at ten schools managed by Edison in Massachusetts, Michigan, Florida, Kansas, Texas, and Colorado, Gary Miron and Brooks Applegate of Western Michigan University concluded in 2000 that Edison students did not do as well as Edison had claimed but rather made average progress. Miron and Applegate argued that Edison looked solely at criterion-referenced tests (measuring gains in knowledge over time) when it should have also examined norm-referenced tests (assessing progress relative to comparison groups). The latter approach showed Edison's schools to be in the middle of the pack, not out front.[62] Likewise, longitudinal studies commissioned by Edison of reading scores at Edison's first four schools done from 1995 to 1998 by Robert Mislevy, a statistician at the Educational Testing Service, exhibited mixed results.[63]

Edison nevertheless maintained in its annual reports that its schools achieved significant academic gains.[64] And Whittle and Schmidt maintained that on account of streamlined operations, top managerial talent, and high-quality professional development, Edison would with growth achieve the economies of scale necessary for the company to earn a profit. Edison had indeed hired top managerial talent. It had centralized purchasing and professional development. It had adopted state-of-the-art data management systems and trained school administrators to make proficient use of them. All Edison schools, for example, were equipped with SASI, arguably the best software at the time for maintaining student records and scheduling classes, as explained earlier, and all Edison programmers responsible for running SASI received a week of hands-on training; by contrast, programmers in such school systems as New York City's got little, if any, training.[65] Edison's well-appointed headquarters at Fifth Avenue and Forty-Third Street in New York likewise gave every impression of order and efficiency, standing in sharp contrast to the typical central office of a large school department. The switchboard was open from 8 a.m. to 6:30 p.m., Monday through Friday. Telephone calls were promptly returned. The staff treated visitors with exceptional courtesy; even company executives, from Whittle and Schmidt to Chubb, greeted visitors at the front desk and escorted them out.[66]

With this professionalism and operational efficiency, economies of scale did grow, but not to the point of generating profits. Whittle and Schmidt repeatedly pushed back target dates as they approached. For example, in December 1996, when Edison was running twelve schools, they predicted the company would become profitable once it had twenty-five schools.[67] By 1998 Edison was running twenty-five schools and posted losses of $11.4 million on revenue of $38.5 million.[68] In June 1997, Whittle and Schmidt told the *New York Times* that Edison would be profitable with fifty to seventy schools, which they said they expected to have under management in two years.[69] By 1999 Edison was running fifty-one schools and posted losses of $21.9 million on revenue of $69.4 million; by 2000 Edison was running seventy-nine schools and posted losses of $49.4 million on revenue of $125 million.[70] In July 2001, Whittle told *Businessweek* that Edison would be profitable by 2005 with 250,000 students in its schools.[71]

■

To remain in business, Edison executives concluded that the company had to change its business. While the company could achieve volume in running public schools across the country as a subcontractor, the margins were at best slim. In fact, the margins were so slim in some states that Edison accepted philanthropic funding from privatization advocates to subsidize the operation of many schools.[72]

The family foundation of Donald Fisher, the founder of Gap Inc., donated $1.8 million in 1998 to fund the start-up of an Edison charter school in San Francisco and pledged $25 million more to California school districts that signed on with Edison.[73] Business groups and foundations in Denver the same year contributed more than $4 million to transform an old school building into a new home for an Edison school.[74] In Peoria, Illinois, an heir to the Caterpillar Company fortune provided $1 million in 1999 to help finance the opening of two Edison schools.[75] In suburban Indianapolis, the Lilly Endowment gave a school district $3.3 million in 2001 to subsidize a five-year contract with Edison to run two schools.[76] That same year, the Fisher Foundation combined with the Thompson Family Foundation of Knoxville, Tennessee, in providing $2.8 million to the school district of Clark County, Nevada, to subsidize a five-year contract with Edison to run seven schools.[77] In sum, according to Edison's filings with the SEC, philanthropies supported nineteen of the 113 schools under company management in 2000–2001.[78]

To reorient the company, executives made use of its brand and its intellectual property to develop higher-margin divisions. In 1999 Edison introduced a summer school component with nonunion staff. By 2001 the company had 12,000 students enrolled in its summer programs. In 2002 summer enrollment climbed to 35,000. That same year Edison rolled out Edison Extra, combining after-school and summer programs, as well as Edison Affiliates, offering school districts a light version of its whole-school management model in providing professional development, curriculum guidance, and computer software for assessing student progress.[79]

To what degree these higher-margin divisions drove down costs cannot be discerned from the company's filings with the SEC, as the company did not break out revenues and costs by division. But it is clear that they played a role. Jim Howland, the CEO of Edison's Educational Services Group and a former McKinsey consultant, said in a 2005 interview that the company's supplementary divisions had quickly evolved into the company's strongest.[80]

In adhering to its core mission, Edison continued to pursue more management contracts but concentrated its efforts on signing multiple schools within a district to reduce oversight costs and improve academic supervision.[81] To that end, Edison in 1999 was already running four schools in each of six cities: Flint and Mount Clemens, Michigan; Peoria, Illinois; Wichita, Kansas; San Antonio, Texas; and Washington, DC. The following year, Edison had three schools in Baltimore, seven schools in Dallas, and all three schools in

Inkster, Michigan, making it the company's first wholly run district and the nation's first district run by a private company.[82]

But it was Baltimore that presented Edison with its best opportunity yet to prove its promise. In Flint, Mount Clemens, Peoria, Wichita, San Antonio, Dallas, and Inkster, Edison was managing traditional district schools, which meant working within the constraints of teacher union contracts. In Washington, D.C., Edison was running four charter schools launched by Friendship House, a local social services agency. Working for a charter board under Friendship House freed Edison from such staffing constraints yet placed the company one remove from the city's department of education and thus necessarily limited its influence on municipal policy and its capacity to grow.

In Baltimore, Edison likewise had no such staffing constraints. In an effort to catalyze change throughout the Baltimore system with an injection of competition, the Maryland State Department of Education in February 2000 took the nationally unprecedented step of taking over three struggling schools and hiring a commercial operator to manage them. Six other states to date had taken over failing school districts. Most prominently, New Jersey had assumed control of the school systems of Jersey City in 1989, Paterson in 1991, and Newark in 1995. But no state so far had assigned management of any schools to a commercial operator.[83] As state takeover schools, the three schools Maryland assigned to Edison—Gilmor Elementary, Furman Templeton Elementary, and Montebello Elementary—were off limits to the Baltimore Teachers Union. Edison had the same freedom of a private or nonunion charter school to hire and fire staff and to fully implement its program. In contrast to typical arrangements in running charter schools, Edison did not have to lease or buy property. Moreover, as Edison's contract was with the state school board, the company was well positioned to influence state as well as municipal policy and thereby take on more schools.[84]

Granted significant administrative liberty and placed squarely within a public school system, Edison now had the opportunity to manage a miniature district in the manner Myron Lieberman had long ago prescribed.[85]

3

ON THE WIRE

This is the first time that a state, in a sense, has assumed this responsibility, and it's not been a decision by a local system. We have no model. We're creating a model. And there's a lot at stake.

Nancy S. Grasmick, Maryland Superintendent of Schools, *Baltimore Sun*, July 30, 2000

■ UPON ENTERING Edison's Montebello Elementary School in Northeast Baltimore in 2005 and again in 2009, I left behind a quiet working-class neighborhood for an orderly, vibrant school governed by a charismatic principal, Camille Bell, who collected hugs from students everywhere she went. "Give me some sugar, pumpkin," Bell said to one student after another upon inviting them into a warm embrace. "Are you feeling fine," she followed up, "or fabulous?"[1]

At each turn, Montebello fulfilled Edison's promise of immaculate, bright schools with dedicated teachers leading well-behaved students through focused lessons. The hallways and classrooms were sparkling clean and decorated with colorful bulletin boards. All students were neatly attired in navy polo shirts and khaki pants. They sat politely attentive in class and marched quietly in single file between periods. Reflecting Bell, the teachers and staff were universally upbeat.

Four miles across town in West Baltimore sat the two other schools turned over to Edison by the Maryland State Department of Education in 2000: Furman Templeton Elementary and Gilmor Elementary. West Baltimore, rendered iconic by the acclaimed HBO series *The Wire*, is a neighborhood of boarded-up row houses, empty storefronts, and frequent police sirens. One block from Furman Templeton Elementary is McCulloh Homes, a sprawling maze of two- and three-story red-brick public housing anchored by two high-rises and checkered by courtyards, some of patchy grass, others of concrete laced by clotheslines. In *The Wire,* this is home turf to Avon Barksdale and his crew of drug dealers. Across the street from nearby Gilmor Elementary is Gilmor Homes, a smaller but equally impersonal assemblage of three-story red-brick public housing where twenty-five-year-old Freddie Gray would be arrested in April 2015 and soon after slip into a coma while in police custody and die, setting off a night of violent protest and several days of marches and rallies.[2]

When Jeff Wahl, who became CEO of Edison in 2008, recalled his first trip from Baltimore/Washington International Thurgood Marshall Airport to this neighborhood, he shook his head in disbelief and said he had never seen such a sudden and sustained shift in urban landscape.[3]

■

While Baltimore pays homage to Maryland's most famous jurist, Thurgood Marshall, with an airport on the city's edge and a prominent statue downtown outside the Garmatz Federal Courthouse, its most infamous, Roger Taney, casts a larger shadow. Though unmentioned in city guidebooks and unknown to countless lifelong residents, Taney, chief justice of the Supreme Court from 1836 to 1864 and author of the 1857 decision *Dred Scott v. Sandford* that denied blacks citizenship and fueled the sectionalism basic to the Civil War, sits squarely in bronze in a park several blocks from Marshall's stately image.

The world Marshall fought and appeared to defeat in 1954 as lead counsel for the National Association for the Advancement of Colored People in *Brown v. Board of Education of Topeka* implicitly persists here, as in cities across the country. Furman Templeton, Gilmor, and Montebello are each 99 percent black. Though Baltimore's schools are not technically segregated, they reflect a metropolitan area rigidly divided by race. Because of white flight in the 1960s and 1970s, the city's schools fifty years after *Brown* were 89 percent black, up from 51 percent in 1960. Because of divisions within the city, the neighborhoods of Furman Templeton, Gilmor, and Montebello are even more segregated.[4] Moreover, the students at these three schools are poor: 91 percent of Furman Templeton's 448 students qualified for free or reduced-price lunch when Edison took over in September 2000, as did

89 percent of Montebello's 699 students and 96 percent of Gilmor's 486; and these figures changed little in the ensuing decade.[5]

A midday walk through the neighborhood surrounding Furman Templeton in 2009 with the school's principal, Ken Cherry, revealed a playing field littered with broken glass, buckled sidewalks dotted with discarded crack vials, a bloated dead white cat by a curb, three prostitutes on a corner smiling at passersby, and a black Baltimore Police helicopter locked in the sky some 500 feet above.

"Every job candidate gets this tour," Cherry said. "They have to know the school beyond the classroom and the parking lot. Quite a few afterward withdraw from consideration."[6]

Though Cherry and Gilmor's principal, Ledonnis Hernandez, exhibited the same focus and determination as their crosstown colleague Bell, their schools by comparison lacked the vibrancy and warmth of Montebello. And their students' scores on the state's standardized exams year after year lagged far behind. Along with recycled claims that Edison received more money per pupil than other Baltimore schools, the low test scores at Furman Templeton and Gilmor repeatedly subjected Edison to scrutiny and put the company's contract in jeopardy.

■

The story of Maryland's takeover of Furman Templeton, Gilmor, and Montebello goes back to 1993, when the state school board introduced an accountability system based on annual tests given to third-, fifth-, and eighth-graders in the following subjects: reading, writing, language usage, math, science, and social studies. Student scores were categorized as excellent, satisfactory, or unsatisfactory. Schools with low rates of proficiency were labeled "reconstitution eligible." With passage in 1997 of a bill in the Maryland legislature giving Baltimore schools $254 million in additional funding over the ensuing five years in exchange for joint control of the Baltimore School Board by the governor and the mayor, the state gained authority to take over persistently underperforming schools.[7] By 1999, 83 of Baltimore's 180 elementary, middle, and high schools were labeled "reconstitution eligible," though Maryland superintendent of schools Nancy Grasmick said that only schools on this list since 1994 would be considered for state takeover.[8]

For Grasmick, the time for intervention was overdue. "Any accountability system has to have a bottom line," she said at a meeting of the state school board in September 1999 where members voted unanimously to identify persistently underperforming schools for management by outside operators. "We have an obligation to the children in those schools. We can't wait." Grasmick conceded that Baltimore's experiment in outsourcing the management of nine schools to Minneapolis-based Educational Alternatives Inc. (EAI) from 1992 to 1996 was a disappointment but contended that the state's application of privatization would be different. EAI had neither been granted the freedom to hire and fire staff, she said, nor introduced a distinct, comprehensive curriculum. Any contractor working with the state would have such freedom and would be expected to introduce a genuinely new academic program.[9]

In an editorial following Grasmick's announcement, the *Baltimore Sun* backed her up:

> Several things make this an entirely different proposal than the EAI mess, but the most important is that this privatization venture would be part of the existing plan to improve the lowest-performing schools. . . . A third-party manager would step into that process, acting as an agent of the state in the takeover. If the state does its job, that contractor would comply with the same meticulous documentation demanded of the schools. . . . EAI didn't face those kind of strictures in Baltimore. Nor did it operate as part of a well-functioning structure. The company's academic improvement plans were sketchy, and its efforts were not well-supervised. Then-Superintendent Walter G. Amprey acted more as EAI's cheerleader than as the school system's guardian. . . . If the state proceeds cautiously with this plan, and ensures that safeguards are in place to prevent abuses, this plan might just work. EAI's crash and burn in Baltimore soured a lot of people on privatization, and the state has an opportunity to show that it's not a taboo.[10]

Following several months of study, Grasmick announced at a meeting of the state school board in February 2000 that Furman Templeton, Gilmor, and Montebello would be taken over and that interested school management firms should submit detailed proposals. Two board members dissented, one of whom, Reginald Dunn, a marketing executive appointed to the board in August, asked, "What have we done in the previous years to help these three schools to achieve before we got to the point of a takeover?" Dunn's question went unanswered.[11] The reaction after the meeting from Baltimore officials was mixed. "I cannot say strongly enough how much I feel they have made an error," said Samuel C. Stringfield, a member of the Baltimore School Board and an educational research scientist at Johns Hopkins University. "I'm not happy," responded State Senator Charles M. Mitchell IV of West Baltimore. "We lived through the EAI experiment, and look where that got us." Conversely, J. Tyson Tildon, the president of the Baltimore School Board and a neuroscientist at the University of Maryland, welcomed the decision: "While there are concerns, I think one has to use this as a wake-up call."[12]

Appearing before the Maryland State House Ways and Means Committee the next day, Grasmick had some explaining to do. House delegate Clarence Davis, representing Northeast Baltimore, echoed Mitchell in citing the confidence a decade earlier in EAI and the ensuing disappointment. Grasmick guaranteed that the state takeover would differ significantly from Baltimore's experience with EAI: the school manager would be bound by a "performance-based" contract stipulating "very strict benchmarks." Testifying before the same committee, Baltimore Teachers Union (BTU) president Marietta English built on the concerns raised by Davis: "How can a third party do better than those of us who live here, who went to Baltimore city schools, who send their children to Baltimore city schools, and who will still be here when the contractor fails and goes home?" Baltimore's new school chief, Robert Booker, sidestepped the matter of outsourcing to underscore the considerable needs of the city's children and to lobby the committee for more state aid. Booker said that in his many years as a school administrator in Los Angeles, he had never seen children as underserved.[13]

■

The only other company to compete with Edison for the contract to run Furman Templeton, Gilmor, and Montebello was Mosaica, an educational management organization running eight schools at that time—five in

Michigan, two in Pennsylvania, and one in New Jersey.[14] Founded in 1997 by the husband-and-wife team of Gene and Dawn Eidelman—who had previously operated a network of child-care centers for corporations—and based in New York, Mosaica pitched an integrated curriculum, called Paragon, applying several disciplines to the study of a series of civilizations in chronological order in each grade. Mosaica also promised individualized lesson plans for all students, Spanish instruction in kindergarten and beyond, abundant use of technology, and a longer school day (by one hour) and year (by twenty days).[15]

Edison made the same promises of abundant technology and a longer day and school year. Moreover, Edison promised brisk improvement. After touring Furman Templeton, Gilmor, and Montebello in February, Richard O'Neill, the Edison vice president for development who later soured on the company's marketing strategy, predicted that the Edison model would produce quick results. "I think this idea that reform takes years is bogus," O'Neill said. Should Edison fail to turn the tide in one year, he added, "we should have our feet held to the fire."[16]

The Maryland School Board settled unanimously in March on Edison, citing the company's wider experience, better results, and more detailed plans. The state awarded Edison a five-year renewable contract and committed to paying the company the same amount per student spent throughout the Baltimore system, which in 2000 amounted to $7,400. With 1,400 students in total at Furman Templeton, Gilmor, and Montebello, Edison stood to collect $10.4 million a year, though the company had only nominal control over much of that sum. Even with the unprecedented autonomy conferred by the state to operate free from union regulations, Edison had to pay competitive salaries to attract and retain good teachers and moreover couldn't economize by increasing class size for fear of both provoking yet more criticism and undermining the performance of their students, whose test results would be the key determinant of the company's effectiveness.[17]

Aiming to thwart the takeover, the BTU revived an ill-fated lawsuit it had filed in Baltimore Circuit Court in 1993 against the city for having hired EAI. The BTU alleged that the state had improperly delegated to Edison the authority to set salaries and implement disciplinary procedures; dispensed more money to Edison per student, a charge that would be henceforth debated repeatedly; and, most fundamentally, violated its commitment to the city's schoolchildren by diverting funds to a commercial school operator. "A fair allocation of the city's limited resources," the BTU contended, ". . . does not include a profit to a private sector company."[18]

Backing Grasmick again, the *Baltimore Sun* weighed in derisively against the BTU:

> At least the Baltimore Teachers Union is consistent. Consistently against change and innovation, that is. Consistently blocking progress and yammering about how the status quo works just fine. . . . There are legitimate questions about what would happen to teacher pensions and benefits in the Edison schools. Edison must provide good answers to those questions, and reassure potential employees that fairness will prevail. But the BTU is way off base with its lawsuit. It sends the wrong message—to the public and to city kids, who desperately need a better education. Unfortunately, the union is all too consistent in that regard.[19]

While this BTU lawsuit against privatization, like the last one, went nowhere, it was grounded not in fear, as before, but in bitter experience that both the *Sun* and Grasmick acknowledged as substantial.[20] The *Sun* declared that the state's venture with Edison would have to be different from Baltimore's alliance with EAI. And Grasmick had vowed it would. In addition to the state's new accountability measures, Edison's freedom to hire and fire and its distinctive curriculum, Grasmick had declared, made this second experiment in privatization far different.[21]

As Edison introduced its new teachers to its philosophy and methods in a weeklong program at Towson University in July, Grasmick underscored the singularity of this undertaking: "This is the first time that a state, in a sense, has assumed this responsibility, and it's not been a decision by a local system. We have no model. We're creating a model. And there's a lot at stake." To Dwight D. Jones, an Edison regional vice president overseeing the program at Towson University, the company's model was likewise unique, and quality control at each school was of paramount importance. "It has to look like what we call the Edison brand," said Jones, who would go on to become Colorado's commissioner of education and then superintendent of the Las Vegas school system. "It's going to be clean. It's going to be well lit. It's going to be organized in a certain way. . . . We leave nothing to chance."[22]

■

When EAI arrived in Baltimore in 1992, the company received a warm reception from many corners. The *Sun,* the BTU, the Baltimore School Board, Mayor Kurt L. Schmoke, Superintendent Walter G. Amprey, and the city's esteemed Abell Foundation all welcomed EAI. In fact, Robert C. Embry Jr., the president of the Abell Foundation, who would a decade later become an adamant opponent of Edison, had invited John T. Golle, EAI's founder and president, to Baltimore in 1991 to learn more about the company. Impressed with Golle's message, Embry recommended EAI to Schmoke and had the Abell Foundation pay for a group of school and union officials to tour a private school in Minnesota and a public school in Florida run by EAI.[23] BTU president Irene Dandridge and Assistant School Superintendent Charlene Cooper Boston returned with an enthusiastic report to the city's school board. Dandridge was especially impressed with Golle. "He's very personable, very committed," Dandridge said. "If you just listened to him, you'd turn all your schools over to him."[24]

With Schmoke's endorsement, Amprey proposed turning over one middle and eight elementary schools to EAI. The *Sun* lauded both Schmoke and Amprey for venturing to work with the private sector to streamline operations and deliver better results.[25] Leaders of the Interdenominational Ministerial Alliance nevertheless expressed anger with Schmoke and Amprey for failing to consult them and protested the diversion of funds to a for-profit school operator.[26] More resistance followed. Baltimoreans United for Leadership Development (BUILD) held a forum on the deal that was attended by nearly 500 BUILD delegates as well as Schmoke.[27] "We will fight you on this," BUILD cochair Reverend Robert Behnke said to Schmoke at the forum, "because the whole thing is contrary to public education."[28]

BTU president Dandridge subsequently backpedaled to caution that the contract's language was too loose, especially regarding EAI's freedom to replace $12-an-hour BTU teacher aides with $8-an-hour college interns. And City Comptroller Jacqueline McLean voiced concern about EAI's financial stability. With McLean and another member of the city's board of estimates dissenting, Amprey's proposal was approved by a vote of 3–2, granting EAI a five-year contract three times the size of the contract awarded Edison eight years later. EAI got all nine schools Amprey had listed, with a total enrollment of 4,815 students. With per-pupil expenditure in Baltimore at $5,549 in 1992–1993, the contract was worth $26.7 million in its initial year, though all but 10 percent of that amount, reported the *Sun,* went to the city for administrative costs and to teacher salaries and benefits.[29]

Golle, like Chris Whittle, had no background as an educator. After graduating from the University of Minnesota in 1966 with a bachelor's degree in business, Golle (pronounced goal·ie) joined Xerox in corporate sales. Four years later, he cofounded a consultancy providing human resources advice to Fortune 500 companies. In 1986, dissatisfied with the lockstep curriculum his two sons went through in Minnesota public schools, Golle decided to develop a network of moderately priced private schools with individualized curricula so that students could proceed at appropriate paces. Golle hired David A. Bennett, who had twenty-four years of experience as a public school administrator, away from the superintendency of the St. Paul, Minnesota, school system to be his president. Golle and Bennett began with one school in Minnesota and another in Arizona, each charging about $5,000 a year. However, start-up costs proved too steep to take the plan to scale. So Golle and Bennett, like Whittle and Schmidt after them, reconceived their company as a subcontractor working with public school districts. In 1991 they took on their first client: South Pointe Elementary, a school with 720 students in a poor neighborhood of Miami. To boost the adult-to-student ratio while keeping costs down, EAI hired University of Miami students as teacher aides at $7 an hour. To enhance self-paced learning, EAI invested in classroom computers and retraining of staff.[30]

For Golle, as with Whittle, the rigor of business methods would pave the way to better schooling. Through efficiencies in administration, maintenance, food preparation, and purchasing, Golle claimed that he would reduce noninstructional spending in Baltimore by 25 percent, plow 80 percent of the savings back into the classroom, and retain 20 percent of the savings as profit.[31] In particular, Golle contended, such savings would be achieved through bottom-up budgeting overseen by KPMG Peat Marwick and sophisticated building maintenance carried out by Johnson Control Services. The resulting difference in the classroom would include, as in Miami, a "personal education plan" for every student designed in consultation with parents; an instructional assistant for every teacher to facilitate small-group learning; several computers in every classroom; and a computer, phone, and desk for every teacher.[32] Like the New American Schools Development Corporation before him and Benno Schmidt after, Golle predicted remarkable gains at average costs. "We pledged to Baltimore," Golle said as the school year was about to begin, "that without spending any additional dollars, we will dramatically improve the quality of education for children."[33]

Golle's optimism notwithstanding, the chorus of skeptics grew. Teachers picketed outside City Hall a week before schools opened. An art teacher in the picket line complained that she had been involuntarily transferred from two schools taken over by EAI because art had been dropped from the curriculum. "We were deceived," she said. "We were not treated as professionals." Meanwhile, 37 of the 160 teachers at EAI's nine schools requested transfers. Three weeks into the school year, company officials parried two hours of angry questions at an evening gathering of approximately eighty parents. One complaint concerned the unauthorized mainstreaming of children with special needs. Company officials vowed that no steps would be taken without parental approval. Another complaint concerned the replacement of roving teachers of art and music with low-paid interns functioning as teacher aides. While teachers registered their praise by November for EAI's significant improvement of both building maintenance and purchasing protocol, they faulted EAI's individualized curriculum for lack of structure.[34]

Despite implementation problems, Wall Street responded to EAI's first year in Baltimore with enthusiasm. From June 1992 to June 1993, the company's stock climbed from $7 a share to $33. The company had gone public in April 1991 at $4 a share.[35] Basic to this enthusiasm, however, was a basic misreading of company financials by EAI executives, analysts, and investors. This same mistake would be repeated several years later by Edison executives, analysts, and investors in assessing the company's progress. The damage for both companies would be irreparable. The issue concerned revenue recognition. EAI booked as revenue budgetary allocations for teacher salaries and other costs over which the company had no control. Company revenue accordingly appeared to be as much as ten times the actual figure.

While this representation of revenue didn't alter the reportage of company earnings, it necessarily gave the impression of far greater volume and growth. In an article entitled "Schools Manager Aces Market Test," the *Sun,* for example, incorrectly reported in June 1993 that EAI "now averages $8 million in quarterly revenues vs. $800,000 a year ago."[36] Yet, as noted above, the *Sun* had reported a year earlier, after the board of estimates approved EAI's five-year contract, that EAI retained only 10 percent of the per-pupil allocation: in the first year, $3.4 million went back to the city for administrative expenditures and $20.6 million went directly to teachers' salaries and benefits, leaving EAI $2.7 million to manage its nine schools. By September, the *Sun* reported grumblings from some analysts about EAI's accounting methods but proceeded regardless to report revenue as the company had presented it.[37]

The tide turned in November, by which time EAI's stock had soared to $48.75 a share. City comptroller Jacqueline McLean, who had voted against the EAI contract in July 1992 because of concerns about the company's balance sheet, spoke up against turning over additional Baltimore schools to EAI. McLean accused EAI of misleading investors on revenue, falling far behind in submission of audited financial statements, and distorting the impact of its pedagogical strategies. "They have a good dog and pony show," McLean said. Broadcast on CNBC, McLean's comments sent the stock down 14 percent in one hour. While the stock recovered much lost ground by day's end, a new narrative had taken hold and would in time prevail.[38] A month later, the *Sun* ran a 1,600-word analysis of EAI's accounting practices. One professor of finance was quoted in the story as describing EAI's methods as "nonsensical." Another was quoted as describing the methods as "very misleading." At the end of February, the stock closed at $21.25, down 64 percent from its peak three months before and never to rebound.[39]

More troubling for EAI than its misrepresentation of revenue was its misrepresentation of academic progress and its failure to provide sufficient assistance to children with special needs. The company reported in an ebullient press release in August 1993 that the 4,800 students at its nine schools had advanced almost a full grade level after just three months of new management. The company backtracked in June 1994 to concede that such progress applied only to a subgroup of 954 underperforming students at five schools. EAI lost more credibility and saw its stock plunge 18 percent on the day of this concession.[40] Allegations that EAI shortchanged learning-disabled students moreover led to both state and federal investigations. At one school, it was discovered, EAI dismantled remediation programs for almost 300 students and decreased the special education staff from twenty-four teachers to eleven. The director of special education for the U.S. Department of Education concluded that EAI had violated procedures at six of its nine schools and issued the state a stern warning to exercise more vigilant oversight. Ultimately, a federal judge found Superintendent Amprey in contempt for failing to properly supervise EAI and removed special education—one-third of the superintendent's bailiwick—from his control.[41]

Making matters worse, reading and math scores dropped from 1992 to 1994 at the eight elementary schools managed by EAI while scores in both subjects climbed over the same period for the city's other elementary schools as a whole. On these tests—with scores ranging from 1 to 99, with 50 as the national average—scores in reading at EAI schools dropped from 39.8 to 37 while they rose for Baltimore schools as a whole from 42.3 to 44.8; scores in math dropped for EAI schools from 41.7 to 40 while they rose for city schools from 44.4 to 47.7. Meanwhile, scores at EAI's elementary school in Miami failed to advance during three years under the company's management.[42]

Persisting in EAI's corner, Mayor Schmoke and Superintendent Amprey contended that EAI's presence in Baltimore should be credited with catalyzing the city's overall improvement.[43] Amprey was so enamored of EAI that he had flown to Connecticut in May on behalf of the company to lobby the Hartford City Council to hire EAI to run the state capital's school system, with thirty-two schools and a total enrollment of 26,000 students. In praising EAI, Amprey went so far as to say that Baltimore would have been better served had it hired the company to manage all of its schools. "I asked for nine," Amprey said. "I wish I asked for 178."[44]

While EAI landed a five-year contract to run all of Hartford's schools, the company soon acknowledged its limitations and scaled back its role to managing five schools while overseeing only maintenance and business operations at the remaining twenty-seven. Questions about spending and effectiveness nevertheless dogged the company, and Golle in particular. A report issued by the Center for Educational Research at the University of

Maryland in August 1995 concluded that EAI received 11 percent more in funding per pupil than Baltimore schools in a comparison group and yet posted no better results; in an analysis published a year later, Craig E. Richards of Teachers College, Columbia University, determined that EAI received 26 percent more in funding per pupil for students in elementary school and 36 percent more per pupil for students in middle school.[45] Meanwhile, in Hartford, Golle came to be derided as the Music Man, referring to the con artist in the play and movie by that name who sells band instruments and uniforms to innocent folk in a small Iowan city with the false promise he would lead a boys' ensemble that would give the city new life.[46]

By the spring of 1996, EAI was out of Baltimore and Hartford as well as Miami and done as a subcontractor. Renamed the Tesseract Group, the company moved on to manage preschools, private schools, and charter schools. Yet even in this safer space, the company failed to make money. In 2000 the Tesseract Group filed for bankruptcy.[47]

Amprey was also soon out of Baltimore and done as a school administrator. In the spring of 1997, following a thirty-one-year career in the Baltimore school system begun as a social studies teacher at a junior high, Amprey stepped down as superintendent, earning from the *Sun* an A for effort, an A for style, and a C– for effectiveness, and took a job as national vice president of an education subsidiary of Tele-Communications Inc., the cable TV giant soon after absorbed by AT&T before being spun off to Charter Communications and Comcast.[48]

Reflecting on his struggles, Golle concluded that for-profit management of district schools was a lose-lose proposition: "Sometimes I feel that I'm between the hydrant and the dog. If you make too much money, they say, 'How dare you make too much money off these children?' If you don't make any money, they say, 'You're a bad businessperson.'"[49]

■

Of the eight elementary schools run by EAI, two—Graceland Park and Mary E. Rodman—appeared on the same list of persistently underperforming schools from which Grasmick in 2000 chose Furman Templeton, Gilmor, and Montebello to be taken over by the state. Students at Graceland Park and Mary E. Rodman, in fact, posted lower scores in reading and math

Table 3.1 Percentage of students graded proficient on the 1999 Maryland School Performance Assessment Program (MSPAP)

Elementary school	Grade 3		Grade 5		Mean proficiency
	Reading	Math	Reading	Math	
Arundel	6.8	0	11.4	5.3	5.9
Bay-Brook	4.7	0	4.5	18.5	6.9
Dr. Martin Luther King, Jr.	3.4	2.0	14.2	0.8	5.1
Furman Templeton*	5.6	3.6	0	23.9	8.3
Gilmor*	9.4	5.0	10.1	2.6	6.8
Graceland Park	6.6	1.6	11.3	4.7	6.1
Lafayette	8.3	4.8	6.4	6.3	6.5
Mary Rodman	4.3	4.3	10.9	6.3	6.5
Montebello*	5.3	1.9	5.6	2.4	3.8
William Paca	4.0	2.3	6.1	14.3	6.7
Mean of future Edison schools	6.8	3.5	5.2	9.6	6.3
Mean of remaining seven	5.4	2.1	9.3	8.0	6.2
Baltimore City	17.0	21.4	17.5	18.8	18.7

Data source: MSPAP data obtained from the Maryland State Department of Education by e-mail, July 2012.

Note: Mean figures are unweighted by student population except in the case of grade-level scores for Baltimore City.

*Schools taken over by Edison in 2000.

than their peers at Furman Templeton in 1996, 1997, and 1999. More surprising, students at Montebello, which would soon become Edison's flagship, posted lower scores in reading and math than their peers at Furman Templeton from 1996 through 1999. Montebello, in fact, ranked at the very bottom of Baltimore's 121 elementary schools in both 1998 and 1999. Taken together, the proficiency levels for third- and fifth-graders at Montebello in 1998 in reading and math stood at 3 percent; in 1999 the figure was 4 percent for the same grades in the same subjects. Furman Templeton and Gilmor recorded averaged proficiency levels in 1999 of 8 and 7 percent, respectively (see Table 3.1).

Still more surprising, the seven other schools at the bottom of the city recorded a combined proficiency level just below that of Furman Templeton,

Gilmor, and Montebello. The students at these seven schools likewise came from disadvantaged homes: 84 percent of the students at the three schools to be turned over to Edison qualified for free or reduced-price lunch in 1999; 89 percent of the students at the other seven qualified for the same.[50]

These differences would become central to the argument against Edison waged by the Abell Foundation, the BTU, and community activists rattled by Baltimore's bad experience with EAI. Furman Templeton, Gilmor, and Montebello were indeed failing schools serving poor children, but no more so than these seven other schools in 1999. In 2000, after Grasmick had issued her decision and before Edison took over, reading and math scores at Furman Templeton did drop steeply, from 8 percent proficient to 1 percent, but they went up modestly at both Gilmor and Montebello. The central issue is what happened from 2001 onward. Edison turned things around at Montebello in one year, as Richard O'Neill, the Edison executive, had predicted the company would, or its feet should be held to the fire. Yet reading and math scores dropped at Furman Templeton and Gilmor during their first year under Edison.

Over the next four years, from 2002 to 2005, Edison's three schools collectively exhibited improvement, and in 2002, 2003, and 2005 they together outperformed the seven others with which they were grouped in 1999. In 2006, however, the tide turned. Though Edison's personnel and practices were firmly in place, its schools slipped and continued to slip. Grasmick remained solidly in Edison's corner, much as Amprey persisted in praising EAI despite bad news. But the *Sun* and North Avenue, the metonymical term for the Baltimore City Public School System (BCPSS), eventually joined the Abell Foundation and the BTU in taking up O'Neill's challenge to put Edison's feet to the fire.

4

REPRISE

We turned around three schools on the state takeover list in Baltimore,
and they hate us in Baltimore.

Jim Howland, CEO, Educational Services Group, Edison Schools,
October 18, 2005

■ BEFORE ACADEMIC RESULTS for Edison's three schools in Baltimore
became a cause for concern, Edison's critics, picking up where analysts of
EAI had left off, charged that the company received much more money per
pupil than other Baltimore schools. A former Baltimore School Board member
and Maryland secretary of human resources named Kalman Hettleman
made this argument repeatedly. Just as Edison was putting down roots in
Baltimore in July 2000, Hettleman wrote in an op-ed in the *Sun* that Edison
would be getting as much as $2,400 more than the average Baltimore alloca-
tion of $5,000 per student. Hettleman made this case again in response to a
laudatory article two weeks later in the *Sun* about summer preparations and
professional development at Furman Templeton, Gilmor, and Montebello.[1]

In Edison's defense, Nancy Grasmick fired back with her own op-ed in the
Sun that Edison's payment appeared larger only because Edison would be
responsible for its own administrative expenditures, meaning that the additional $2,400 simply matched Baltimore's per-pupil overhead. Grasmick ex-
plained that while Baltimore would cover the cost of some technical support
and health services, Edison would otherwise receive "virtually no centralized services free of charge" and moreover would keep its schools open for a
longer day and year without any subsidy. In turn, Grasmick's op-ed provoked
an angry letter from the leaders of the BTU, contending that Edison's fees
came at the expense of Baltimore's other schools.[2]

Like the leaders of the BTU, Hettleman didn't buy Grasmick's explanation and responded with another op-ed in the *Sun* in December reiterating his claim and adding to it that Edison benefited in two significant ways from a special arrangement with the state for provision of services to its eighty-five students with serious learning disabilities: first, the state would pay the highly regarded Kennedy Krieger Institute $2.1 million—or $25,000 per student—for instruction of learning-disabled children in self-contained classes at Edison's three schools, while other Baltimore schools had to make do with half that allocation for children with the same needs; second, in doing so, the state conferred on Edison a hidden advantage by relieving its teachers of a significant instructional burden and thereby boosting the likelihood of better results on standardized exams.[3]

Instead of Grasmick, Richard O'Neill, Edison's vice president for development, replied this time to Hettleman, reiterating the point that Edison's payment covered administrative costs and countering that the state had encouraged other Baltimore schools to make the same arrangement with Kennedy Krieger. Sticking to his guns, Hettleman responded to O'Neill's letter, contending that the state had shown Edison preferential treatment.[4]

This conflict over costs climaxed in September 2005 when the Abell Foundation issued a 4,500-word report buttressing Hettleman's claims and asserting that several schools in equally tough straits had outperformed Edison's schools without Edison's additional funding. The facts remained long in dispute, but one thing was clear: both sides had come to distrust, if not detest, each other. Grasmick vehemently rejected the report, arguing that Edison had transformed Furman Templeton, Gilmor, and Montebello with no monetary advantage and questioning whether any of the schools listed in the Abell report had ever been in such bad shape. When asked to comment on the Abell report in October 2005, Benno Schmidt said, "I don't believe a word those people print."[5]

When asked the same question several days later, Jim Howland, the CEO of Edison's Educational Services Group, shook his head and attributed the negative assessment of the company to entrenched opposition to the concept of for-profit management of schools. "We turned around three schools in Baltimore on the state take-over list," Howland said, "and they hate us in Baltimore." Howland said that the distrust of for-profit educational management in Baltimore and elsewhere had become so intense that he saw Edison's future confined to the provision of ancillary services, from after-school tutoring and summer enrichment programs to professional development, curriculum guidance, and test preparation. Managing some schools, Howland said, made sense to keep the company in the public eye and to hone services that could be sold in supplementary form to a wider market, but the number of schools would have to be limited. A year later, following four years at Edison, Howland left the company to become president of the international division of Dun & Bradstreet, a leading corporate information conglomerate.[6]

Like Howland, Chris Whittle too contended that entrenched opposition to for-profit educational management made it hard for Edison to get a fair shake. When asked during an interview in his corner office overlooking Manhattan's Fifth Avenue in November 2005 if John Golle was right to compare an EMO to a man between a fire hydrant and a dog, Whittle grimaced and nodded. "When I appeared before the Maryland State School Board when the company's stock was high," Whittle added, "I got beaten up as a profiteer. When I appeared before the same people a year later when the stock was low, I got beaten up as a bad businessman."[7]

Yet unlike Howland, Whittle maintained that for-profit educational management had a robust future, both in that interview and in a book he wrote on education that was published the same month as the Abell report. In *Crash Course: Imagining a Better Future for Public Education,* Whittle described the nation's schools and many abroad as being run by 2030 by mammoth competing EMOs with such names as Grawson Schools (an apparent conflation of McGraw Hill and Pearson Education or Edison) and Horizon Schools (an apparent transmutation of child-care giant Bright Horizons Family Solutions). Whittle not only predicted that the nation would move "rapidly" in this direction between 2005 and 2015, but he also reclaimed the language of historical necessity he used in trumpeting Edison in 1992 as the free-market answer to the nation's educational ills. Whittle asserted that, in his view, "the changes proposed in this book are as inevitable as the fall of the Berlin Wall."[8]

The changes Whittle proposed in *Crash Course* comprised boosting teacher quality by doubling pay and covering the cost by substantially cutting the number of teachers; reducing instructional time significantly by devoting an increasing portion of the school day to independent learning (so that third-graders, for example, would be "on their own" two hours a day, while high school students would spend only one-third of their day in a conventional classroom); and putting students to work as corridor, cafeteria, and study-hall monitors, as receptionists answering phones and giving school tours, as graders of papers and exams, and as tutors ("with fifth-graders helping first-graders, eighth-graders helping fifth-graders, and so forth").[9]

Whittle won praise as a visionary in blurbs from Wendy Kopp, the founder of Teach for America (TFA), and Lamar Alexander, the former governor of Tennessee and U.S. secretary of education who, as noted earlier, was previously a stakeholder in Whittle Communications and a member of Channel One's advisory board. In separate forewords, Walter Isaacson, the president and CEO of the Aspen Institute and former managing editor of *Time*, and Tom Ridge, the former governor of Pennsylvania and U.S. secretary for homeland security, likewise lauded Whittle. The only significant response from education scholars came from Henry Levin in a critical essay in *Education Next* entitled, in the immortal words of Yogi Berra, "Déjà Vu All Over Again."[10]

In updating Hettleman's argument, William S. Ratchford II, the author of the Abell report and the former director of the Maryland Department of Fiscal Services, wrote that in fiscal year 2005, Edison posted $3.2 million as retained revenue (or profit), equivalent to $1,425 per pupil and nearly 16 percent of its contract payment of $20.1 million. In refutation of those contending that the private sector is more efficient, Ratchford noted that while the Baltimore City Public School System (BCPSS) spent $647 per pupil on central administration, Edison spent $1,059. And echoing Hettleman, Ratchford argued that the state's contract with Kennedy Krieger for learning-disabled students at Edison's three schools indeed amounted to a significant subsidy.

Reflecting four years later on the controversy over costs, Laura Weeldreyer, the deputy chief of staff under Andrés Alonso, the CEO of the BCPSS, dismissed objections to Ratchford's analysis with a shake of her head. "As a huge charter advocate," Weeldreyer said during a March 2009 interview in her office on the fourth floor of the BCPSS headquarters on North Avenue, "I know charters contend they have their own administrative costs. But they use so many of our administrative services and must: we provide transportation, lunch, testing, and data analysis, as their scores are our scores. They use our office of student placement, our office of suspension services. They can't suspend students and not report the suspensions through us. Whether they like our services or not, they have to use them."[11]

Weeldreyer knew Baltimore and its schools well. Following three years as an elementary school teacher in New Orleans through TFA from 1991 to 1994, Weeldreyer taught middle school in Baltimore for one year and then worked for Baltimore's Citizens Planning and Housing Association and Maryland's Advocates for Children and Youth. Weeldreyer moved to BCPSS headquarters in 2000, serving first as executive director of the Office of New and Charter Schools and, after that, as a regional superintendent before becoming deputy chief of staff in 2008. In addition, her husband had been a middle school teacher in the Baltimore system since 1993. Without pause, Weeldreyer reeled off budgetary figures distinguishing charter from district schools. "Since we moved to per-pupil expenditures last year," she said in 2009, "we can show definitively that charters get more than district schools, so long as they don't have location or building costs, and Edison does not have those costs in Baltimore. Last year, charter schools received $9,115 per student; this year, $9,006. For the conventional district school, we have a weighted system, starting with $4,800 per student; for needy or gifted students, there's an additional allocation of $2,200; for students getting free or reduced-price lunch, there's an extra allocation of $900. For a student qualifying in all categories, the per-pupil expenditure is $7,900. That's the top."[12]

Yet of greater concern to Ratchford than cost was academic achievement. Ratchford's study was a cost-benefit analysis, and he didn't see the benefit, though his assessment of outcomes was brief. Ratchford wrote that though student performance on state exams at Furman Templeton, Gilmor, and Montebello improved under Edison, it didn't improve as much as at three of the other seven persistently underperforming schools with which Edison was grouped in 1999.[13]

Ratchford failed to describe the results in much detail, but an examination of test scores confirms his conclusion and furthermore buries doubts raised by Grasmick that the three schools Ratchford cited—Dr. Martin Luther King, Jr., Bay-Brook, and William Paca—had not been in as bad shape (see Table 3.1). These three schools were in addition, in sum, even more underprivileged, according to data from the National Center for Education Statistics: whereas the percentage of students entitled to free and reduced-price lunch in 1999 at Furman Templeton, Gilmor, and Montebello was 91, 95, and 68, respectively, it was 91, 95, and 94 at Dr. Martin Luther King, Jr., Bay-Brook, and William Paca.[14]

Without any external intervention, Ratchford wrote, Dr. Martin Luther King, Jr., Bay-Brook, and William Paca outperformed Edison's three schools. In 1999 students at these three schools collectively posted an averaged proficiency level of 6 percent in third- and fifth-grade reading and math, as did students at Furman Templeton, Gilmor, and Montebello. The schools, in other words, started at the same place. In 2003 Maryland changed its exam in response to No Child Left Behind (NCLB). The Maryland School Performance Assessment Program (MSPAP) became the Maryland School Assessment (MSA), and, as in states across the country, proficiency levels soared. Baltimore's citywide proficiency level in reading for third-graders, for example, was 13 percent in 2002. In 2003 it was 39 percent. A year later, it jumped to 55 percent. By 2005 it was up to 61.[15]

The only compelling explanation for this dramatic improvement was that NCLB stipulated that the federal government would cut educational funding to states whose schools didn't reach proficiency targets, as defined by Adequate Yearly Progress (AYP). States consequently lowered the bar to make AYP and in the process made a mockery of the definition of proficiency. Regardless, the performance of schools within states still revealed relative achievement. In compliance with NLCB, the MSA was administered to students in grades three through eight, but for purposes of consistency with analysis of results for the MSPAP, which was administered to elementary students in the third and fifth grades, only scores for third and fifth grade are examined here. For the non-Edison trio cited by Ratchford, the averaged proficiency level for 2005 in third- and fifth-grade reading and math was 71 percent. For Edison's three schools, it was 56 percent (see Table 4.1).[16]

Table 4.1   Percentage of students graded proficient on the 2005 Maryland School Assessment (MSA)

Elementary school	Grade 3		Grade 5		Mean proficiency
	Reading	Math	Reading	Math	
Arundel	40.7	22.2	36.6	12.2	27.9
Bay-Brook	80.9	78.7	74.4	51.2	71.3
Dr. Martin Luther King, Jr.	81.9	73.5	83.5	65.6	76.1
Furman Templeton*	52.9	60.8	37.2	37.2	47.0
Gilmor*	64.2	62.7	38.9	41.1	51.7
Graceland Park	34.6	26.9	51.3	30.8	35.9
Lafayette	58.5	37.5	58.3	25.0	44.8
Mary Rodman	33.8	47.9	75.9	26.4	46.0
Montebello*	69.0	71.0	69.7	71.0	70.2
William Paca	79.7	74.4	49.2	63.6	66.7
Mean of Edison schools	62.0	64.8	48.6	49.8	56.3
Mean of remaining seven	58.6	51.6	61.3	39.3	52.7
Baltimore City	61.0	56.5	57.6	48.5	55.9

Data source: Maryland State Department of Education, accessed at http://www.maryland publicschools.org/MSDE.

Note: Mean figures are unweighted by student population except in the case of grade-level scores for Baltimore City.

*Edison school

Students at Edison's three schools in 2005 still outperformed peers in sum at the seven schools with which they had been grouped in 1999—something Ratchford neglected to mention—but that too would change the following year, and the gap would only grow wider before closing somewhat in 2009. In 2006 these seven schools outperformed Edison's three by 6 percentage points, and in 2007 by 11. In 2008 these schools (down to six, as Lafayette Elementary was closed in 2007) not only outperformed Edison's three by 25 percentage points but also surpassed the city average, as they would again in 2009 (see Table 4.2).

The man behind William S. Ratchford's report was Robert C. Embry Jr., the president of the Abell Foundation since 1986 and, in the opinion of

Table 4.2 Mean proficiency rates for third- and fifth-graders in reading and math on the MSPAP for 2001–2002 and on the MSA for 2003–2009

Elementary school	2001	2002	2003	2004	2005	2006	2007	2008	2009
Arundel	8.5	6.4	28.8	36.6	27.9	27.9	45.3	63.3	83.5
Bay-Brook	4.6	33.6	45.2	79.1	71.3	88.5	84.7	84.9	77.4
Dr. Martin Luther King, Jr.	23.1	17.6	43.7	54.9	76.1	65.7	54.8	65.8	78.1
Furman Templeton*	0.5	3.0	19.8	55.5	47.0	48.2	46.6	43.4	60.7
Gilmor*	7.5	14.7	33.9	47.2	51.7	43.9	41.8	38.2	64.2
Graceland Park	11.1	8.4	30.6	44.6	35.9	74.2	65.8	84.6	86.6
Lafayette	17.8	21.7	36.0	63.4	44.8	53.5	41.7	n/a	n/a
Mary Rodman	14.8	8.2	31.1	28.3	46.0	36.8	50.1	56.9	74.5
Montebello*	31.5	63.5	49.7	69.8	70.2	63.3	56.4	61.5	73.3
William Paca	3.5	11.1	27.1	48.7	66.7	60.2	71.5	81.6	86.6
Mean of Edison schools	13.2	27.1	26.9	57.5	56.3	51.8	48.3	47.7	66.1
Mean of remaining seven	11.9	15.3	34.6	50.8	52.7	58.1	59.1	72.8	81.1
Baltimore City	23.1	17.2	39.2	50.6	55.9	59.5	63.8	72.2	77.9

Data source: Maryland State Department of Education, http://www.marylandpublic schools.org/MSDE.

Note: Mean figures are unweighted by student population except in the case of Baltimore City.

*Edison school

several local officials, Baltimore's shadow mayor. It was Embry, as previously noted, who recommended EAI to Mayor Schmoke in 1991 and then had the Abell Foundation fund visits by Baltimore school officials to schools run by EAI in Minnesota and Florida. The Abell Foundation itself is the city's local version of the Ford Foundation, making grants of more than $263 million to community initiatives and research projects since its establishment in 1953.[17]

Embry was born in Baltimore in 1937, graduated from its public schools, went to Massachusetts for his bachelor's degree at Williams College and his law degree at Harvard, returned to Baltimore to clerk for a U.S. Appeals Court judge, and then worked several years for a local law firm before becoming Baltimore's commissioner of housing and community development in 1967. Ten years later, President Jimmy Carter named Embry assistant secretary of housing and urban development. As important to Embry as good housing and thoughtful city planning were solid public schools. In addition to financing educational initiatives as head of the Abell Foundation to improve Baltimore's schools, Embry served during his free time as president of the Baltimore Board of School Commissioners and then the Maryland State Board of Education.

As his endorsement of EAI made clear, Embry wasn't instinctively opposed to for-profit school management. Moreover, Embry supported not only Baltimore's partnership with EAI for school management but also the city's contract with Sylvan Learning Centers, the tutoring company, for supplementary assistance to learning-disabled children at six city schools. Embry declared to a reporter for the *Sun* in 1993 that just as Harborplace made Baltimore "a model for physical development," the city's collaboration with EAI and Sylvan stood to make it a model for educational reform.[18]

Sitting in his office on the twenty-third floor of a downtown skyscraper with a panoramic view of the Baltimore Harbor, Embry explained in March 2009 that on top of EAI's failure, it was a combination of the 2004 MSA results at Edison's three schools and subsequent reports from teachers at Montebello about test tampering that led him to change his mind about for-profit educational management. Embry had already been concerned about how simple it was for schools to cheat on statewide exams and sent an op-ed to the *Sun* in August 2004 making his case in detail, explaining that teachers can easily give students extra time, point out correct responses as they walk about classrooms, and afterward change incorrect responses on bubble sheets and finish unanswered questions; moreover, teachers are allowed to view the exams in advance. But the *Sun* declined to publish Embry's submission.[19]

A month later, Embry wrote Grasmick that he had just reviewed Edison's 2004 MSA results for third- and fifth-graders, had doubts about their authenticity, and urged her to recall the case of two Baltimore elementary schools—Glenmount and Tench Tilghman—whose extraordinary 1995

MSPAP scores plummeted when independent monitors from the state oversaw the examination the following year. The percentage of fifth-graders at Glenmount scoring proficient in math, for example, dropped from 88 in 1995 to 27 in 1996. "If the scores are accurate," Embry wrote Grasmick about the 2004 MSA results at Edison's three schools, "they have significant implications for the future of city schools. To validate these successes, you might want to have the 2005 tests independently monitored. . . . If you are interested . . . we would be delighted to pay any associated costs or provide the monitors." In a 409-word response explaining the state's protocol and, in particular, its careful oversight of Edison's three schools in 2003–2004, Grasmick thanked Embry for the offer but declined.[20]

Upon subsequently hearing from a teacher at Montebello that the school suffered from widespread cheating on statewide exams of just the nature he had described in his rejected op-ed submission and that several of this teacher's colleagues had written Grasmick about the problem to no avail, Embry in March 2005 revised his op-ed, changed the title from "Test Security" to "Catching the Cheaters," and resent it. This time, the *Sun* ran Embry's submission. Embry alleged that weak supervision by the Maryland State Department of Education had permitted significant cheating by school administrators and teachers to boost student scores. "Particularly troubling," Embry wrote, "is when a for-profit firm such as Edison Schools, Inc., which operates three schools in Baltimore, is compensated in part based on its test scores—information that is solely under Edison's control with no external monitoring."[21]

The day after the *Sun* published the op-ed, Embry e-mailed Ben Feldman, chief accountability officer of the BCPSS, to find out the test results for Montebello before the arrival in 2000 of its celebrated principal, Sarah Horsey, as well as the test results for the two Baltimore elementary schools she had previously led—Rognel Heights and Pimlico—before, during, and after her tenure. Feldman e-mailed Embry a spreadsheet with data inexplicably going back only as far as 2002—Horsey had led Rognel Heights from 1989 to 1996 and Pimlico from 1996 to 2000—and claimed he was unable to "cull a telling pattern." Embry dropped that path of inquiry and wrote Grasmick several days later about his conversation with the teacher at Montebello. Grasmick wrote Embry back that "all allegations regarding cheating on state tests received by the Maryland State Department of Education are taken very seriously and are carefully investigated."[22]

Still unpersuaded, Embry appealed to Grasmick at the end of April to meet with the teacher in question and to authorize an independent re-administration of the MSA exam just given in March. To provide urgent cause for his concern, Embry attached to his letter an article published that morning by the Associated Press about a celebrated principal at an Edison school in Chester, Pennsylvania, alleged to have given eighth-graders at her school answers to the state's standardized exam. Grasmick responded to Embry that while it would be inappropriate for her to meet with the teacher, the head of the Assessment Branch of the Division of Accountability and Assessment would be more than willing to do so and provided the man's name and number; Grasmick didn't acknowledge Embry's recommendation that the MSA be re-administered by independent monitors.[23]

While Embry didn't get anywhere with Feldman or Grasmick, an examination of MSPAP data as well as newspaper archives makes clear that Embry's suspicions were justified. Montebello's scores did indeed spike after Edison and its inaugural principal, Horsey, took over the school in 2000. In addition, on top of the allegations of test tampering at an Edison school in Chester, Pennsylvania, in 2005, an investigation of an Edison school in Wichita, Kansas, in 2001 found the principal and assistant principal guilty of instructing teachers to give third- and fifth-graders extra time on state exams, to read aloud reading comprehension passages, and to point to correct answers.[24]

While scores at Furman Templeton and Gilmor dropped in their first year under Edison, scores at Montebello went up as follows: in third-grade reading and math, the percentage of students graded proficient jumped from 10 and 4, respectively, in 2000 to 27 and 40 in 2001; in fifth-grade reading and math, the percentage of students graded proficient jumped from 8 and 2, respectively, in 2000 to 29 and 31 in 2001. This hike in scores repeated itself the following year, to the degree that 90 percent of fifth-graders scored proficient in math (see Table 4.3).

More troubling still is that Horsey had been extolled for dramatically improving results at her previous school, Pimlico Elementary, which eighteen months after her departure was exposed for test tampering. Horsey took over as principal at Pimlico in 1996. Under Horsey, Pimlico saw its scores

Table 4.3 Percentage of students graded proficient on the MSPAP for 2000–2002 and on the MSA for 2003–2009

	2000	2001	2002	2003	2004	2005	2006	2007	2008	2009
Furman Templeton										
Third-grade reading	0	0	2.8	23.9	58.3	52.9	43.5	37.3	43.9	63
Third-grade math	0	0	1.8	18.2	61.2	60.8	45.7	45.2	40.8	52.1
Fifth-grade reading	2.3	1.9	4.9	23.7	46.5	37.2	47.1	50.0	47.2	72.1
Fifth-grade math	2.0	0	2.3	13.4	56.0	37.2	56.3	53.8	41.7	55.7
Gilmor										
Third-grade reading	14.0	5.1	5.2	19.8	46.2	64.2	49.3	35.6	48.6	63.6
Third-grade math	18.0	7.6	20.0	25.7	51.9	62.7	41.1	39.7	41.7	60.4
Fifth-grade reading	5.0	6.3	10.3	55.4	34.7	38.9	37.8	33.3	39.3	65.5
Fifth-grade math	9.4	11.0	23.4	34.8	56.0	41.1	47.3	58.7	23.0	67.2
Montebello										
Third-grade reading	9.6	27.0	51.7	48.5	82.3	69.0	71.4	57.5	60.2	74.4
Third-grade math	3.6	39.7	60.3	53.8	70.7	71.0	81.0	47.9	60.5	57.9
Fifth-grade reading	8.2	28.7	52.2	53.7	70.1	69.7	46.9	53.1	70.0	87.8
Fifth-grade math	1.7	30.7	89.9	42.9	55.9	71.0	53.8	67.2	55.4	73.0
Baltimore City										
Third-grade reading	20.3	18.5	12.9	39.1	54.6	61.0	65.1	68.8	73.1	76.7
Third-grade math	22.3	22.0	13.1	41.9	54.3	56.5	60.4	62.0	72.2	78.0
Fifth-grade reading	22.3	24.6	20.9	44.4	49.9	57.6	58.7	60.3	75.9	82.3
Fifth-grade math	24.5	27.1	22.0	31.2	43.7	48.5	53.7	63.9	67.4	74.6

Data source: MSPAP data obtained from the Maryland State Department of Education by e-mail, July 2012. MSA data come from the Maryland State Department of Education, http://www.marylandpublic schools.org/MSDE.

Note: Baltimore City ran Furman Templeton, Gilmor, and Montebello in 1999–2000, while Edison did so the ensuing years.

soar. After one year, the percentage of third-graders ranked proficient in reading and math on the MSPAP jumped from 5 and 3, respectively, to 25 and 15; and the percentage of fifth-graders ranked proficient in reading and math on the MSPAP jumped from 10 and 3, respectively, to 21 and 35. By 2000, the percentage of third-graders ranked proficient in reading and math was up to 73 and 85, respectively; and the percentage of fifth-graders ranked proficient in reading and math was up to 85 and 80, respectively. Horsey was hailed in a long front-page profile in the *Sun* as a turn-around genius: "In the past four years under Horsey, Pimlico has become the proverbial rose in the forest. Rare is the inner-city school that has risen from the depths of failure to compete on Maryland tests with the average performance of schools in much more well-off suburbs."[25]

In January 2002, however, the *Sun* reported as an aside in a story about citywide test results that a significant portion of the 2001 MSPAP exams at Pimlico were ruled illegitimate due to discovery of improper assistance from teachers, precisely the activity Embry had been told was taking place at Montebello. Those results deemed legitimate were markedly below results from 2000 (see Table 4.4 and Figure 4.1). Horsey's successor and two additional administrators were reprimanded, and five teachers were suspended for twenty days without pay.[26] The 2002 MSPAP results for Pimlico plunged further, landing just above the school's 1996 results. Likewise, Rognel Heights Elementary, which Horsey led from 1989 to 1996, was one of six Baltimore schools, the *Sun* reported in January 1997, along with the two Embry cited in his September 2004 letter to Grasmick—Glenmount and Tench Tilghman—found guilty by a state probe of test tampering in 1995. The percentage of fifth-graders at Rognel Heights graded proficient in 1995 on the MSPAP in math, for example, was 100. The next year, with state monitors proctoring the exam, the percentage was 30.[27]

Table 4.4   Percentage of students graded proficient on the MSPAP at Pimlico Elementary School

	1995	1996	1997	1998	1999	2000	2001	2002
Third-grade reading	3.1	5.1	24.7	18.8	33.8	73.1	21.7*	8.1
Third-grade math	5.2	3.0	15.4	14.3	43.0	85.3	9.5*	13.1
Fifth-grade reading	5.4	10.1	21.4	15.8	45.9	77.0	37.5*	18.4
Fifth-grade math	4.1	2.5	35.3	32.7	60.2	80.4	21.3*	7.9

Data source: MSPAP data obtained from the Maryland State Department of Education by e-mail, July 2012.

Note: Scores for 1997 through 2000 were posted while Sarah Horsey was principal; because the state voided the scores of more than half of the school's students in 2001, the results for that year are qualified with an asterisk.

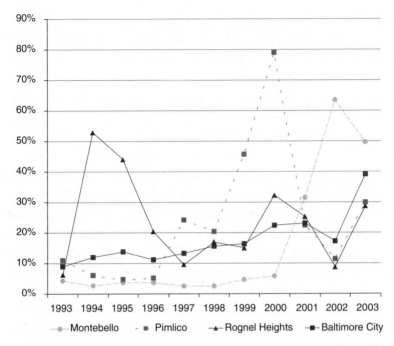

Figure 4.1 Percentage of third- and fifth-grade students graded proficient in reading and math combined on the MSPAP from 1993 to 2002 and on the MSA in 2003. Citing suspiciously high scores at Rognel Heights in 1994 and 1995, state officials monitored exams at the school in 1996. Scores of more than half of the students at Pimlico in 2001 were voided by the state because of reports of improper assistance from teachers. In the case of 1993, Maryland data do not reflect a reading exam given to third-graders. MSPAP data obtained from the Maryland State Department of Education by e-mail, July 2012. MSA data come from the Maryland State Department of Education, accessed at http://www.marylandpublicschools.org/MSDE.

Worse yet, the grounds for suspicion don't stop there. In 2003, the first year of the MSA—which on account of NCLB, as explained earlier, made attaining proficiency much easier than the MSPAP—proficiency levels at Montebello mysteriously dropped, and by a significant degree: from 64 percent for combined proficiency in third- and fifth-grade reading and math to 50 percent. Horsey was in her third and final year at the helm of Montebello before becoming a regional supervisor. Proficiency levels meanwhile jumped for Baltimore as well as Furman Templeton and Gilmor (see Table 4.3 and Figure 4.1). For the city as a whole, the mean rate of proficiency in third- and fifth-grade reading and math climbed from 17 percent to 39 percent. Only

Montebello and four other of Baltimore's 114 elementary schools posted declines; and only Montebello and one other school posted double-digit declines. Either the capacity of teachers and students at Montebello—and the other four schools—plummeted in one year or the consequences at Pimlico led administrators and teachers into proctoring exams according to the rules.[28] Efforts to seek comment from Horsey produced no results.[29]

In sum, the test results at Rognel Heights, Pimlico, and Montebello from 1993, the first year the MSPAP was administered, to 2003, the first year of the MSA, exhibit a striking pattern (see Figure 4.1). According to a former Edison administrator in Baltimore, who would speak only on condition of anonymity, principals and teachers in Baltimore knew scores at Montebello had been cooked. This former administrator also contended that Edison officials, with all their statistical expertise, had to know this as well, but they needed the Montebello success story as a selling point. Indeed, amid Edison's campaign to win a major management contract in Philadelphia, a front-page story in the *Philadelphia Inquirer* in November 2001 about Edison's first year in Baltimore highlighted the spike in scores at Montebello, noting in particular that "the percentage of first graders who passed the state reading test went from 42 to 93, the highest in the city."[30]

In pushing for that contract, Edison spokesperson Adam Tucker deflected news in the Philadelphia press of disappointing outcomes at Edison schools in Trenton and Wichita by pointing to the test scores at Montebello.[31] Edison even bused parent activists in Philadelphia to Baltimore to see Montebello as well as Gilmor in action.[32] In addition, Montebello was showcased as one of Edison's finest schools in a July 2003 PBS *Frontline* documentary about the company. *Frontline* host John Merrow reported that when he asked Whittle to see Edison at its best, Whittle sent him to Montebello.[33]

The 2003 MSA results were published in August. Had they been published earlier or the *Frontline* documentary aired later, Merrow could not have told such a laudatory story. Had the odd pattern of test results at Rognel Heights, Pimlico, and Montebello been discovered, Merrow likewise could not have told such a laudatory story: the news of cheating at Rognel Heights and Pimlico, on top of the statistical improbability of such radical improvement at all three schools, would have provoked disturbing questions.

In aggressively coaching students for standardized tests, school leaders have significantly raised scores without any allegations of wrongdoing— other than that of teaching to the test, which is itself considered wrong by many educators but certainly not illegal. Rudy Crew, chancellor of New York City's schools from 1995 to 1999 and superintendent of Miami-Dade County Public Schools from 2004 to 2008, had risen to prominence as superintendent of schools in Tacoma, Washington, by doing just that with the assistance of a teacher-training firm he brought in from Lexington, Massachusetts, called the Efficacy Institute.[34] In the autumn of 1994 in Tacoma, the average score of fourth-graders on the Comprehensive Test of Basic Skills (CTBS) was the 42nd percentile and that of eighth-graders the 45th percentile. Disgusted with these results, Crew took the unusual step of arranging a second administration of the CTBS in the spring and ordered workshops across the district in test preparation for principals and teachers. Many teachers went on to tailor their curricula to the CTBS and regularly administer practice tests. On the spring administration of the CTBS, the average score of fourth-graders climbed to the 63rd percentile and that of eighth-graders to the 58th percentile.[35]

While significant, this improvement in Tacoma paled in comparison to the gains in Baltimore. The gains in Tacoma in the spring of 1995, after all, were achieved by the same students on exams of the same level of difficulty given after six more months of schooling. And despite the district-wide shift in strategy, the CTBS scores in the autumn of 1995 and 1996 represented only modest improvement over the 1994 scores: fourth-grade scores over these three years went from the 42nd to the 49th and 48th percentile; eighth-grade scores went from the 45th to the 51st and 49th percentile.[36] The context and magnitude of gains in Baltimore, by contrast, suggested that Embry was indeed right to conclude that more than concentrated test preparation was taking place at Montebello.

■

For Edison officials, Embry's op-ed in March 2005 and Ratchford's report six months later were mere distractions. Of far greater import was finding an explanation for the downturn in results from 2005 onward and reversing course. After all, Edison had been granted the freedom to hire and fire that

Whittle—and Lieberman—had claimed was critical. And the company exercised that freedom vigorously. Edison, to start, brought in Horsey and two other seasoned principals—JoAnn Cason from Baltimore and Darryl Bonds from Wichita, Kansas—to run its three schools. Edison paid these principals significantly more than North Avenue compensated principals and included provisions in their contracts for substantial performance-based bonuses. Horsey brought with her eight teachers from Pimlico. Cason, the new principal of Gilmor, brought five teachers with her from the school she had led in South Baltimore, Carter G. Woodson Elementary. Following her second year, Cason would receive a $20,000 bonus for meeting Edison goals, and following her fifth year, she would receive a bonus in excess of that. Horsey would earn several bonuses and, like several top performers, a Mustang convertible presented at the company's annual summit. Because of disappointing results, Bonds would be replaced after one year in charge of Furman Templeton.[37]

Even with such freedom to hire and fire, Edison couldn't fill positions, hold on to valued staff, or get the right leaders. Bonds confessed to being overwhelmed as the principal of Furman Templeton. "I've seen some stuff I've never seen kids do before," he told a reporter for the *Sun* six weeks into the school year. And in that time, he lost his assistant principal, business manager, office manager, and two teachers. Horsey's successor at Montebello moved on after only two years. Following her first year as principal of Montebello, in 2005–2006, Camille Bell said, thirty of forty-five staff members left, some because they were asked to go and others of their own volition. Cason's successor at Gilmor nearly provoked a revolt by teachers and parents, according to Laura Weeldreyer, the deputy chief of staff for the Baltimore City Public Schools. "We did a site review and were appalled," Weeldreyer recalled in 2009. "The teachers and parents hated this woman. We feared her head would soon be on a stick." Weeldreyer explained that she immediately called Marlaina Palmeri, Edison's regional vice president, to voice her concern. Palmeri conceded Edison had chosen the wrong person to head Gilmor and had the principal replaced. When asked how Edison could make such a mistake, Palmeri said it was harder than expected to get people to work in West Baltimore.[38]

Indeed, when Ken Cherry took over as principal of Furman Templeton in July 2007, he had to hire half a faculty, and by mid-October, nine of twenty-seven teachers resigned. Cherry said teachers didn't feel safe. In describing a scene that could have easily appeared in *The Wire* but never did, Cherry's predecessor, Evelyn Randall, recounted at a March 2007 City Hall meeting on school neighborhood violence how one of her crossing guards had been told by a drug dealer at gunpoint to get off his corner.[39]

Palmeri's life was urban education. She had been an educator in Rochester, New York, for twenty-eight years: twelve as an elementary school teacher, five as a vice principal, eight as a principal of a Title I elementary school, and three as the director of the city's magnet schools. She earned a doctorate in educational administration from the University of Rochester in 1998 and joined Edison in 1999 as a regional supervisor. At once elegant, diplomatic, and encyclopedic, Palmeri could be mistaken for a senior State Department official. She said she had never seen a neighborhood as underserved and dangerous as West Baltimore.[40]

Yet Edison had embraced this challenge of working in the nation's toughest neighborhoods. Company officials maintained that its longer school year (195 days instead of 180) and day (from 8:00 to 3:40 rather than 2:40), its house system, administrative freedom, and research-based curriculum would all have a compensatory effect. Though Edison terminated its policy in 2002 of giving every student a home computer on account of the high cost, it invested heavily in technology. During a tour of Montebello in 2009, Bell, the school's ebullient principal, cited in this regard the school's twenty-one Promethean interactive whiteboards, each costing about $6,000, and noted that Edison had never denied her requests for resources of any kind. Bell, who had taught in public schools for seven years and served as a vice principal for one year in Rochester, New York, where she had come to know Palmeri, said that such responsiveness from above, along with the latitude she had on site, made Edison's model special. "At an Edison school," Bell said, "I have the liberty to do what I need to do for my children. I remember at my district school, you had to fight to do right by children."[41]

Edison was, moreover, granted the freedom in 2001 by the state board of education to enroll out-of-zone students and year after year waged an impressive publicity campaign with glossy mailings to entice top students from beyond each school's official boundaries. Furman Templeton, Gilmor, and Montebello by law had to accept zoned students, but they could enroll out-of-zone students whose parents had filled out applications. According to

Weeldreyer, about 60 percent of the 556 students at Furman Templeton in 2009 came from beyond the school's official zone. This privilege, however, came with a downside: resentment and distrust. Baltimore School Board member Kenneth A. Jones, for example, accused Edison of skimming the best students from neighboring zones and rejecting or pushing out "difficult and expensive" students.[42]

Edison's schools, in addition, had the advantage of a rigorously developed monthly benchmark testing system to evaluate the progress of its students and prepare them for annual statewide exams. Every four weeks, students filed into a computer lab to sit at terminals to take reading and math assessments designed and analyzed by specialists at Edison's national headquarters. The company long prided itself on its methodical use of this system to monitor student development and diagnose strengths and weaknesses. To track results on site, each Edison school had a "mission control center," as several Edison administrators put it, where walls were covered with color-coded charts listing every student and his or her score on the monthly assessments. At Furman Templeton, blue denoted Advanced; green, Proficient; and black, Basic. At Montebello, the corresponding colors were purple, green, and red. In explaining the numbers covering the walls of her data room, perched in an isolated space above the school's gymnasium that appeared to have once served as a physical education office, Bell said, "My mission is to grow the purple population." Moreover, in the lobby of each Edison school were charts listing the monthly scores in reading and math of each class section lest any teacher or student forget the importance of statewide exams.[43]

Assisting in the benchmark assessment process were regional experts in testing who concentrated on aligning Edison's monthly routine with statewide exams, much like the outside consultants Rudy Crew brought to Tacoma. Their purpose was singular, as was evident at a meeting of administrators after school in the library at Montebello in November 2005 run by Kent Luetke-Stahlman, at the time Edison's community technical services manager.

Operating a projector and taking the small audience through one slide after another about the MSA, Luetke-Stahlman explained what students at each grade level would be expected to know. The principals, assistant principals, and several learning specialists from Furman Templeton, Gilmor, and

Montebello silently took notes; also in attendance was Sarah Horsey in her role as a regional supervisor. The MSA would be administered in early March, more than three months away. The mood in the library was nevertheless grim.

In reviewing the math exam for fifth-graders, Luetke-Stahlman said: "The kids will have to know how to convert the following fractions into percentages: one-fourth, one-third, a half, two-thirds, and three-fourths. Don't worry about five-eighths. That's not on the test. Focus on what's on the test. The kids have to do well on the test."[44]

"That's right," chimed in JoAnn Cason, the celebrated principal of Gilmor. "Remember what Mr. [John] Chubb [then Edison's chief education officer] said here last month. We have to beat the competition. If we don't, there's no reason for Edison."[45]

Luetke-Stahlman's instructions, no doubt, echo those of school administrators across the country in this era of high-stakes testing.[46] Luetke-Stahlman's counsel, in fact, bears an uncanny resemblance to the repeated words of admonition uttered by the assistant principal in *The Wire* to Roland "Prez" Pryzbylewski, the detective-turned-teacher, to focus on preparing his students for the MSA. "Stay on the curriculum, Mr. Pryzbylewski," she says, for example, upon learning of his interest in integrating board games like Parcheesi and Monopoly into his lessons, "or you'll have an area superintendent on our backs."[47] But the pressure on a company like Edison to teach to the test stands to be that much greater, and its method more systematic, for precisely the reason articulated by Cason: EMOs must exhibit concrete gains to justify contract renewals, never mind earn performance-based payments, as Embry had argued.

The same, in turn, holds for principals of EMO schools. In July 2006, Edison terminated Cason on account of persistently low test scores at Gilmor. Though lauded for bringing peace and efficiency for five years to a school previously notorious for disorder, Cason did not make Edison's numbers.[48]

According to Weeldreyer, Cason sank her heart into her job and transformed the school climate, but that was not enough for Edison. Todd McIntire, an Edison senior vice president for operations, confirmed Weeldreyer's take and added that Chubb's focus on test results often meant abrupt terminations. "When numbers came in in July or August," McIntire recalled, "there was always a lot of tension. Chubb would examine the test results and then shuffle people in and out. And many good people got shuffled out."[49]

■

The science of methodical benchmarking, the liberty to enroll selected out-of-zone students, the longer school year and day, the research-based curriculum, the house system, and the freedom to hire and fire nevertheless had no enduring impact. When the 2006 MSA results were published in July, this became clear. For the first time, scores dropped at all three Edison schools in Baltimore. Meanwhile, scores climbed not only for the seven schools with which Furman Templeton, Gilmor, and Montebello had been grouped in 1999 but also for Baltimore City schools in general (see Tables 4.1 and 4.2).[50]

The best answer Edison could muster contradicted the sales pitch made by its own Richard O'Neill in February 2000 that reforming schools doesn't take years; Edison's response moreover distorted the relative straits of its three schools before the company took them over. "School improvement is a long process," Chubb said to a reporter for the *Sun*. "We started working in the schools six years ago when there were no worse schools in Baltimore."[51] Again, Gilmor, Furman Templeton, and Montebello had indeed been persistently low-performing schools, but no more so than seven other Baltimore schools with which they had been grouped in 1999 that had subsequently exhibited greater improvement without additional funding or administrative latitude (see Tables 3.1 and 4.2).

Breaking from six years of consistent support of Edison, the *Sun* cited the low test scores at the three schools in an editorial the following day entitled "No Magic Bullet" and turned on the company: "Arguments for privatizing government functions often raise legitimate and practical issues—expediency, economic savings, a higher degree of professionalism. But privatizing public schools is nothing more than an act of desperation. . . . There are some school privatization success stories around the country, but what matters here is that Baltimore is not among them."[52]

The editorial page of the *Sun* had endorsed Grasmick's plan to privatize underperforming schools in Baltimore in September 1999, praised her selection of Edison in April 2000, and lauded Edison in May 2001 after its first year of managing Furman Templeton, Gilmor, and Montebello.[53] In addition, the paper had run a five-part series about the first year of Furman Templeton under the company.[54] Only once before had the *Sun* questioned Edison's wherewithal. In a June 2002 editorial, the paper opposed Edison's petition to add grades seven and eight to Furman Templeton, Gilmor, and Montebello. The state board of education had allowed the company to add grade six the previous year. The issue for the paper's editors was news of Edison's financial predicament.[55]

Just as EAI's stock went into a tailspin following charges in November 1993 that the company had booked as revenue money that went directly from the district to staff and thus gave the impression of much greater volume and growth of business, Edison's stock took a nosedive following revelations in February 2002 that Edison employed the same form of inappropriate revenue recognition. Along with stock analysts, Baltimore's city comptroller, Jacqueline McLean, had exposed EAI.[56] *Bloomberg News* exposed Edison. Adam Feild, Edison's chief financial officer, conceded in a conference call with analysts that Edison received only about 50 percent of the $375.8 million reported in revenue for fiscal 2001 and moreover admitted that the company's practice of sending client school districts two invoices—representing "gross" and "net" amounts—did not make sense, as school districts pay only the net amount.[57] Edison's stock had closed in December 2001 at $19.65 a share and in March 2002 at $13.90 a share. After the SEC confirmed the *Bloomberg* allegations in May, the stock cratered.[58] By the end of June, the company's stock had fallen to $1.01, representing a second-quarter decline of 93 percent, the second-worst performance that quarter of all NASDAQ companies, worse even than that of WorldCom, the telecom giant exposed as an accounting mirage.[59]

For the editors of the *Sun,* permitting a company under such financial duress to add two grades to each of its three schools in Baltimore would be irresponsible. And yet they maintained their confidence in the company, so much so that they suggested Edison be allowed "to add another grade to one or more of these schools," and if the company's financial house were put back in order, another grade later in time.[60]

After the report of the 2006 MSA scores, however, the *Sun* gave up on Edison. When Grasmick urged Baltimore to take over the state's contract with Edison in 2007—following fulfillment of the initial five-year contract with the state and a two-year extension—the *Sun* firmly rejected the recommendation. Grasmick would have pursued another extension of the state contract, but she encountered stiff resistance from the Maryland General Assembly. "Given Edison's lackluster record," the *Sun* intoned in an April 2007 editorial, "city school officials should resume managing the schools. . . . Edison does appear to have done a good job of engaging parents and communities in its reform efforts. . . . But its achievements have been inconsistent."[61]

In agreement with the *Sun*, Weeldreyer contended that Edison's impact on balance was negative. While Edison staffers brought budgetary discipline to each school and helped shape citywide practice with their insights, Weeldreyer said, the company failed to improve instruction. In large part, Weeldreyer attributed this failure to the company's inability to nurture or retain talented teachers:

> Edison had business managers for all their schools, and that seemed to help their schools work much better. In fact, when the city school system moved to a per-pupil expenditure formula, we invited Edison to show us how they coached principals through the budgeting process. And they have some great decision-tree tools. Those were helpful to us in preparing principals to take on a zero-based budgeting process. But did it really help for the schools to have business managers? Two of Edison's schools last year were in utter chaos because of massive teacher turnover. It seemed from an adult vantage point that the schools had better infrastructure, but that didn't change what the kids were experiencing in the classroom. . . . I don't think from a kid's perspective, business managers did squat for them, since twenty-five classrooms had first-year teachers who didn't know what they were doing.[62]

Rather than heed the *Sun*, the Baltimore School Board complied with Grasmick and other Edison advocates—including 250 Edison parents, schoolchildren, and staff members who had attended a school board meeting in January to lobby for the extension—and voted in May to issue the company a new contract that would run through 2009. But the city allocation for Edison would be less than what the state had provided, confirming the case made by both Hettleman and Ratchford. Edison's 195-day school year and seven-hour-and-forty-minute day would consequently be reduced to the city standard of 180 days and six hours and forty minutes.[63]

With MSA results at Furman Templeton and Gilmor considerably lower in 2007 and 2008, BCPSS CEO Andrés Alonso announced in March 2009 that he would urge the school board at its upcoming meeting on the twenty-fourth of the month to let the contracts with the company expire. Only Montebello met the federal standard of AYP in 2008. Edison officials protested that Alonso should take the long view and not focus on merely the past two years.[64]

Palmeri made precisely this case as I accompanied her to this meeting of the school board at the BCPSS headquarters on North Avenue, a five-story gray stone edifice with Ionic columns supporting decorative entablatures above the building's southern and northern wings. As we exited her car in the abutting parking lot, Palmeri nodded in the direction of a nearby yellow school bus. "Good, they got here," she said and went on to explain that Edison had paid for the bus to transport parents and children to show support for the company at the meeting; Edison had likewise funded school buses to get parents and schoolchildren to rally on behalf of the company at a school board meeting of a similar nature in San Francisco in 2001.[65]

More than 120 Edison parents, schoolchildren, and staff members filled the building's largest hall. Many of the Edison contingent sat on the floor, including Furman Templeton's principal, Ken Cherry. Nearly all wore T-shirts reading Furman Templeton or Gilmor across the front and Attitude = Altitude across the back. From Edison headquarters in New York and seated in the front row of the audience were Roberto Gutierrez, senior vice president for communications, and Michael Serpe, senior vice president for public affairs, both in dark suits.[66]

The central item on the meeting's agenda was Alonso's $1.27 billion budget proposal for fiscal 2010, intended to close a $55 million shortfall. If the board approved the budget, the North Avenue staff would be cut from 1,189 workers to 1,007, and Edison would lose its contract to manage Furman Templeton and Gilmor.[67]

The meeting began promptly at 6 p.m. with board chair Brian A. Morris calling for order and asking everyone to rise for the color guard presentation by a stoical uniformed array of flag-bearing students from Edmondson

High School. Following approval of minutes from last month's meeting, Alonso and the ten board members patiently listened during a public comment period to ten speakers voicing a range of concerns. Among them, local civil rights advocate Edna Lawrence, addressed by Morris as Grandma Edna, complained that her ten-year-old granddaughter had been dragged into a bathroom by three boys at an unidentified school, wrestled herself free to report the incident to her teacher, and yet nothing was done about it. Latasha Peterkin next rose to the microphone and asserted that she had repeatedly complained to the principal of Carter High School that her sophomore son wasn't learning anything in science class; she got nowhere, then took her concerns to North Avenue's head of secondary schools, and yet nothing was done about it. "I'm just tired of being pushed around," Peterkin said. "I'm tired of being ignored." Both Lawrence and Peterkin far exceeded the three minutes allotted to each speaker and had to be coaxed by Morris into wrapping up their grievances.[68]

From Gilmor, fifth-grader Isaiah Reese, fourth-grader Shamiria Darby, and third-grader Tykera McDowell each read a statement about how much they valued Edison's approach to learning, highlighting the company's monthly benchmark method of assessment and its core values of perseverance, respect, integrity, determination, and excellence. McDowell closed with a wide-eyed appeal: "Can you please, please, please keep Gilmor an Edison school?" The Edison crowd burst into a standing ovation. Leslie Sturdevant, the mother of a fifth-grade boy at Furman Templeton, followed with a glowing account of her son's success in the school's gifted and talented program. "These children cannot be left behind," she said to loud applause.[69]

At 8:02 p.m., the board voted on Alonso's budget proposal, approving it 9–1. North Avenue would resume management of Furman Templeton and Gilmor. The Edison crowd returned to its feet and quietly filed out of the hall, defeated. Alonso and the board moved on to renew the contract of a struggling charter high school and to agree to set aside funds to rent trailers outfitted as classrooms should the need arise.[70]

In the corridor outside, Bell hugged Palmeri.

"It's the end of an era," Bell said. "Nine years."

"I feel kind of numb," Palmeri responded.

Gutierrez and Serpe meanwhile fielded questions on camera with a reporter from Baltimore's ABC affiliate, Channel 2.

■

With the loss of Furman Templeton and Gilmor, Palmeri was relieved of her responsibilities as a regional supervisor. Offered a role within Edison with less authority, Palmeri declined and left the company in April. In January 2010 she took a job as an executive with a New York–based competitor called Global Partnership Schools, founded by Sunny Varkey, an educational entrepreneur in Dubai, and coheaded by Manny Rivera, former Rochester superintendent and Edison vice president for development, and Rudy Crew, following his leadership of Miami-Dade County Public Schools.[71]

While Edison would see its contract renewed in 2010 and 2011 to continue managing Montebello, the school had failed to make AYP in 2009 and each subsequent year. On June 27, 2011, Bell, Montebello's leader since 2005, was abruptly let go by the company. Upon emerging from a meeting at Montebello with Councilwoman Mary Pat Clarke about neighborhood violence, Bell was handed a letter of termination. According to Bell, the letter provided no explanation. According to a company spokesperson, the decision concerned a personnel matter that could not be disclosed. Parents waged a protest on Bell's behalf, but to no avail.[72]

Bell had been meeting with Clarke to discuss, in particular, the ramifications of the drive-by shooting death in May of a twelve-year-old seventh-grader at Montebello named Sean Johnson. With three friends, Johnson was sitting on the front porch of a home one mile from Montebello watching an NBA playoff game on television on a Tuesday evening. Bullets hit all four, but the others survived. Johnson was hit four times, twice in the chest, twice in the head.[73]

5

THE GOVERNOR'S PROPOSAL

I ask you all to commit yourselves to helping Governor Schweiker turn around the Philadelphia School District. Nearly a quarter million children are educated in it—or, truth be told, not educated.

Governor Tom Ridge, Farewell Address, Pennsylvania General Assembly, *Philadelphia Inquirer*, October 2, 2001

■ HOURS BEFORE ANDRÉS ALONSO and the Baltimore School Board convened on March 24, 2009, to determine, among other things, Edison's role in managing Furman Templeton and Gilmor, the *Philadelphia Public School Notebook* ran a story on its Web site entitled "Edison on the Ropes in Baltimore; Is Philly Far Behind?" Complementing the article was a vintage photo of Tommy Murphy driving Adolph Wolgast into the ropes in their legendary twenty-round 1913 boxing match in San Francisco.[1]

While Edison's entry into Baltimore in 2000 generated headlines and conflict, the company's move into Philadelphia in 2002 brought news coverage and discord of an entirely different dimension. And the ensuing years brought no peace. Much akin to the Murphy-Wolgast fight, the company's long battle in Philadelphia would make its time in Baltimore look like a preliminary bout.

Four critical factors explain the difference between Edison's experiences in Baltimore and Philadelphia: transparency, scope, timing, and labor relations. While Maryland selected Edison in an open process, Pennsylvania signed an agreement with Edison behind closed doors to produce a study of the Philadelphia school system that would in turn pave the way to a significant managerial role for the company. While Edison entered Baltimore to manage three schools, the company entered Philadelphia, in accordance with its study, to manage as many as forty-five schools and run the district's central office itself. When Edison competed for the contract in Baltimore, the company was robust and untarnished. The company at that point had lost only one of the seventy-one contracts it had signed since 1995. When Edison tried to market itself two years later in Philadelphia, the company had lost its sheen. It had lost six more contracts and, more importantly, had suffered an ugly defeat in New York, failing to gain the support of parents in a prominent quest to take over five underperforming schools; in the process, the company got drubbed in the press as avaricious and out of touch. Finally, while in Baltimore, Edison was granted a waiver by the state to operate outside the rules and regulations of the teachers' union contract; in Philadelphia, Edison, despite all of its support in Harrisburg, obtained no such freedom.[2]

Edison was not new to Pennsylvania. In 2000 the company started operating one charter school in Phoenixville, a middle-class suburb northwest of Philadelphia, and another in York, a struggling city south of Harrisburg. In 2001 Edison assumed a significant role in the Chester Upland School District, encompassing Chester, a factory town south of Philadelphia in steep decline, and two small neighboring townships. Pennsylvania had outdone Maryland and turned over all ten schools in Chester Upland to commercial operators. This marked another national first. While Maryland had made history in 2000 in turning over three of Baltimore's schools to Edison, and while Inkster, Michigan, had likewise made history in 1999 in turning over all three of its schools to Edison, never before had a state outsourced the management of all of a district's schools to commercial operators.[3]

At the outset, Edison was contracted to run six of Chester Upland's ten schools; LearnNow, a for-profit operator of charter schools, was contracted to run three; and Mosaica, another for-profit operator of charter schools, one.[4] Within three months, Edison had purchased LearnNow for $36 million in stock. Edison in the process increased its presence in Chester Upland to nine schools and took over eight charter schools under LearnNow management.[5] LearnNow's cofounders, Jim Shelton and Eugene Wade, served for a year as Edison executives and then headed their separate ways (Shelton moved on to positions with the NewSchool Ventures Fund, a philanthropy dedicated to educational entrepreneurship, and the Gates Foundation before joining the Obama administration in 2009 as deputy secretary of education for innovation and improvement; Wade went on to found and lead Platform Learning, a company providing after-school and summer tutoring to students at schools deemed in need of improvement by No Child Left Behind, and then in 2013 UniversityNow, a for-profit tertiary institution delivering low-cost degrees via online and conventional instruction).[6]

Mosaica joined Edison as the only other EMO in Chester Upland but in a sharply reduced capacity. Mosaica retreated to a minimal role just before the school year began, agreeing to employ only the school's principal and vice principal. Mosaica's president, Michael J. Connelly, said the company had concluded that it could take over the school only if conferred the authority to manage it as a charter, with all the autonomy over staffing and finances such authority implied.[7]

Though lacking the administrative freedom it was granted in Baltimore, Edison forged ahead in Chester Upland, promised great results, won support from the Chester Upland Education Association (the 500-member local union affiliate that had failed months earlier in court to block the state takeover), and garnered praise from many teachers learning the company's pedagogical strategies at workshops conducted over the summer.[8] Achieving success in Chester Upland would be a tough challenge, though. Chester Upland had been designated by the state in 2000 as one of twelve failing school districts and was the only one in that group immediately placed under the supervision of an external governing board; the Harrisburg School District was also taken over immediately by the state, but it was turned over to the city's mayor, Stephen R. Reed.[9]

Philadelphia was by far the biggest school district on this unenviable list and the next one slated by state officials for external oversight. While Edison prepared in the summer of 2001 for the upcoming school year in Chester Upland, the company was commissioned by Pennsylvania governor Tom Ridge to produce a report on how to boost test scores and contain costs in Philadelphia. Of the city's 264 schools, 176 were judged by the state to be failing; only 12 percent of the city's 210,000 students scored "proficient" on state exams; truancy averaged 20,000 students a day; school buildings were crumbling; the district struggled to fill teaching positions; violence plagued many schools; and the system was on course to overspend its annual budget of $1.7 billion by $216 million and faced a $1.5 billion deficit over the next five years.[10]

Ridge ordered the study on August 1 after striking a deal with Philadelphia mayor John Street. According to the deal, Ridge agreed to lend the city enough money to pay its bills through the summer, while Street, in return, consented to suspend a federal lawsuit initiated by the city in 1998 claiming the state's formula for funding schools to be racially discriminatory and to allow an external team of experts to study the district and develop a long-term plan to cover costs. In addition, Street and Ridge concurred that if no such plan were agreed upon within ninety days, the state would take over the school system.[11]

Pennsylvania Republican and Democratic lawmakers alike, however, saw little reason for optimism. Whether the city's federal lawsuit was justified on racial grounds or not was moot. What was clear was that Pennsylvania's school funding formula placed low-income districts—from hard-pressed cities to poor inner-ring suburbs and rural townships—at a distinct disadvantage. Bringing in a team from a company like Edison to find efficiencies stood to accomplish little; turning the city's school system over to the state likewise stood to dodge a glaring problem. Wallace Nunn, a Republican serving on the Pennsylvania State Board of Education and the County Council of Delaware County, comprising forty-nine municipalities outside of Philadelphia, contended that Philadelphia's budgetary crisis could be solved only if the state significantly raised the personal income tax and applied the money to equalizing disparities between school districts. Both James Rhoades, a Republican in the state senate and head of the Senate Education Committee, and Mario Civera, a Republican in the state house and chair of a bipartisan select committee on school funding, echoed Nunn. "You cannot let Philadelphia fall into the Delaware River," said Civera. "The way we fund education is an antiquated system. The state is just going to have to step up to the plate and provide more money."[12]

In the wake of Ridge's agreement with Street, Civera's committee recommended precisely what Nunn had endorsed. In a bill crafted by committee member Nicholas Micozzie, a Republican representing Delaware County, the committee proposed shifting the burden of school funding from local property taxes, which pegged educational spending to the value of housing, to state-wide personal income taxes. "Pennsylvania's system for funding public education is one of the worst in the nation," Micozzie said. "It's unfair to students, unfair to taxpayers, and it's inadequate to ensure a quality education for every child." Micozzie's hybrid bill called for raising the state personal income tax rate from 2.8 percent to 4.6 percent, lowering local property taxes, tying the statewide per-pupil expenditure to the average spent in the thirty-three best-performing districts, and providing additional funds to districts with more low-income students and greater special-education needs. With this reformulation, Micozzie said, Philadelphia's annual state subsidy for schooling would climb from $807 million to $1.5 billion and thus end the city's budgetary woes and afford Philadelphia students the education they deserved.[13] Yet Micozzie's proposal ran into immediate opposition from House majority leader John Perzel, a Republican representing Philadelphia, and got deflected for months of study and hearings.[14]

█

To many outsiders as well, the Philadelphia school crisis had little if anything to do with managerial or pedagogical strategy and much more to do with insufficient funding. "Few disagree," wrote Catherine Gewertz in *Education Week* amid this battle between Harrisburg and Philadelphia, "that Pennsylvania's system needs changing. In the past 30 years, the state's share of public school funding has dropped from 54 percent to 37 percent." Placing Pennsylvania in the context of the nation as a whole, Gewertz cited a report published by the Education Commission of the States (ECS) the same month Ridge turned for help to Edison. According to the ECS, a nonpartisan research center based in Denver, states on average in 2001 covered 48 percent of school budgets, while only thirteen states provided under 40 percent; in addition, forty states used a foundation formula akin to Micozzie's proposal, whereby spending in all districts could go no lower than a standard determined by spending in well-performing districts.[15]

The differences in per-pupil expenditure in Pennsylvania were indeed striking. While Philadelphia, for example, spent $7,944 per student in 2000–2001, the five school districts along the Paoli/Thorndale Line—traditionally known as the Main Line—of the region's commuter rail system, taking suburbanites southeast into Philadelphia and back, spent, on average, $11,437 per student; if treated as one school district, with 24,003 K–12 students in total, the Main Line suburbs spent $11,421 per student (see Table 5.1).[16]

Philadelphia was, in other words, expected to educate its children spending 70 percent as much per pupil as the school districts of Great Valley, Haverford, Lower Merion, Radnor, and Tredyffrin-Easttown. Making matters worse, children in Philadelphia came to school with many more needs than their peers in the leafy Main Line suburbs, inspiration long ago for *The Philadelphia Story,* the Broadway play that became a film classic starring Cary Grant, Katharine Hepburn, and Jimmy Stewart. This inequality had endured for some time. Over the previous five years for which data are available, Philadelphia spent, on average, 68 percent as much per pupil as its neighboring Main Line school districts. This disequilibrium likewise applied to nearby Chester Upland, though to a lesser degree. In 2000–2001, when Edison moved in to manage nine of the district's schools, Chester Upland was spending 85 percent as much per pupil as the Main Line school districts. Over the previous five years, Chester Upland spent, on average, 75 percent as much per pupil (see Table 5.1 and Figure 5.1).[17]

While Edison officials had claimed from the company's start and persisted in claiming that on account of streamlined operations, top managerial talent, research-based curricula, and high-quality professional development, they would efficiently deliver a world-class education,[18] they never contended that they could take a high-poverty urban school district to the level of, say, Lower Merion at 60 percent of the cost. No amount of professionalism, operational efficiency, and technological savvy could compensate for the funding gaps evident across Pennsylvania and many other states.

Clearly, comparable funding is not the sole determinant of comparable schooling. Chester Upland, in fact, spent more per pupil than Haverford in the last three of the six school years listed in Table 5.1. Moreover, disparity in interdistrict funding was not an issue two years earlier when Edison took over three schools in Baltimore, because per-pupil expenditure in Baltimore was relatively high. In spending $7,963 per pupil in 1999–2000, the school district of Baltimore City spent 90 percent as much as the state's richest district, Montgomery County, and 109 percent as much per pupil as neighboring suburban Baltimore County.[19] Yet it is hard to fathom how comparable

Table 5.1 Per-pupil expenditure for the school districts of Chester Upland, Philadelphia, the Main Line suburbs, and Pennsylvania as a whole

School district	1995–96	1996–97	1997–98	1998–99	1999–2000	2000–2001
Great Valley	$8,416	$8,849	$8,910	$9,304	$9,876	$10,783
Haverford	$7,772	$7,399	$7,491	$7,752	$8,061	$8,460
Lower Merion	$10,848	$10,134	$11,681	$12,123	$12,875	$13,955
Radnor	$11,950	$11,964	$12,689	$13,402	$13,038	$13,149
Tredyffrin-Easttown	$9,935	$10,345	$9,822	$9,907	$10,300	$10,839
Main Line weighted average	$9,569	$9,559	$9,995	$10,348	$10,763	$11,421
Chester Upland	$6,891	$6,981	$7,365	$8,096	$8,812	$9,696
Philadelphia	$6,550	$6,810	$6,720	$7,105	$7,378	$7,944
Philadelphia/ Main Line	0.68	0.71	0.67	0.69	0.69	0.70
Pennsylvania average	$6,421	$7,013	$7,123	$6,998	$7,309	$7,672

Data source: Pennsylvania Department of Education, Current Expenditures for All LEAs, accessed at http://www.portal.state.pa.us.

Note: Figures for the Main Line suburbs are collectively presented as averages weighted by student population; figures for Pennsylvania are presented as unweighted averages for the state's 501 school districts.

funding could not be considered a necessary condition for comparable schooling, especially for children from disadvantaged families. After all, the logic behind additional funding from the federal government (in the form of Title I allocations) to schools where 40 percent or more of the children come from low-income homes derives specifically from the concept of positive discrimination to counteract the forces of poverty. This was the logic behind Micozzie's sidelined bill as well.

■

The turning point for Philadelphia and similar school districts came in 1993, when Pennsylvania froze its school-funding formula. While the population of poor and immigrant children in inner-cities grew and local

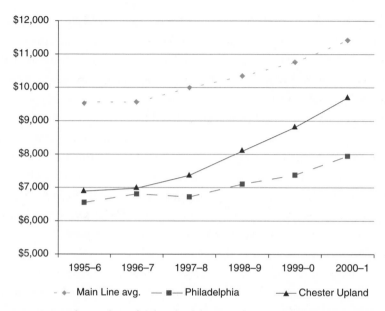

Figure 5.1 Per-pupil expenditure for the school districts of Chester Upland, Philadelphia, and the Main Line suburbs; the averages for the five school districts of the Main Line are weighted. Pennsylvania Department of Education, Current Expenditures for All LEAs, accessed at http://www.portal.state.pa.us.

tax revenue declined, state assistance failed to compensate.[20] By 1998 the financial situation of the Philadelphia School District had grown so severe that the mayor and superintendent at that time—Edward Rendell and David Hornbeck, respectively—threatened to shut the system down unless the state agreed to contribute more funding. The state legislature's response was Act 46, a law empowering the state to take over the district if it slid into financial or academic "distress." Lawsuits calling for a more equitable funding formula met with similar defeat, as the Pennsylvania Supreme Court ruled in 1999 that the issue belonged to the legislature, not the judiciary.[21]

It was this deadlock that led to Hornbeck's resignation in August 2000 and ultimately to Ridge's deal with Street and Edison.[22] Adding fuel to the crisis, Ridge not only hired Edison to produce a study of the Philadelphia school system without seeking competitive bids but also agreed to pay the company $2.7 million.[23]

Even Brandon Dobell, an analyst at Credit Suisse First Boston who was bullish on Edison, expressed disapproval of the arrangement. Along with Howard M. Block, an analyst at Banc of America Securities, Dobell took the consulting contract to mean that Edison would end up running a cluster of the city's schools and, on that account, forecasted greater earning potential for the company. A report Dobell coauthored termed the contract "a strong endorsement for the Edison value proposition—perhaps the strongest we have seen thus far in Edison's lifetime."[24] Indeed, Edison's stock spiked 6 percent on the day of the announcement of the contract.[25] Yet Dobell saw the conflict of interest inherent in commissioning a study from a company that stood likely to recommend its own services. "This contract is a bit strange," Dobell said to a reporter for the *Philadelphia Inquirer.* "It is kind of like putting a fox in charge of the henhouse."[26]

Instrumental to Ridge's agreement with Edison was Floyd Flake, yet another example of Whittle's hiring acumen. Much as Whittle long before won clout in the political and publishing worlds by making Hamilton Jordan and William S. Rukeyser senior executives of Whittle Communications, and much as he achieved academic credibility for Edison by naming John Chubb chief education officer and Benno Schmidt president and CEO, Whittle scored a strategic coup in bringing Flake aboard in May 2000 as president of Edison's charter school division and the company's chief spokesperson.

The appointment of Flake generated a detailed story in the *New York Times.* Flake had not only been a Democratic congressman for eleven years, representing a portion of Queens, New York, from 1986 to 1997, but also was and would remain senior pastor of the Allen African Methodist Episcopal Church in Queens. With 12,000 members, Flake's congregation was one of the biggest churches in the state. Moreover, Flake was famously nonpartisan. Flake had endorsed such Republicans as Senator Alfonse D'Amato, Mayor Rudolph Giuliani, and Governor George Pataki in their runs for office. Flake even prefaced a talk on educational policy by George W. Bush in 1999 at the Manhattan Institute, a conservative think tank, with a warm introduction, going so far as to call Bush "my homeboy."[27] And Flake had worked closely in Congress with Ridge, his colleague in the House for nine years.[28]

While Flake's bipartisan flair may have worked magic in Harrisburg, the $2.7 million contract was a public relations disaster in Philadelphia. Flake's role as Edison's chief spokesperson and ex officio liaison to African American communities made no difference. The response from nearly every corner was indignant and relentless. Whereas the Maryland School Board's designation of Edison to run three schools in Baltimore a year before provoked little more than a lawsuit by the Baltimore Teachers Union, which the *Baltimore Sun* dismissed as groundless and went nowhere,[29] Ridge's contract with Edison triggered protest from the Black Clergy of Philadelphia and Vicinity; the local affiliates of the National Association for the Advancement of Colored People (NAACP) and the Association of Community Organizations for Reform Now (ACORN); Philadelphia Citizens for Children and Youth; the Parents Union for Public Schools; the Philadelphia Home and School Council; Parents United for Better Schools; Asian Americans United; the Public Interest Law Center; the Philadelphia Student Union; Youth United for Change; the Philadelphia Federation of Teachers; the Philadelphia Board of Education; the interim superintendent (titled CEO in keeping with a growing trend); the city budget director; the city secretary of education; the state auditor; Mayor Street; former mayor Rendell; and city councilman and future mayor Michael Nutter. And in contrast to Baltimore, the local press sided with the opposition.

■

Among the first groups to protest Governor Ridge's agreement with Edison was the Philadelphia chapter of ACORN, a national antipoverty organization focused on voter registration and housing advocacy.[30] A day after the announcement on August 1, Jeff Ordower, chief organizer of Philadelphia's ACORN, told the *Philadelphia Inquirer,* "We will not let Edison come into the district without a fight. Through privatization, you lose accountability."[31]

ACORN had played a decisive role five months earlier in preventing Edison from entering New York to take over five persistently underperforming schools. Yet the terrain in New York differed significantly. While New York's mayor, Rudolph Giuliani, adamantly supported Edison and was an ally of Floyd Flake, much as Governor Ridge strongly backed Edison and was a friend of the company's new spokesperson, Giuliani was powerless. All Giuliani could do was urge his schools chancellor, Harold O. Levy, to endorse

Edison as the EMO parents of students at these five schools should choose in a referendum.[32] In fact, Edison had aimed to take over forty-five schools in New York, the same number it vied to manage in Philadelphia. Though headquartered in New York, the company ran no schools in the city and was eager to exhibit its managerial and pedagogical know-how on the nation's biggest educational stage.[33]

According to New York State law, the only way Edison could take over any of these five schools was if the parents of more than half of the students first voted to convert the school to charter status. In Edison's battle in New York City, the state was not pushing privatization, as had been the case in Maryland and as would be the case in Pennsylvania. Rather, it was the mayor, and he had to play by the state's rules. Levy followed Giuliani's call to recommend Edison, gave company officials the names, addresses, and phone numbers of all the parents of the 5,000 children in the five schools, and saw to it that the board of education funded a mailing from Edison to the parents explaining the company's merits. ACORN, led by the career agitator Bertha Lewis, lashed back that Levy had tilted the playing field. Levy relented, agreeing to fund a mailing from ACORN to the same parents explaining the downside of outsourcing to Edison the management of their children's schools and to postpone the referendum period by one week—from the second and third weeks of March to the third and fourth weeks.[34]

Yet Lewis was not alone in blasting Levy and Edison. Nor was she done. Though more than thirty years had passed since racial tensions over school staffing and curricula in the Ocean Hill and Brownsville neighborhoods of Brooklyn led to a series of citywide teacher strikes that bitterly divided New Yorkers, distrust of City Hall and the board of education in some quarters still burned. At a forum in Harlem featuring representatives from Edison and community organizations, Hazel Dukes, president of the New York chapter of the NAACP, declared that Levy should "be put in a dungeon, and let us get on with the education of our children." Irving Hamer Jr., himself a member of the board of education, compared the privatization of underperforming schools to the infamous Tuskegee experiment, a clinical study of the development of untreated syphilis in black men told by the U.S. government they were getting free medical checkups.[35]

Lewis likewise decried the privatization proposal as "race and class to the max" and along with her ACORN staff and volunteers canvassed hard and wide to defeat it.[36] In some cases, reporters from the *New York Times* learned after the vote, ACORN staff and volunteers canvassed too hard, misrepresenting Edison as a company that charges tuition at its charter schools, does not make accommodations for bilingual students, and expels underperformers.[37]

Despite the negative publicity, Edison officials expected to win the support of more than half the parents at two schools at least and thereby gain the foothold in New York that had long eluded them.[38] Whittle, in particular, exuded confidence. In late March, the day before the ballots were counted, Whittle again expressed his mission and conviction in Cold War terms, saying to a major Edison investor, "The Kremlin of American education is about to crumble."[39]

Of 5,000 ballots, only 2,286 were cast. And of those cast, only 453 were for Edison. Not one school came close to the plurality necessary for conversion to charter status. In sum, 9 percent of eligible parents voted for the proposal. Flake was both incredulous and disgusted. "Given the energy and effort and sacrifice our team put into this, I certainly thought we would have more votes," he said. "It got caught in a cloud of misinformation. In the end it was a matter of parents misunderstanding what we do."[40] With the defeat at the polls, the company's stock took a beating, dropping from an all-time high of $38.75 on February 8 to $19.50 on March 30, when the results were announced.[41]

Editorials in the *New York Daily News* and the *New York Post* along with columns by Joyce Purnick and John Tierney in the *New York Times* and by Michael Kramer in the *New York Daily News* took Flake's frustration to another level. In an editorial entitled "The Kids Lose Again," the *New York Post* rebuked Edison's opponents: "Look for broad smiles on the faces of Edison's institutional enemies—politicians whose parochialism is exceeded only by their cynicism, and union leaders utterly incapable of subordinating their own interests to those of children whose only real hope is a decent education." Elaborating on the case made by the *Post,* the editors of the *Daily News* three days later concluded: "It was a no-brainer, an effort to pluck some of the city's worst schools from the educational gutter and give their students a real shot at both learning and success in life. But thanks to a union, a chancellor, a platoon of tired politicians and an army of apathetic and/or misguided parents, those students will continue to be shackled by illiteracy and hopelessness."[42]

Kramer, Purnick, and Tierney conveyed similar dismay and derision. "Uninvolved parents share the blame," wrote Kramer, "and the evidence suggests that most of the parents of the kids in the five schools are indeed uninterested in their children's education. If they cared, they would have turned out in droves." Purnick went further: "What an embarrassing time for New York City. Students in five failing schools are thrown a life preserver and their parents opt for drowning." Likewise convinced of Edison's effectiveness, Tierney deplored an opportunity lost and questioned the integrity of Edison's adversaries: "It would be interesting to see how the black politicians, organizers and parents who rallied against Edison would react if middle-class white students ended up with the new computers, textbooks and refurbished classrooms promised by Edison. Would the Rev. Al Sharpton wish the white students well in their improved schools? Or would he be organizing rallies against this new evidence of racism?"[43]

Of academics, Diane Ravitch was cited in the *Times* as a critic of the outcome. Ravitch, who, as previously noted, would later become a leading opponent of market-based reforms, claimed that Edison stood to run exemplary schools in the city to showcase to policy makers as well as shareholders its managerial and pedagogical expertise.[44]

Yet nothing had been lost in the opinion of the prominent school choice advocate Seymour Fliegel. The city did not need Edison to know how to run schools, Fliegel said in the *Times*. As one example of a successful model readily available for replication, Fliegel cited an experiment in which he partook in the 1960s, the More Effective Schools (MES) program, orchestrated by the United Federation of Teachers (UFT) and implemented at twenty-one schools in New York City: class size was capped at twenty-two; teachers were given additional planning time; principals were freed from paperwork by administrative assistants; and wraparound services included a guidance counselor for every two grades, a social worker and psychologist on staff at each school, and a psychiatrist making weekly visits.[45] In lamenting the termination of the MES program, Fliegel later recalled that Albert Shanker, president of the UFT, had explained to him that he had to choose between endorsing continued funding of the program and higher salaries for teachers throughout the system and opted for the latter.[46]

∎

In Philadelphia, parents would not be polled, and nothing akin to the MES program was being offered. Parents would have no say beyond voicing their concerns at four forums cosponsored by the Philadelphia chapter of the Black Alliance for Educational Options and the Greater Philadelphia Urban Affairs Coalition. The decision would ultimately rest with a five-member commission appointed jointly by Pennsylvania's governor and Philadelphia's mayor. ACORN in Philadelphia was accordingly toothless by New York standards. Yet the organization and like-minded opponents of privatization nevertheless persisted in protesting.

The protesting began immediately. Two days after the announcement of Ridge's deal with Edison and a day after ACORN's Ordower vowed to battle Edison, the NAACP, the Black Clergy of Philadelphia and Vicinity, the Parents Union for Public Schools, and Parents United for Better Schools together filed an appeal with U.S. District Court judge Herbert Hutton to reject Mayor Street's request for a ninety-day stay of the city's federal lawsuit against the state, claiming the state's formula for funding schools to be racially discriminatory. "This delay is depriving Philadelphia children of any opportunity for fair educational achievement," said Michael Churchill, a lawyer with the Public Interest Law Center who was representing the four groups. "Privatizing schools at the same level of funding will not give Philadelphia students a fair chance to compete with suburban students, where they are spending, on average, $2,000 more on each child's education."[47] Acknowledging this significant disparity in funding, the editorial page of the *Philadelphia Daily News,* the city's afternoon paper, echoed Churchill on the same day, scoffing at the contention that "Edison has a magic bullet for public education that has eluded the district—and everyone else in the country."[48]

One week later, approximately thirty-five parents and community activists affiliated with ACORN and the Alliance Organizing Project (AOP) stormed the Edison suite in the State Office Building in Philadelphia and demanded a meeting with Whittle. Construction workers had yet to finish laying carpet and painting walls for the new work space for the twenty-five

Edison employees dispatched to Philadelphia to study the city's school system. State troopers and city policemen intervened to break up a one-hour standoff and steered the protesters outside into the 101-degree heat while ACORN and AOP representatives met with Edison officials to arrange a meeting. Edison executive vice president Eugene Wade was flummoxed: "You don't have to take over our office to get a meeting with us. Just pick up the phone."[49]

In addition to meeting afterward with ACORN and AOP members, Edison officials appeared at the four forums cosponsored by the Philadelphia chapter of the Black Alliance for Educational Options and the Greater Philadelphia Urban Affairs Coalition and parried gibes at each. At the first forum, held the evening of August 30 in the basement of Mount Carmel Baptist Church in West Philadelphia and moderated by Democratic state senator Anthony Hardy Williams, many of the 250 parents and community activists showed up to shout down Edison. Williams, himself the cofounder of a K–8 charter school run by the EMO Mosaica, sought with marginal effect to deflect criticism of Edison and to guide the discussion to discovering solutions for the city's schools.[50]

"Speaker after speaker," recounted *Philadelphia Inquirer* columnist Larry Eichel, "said you didn't need a $2.7 million report to tell you that the schools don't have enough money. Or that buildings are decrepit, that classes are too big, that there aren't enough textbooks and that computers aren't sufficiently available."[51] Elmer Smith, a columnist for the *Philadelphia Daily News,* dismissed this forum and the following three held over the next two weeks as "show hearings" and cited a poll conducted by Hart Research Associates finding 65 percent of Philadelphia's public school parents strongly opposed to Edison's management of city schools.[52]

With his parting words to the General Assembly upon leaving Harrisburg for Washington, D.C., in October to head the new Office of Homeland Security, Ridge fanned the flames of discontent. In exhorting the General Assembly to help his successor, Lieutenant Governor Mark Schweiker, in turning around the Philadelphia School District, Ridge added, "Nearly a quarter million children are educated in it—or, truth be told, not educated." The CEO of the Philadelphia School District, Philip Goldsmith, called Ridge's comment "a kick in the gut."[53] Schweiker proved no less brusque. Dismissing concerns about criticism in the press of his stance on the Philadelphia school crisis, Schweiker said he wasn't worried: "After all, only 13 percent of the district's high school juniors are able to read the newspapers with basic comprehension. And that's not counting those who drop out."[54]

With no vote, little confidence in forums and hearings, and no affection for Schweiker, Edison opponents took to demonstrating—at teach-ins, rallies, and marches. At a teach-in in late October organized by Youth United for Change the day after Schweiker's swipe, 200 students, teachers, administrators, and parents voiced their anger with the process playing out and the prospect of Edison taking a managerial role in Philadelphia. Echoing many at the teach-in, Daniel Pena, a high school sophomore, called Edison "a cold-hearted monster" and Schweiker ignorant.[55]

In the wake of Schweiker's endorsement of Edison's eighty-page report at the end of the month, the demonstrations would intensify. Synthesizing the report as his blueprint for transforming the Philadelphia School District, Schweiker called for abolishing the board of education, made up of nine members appointed by the mayor; replacing it with a five-member School Reform Commission (SRC), with four members appointed by the governor and one by the mayor, as stipulated by Act 46; and turning over the district's central office to a private firm, which would, in turn, replace some or all of the district's top fifty-five administrators and report to the SRC.[56]

Schweiker also proposed dividing the city's 264 schools into three groups: some 30 or 40 high-performing schools would simply be monitored, but not controlled; from 60 to 80 low-performing schools would be managed by local community organizations or outside operators, like Edison, with 45 schools going to a "lead provider"; and the remaining 170 or so schools would be retrofitted with a choice of one of three curricula. In addition, Schweiker recommended offering principals performance-based bonuses worth up to 30 percent of their salaries; creating a new corps of approximately 1,500 master teachers—or 15 percent of the district's total—and paying them an additional $7,500 a year; outsourcing custodial work; upgrading information systems; and selling the board of education's downtown nine-floor art deco headquarters.[57]

With Schweiker's announcement came Edison's commitment to take control. Adam Tucker, the company's vice president for communications, expressed confidence in the company's understanding of the Philadelphia School District and affirmed its capacity to turn it around: "We spent ninety days studying Philadelphia, and we know we can absolutely deliver on the governor's proposal. We hope to be a partner, and we know we're up to the challenge."[58] Whittle underscored the company's qualifications: "There's not another organization in America that can take something like this on. We've been training for this."[59]

6

WATERLOO

If you're part of a hostile takeover, you and your shareholders will regret it.

Pedro Ramos, President, Philadelphia School Board, to Chris Whittle,
Philadelphia City Hall hearing, *Philadelphia Daily News,* November 9, 2001

■ IN RESPONSE TO Governor Mark Schweiker's proposal on October 30, 2001, and Edison's ambitions, opponents massed and chanted the next day on the steps of the art deco landmark building Edison had recommended putting up for sale. After attending the rally, Pedro Ramos, the president of the school board, said, "This is a bad Halloween story. People are coming to town with Frankenstein trying to convince us that it's Prince Charming." Mayor Street, who had agreed in August to welcome Edison to conduct its study in exchange for emergency funding from Governor Ridge, likewise professed shock: "A plan like this would literally take control of our system and turn it over to a corporate entity."[1] Especially troubling to some critics was the prospect of a firm like Edison running the central office at the same time it ran a cluster of schools. To these critics, a conflict of interest was inherent. "Nobody can contract with themselves and be expected to do a credible job," said school board member Michael Masch after Schweiker had outlined his plan two weeks earlier.[2]

City councilman and future mayor Michael Nutter would contend that Street had only himself to blame: "It seems to me you invited the fox into the henhouse. Now the complaint is the fox is having dinner."[3] Street would, in turn, claim he had been duped by Harrisburg into thinking Philadelphia would be an active partner, not a voiceless domain.[4]

One week later, on the first Wednesday of November, 350 students, teachers, parents, and politicians massed and chanted outside City Hall on the eve of the first of two daylong hearings bringing together state, city, and Edison officials as well as academic experts and community leaders. One organizer of the rally, Helen Gym, of Asian Americans United, directed a question at the heart of the funding debate: "If this [privatization] is so innovative, why aren't they doing it in Lower Merion?"[5]

During the first day of the City Hall hearings, on November 8, U.S. Representative Chaka Fattah tangled with Whittle and left him with a warning: "You need to think about whether you're prepared to come into this city absent the support of the mayor or any major elected officials and run a school system." Ramos went a step further in addressing Whittle: "If you're part of a hostile takeover, you and your shareholders will regret it." Ramos's grim forecast sparked a standing ovation.[6]

While Edison indeed lacked much political support in Philadelphia, Fattah overstated the case. Two prominent Democratic lawmakers had endorsed Edison: State Senator Anthony Hardy Williams, who moderated the first Edison forum, at Mount Carmel Baptist Church in August, and who had cofounded a charter school and expressed interest in managing some of the schools designated as underperforming; and State Representative Dwight Evans, who had also started a charter school and expressed interest in managing schools in this same category.[7]

In addition, Kenny Gamble, the legendary R&B artist and producer, had endorsed Edison, as had the president of the Philadelphia chapter of Nueva Esperanza, Reverend Luis Cortez. Like Evans and Williams, Gamble had already started a charter school, through his nonprofit community organization, Universal Companies, and was intent on running more charter schools. Gamble had, in fact, been in talks with Edison officials as early as April to join forces, and his organization had undertaken work from the company to study parent and community involvement in Philadelphia schooling (the product of that endeavor would become a fifty-four-page appendix to Edison's report to the governor).[8]

Cortez had also founded a charter school and saw privatization as an opportunity for improving community engagement. For all four men, funding was not the central problem for Philadelphia's schools, but rather bureaucratic complexity and union work rules. What John Chubb and Terry Moe had articulated a decade earlier in theory in *Politics, Markets, and America's Schools,* Cortez, Evans, Gamble, and Williams put in local everyday terms.[9] "The failure [of the Philadelphia School District] is so blatant and so severe," Cortez said at a gathering chaired by Gamble on the day of Schweiker's announcement of his privatization plan, "that if you live in our community, you have no choice but to see this as an opportunity, a right—a civil right— to defend our children."[10]

Fattah was in essence right, though. While Evans and Williams were major elected officials, their support of Edison, along with backing from notable Philadelphians like Gamble and Cortez, would not give Schweiker the authority to turn over the school system to Whittle. In protest against Schweiker's proposal, Mayor Street started working out of an office in the board of education building the day after Fattah and Ramos had admonished Whittle in City Hall, refused to negotiate with Schweiker until privatization of the central administration was off the table, and dared state officials to carry him out.[11]

Within two weeks, Schweiker conceded. The governor was technically empowered by Act 46 to follow through in taking over the Philadelphia School District in the manner he wished, "with or without Street on board," observed *Philadelphia Inquirer* columnist Larry Eichel, but doing so appeared politically untenable. Street had already provoked significant pushback. If Schweiker persisted in implementing Edison's recommendation to outsource management of the school system, Street stood to sabotage the effort, however costly to the city.[12]

■

Territorial jealousy clearly explained some of the resistance to the Edison report and Schweiker's endorsement. Forfeiture of local control naturally constitutes a blow to civic pride, no matter the wisdom of an outsider. Edison, after all, made several constructive recommendations in its eighty-page report. Edison made a compelling case to create a widespread corps of mentor teachers; to upgrade and coordinate the district's archaic and disparate information systems; and to rationalize purchasing. The company moreover advised the district to substitute a "dizzying array" of more than seventy different reading, math, and science curricula throughout the district with a choice of three programs. Such consolidation, the company contended, would make it easier for students to move from one classroom or school to another without falling behind; Edison reported several cases of classes at the same grade level within the same building using different curricula. Such consolidation, Edison maintained, would also assist teachers in getting support and guidance from district subject administrators. Lastly, Edison made a strong argument to give principals more freedom in how they staffed their schools.[13]

Yet these recommendations, however meritorious and lucidly expressed, were obscured by Edison's evident purpose of taking over the district, by the report's tone, and by several telling lapses in research and argumentation. In implicitly endorsing itself to take over the school district, Edison provoked immediate distrust. Columnists for the *Philadelphia Inquirer* and the *Philadelphia Daily News* dismissed the company's role as a consultancy issuing impartial advice as a charade.[14] Moreover, the tone of the report was judged derisive. With its headline for an article assessing the report, the typically urbane *Philadelphia Inquirer* made this point clear: "Edison Rips District over 'Accountability.'"[15]

The language throughout the report was indeed damning. Regarding accountability, in particular, Edison slammed the district on the first page of the executive summary: "Over the past decade, the district's management has overseen the expenditure of more than $10 billion with no clear accountability for the results."[16] Edison went on to call these results "dismal."[17]

Edison conceded that these results were, in part, the consequence of economic disadvantage but proceeded to sidestep the role of life outside of school. Instead of digging deeper, Edison pointed out that students in three districts of comparable size (Clark County, Nevada; Houston, Texas; and Broward County, Florida) did 18 percent better on the SAT in 1999–2000 while their districts in 1998–1999 spent 7 percent less per pupil.[18] Edison concluded, "Based on such comparisons, we believe student achievement in the P[hiladelphia] S[chool] D[istrict] can be improved dramatically."[19]

In comparing school districts by size without reference to demographic data or costs of living, Edison denied readers important context for understanding the challenges facing the Philadelphia School District. Philadelphia's students were and remain significantly poorer than their counterparts in the comparison districts; and in cost-adjusted dollars, Philadelphia spent considerably less per pupil than the comparison districts.[20]

Despite assistance on the report from prestigious firms—including IBM, McKinsey, MetaMetrics, and Public Financial Management—Edison made an incomplete case.[21] Edison neglected to acknowledge that the portion of students in Philadelphia qualifying for free or reduced-price lunch, a standard measure for economic disadvantage, was much higher than in the three other districts it had cited: 69 percent in 2000 in contrast to a weighted average of 46 percent for the three other districts. The portion of Philadelphia's children ages five to seventeen living below the poverty line in 2000 was likewise 24 percent in contrast to a weighted average of 18 percent for the same cohort in the three other districts.[22] Furthermore, while Edison was right that the three other districts spent, on average, 7 percent less per pupil than Philadelphia in 1998–1999, the report failed to acknowledge that the cost of living in these three other districts at that time was, on average, 16 percent lower than in Philadelphia.[23] This means, by extension, that the other three districts were spending, on average, not 7 percent less per pupil than Philadelphia but 11 percent more; conversely, Philadelphia was spending 10 percent less.[24]

In an op-ed in the *Philadelphia Inquirer* entitled "Company's Report Doesn't Inspire Trust," published several days after the release of the Edison study, Michael Casserly, executive director of the Council of the Great City Schools, faulted Edison for overlooking such demographic and economic distinctions. Casserly also contended that while Edison was right that district students performed poorly on state and national standardized exams, the company painted a bleaker picture than necessary. Edison could and should have noted, Casserly wrote, that since the implementation six years earlier of the district's reform program, Children Achieving, elementary school students had recorded significant progress: from 1996 to 2000, the portion of fourth-graders reading at or above the basic levels, according to the nationally normed SAT-9 test, climbed consistently from 44 percent to 60; fourth-graders were also outpacing their peers on the state exam over this same period; and the district's fourth- and eighth-graders posted average scores on the SAT-9 in comparison to their peers in eleven other major cities with similar levels of poverty and school spending, with students in six cities doing better and five doing worse. Casserly elaborated on his critique of the Edison report in a thirty-five-page analysis in December.[25]

For a company censuring a school district for poor accountability, such porous analysis made Edison an easy target for critics. The oversights amounted, at best, to a rushed job and, at worst, to a deliberate effort to exaggerate the underperformance of the school district in order to win a major managerial contract. On top of Casserly's corrections, allegations of misrepresentation piled on: the district's chief financial officer, Rhonda Chatzkel, claimed that the student-teacher ratio was not 16.9 to 1, as Edison had reported, but 17.6 to 1, in line with districts of similar size; the district's chief operating officer, Thomas McGlinchy, argued that Edison had significantly underestimated the efficiency of school custodians by failing to note that many worked five-hour, not eight-hour, shifts; and the district's interim CEO, Philip Goldsmith, countered in a scathing six-page rebuttal he read before the soon-to-be abolished board of education that Edison had brought no insights but had merely studied the district's plans and then spun them as the company's own prescriptions.[26]

Whether the critics were right or wrong about these additional matters—no letters of correction from Edison officials ran in the newspapers printing these charges—became moot. The reaction by Street, school board and city council members, local newspaper columnists, and community activists forced Schweiker's decision. The editorial page of the *Wall Street Journal* repeatedly weighed in from afar for full privatization—calling Edison a trailblazer and Schweiker the state's greatest revolutionary since 1776—but to no avail.[27]

■

Schweiker surrendered at the end of a day in late November marked by a rally at the Capitol of 800 high school students bused in from Philadelphia by the Philadelphia Student Union and Youth United for Change to protest his privatization plan. Eugene Tinsley, a junior in the crowd, remade in plain language the funding argument long ago articulated by state lawmakers Nicholas Micozzie, Wallace Nunn, James Rhoades, and Mario Civera: "We are sick and tired of going to classes with no books. The state has set up an unfair way of funding our schools and then blamed us for the results."[28]

Following a two-hour impromptu meeting with Street that evening in Philadelphia, Schweiker announced that he had agreed to drop his insistence on privatizing the management of the district's central office. Schweiker's compromise with Street called instead for employing Edison as a consultant to the district.[29] While this concession satisfied Street enough to return to the negotiating table, it was a hollow victory to many on the left. "I think we didn't get a new deal," said J. Whyatt Mondesire, president of the Philadelphia chapter of the NAACP. "We got a raw deal. There was no victory here. Nothing's changed. It's really privatization through the back door instead of coming through the front door."[30]

More demonstrations followed. Mondesire one week later, on Wednesday, November 28, led hundreds of protesters in a march from the State Office Building, temporary home to Edison's team of twenty-five staffers, one mile south on Broad Street to City Hall, where they blocked traffic on Market Street and drowned out the choir singing for spectators at the annual lighting of the city's Christmas tree.[31] The next morning, hundreds of high school students organized by the Philadelphia Student Union and Youth United for Change walked out of class. Many marched on the school board headquarters, guarded by a phalanx of police officers to prevent their entry. Meanwhile, school-employee unions and community allies brought suit in Pennsylvania Supreme Court to overturn Act 46, declaring it unconstitutional and requesting an injunction to bar a state takeover until the issue was resolved. In the afternoon, approximately 200 students gathered at City Hall. A delegation met with Street. The protesters then marched to the school board headquarters and linked hands to form a human chain encircling the whole building while chanting, "Hey, hey! Ho, ho! Edison has got to go" and "It's not hard, it's not funny, all the other kids have money. Like the kids across the nation, we just want our education."[32] The following day, twenty-five ministers, all members of the Black Clergy of Philadelphia and Vicinity, joined the protest by blocking traffic at the intersection of Broad and Vine Streets, two downtown arteries, as well as the entrance and exits to the Vine Street Expressway.[33]

While Street and Schweiker continued to meet to hammer out an agreement, Edison responded to the series of protests with a $430,000 public relations campaign, featuring eight days of newspaper ads and TV commercials, commencing on December 12, as well as a Web site and telephone hotline for more information about the company.[34] Discontent nevertheless persisted. On December 18, the Philadelphia Student Union and Youth United for Change carried out their biggest protest so far. At 10:30 a.m., more than 1,000 students walked out of class at high schools across the city and made their way to City Hall. After a rally at City Hall, the crowd grew and marched up Broad Street to rally again outside the State Office Building.[35]

■

Much as the lawsuits filed by teachers' unions against state interventions involving Edison in Baltimore in 2000 and in Chester Upland in 2001 gained no traction, the same held for the suit filed by the coalition of opponents to privatization on November 29 against Act 46. Meeting the same fate was a preemptive suit filed by the same group—on the same day as the massive student walkout—against Schweiker for violating conflict-of-interest regulations in hiring Edison as a consultant and then using its recommendations to contract with the company itself.[36] A fifty-nine-page critique of the Edison consulting deal on the same conflict-of-interest grounds by the state auditor general, Robert P. Casey Jr., several months later likewise garnered significant press coverage but generated no legal repercussions.[37]

Reflecting on the futility of these challenges, Len Rieser, executive director of the Education Law Center in Philadelphia and a lawyer who had contested the state takeover, observed in 2009 during an interview in his office in a century-old brick-and-limestone building four blocks from City Hall, "When you get rescued, you don't get to choose what kind of life preserver you want. The public got bumped out of the discussion."[38]

In the end, while Street did not get everything he wanted, he negotiated a much better rescue than many had expected. In addition to saving the central office from privatization, Street talked Schweiker into granting him two appointments, instead of one, to the five-member SRC and into accepting $45 million from the city in additional annual school funding instead of the $75 million Schweiker had sought to match the $75 million in additional annual school funding the state would be allocating to the city. The deal was announced by Schweiker and Street at the Convention Center the afternoon of Friday, December 21, making Philadelphia by far the largest school district in the nation ever taken over by a state government.[39] In keeping with their practice of protesting every step of the takeover process, students afterward blocked traffic outside the Convention Center.[40]

Schweiker the next day named James Nevels to lead the SRC. Nevels was chair and CEO of the Swarthmore Group, the nation's eighth-largest minority-owned investment company, as well as a member of the board of control for the Chester Upland School District, which chose Edison the previous March to run six of its ten schools.[41] While Nevels called Edison "a great company," he did not use his blanket authority over his first thirty days to commit to Schweiker's plan to sign a six-year, $101 million consulting deal with the company.[42] Nevels instead waited for the other four SRC members to be named and then with them on March 26, 2002, agreed on a smaller contract with Edison, naming the company lead consultant, among twelve consultants, for a period running no longer than two years and on undisclosed terms.[43]

This diminishment of expected authority, however, paled in comparison to the news three weeks later. On April 17, the SRC announced its plans for the schools in greatest need of improvement. Edison was awarded management of twenty schools instead of the expected forty-five. Twenty-two additional schools were assigned to a mix of two universities, two smaller for-profit EMOs, and two local nonprofit community organizations: Temple University got five schools; the University of Pennsylvania, three; Florida-based Chancellor Beacon Academies Inc., five; New York–based Victory Schools Inc., three; Kenny Gamble's Universal Companies, two; and Foundations Inc., four. The panel decided on more modest intervention at twenty-eight additional schools under consideration: nine would become charter schools, which were free to seek corporate partners, and nineteen would be reorganized but would most likely remain under district auspices.[44]

The announcement came at the end of a day fraught with tension. Members of the Philadelphia Student Union had camped overnight outside the district headquarters and then locked arms in the morning to form a human barricade to prevent the SRC from holding its meeting inside.[45] The SRC relocated a mile away to the African American Museum and deliberated for three hours at the front of a room filled with more than one hundred parents, students, and community activists intermittently protesting as members voiced opinions and cast their votes.[46]

While local opponents derided the SRC for doing the governor's bidding, the editors of the *Wall Street Journal* accused the SRC of caving in to populist pressures by allotting Edison twenty schools instead of forty-five. "The latest move is a compromise of the compromise," the editors concluded: first, Schweiker backed down on turning over the district's central office to Edison; next, the SRC gave Edison under half the number of schools expected.[47]

Investors, in turn, bailed. Edison's stock had recovered since *Bloomberg News* reported in February that the company had misrepresented revenue in much the same way EAI had a decade earlier in Baltimore. The stock dropped 11 percent the day the *Bloomberg* story appeared, from $13.45 to $12 a share, but in the ensuing two months it climbed as high as $14.25. When the SRC announced that Edison would be getting twenty schools, not forty-five, the stock dropped 8 percent, from $12.79 to $11.78. Two weeks later, after Merrill Lynch and Bear Stearns had both downgraded the stock, it was down another 56 percent, closing April at $5.23. The consensus on Wall Street was that without the share of business in Philadelphia that Edison had projected, the company would not be able to achieve the economies of scale necessary to become profitable in the foreseeable future. Investors also appeared nervous about the SEC's pending ruling on Edison's definition of revenue. How much of the decline in share value derived from the Philadelphia news and how much from fears of a negative determination from the SEC is hard, if not impossible, to know. What is certain is that the SEC ruling, as previously explained, was devastating. When the SEC issued its report on May 15 validating the *Bloomberg* story, Edison's stock had already fallen to $3.34. News of the SEC report drove the stock down another 33 percent in one day, to $2.25.[48]

In the wake of the SEC report, which required that Edison revise past revenue reports and hire an internal audit manager, Edison not only suffered a black eye for the sloppy bookkeeping for which it had faulted public school districts but also provoked ten class action shareholder lawsuits.[49] Edison correctly contended that it had accounted for all expenses in reporting revenue. But the company had to concede—after having vigorously disputed the *Bloomberg* account—that its practice of booking money designated by districts for school employees as company revenue exaggerated the scale of its business; of equal importance, this practice substantially diminished the ratio of the company's losses.[50]

Revenue for managing its seven schools in Las Vegas, for example, should have been limited to the money paid by the district to Edison for running the schools and compensating the company administrators hired to do that job. Instead, in perhaps its most egregious case of revenue misrepresentation, Edison reported $30 million in revenue for its 2001–2002 contract with Las Vegas while $21.3 million of that sum went directly to teachers, secretaries, custodians, bus drivers, and cafeteria workers, meaning that Edison had overstated its revenue for this contract by 244 percent.[51] For its business as a whole that year, Edison reported $465.1 million in revenue when $178.7 million of that sum bypassed the company, meaning Edison had overstated its revenue in sum by 62 percent.[52]

■

Achieving economies of scale had been Edison's central fiscal challenge. Edison appeared in 2001 to be on its way to achieving economies of scale. Yet the SEC report made clear that the appearance was an illusion. According to its annual reports to the SEC, the company's losses over revenue had declined to 11 percent by 2001. But for an impairment charge of $36.9 million in company stock the following year for its acquisition of LearnNow, the company's losses over revenue would have allegedly been 11 percent again, not 19 percent. By 2003 the loss appeared to be down to 6 percent (see Table 6.1).

However, because much of what Edison tallied as revenue went directly from school districts to employees, its alleged rate of growth was greatly exaggerated. While it was still accurate for Edison to calculate its administrative costs as a portion of total operating costs to determine its efficiency as a school operator, it was misleading for the company to depict as revenue money it never touched. In the case of fiscal year 2002, for example, company revenue would be lowered from $465.1 million to $286.4 million. This

Table 6.1 Edison's schools, enrollment, reported and amended revenue, and net income, 1995–2003

Fiscal year	Schools (company count)	Estimated enrollment	Revenue	Amended revenue	Net income	Loss/revenue and amended loss/revenue
1996	4	2,250	$ 11,773	n/a	$ (10,103)	86% & n/a
1997	11 (12)	7,150	38,559	n/a	(11,422)	30% & n/a
1998	22 (25)	12,600	65,630	$ 37,251	(26,483)	40% & 71%
1999	43 (51)	23,900	125,085	68,570	(49,433)	40% & 72%
2000	61 (79)	37,500	208,971	125,061	(50,630)	24% & 40%
2001	88 (113)	57,000	350,508	221,336	(38,512)	11% & 17%
2002	114 (136)	74,000	465,058	286,356	(86,040)	19% & 30%
2003	133 (149)	80,000	425,628	281,959	(25,028)	6% & 9%

Data sources: The school counts come from Brian Gill et al., *Inspiration, Perspiration, and Time: Operations and Achievement in Edison Schools* (Santa Monica: RAND, 2005), 13. Enrollment, the company's school count, and financial figures come from Edison Schools Inc., "Securities and Exchange Commission File No. 000-27817 (Form 10-K)," September 28, 2000, September 30, 2002, and September 29, 2003.

Notes: The difference in school counts is explained by Edison's policy of tallying divisions within one building, such as K–5 and 6–8, as separate schools; revenue was revised downward considerably by order of the SEC in 2002 to exclude funds allocated by districts directly to employees; revenue and income in thousands; the difference between revenue and amended revenue amounts to school district expenditures that bypassed Edison.

meant that company losses of $86 million amounted to 30 percent of revenue, not 19 percent.

Administrative costs over total operating costs did nevertheless exhibit a steady decline. For economies of scale to set in, this is precisely where progress was required. Whittle was keenly aware of this. In a PowerPoint presentation at an investor conference in July 2000 at the St. Regis Hotel in New York before Edison's second public offering, Whittle displayed a graph showing an inverse relationship between revenue growth and administrative costs. Whittle predicted that within three years administrative costs would drop from 15 percent of total expenditures (the figure for the nine months ending March 31, 2000) to 7 percent. With public school districts spending on average 27 percent of their budgets on administration, Whittle said, Edison would record earnings of 20 percent, send 13 points of the difference back into the classroom, and retain 7 points as profit.[53]

Table 6.2 Edison's administrative costs in relation to total costs, 1996–2003

Fiscal year	Administrative costs	Total operating costs	Costs incurred by Edison	District expenditures bypassing Edison	Administrative costs over total operating costs
1996	$ 7,717	$ 21,774	n/a	n/a	35%
1997	12,755	49,944	n/a	n/a	26%
1998	18,258	86,499	$58,120	$28,379	21%
1999	49,984	174,755	118,240	56,515	29%
2000	54,232	260,506	176,597	83,909	21%
2001	57,851	392,436	263,264	129,172	15%
2002	71,230	509,703	367,879	178,702	14%
2003	67,809	439,379	295,710	143,669	15%

Data source: Edison Schools Inc., "Securities and Exchange Commission File No. 000-27817 (Form 10-K)," September 28, 2000, September 30, 2002, and September 29, 2003.

Notes: All costs in thousands; total operating costs for 2002 do not include an impairment charge of $36,878,000 listed by Edison in its 2002 10-K, as this charge was not for operating costs but for its acquisition of LearnNow, another EMO; total revenue plus losses in Table 6.1 do not add up to total operating costs in Table 6.2 because other income (or expenses), state and local taxes, and preferred stock accretion are not included.

Yet Edison's spending on administration ("Administration, curriculum, and development" in its filings with the SEC) never reached single digits, instead rising to 21 percent for the fiscal year ending 2000, dropping to 15 percent for 2001 and then to 14 percent for 2002, and returning to 15 percent for 2003, 8 points above what Whittle had forecasted (see Table 6.2).[54]

Adding to Edison's pain in the spring of 2002 was news of contract terminations. On May 16, Edison's largest school and one of its original four, the Boston Renaissance Charter School, announced it would terminate its relationship with the company at the end of June, citing inadequate improvement in test scores and curricular inflexibility; Boston Renaissance had 1,300 students in kindergarten through eighth grade and paid Edison $9 million a year. A month later, on June 18, another of Edison's original four clients voted to terminate its contract at the end of the school year as well. The school board of Mount Clemens, Michigan, which had outsourced the management of one of its schools to Edison in 1995 and subsequently added three more schools, concluded that the company's fee was too high. Edison officials countered that the company was owed money by the district and could no longer run the four schools at the current rate. Chris Cerf, Edison's president and chief operating officer, who would a decade later become New Jersey's commissioner of education, claimed that given the cost of the contract to the company, this parting of ways should be viewed as "positive to the company's finances." The market disagreed, sending Edison's stock down 34 percent in three days, from $1.52 to $1.00.[55]

Making matters worse still was the SRC's selection of Paul Vallas in July as the new CEO of the Philadelphia School District. Within weeks of assuming office, the former CEO of the Chicago Public Schools, who had just lost to Rod Blagojevich in the Democratic primary race to become governor of Illinois, nullified the SRC's contract with Edison as the district's lead consultant. "There's no need for a lead consultant," Vallas said on August 1. "That's what I'm here for."[56]

With the stock tailspinning, Edison's very presence in Philadelphia as a school manager was in jeopardy. As the company averaged $2,500 in start-up costs for each student at its new schools, the bill in Philadelphia for upgrading twenty schools serving 14,500 students would amount to $36,250,000. Given its negative cash flow, lack of assets, and plummeting market value, the company would have a hard time raising that sum through loans.[57] Raising funds as Edison had three times before with public offerings was out of the question with the share price so low.

To the rescue came Merrill Lynch, Edison's lead underwriter in 1999, and Leeds Weld & Co. The same day Vallas rejected the need for Edison's input as a consultant, Edison announced that Merrill Lynch would expand a $35 million revolving-credit agreement with the company by $20 million and that Leeds Weld would lend the company another $20 million. Merrill Lynch and Leeds Weld would in turn receive rights to buy up to 10.7 million new shares of Edison at $1 a share; if the two New York–based firms exercised these options, they would own a 17 percent stake.[58]

While the new funding kept Edison's plans alive in Philadelphia, more bad news soon after streamed in from Georgia and Texas. On August 15, the Bibb County Board of Education in Georgia voted unanimously to terminate its five-year contract with Edison, commenced in 1999, to run two of the district's schools two years early; the board cited stagnant test scores, declines in enrollment, and high teacher turnover.[59] Much worse for Edison, a week later, at the recommendation of their superintendent, the trustees of the Dallas Independent School District also voted unanimously to terminate its five-year contract with Edison, commenced in 2000, two years early, but this contract was for running seven schools; Superintendent Mike Moses cited low test scores and budget constraints.[60] The following week, Edison shares were trading below 50 cents. The same bold accounting practices and grand expectations that doomed Whittle Communications in 1994 appeared to be undoing Edison eight years later. On August 27, Edison was put on notice by NASDAQ that it would be delisted if the company's stock did not close above $1.00 for ten trading days in a row before November 25.[61]

■

In the course of twelve months, Edison's administrative profile in Philadelphia had dropped from potentially running the district's central office to potentially serving as the sole consultant to the district with a six-year $101 million contract, to serving as the lead consultant among twelve consultants with a two-year, $36 million contract, to having no consulting role at all.[62] Moreover, though Edison was awarded far more schools to run in Philadelphia than the company had ever won in any city, the total numbered less than half what many had expected.

"The Philadelphia School District was once touted as the big-ticket contract that would rescue Edison Schools Inc. from its never-turned-a-profit troubles," wrote reporter Chris Brennan in the *Philadelphia Daily News* the day after Vallas had said he would not keep Edison as a consultant. "Now it could be Edison CEO Chris Whittle's Waterloo."[63]

Edison's first months in Philadelphia validated Brennan's assessment. Bad press came early and kept appearing for one matter after another: the company's botched management of inventory; its dismissal of nonteaching personnel; Vallas's indignant reversal of some of these dismissals; disorder and violence at several schools under company management; the midyear resignation of a veteran principal; failure to submit financial reports on time; delay of payment by the district for this tardiness; and lavish administrative spending. In addition, bad news from neighboring Chester Upland about

Edison's management of nine schools in the district since September 2001 deepened doubts about the company's capacities.

Expecting a premium of $1,500 per student in Philadelphia, Edison ordered new musical instruments, physical education equipment, textbooks, workbooks, science materials, and art supplies for all twenty of the schools it was taking over. While Pennsylvania secretary of education Charles Zogby had endorsed this premium, the SRC needed to approve it.[64] Vallas and countless Edison critics, including Mayor Street, Congressman Fattah, and columnist Elmer Smith of the *Philadelphia Daily News*, made such approval difficult. Street, Fattah, and Smith challenged the premium, issuing variations on a bitter argument: if Edison found the school district inefficient, it should not get a per-pupil premium at all.[65] "This is the same Edison Schools, Inc., that authored a report claiming reform is not about money," wrote Smith. "They pocketed $2.7 million for that wisdom."[66] Zogby countered that Edison and other EMOs were taking over historically underfunded schools in need of compensatory resources. Vallas and Philadelphia secretary of education Debra Kahn accused Zogby of misunderstanding basic school finance: because the takeover schools had been predominantly staffed by junior faculty, payrolls had been lower, but not allocations for materials and services.[67]

The SRC heard both sides and agreed unanimously at the end of July to give Edison an extra $881, not $1,500, per pupil.[68] Edison's response to this unexpected cut in funding was twofold. In the final week of August, the company sent in trucks to load up the new instruments, books, equipment, and materials and return them to their vendors. Edison's critics in Philadelphia professed disbelief. The company's supporters in Harrisburg refused to comment. Chris Brennan of the *Philadelphia Daily News* took the move to be an embarrassing sign of the company's financial frailty, ultimately having nothing to do with the cut in funding and everything to do with the plunge in the company's market value and the recent loss of fourteen contracts in Georgia, Massachusetts, Michigan, and Texas.[69]

Edison's second cost-cutting measure caused far more controversy and trouble. The same week Edison hauled away its new inventory, the company announced the layoff of nearly 200 school secretaries, supportive services assistants (SSAs), who help teachers in running classes with struggling or unruly students, and nonteaching assistants (NTAs), who monitor hallways as well as libraries and cafeterias to keep order. Edison declared that it would use just one secretary per school instead of three or four, and would use disciplinary strategies it had effectively implemented in schools across the country to make up for the dismissed SSAs and NTAs.[70]

Edison spokesperson Adam Tucker explained, "We know, because we've done this in schools across the country, that our staffing model, curriculum and professional development, when combined with successful existing school strategies, do not require NTAs." One ten-year veteran NTA who was laid off shot back that Tucker knew nothing about the role played by NTAs or the nature of Philadelphia schools. Jerry Jordan, the vice president of the Philadelphia Teachers Union, expressed concern about children's safety and vowed to fight the layoffs: "Children need supervision. We're attempting to talk to the administration, to anybody who will listen, saying this is not a good model; it's going to be harmful for kids."[71] Tucker defied such objections: "Edison was not hired in Philadelphia to perpetuate the status quo. Reform means change. The staffing model we are putting in place, we believe, will increase student achievement and help the district financially."[72] The consensus among Edison executives, according to one company official, was that the NTAs and SSAs were merely beneficiaries of an "urban patronage mill," doing little for an easy check: this arrangement had to go for the school system to operate more efficiently.[73]

Yet Vallas disagreed and did not let Tucker have the final word. Vallas summarily ordered Edison to hire back one full-time NTA and two part-time SSAs for each school.[74] "I want to make sure they have enough backup," Vallas said.[75]

Philadelphia, after all, was not Baltimore. As a miniature district unto itself in Baltimore from 2001 to 2007, Edison received its additional funding directly from the state and had significant autonomy in operating its schools. But in Philadelphia, Edison received its additional funding from a commission jointly appointed by state and city officials and had limited freedom in deciding resource allocation. While the CEO of Baltimore's schools from 2001 to 2007 had to treat Edison like a school district within a school district, the CEO of Philadelphia's schools ruled Edison like an experimental project with its own curriculum and supplementary funding from an external source. If Vallas deemed a personnel decision imprudent, he could intervene and did.

Within one month of the start of the school year, however, it was clear that Vallas had not intervened enough. Edison did not have enough backup. In the course of two weeks at Shaw Middle School in West Philadelphia, a thirteen-year-old girl suspended for fighting returned to school and started another fight; four thirteen- and fourteen-year-old boys were charged by the police with disorderly conduct for fighting right after dismissal; and two girls were arrested for setting a fire in a girls' bathroom. Edison spokesperson Tucker tried to downplay the significance of these events by noting that Shaw had a long history of disciplinary problems. But that explanation did not square with Edison's decision to cut the positions of four NTAs and two secretaries at Shaw. Vallas responded by dispatching a veteran administrator to coach Shaw's principal and demanding Edison rehire the dismissed NTAs.[76]

At the same time fights were breaking out at Shaw, a vicious battle between two fourth-graders ruptured class across the Schuylkill River at Edison's Waring Elementary School. Desks were overturned. Classmates were cheering and jeering. The teacher, age twenty-two, 5'2", and several months out of college, called the office for help, but no one picked up. The fight's instigator, who had already been in two classroom skirmishes that same week, then grabbed a pair of scissors off the teacher's desk and threatened to stab the other student in the face. Two teachers from neighboring classrooms heard the commotion and ran in to restore order. Making matters worse, Waring's principal took six days to report the incident to district personnel and failed to mention in her report the scissors or the threat. Vallas launched an investigation. Shaken up, the teacher did not return to Waring and resigned a week later.[77]

Hallway disruptions and fires meanwhile plagued Edison's Gillespie Middle School in North Philadelphia. Vallas responded at the beginning of October by temporarily adding fifteen NTAs and five school police officers.[78] Four miles away, at Edison's Penn Treaty Middle School, just blocks from the Delaware River, teachers complained that the dismissal of five NTAs rendered hallway conduct chaotic. "What was Chris Whittle thinking?" asked one veteran teacher, reflecting on the company leader's assertion that Edison's core values of respect, compassion, and integrity, along with better instruction, would obviate the need for customary supervision. "They don't expect us to do discipline because they don't expect discipline to be an issue. I think they have their head in the sand."[79]

Even an Edison principal who firmly believed in the company's model concluded that it could not work without the funding initially expected. Janice Solkov, a veteran school administrator with a doctorate and thirty years of experience as an educator, found herself so overwhelmed as the principal of Edison's Morton McMichael Elementary in West Philadelphia that she informed the company in mid-November that she would step down at the end of December. Solkov explained her sense of defeat in a long article in the *New York Times* and again in an op-ed in the *Washington Post*.[80]

Without the business manager Edison had promised and the second school secretary that the company had laid off, Solkov said she could not keep up with paperwork. Compounding this managerial challenge was the requirement that she report to both district and company supervisors, meaning twice the number of meetings and twice the number of forms to fill out. For this redundancy, Solkov faulted the district for failing to give Edison sufficient autonomy and thus made clear how hard it can be for an EMO to operate within a school district. Moreover, the shortfall in funding kept Solkov from opening the school library and negated the company's signature policy of providing home computers for all students in third grade and above as well as laptops for all teachers, making implementation of Edison's curriculum all the more difficult.[81]

Graver still, Solkov's teachers were overwhelmed. Within the first two weeks of the school year, a first-year sixth-grade teacher quit, and a veteran fifth-grade teacher, who suffered from multiple sclerosis and used a cane, was struck by a student and taken to the hospital in an ambulance. With a teacher shortage in the district, Solkov had to make do with serial substitutes. "I felt like I was drowning, and I did not see a way to stay afloat," Solkov confessed to the *Times* reporter. "Maybe in some other real world, it [the Edison model] can work. I'm not sure it can work in the Philadelphia real world." Richard Barth, the company's senior vice president for Philadelphia, acknowledged to the same reporter the burden of running an Edison school: "This is a bear of a job. It is not for everyone."[82] Three years later, Barth left Edison to become CEO of the Knowledge Is Power Program, the nonprofit charter network.[83]

■

While Edison did not hire back more NTAs and SSAs than Vallas ordered, the company eventually admitted the need for more adults in its schools. With Vallas, Edison devised a work-around. Through the school district, Edison was permitted to hire employees of eight community-based organizations—such as We Overcome, West Philadelphia Coalition of Neighborhoods and Businesses, and Security Universal—as hall monitors for half the cost of unionized NTAs.[84]

Keeping down costs was not Edison's only bookkeeping problem. The company was seven weeks late in submitting three required documents: an audited financial statement for the past fiscal year; a guarantee entitling the city to the company's assets, such as computers and textbooks, should the company declare bankruptcy; and proof from the company's creditors of money borrowed.[85] Known for running a tight ship, Vallas, who had worked for fifteen years as a budget analyst for the Illinois legislature before becoming CEO of Chicago's public schools, withheld $5.3 million in scheduled payments to Edison until October 28, a week after all the necessary paperwork was filed.[86]

Edison in addition suffered more bad press for holding a three-day conference earlier in the month for 175 principals at the posh Broadmoor Resort in Colorado Springs at the same time the company was behind in its financial paperwork and borrowing money to stay afloat. Ten principals from Philadelphia and nine from Chester Upland attended the $300,000 retreat. At a news conference about a new after-school initiative, Vallas lambasted Edison for lavish spending. "If a company's in trouble," Vallas said, "the company shouldn't be having expensive sabbaticals or orientations in far-off places." Sidestepping the approximate per-day cost of $550 per principal, travel not included, Edison spokesperson Tucker attempted to deflect Vallas's response: "Any school system that does not invest time, money, and resources in the development of its principals will never reach its full potential."[87]

Yet the cost of the conference was not the only impolitic development to make it into both the *Philadelphia Inquirer* and the *Philadelphia Daily News*. Equally startling was Whittle's recommendation in a keynote address at the conference that students should be put to work as office assistants or technology aides in schools to nurture responsibility and to cut costs. "We could have less adult staff," Whittle said, laying the foundation for the previously cited argument he would flesh out three years later in his book on school reform, *Crash Course: Imagining a Better Future for Public Education*.[88] "I think it's an important concept for education and for economics that Edison needs to raise to another level."[89]

Had there been any doubts about Edison's intentions in laying off NTAs and SSAs in August, Whittle made plain that he believed personnel costs exceeded their value. Whittle said that if each student in a school of 600 worked five hours per week, seventy-five adults could be replaced. Whittle forecasted that such a system could be in place by 2004. Vallas fired back: "It is not going to happen on our watch. . . . Healthy work never hurt anybody, but kids [while in school] need to be in classrooms."[90]

If the turmoil at the beginning of the school year at Shaw, Waring, Gillespie, Penn Treaty, and Morton McMichael did not furnish evidence enough against Whittle's proposal for fewer adults in school buildings, bad news from neighboring Chester Upland conveyed how difficult it would be to put Whittle's theory into practice. In Chester Upland, as in Philadelphia, Edison was faulted for poor school management: behavior problems increased; suspension and truancy rates climbed; and violent incidents at Chester High School, in particular, mounted.[91] Brent Staples reported in a column in the *New York Times* in March 2002 that Edison was on course to issue 3,000 suspensions for the school year in Chester Upland, amounting to one suspension for every two students in its nine schools. Tom Persing, chairman of Chester Upland's state-appointed control board and a retired U.S. Marine, faulted Edison: "That is not working with the problem. That is burying the problem."[92]

Chester school authorities moreover faulted Edison in October 2002 for failing to set up computer labs and provide teachers with laptops, as promised, and threatened termination of its contract with the company.[93] Worse yet, a week later, Edison got bad news from Harrisburg for its schools in Chester: the results on state exams in reading and math given to students in fifth, eighth, and eleventh grades the previous spring declined for nearly every cohort at the nine schools under Edison during the company's first year in Chester Upland. One middle school posted gains in eighth-grade reading yet far more significant drops in fifth- and eighth-grade math; and Chester High School posted gains in eleventh-grade math. The tenth school in the district, and the only one not managed by Edison, meanwhile posted gains in both reading and math. Edison spokesperson Tucker downplayed the drop in scores, claiming that the first year typically involved a transition period for schools under Edison. Persing was unpersuaded. "I'm disappointed and disillusioned," said Persing in an interview with the *Philadelphia Inquirer* in October 2002. "I know this is a difficult situation, but still, I would have expected incremental increases."[94]

■

With authorities in Chester Upland threatening to terminate their contract with Edison, with test scores there sinking rather than rising, and with Philadelphia withholding payment until paperwork had been properly submitted, Edison's stock hit an all-time low, falling to 14 cents a share on October 10. Edison fought back with three identical full-page ads over the next three weeks in the *New York Times* celebrating its first decade. Edison claimed in the ads that the company had boosted student performance "and at historic rates"; had won significant parental support; had grown at a rapid pace to become the nation's thirty-sixth largest school district, with more than 80,000 students; was finally on its way to earning a profit; and had done all of this despite being "the most scrutinized school system in America, bar none."[95]

The company's stock edged up. Yet had NASDAQ adhered to its threat in August that the company would be delisted if it failed to close above $1.00 for ten consecutive trading days before November 25, the company's ticker would have disappeared from computer screens. Leniency prevailed. With a heated run-up in purchasing before the precipice date, November 11, the stock climbed to 68 cents.[96] Two days later, for the first time in four months, the stock closed above $1.00 and stayed north, but for several days the following spring.[97] Whether propelled by Edison's full-page ads in the *New York Times* or engineered by Edison to keep its listing, the buying spree spared Edison yet another embarrassing defeat.

Neither the ad campaign nor the company's retention of its NASDAQ listing meant much, if anything, however, to newspaper editors or school officials in Philadelphia. To the editorial board of the *Philadelphia Daily News*, Edison's time in Philadelphia was up by March 2003.[98] Vallas stood by Edison but called for a 49 percent cut in its per-pupil premium, from $881 to $450.[99] Edison advocates in Harrisburg pushed back and won the company a $750 per-pupil premium for the next two years.[100]

Another EMO did not have such support in Harrisburg. Vallas terminated the district's contract with Chancellor Beacon Academies, which was running five Philadelphia schools, and provoked no opposition. Vallas contended that Chancellor Beacon, which would merge a year later with charter operator Imagine Schools Inc., had no positive impact and brusquely predicted an easy changeover. "Since there wasn't much management going on in the first place [by Chancellor Beacon]," Vallas said at a news conference, "I think the transition is going to be pretty simple." Chancellor Beacon CEO Octavio Visiedo, previously superintendent of schools for Miami-Dade County, expressed dismay at Vallas's decision and tone, asserting that his company had not only fulfilled all terms of its contract but "far exceeded them."[101] Without strong allies in Harrisburg, Chancellor Beacon's fate implicitly conveyed the inherent vulnerability of the EMO model.

Despite this victory for Edison, company executives had no grounds for regaining confidence from analysts and investors. The challenges ahead for Edison in school districts across the country were clearly steep. In particular, the midyear resignation of Janice Solkov, the veteran administrator and Edison believer, made that obvious. The press coverage in Philadelphia as well as New York had been brutal. And Vallas's treatment of Chancellor Beacon sent a blunt message.

In May 2003, Whittle proposed that he and his management team take the company private.[102] In July, Edison's board consented to a $95 million buyout orchestrated by Whittle with Liberty Partners, a New York–based private equity firm managing a portion of the pension fund for Florida's police officers, teachers, and state and county employees.[103] Edison investors received $1.76 a share, under 10 percent of the IPO price of $18 in November 1999. Whittle gained ownership of 3.7 percent of the company (and a commitment to a minimum salary of $600,000), while Liberty Partners assumed possession of the rest.[104] The privately held EMO that went public in order to privatize the management of more public schools had gone private after a beating in the public market.

Chris Brennan of the *Philadelphia Daily News* was right. And Pedro Ramos, the president of the Philadelphia School Board who had a year and a half earlier warned Whittle that he and his shareholders would regret participating in a hostile takeover of the school system, was also right.

Philadelphia could and would be Whittle's Waterloo; and New York could accordingly be seen in retrospect as his Leipzig, a crushing loss portending worse. Whittle had overestimated his company's capacities and spread it too thin. The defeat would unfold in stages, but it would be decisive. And Edison would never again relive its early glory.

7

REDEFINITION

We're now profitable because of what we don't do, not because of
what we do.

Jeff Wahl, CEO and President, EdisonLearning, May 10, 2010

■ AS A PRIVATE COMPANY AGAIN, though this time under the reins
of an investment firm focused on returns—not executives aiming to revo-
lutionize American education—Edison transmuted fully into a multiservice
provider, scaling back its management of schools and promoting the array
of ancillary services it had begun offering in 1999. In 2003 Edison Extra,
which provided after-school and summer programs, was renamed Newton
Learning; Edison Affiliates, which provided school districts with professional development, curriculum guidance, and computer software for
assessing student progress, was renamed Tungsten Learning; and Edison
U.K. was rolled out as a consultancy working with British school districts.[1]
The following year, the company sheared off the consultancy component of
Tungsten Learning and called it Edison Alliance.[2]

Edison Alliance, which could be termed "Edison Light," quickly became
the company's most profitable division. This division responded specifically
to the challenges of No Child Left Behind (NCLB). Edison Alliance staff as-
sisted school principals and teachers in aligning their curricula with state
standards and in constructing monthly assessments to prepare students for
the annual statewide exams in reading and math mandated by NCLB. Edison
Alliance started with thirteen schools in South Carolina in the summer of
2004. The state paid $400,000 as an initial fee plus $327,000 per school per
year (with the annual charge to rise 3 percent each year). In the spring of

2005, Hawaii signed a two-year contract with Edison Alliance for seven schools, valued at $3.9 million per year. The contract in South Carolina was expected to run at least five years but was terminated after three.[3] Edison's contract in Hawaii, however, ballooned. By 2010 the company had thirty-eight Edison Alliance client schools in Hawaii. With twenty-four full-time employees, the company coached administrators and teachers in elementary, middle, and high schools.[4] The annual contract for elementary schools in Hawaii in 2010 cost $300,000; for middle schools, $350,000; and for high schools, $450,000.[5] With a small staff, no brick-and-mortar costs, no liability for untoward events, and a low profile, Edison Alliance proved to be the scalable antithesis to the company's original model of school management.

"Edison Alliance is a much smaller revenue business, with healthy margins and without strife," said Richard Barth, an Edison executive for seven years before leaving the company in January 2006 to become CEO of the Knowledge Is Power Program (KIPP), the nonprofit charter network that would, in turn, prove to be the managerial alternative to Edison.[6] Reflecting on the success of Edison Alliance, Barth said: "If you can be the 'Intel inside,' so to speak, there's a significant opportunity for a for-profit educational company to succeed. McKinsey may help General Mills do a restructuring effort, but McKinsey doesn't issue the press release. General Mills issues the press release. The problem with whole-school management is that the EMO assumes too big a role."[7]

For similar reasons, Newton Learning also evolved into a strong division. But its success would be short-lived. Newton Learning started in 2001 with 20,000 students in its after-school and summer programs. In 2005 Newton Learning served 115,000 students: 50,000 in after-school programs and 65,000 in summer programs.[8] NCLB fueled this business too. NCLB mandated that local education authorities use a portion of their Title I money, allocated by the federal government to assist disadvantaged students, to contract with external organizations to provide supplementary educational services (SES) for students in schools failing to make Adequate Yearly Progress (AYP) for three consecutive years.[9] Yet school districts soon devised ways to dodge the stipulation that they use their Title I funds to hire outsiders to do *all* of this supplementary work and instead provided much of it on their own. The logic behind this stipulation was clear, though the expectations struck many as unreasonable: if schools failed to make AYP, their administrators and teachers should not be hired to assist underperforming students; rather, such work should be outsourced to private entities who might do a better job and who could be easily terminated if they did not.[10]

At the helm of this revolt in 2005 against the U.S. Department of Education was the CEO of the Chicago Public Schools, Arne Duncan, who would four years later become the U.S. secretary of education. Of Chicago's 82,000 students receiving SES, 40,000 took part in the city's own program when all of them, according to NCLB, were supposed to be enrolled in programs run by outside providers. In a sideshow illustrating both how the private sector ran into stiff opposition and how political disempowerment leads to a loose, rather than strict, interpretation of the law, Duncan defied the federal government. "The authors of the law had the best of intentions for kids," Duncan said in a 2005 interview with *Education Week*. "But you can't blindly follow rules that hurt kids, that are absent of logic."[11] Duncan won this battle by diverting funds slated for summer school. Other districts developed different work-arounds to keep SES in house: Philadelphia created an "intermediate unit" within the system to provide SES; smaller districts located tutoring services at schools that had made AYP.[12] The same local resistance to Edison as an EMO got in the way of Edison and other companies as providers of SES.

Beyond these work-arounds, local districts barred outside providers from working within school buildings; made enrollment for tutoring from these providers arduous by requiring that parents fill out multiple forms; and placed low caps on per-pupil funding for services from outside providers (for example, Chicago imposed a limit of $1,500 per student in reimbursement to external providers, though the state had allotted $2,200 for this purpose). By 2006, of the 2.5 million students eligible for tutoring, only 585,000, or 23 percent, received it. Of those students, about 60 percent received their tutoring from school districts, not outside providers, as intended by NCLB. In financial terms, the consequence was blunt: of $2.5 billion in federal funds earmarked in 2005–2006 for SES mandated by NCLB, $400 million went to private-sector organizations, whether for-profit or nonprofit.[13] Edison and many other companies set on a significant share of the SES market got muscled out.[14]

Growth for Tungsten Learning was likewise ephemeral. This division too grew quickly but hit a different wall. At the outset, the market for Tungsten's benchmark assessment software in 2001 was limited to Edison's eighty-eight schools, enrolling 57,000 students. By 2005 the company's software was being used in 377 schools in the United States, enrolling 135,000 students, and in 40 schools in the United Kingdom, enrolling 22,000 students. Yet under pressure from Liberty Partners, Edison had stopped marketing Tungsten Learning. "We're honoring our contracts," said Jim Howland, CEO of Edison's Educational Services Group, in 2005, "but we're not moving forward, though we might down the road. It was a matter of cost. We were fast becoming the number one company in formative assessment, but we couldn't compete with publishing houses that cross-sell software with their textbooks and thereby keep their costs down. We need to be focused. And for a $400 million company, Liberty Partners thought we had too many divisions."[15]

■

With Tungsten Learning squeezed out by major textbook publishers, Newton Learning constrained by politics, and the company's core business of managing schools limited by low margins as well as politics, Liberty Partners took decisive steps to restructure the company. They started at the top. Chris Whittle and Benno Schmidt were pushed out of their administrative roles in December 2006, though they retained their seats on the company's board of directors.[16] Terry Stecz, who had joined Edison as its chief operating officer in 2004 following two decades as an executive in the pharmaceutical sector, became the company's CEO. Under Stecz, Edison Schools in June 2008 became EdisonLearning and marked its transformation with the acquisition of an online education software developer, Provost Systems, based in Santa Clara, California.[17]

With the landscape for school management and supplementary after-school and summer services so forbidding, online education represented a promising alternative. Much like Edison Alliance, an online division is neither labor-intensive nor threatening to local school boards intent on retaining day-to-day managerial authority over their schools; furthermore, the product itself is far easier to assess than day-to-day instruction, as online courses, in the end, constitute discrete goods little different from textbooks. And the demand for online educational services was booming.

One market was homeschooled children who do some, if not all, of their work online. According to the National Center for Education Statistics, the number of American children homeschooled in 2007 was 1.5 million, out of a school-age population of 51 million. The number in 1999 was 850,000, and in 2003, 1.1 million.[18] The annual growth rate from 1999 to 2003 was accordingly 6.7 percent, and from 2003 to 2007, 8.1 percent. By 2012, the latest year for which data is available, the number was 1.8 million. The annual growth rate had slowed to 3.7 percent but remained significant.[19] Another market was schools seeking to offer courses online that they could not provide in person. Schools unable to hire faculty to teach Chinese, Russian, or advanced math could now deliver virtual versions of these courses. In addition, districts seeking to curb costs could likewise replace teachers with online programs. By one estimate, online instruction costs 36 percent less per student than conventional teaching.[20]

But EdisonLearning would be playing catch-up. Far ahead in this new sector were K12 Inc. and Connections Academy. K12 was founded in 1999 by Ron J. Packard, a former McKinsey consultant, with $40 million in capital from Oracle CEO Larry Ellison, the erstwhile bond trader Michael Milken, and Loews Corporation cochair Andrew Tisch. Based in Herndon, Virginia, K12 was already operating twenty-four cyber schools in fifteen states with 31,355 students when EdisonLearning announced its acquisition of Provost in June 2008, and would see enrollment climb to 37,542 the next school year. Founded as a subsidiary of Baltimore-based Sylvan Learning in 2001, Connections Academy was already operating twelve cyber schools in eleven states with 8,615 students when EdisonLearning acquired Provost and would see its enrollment climb to 13,278 the next school year.[21]

By 2011 K12 and Connections had pulled away. EdisonLearning was operating one cyber school in South Carolina, founded in 2009, and another in Colorado, founded in 2010. The combined enrollment was 1,293. By this time, K12 was running forty-nine schools in twenty-three states with 87,091 students. Connections was running nineteen schools in eighteen states with 29,028 students and was poised to mushroom on news in September 2011 of its acquisition for $400 million by Pearson, the London-based multinational media giant.[22]

■

Whittle and Schmidt meanwhile shifted course yet again in pursuit of a for-profit model of school management. Instead of their original plan of running low-budget private schools, tailored for funding through vouchers, and their subsequent strategy of managing district and charter schools as a subcontractor, Whittle and Schmidt embarked on a mission to build a network of premium-quality private schools located in major cities around the world.

These schools would share the same global ethos and dual-language curriculum, compete with established private schools, charge the same amount, if not more, and serve children of parents apt to move among New York, London, Paris, Abu Dhabi, Mumbai, Shanghai, Singapore, Sydney, Mexico City, and Rio. Whittle and Schmidt called their company Nations Academy. They teamed up in 2008 with Sunny Varkey, the aforementioned educational entrepreneur based in Dubai whose company Global Partnership Schools was coheaded by former Edison executive Manny Rivera and former superintendent Rudy Crew. Whittle and Schmidt predicted that Nations Academy would comprise sixty schools around the world by 2021.[23]

After the market crash of 2008–2009 dried up funding, and irreconcilable differences surfaced with Varkey, Whittle and Schmidt in 2011 renamed their company Avenues and secured $37.5 million in funding from Liberty Partners, the same sum from LLR, a private equity group based in Philadelphia,[24] and an undisclosed sum from John Fisher, an early investor in Edison, chairman of the board of KIPP, cochair of the Charter School Growth Fund, and president of Pisces Inc., the financial management organization for the Fisher family, founders of the casual clothing retailer Gap Inc.[25]

In keeping with past practice, Whittle went on a hiring spree and launched a relentless ad campaign. Whittle hired the former heads of three elite private schools—Phillips Exeter, Hotchkiss, and Dalton—as well as the director of the highly regarded 92nd Street Y Nursery School.[26] And as with Channel One and the Edison Project, Whittle promoted Avenues in full-page ads in the *New York Times,* beginning in February 2011 with one full-page ad a week for five weeks in a row.[27] Moreover, the new school was explained in detail in ads on the Internet and in the *Wall Street Journal,* the *New Yorker,* and the *New York Times Magazine* as well as in complimentary neighborhood tabloids such as *Downtown Express, Our Town,* and *West Side Spirit.*[28]

This ad campaign from its beginning until the company's first school opened in the Chelsea section of Manhattan in September 2012 included forty-six newspaper ads, seven magazine ads, and countless ads on the Internet. And Avenues continued to advertise after opening its initial school, publishing another thirty-six newspaper ads and five magazine ads over the next sixteen months. The cost, in sum, according to one advertising database, was $3 million.[29] Some of the ads were basic announcements with clever graphics featuring notebooks depicted as passports and globes opening up as books, the latter of which became the company's ubiquitous logo; others, recalling the ads published by Edison in nearly every issue of *Education Week* from 2004 through 2007, were short essays by school staff or consultants in answer to such questions as "Can success be taught?," "Can children learn language like music?," "Time to reinvent the class schedule?," and "Is the sky the limit for technology in school?"[30] Recalling claims of the Edison Project twenty years before, the company's mission statement published on its Web site was titled "A New School of Thought."[31]

Whittle and Schmidt, in addition, hosted more than fifty elegantly catered wine and cheese information sessions for prospective parents at such venues as the stately Harvard Club in midtown and the posh Crosby Street Hotel in SoHo.[32] Despite these extraordinary efforts, enrollment the first year fell far below projections. In July 2011, Gardner P. Dunnan, academic dean of Avenues, forecasted 1,320 students in nursery through ninth grade.[33] Dunnan knew the private school landscape in New York intimately. He had been headmaster for twenty-three years of the famously progressive Dalton School on the Upper East Side and then founder and director for ten years of the School at Columbia, a Dalton replica constructed as a faculty recruitment and retention device in Morningside Heights for the children of Columbia University professors. In February 2012, Dunnan predicted enrollment of between 800 and 1,100 students.[34] On the opening day of its first school year, Avenues proclaimed in full-page ads in both the *New York Times* and the *Wall Street Journal* enrollment of "over 700." The same full-page ads soon after appeared in the *New Yorker* and the *New York Times Magazine*.[35]

The initial campus, located on 10th Avenue between 25th and 26th Streets, is, as promised in the company's ads, a polished model of a high-tech international school. A former grocery warehouse reconfigured at the cost of $60 million, the building consists of 215,000 square feet spread over ten floors. The building borders the High Line, a former elevated industrial railroad spur reconstructed by the city and philanthropists at the cost of $152 million as a serpentine midair walkway punctuated by gardens and arresting vistas.[36] Inside the school, a wall-sized assemblage of sixteen contiguous rectangular plasma screens flashing maps and news greets students at the top of the central staircase; plasma screens displaying student art and science projects likewise adorn hallways on every floor; all floors are anchored by commodious common areas, many of them filled with natural light; a 20,000-square-foot cafeteria overlooking the High Line resembles a chic minimalist dining room at a modern hotel; the restrooms appear to have been transplanted from a fine restaurant; all signs are in English, Spanish, and Mandarin in keeping with the school's dual-language program, with students in nursery school through fourth grade spending half their day learning in English and the other half in either Spanish or Mandarin; and sound-proof practice rooms for student musicians flank a black-box performance space on the ground floor.

One parent with a son in nursery school and another in kindergarten praised Avenues during a tour he gave in March 2014. A high-tech executive who decades earlier had attended Dalton, he said that he and his wife chose the school for its impressive administrative hires, dual-language program, constructivist curriculum, and pervasive integration of technology. But he confessed concern about insufficient diversity.

This lack of diversity was on prominent display during drop-off that morning in March. Three security staff members, all wearing ties and logoed lanyards with company IDs and combating the cold in three-quarter black coats, stepped in and out of 10th Avenue directing a tangled stream of Range Rovers, yellow cabs, Cadillac Escalades, BMW sedans, and Lincoln Navigators, swung open passenger doors, and escorted children to the curb, frequently scooping them from vehicle to sidewalk like figure skaters practicing a basic maneuver for pairs competition. Had the pace been slower, the staff worn caps, and the passengers been adults rather than children, the scene could have taken place at the Waldorf Astoria or the Plaza. Stranger still, in a juxtaposition that could occur in few if any U.S. cities other than New York, this morning and afternoon ritual happens across the street from a two-square-block housing project comprising seven brick towers for 2,400 low-income residents.[37]

■

If Avenues succeeds, it will do so against great odds. Unlike the leaders of Edison, the leaders of Avenues do not have to battle doubts and barbs from taxpayers, policy makers, unionized teachers, and newspaper columnists. But they must deal with a notoriously vigilant advocacy group: private school parents. In spending so much money on their children and expecting, in return, the best for them, this group will naturally press the leaders of Avenues to provide the same advantages as other high-priced private schools, from small classes and frequent science labs to robust programs in art, music, drama, and sports. Yet, as a for-profit entity, Avenues stands at a distinct disadvantage in meeting these demands. With the exception of a handful of private schools, the competition in the United States are non-profits. In fact, the National Association of Independent Schools (NAIS), the charter organization for private schools, bars for-profit operators from membership.[38] In choosing a domain name ending in .org rather than .com, the leaders of Avenues themselves implicitly betrayed discomfort with the school's for-profit status.[39]

As a for-profit, Avenues cannot receive tax-deductible contributions to subsidize costs, as nearly every nonprofit private school does;[40] and it must pay corporate income taxes, as no nonprofit private schools do. In this corner, Avenues has had no choice but to charge more, offer less financial aid, and increase class size. Tuition and fees in the school's second year, 2013–2014, equaled $43,750 for students in all grades, from nursery through high school. That sum amounted to $3,383, or 8.4 percent, more than the averaged cost of tuition and fees at five well-regarded private schools in Manhattan constituting the competition.[41]

When asked about financial aid, Dunnan said in a 2012 interview that the goal was $2 million in assistance for the upcoming year, given an anticipated enrollment of 1,100, meaning an average abatement of $1,818 per student. Even if Avenues provided such aid, however, this sum would have fallen far short of the aid offered by the five private schools in this comparison group. Based on figures from the latest filings with the IRS, the abatement at these five schools stood to average $6,091 per student in 2012–2013.[42] This difference puts Avenues out of financial reach for many more families and necessarily drives down diversity, which parents like the one who gave the tour of Avenues and educators—NAIS leaders, in particular—consider a critical element of a dynamic learning environment.[43] Finally, leaders of Avenues conceded that classes would be larger. Dunnan said there would be eighteen in a class, rather than fourteen or fifteen at Dalton and similar schools, but contended that research shows and his own experience confirms there is no impact on student outcomes with such a difference.[44]

In other countries with different tax policies, less competition from established private schools, more parents without budgetary concerns, and less interest in diversity, Avenues may generate significant demand. In his annual report in January 2014 on the state of Avenues, Whittle exuded his trademark enthusiasm: enrollment at the first campus was just shy of 1,100 and was expected to exceed 1,300 the following year; a second school developed in collaboration with the highly regarded Rendafuzhong School (known as RDFZ) in Beijing was on schedule to open in the fall of 2016 on a new twenty-five-acre campus; and exploration was under way for building schools in Shanghai, San Francisco, Los Angeles, São Paulo, London, and Delhi. To steer this growth, Jeff Clark, the CEO and president from 2005 to 2012 of National Heritage Academies, the country's biggest charter management organization, had come aboard as the company's president and COO; and to fund this growth, John Fisher had bought out Liberty Partners' stake in Avenues and invested additional money in the company, making Fisher the majority owner.[45]

Yet such demand has yet to materialize. The deal with RDFZ fell through in February 2015, according to a company official with direct knowledge of negotiations. Whittle had spent several months in Beijing trying to cement an arrangement but failed. The *Wall Street Journal* reported in March that Whittle resigned, though the paper conveyed that his departure was involuntary, and the aforementioned company official confirmed it. Much as Whittle was forced out of Edison in 2006, he was forced out of Avenues nine years later. The *Wall Street Journal* reported that the company still planned to open a school in Beijing, though the paper explained that it would not happen until 2017 at the earliest.[46] CNBC reported in November that the "cavernous yet sleek" offices of Avenues in Beijing were nearly empty and that no company officials would commit to setting a date for opening a school in the city.[47]

Beyond the difficulty of establishing commercially operated schools in foreign countries, Avenues faces competition from companies like itself that had arrived first.[48] As of the 2014–2015 academic year, Nord Anglia Education, based in Hong Kong, had six schools across the United States (including one in New York), six across China (including two in both Beijing and Shanghai), and twenty-three more around the world. Meritas, based in Illinois, had seven schools across the United States (including one in New York) as well as one each in Switzerland, Mexico, and China. And GEMS (Global Education Management Systems), based in Dubai and run by Schmidt and Whittle's former ephemeral partner Sunny Varkey, had one school in Chicago and sixty-eight more in thirteen other countries.[49]

This sector has so far appeared quite profitable for some operators. In fact, Nord Anglia paid Meritas $559 million for six schools (enrolling 8,083 students) in June 2015 and went public the same month at $24 a share with 104 million shares outstanding, meaning a market capitalization of $2.5 billion.[50] Yet even if Avenues turns a corner and joins this league, the company's influence will be irrelevant to Whittle's initial ambitions to revolutionize American education. At $45,000 a year per pupil, its model is not close to scalable. In addition, the country abounds with scalable public schools infused with technology, from High Tech High, founded in San Diego in 2000, to Science Leadership Academy, founded in Philadelphia in 2006. And while Avenues and similar companies may increase the privatization of high school foreign-exchange programs, they stand to do so to only a marginal degree, competing at the edges for students who might otherwise study abroad through such established nonprofit programs as AFS (formerly American Field Service) and Youth for Understanding.

Far from this niche market, EdisonLearning continued to struggle. After two years as CEO, Stecz was fired. Much as Stecz moved up from COO to replace Whittle as CEO in 2006, Jeff Wahl moved up from COO to replace Stecz in 2008. And much as Stecz joined the company after more than two decades in consumer health-care marketing rather than education, Wahl came aboard after more than two decades in financial management.

Wahl grew up in Ohio, triple-majored in accounting, finance, and management at Walsh University, a Catholic school in his home state, worked several years as an accountant at KPMG, and then under the training and guidance of Jack Welch climbed the ladder at General Electric, rising to become president and COO of the Great Lakes region of GE Capital. For Wahl, EdisonLearning was in desperate need of financial discipline. In the mold of Welch, Wahl cut costs in myriad ways.

In one of his most visible steps, Wahl moved EdisonLearning's headquarters in August 2009 from 521 Fifth Avenue, on the corner of 43rd Street, three blocks east and up to 485 Lexington Avenue. Wahl said in an interview at the new headquarters in May 2010 that the move would save the company more than $2 million a year in rent and would, in addition, convey a different image. "We already get enough grief for being a for-profit," Wahl said. "We didn't need to be on Fifth Avenue, too." Wahl moreover acquired at no cost the furniture of the previous tenant, *Golf Digest* magazine, from desks and tables to a set of facing white leather Mies van der Rohe Barcelona chairs in his corner office. And Wahl left the layout as is, with one modification: the flags planted in the putting green in the center of the company's new headquarters read EdisonLearning.[51]

Wahl also moved the financial services staff to the company's operations office in Knoxville, Tennessee; ended the company's relationship with the five marketing firms and several consultancies it had on retainer; and cut travel and overhead costs by moving executives from headquarters to their respective regions, implementing a preapproval process for trips, replacing travel agency contracts with a self-service reservation system, and using only limited-service hotel chains. With these latter measures alone, Wahl claimed to have driven down annual costs for airfare, lodging, and meals from $6.3 million in 2007 to $3.9 million in 2010.[52]

Adding that the company was no longer entering school management contracts that did not promise a good return, Wahl cited as an example his recent refusal to take over a charter school in rural Virginia. "We're now profitable because of what we don't do," Wahl said, "not because of what we do."[53]

With EdisonLearning streamlined, Wahl projected significant growth, particularly in working with states competing for slices of the $4.35 billion set aside by President Obama's Race to the Top (RTTT) initiative. Writing in his first year-end message to EdisonLearning staff, a month after congressional passage in November 2009 of the American Recovery and Reinvestment Act authorizing RTTT, Wahl emphasized that the new legislation played to the company's strengths. The focus of RTTT on implementing data systems, raising teacher quality, and turning around failing schools, Wahl wrote, aligned precisely with work done by its Alliance division. Wahl mentioned promising discussions in this regard with education officials in Illinois, Virginia, and Colorado as well as Washington, DC.[54]

Wahl also interpreted the tone and goals of RTTT as both vindication of the company's long-established purpose and justification for optimism. "As I look to the future," he wrote, "I see more opportunity than this company has ever faced. It's as if our crusade has finally been won. When our founders and predecessors were building this organization in the 1990s, they argued ... for choice, competition, accountability and transparency—ideas that were not popular with many educators at that time. We grew rapidly, but faced opposition at every turn."[55]

Wahl grouped EdisonLearning with a tight, interconnected circle of four prominent organizations at the helm of school reform: Teach for America (founded in 1989 by Wendy Kopp); KIPP (founded in 1994 by TFA alumni Mike Feinberg and Dave Levin and headed since 2006 by TFA alumnus and former Edison executive Richard Barth, Kopp's husband); The New Teacher Project (founded in 1997 by TFA alumna and former Washington, D.C., chancellor Michelle Rhee); and New Leaders for New Schools (cofounded in 2000 by RTTT architect Jon Schnur, Kopp's fellow member of the class of 1989 at Princeton). Wahl continued: "It may seem immodest, but I do think that we ... are winning the war of ideas. School reform is moving in the right direction. Now, the challenge is showing that those ideas can truly work, with more students, schools and communities."[56]

Privately, Wahl predicted that the company would soon add eight more cyber charter schools to the two it was already running in Colorado and South Carolina; sign up another twenty-seven schools on top of the sixty-two it currently had under management across the country; and, in partnership with Magic Johnson, the Hall of Fame basketball player turned entrepreneur, announce a national network of credit-recovery centers offering an array of online and conventional courses for high school dropouts working toward diplomas.[57]

In addition to partnering with Johnson, Wahl tried to reach a wider audience by diversifying the company's leadership team and its message. When he joined Edison in 2007, Wahl recalled in May 2010, the company's seven executives comprised six white men and one black man. Wahl said that thirteen of the fifteen members of his leadership team were women and/or people of color.[58] This reorientation was also in evidence two months later at the company's summer summit, a meeting of 300 company executives, financial backers, and school administrators over four days at the Westin Hotel in the Gaslamp District of San Diego. The company for years had been holding fall as well as summer summits, called ELDA (for Edison Leadership Development Academy). The summer summit in 2010 was focused on three Rs: not the conventional three Rs of reading, writing, and arithmetic but rigor, relevance, and relationships.

In his welcome address, Wahl spoke about the low high school graduation rates of inner-city students and the pressing need to boost rigor in their schools, add relevance to their lessons, and foster stronger relationships with their teachers. Wahl closed with reflections about a favorite R&B song, Harold Melvin and the Blue Notes' "Wake Up, Everybody." Wahl explained that the song was a favorite, in part, because of the second stanza, exhorting teachers to inspire their students. On cue, a recording of the song filled the hotel ballroom as Wahl stepped away from the lectern.[59]

The summit's keynote speaker the following day was Cornel West, a professor of African American Studies at Princeton as well as a veteran leader of the Democratic Socialists of America Party who would a year later march in Occupy Wall Street demonstrations in Boston, New York, Washington, D.C., and Los Angeles.[60] Before Wahl's time, keynotes at summer and fall summits were typically given by company executives. Keynotes were given on occasion by outsiders, such as Les Brown, a motivational speaker and radio DJ from Ohio, and Howard Fuller, a professor at Marquette University in Milwaukee and champion of vouchers and charter schools. A keynote by a commentator as progressive and blunt as West was a new development and did not stop with West. Four months later, at Fall ELDA, held in Palm Springs, California, keynotes were delivered by two equally progressive and blunt African American scholars: Michael Eric Dyson, a professor of sociology at Georgetown, and Melissa Harris-Perry, a professor of political science at Princeton.[61]

Though conspicuously out of place at a summit for a for-profit school management company in a ballroom of a grand hotel, West quickly tried to ingratiate himself as a friend of EdisonLearning. West opened by invoking the words of the jazz composer and saxophonist John Coltrane in calling the company "a force for real good" and lauding Wahl as a "courageous and visionary leader." He then embarked on a rambling sixty-five-minute oration, equal parts explication of *paideia* as education of the soul as well as the mind, meditation on musical genius, and condemnation of "the age of Reagan," "market values," "big money," and "indifference to the poor."[62]

Dyson and Harris-Perry four months later delivered more straightforward addresses but likewise hammered away at corporate greed and institutional racism.[63] Like West, Dyson tried at the outset to ingratiate himself with the audience. Dyson said he was honored to be in the "august company of extraordinary pilgrims toward the promised land of educational enlightenment," chuckled that Wahl was "a brother trapped in a white man's body," and went on to praise EdisonLearning for working in inner-city schools and paying close attention to data.[64] But the unmistakable message from Dyson as well as West and Harris-Perry was that educational opportunity for the nation's underprivileged children had much less to do with school choice or managerial methods than with economic and racial justice.

Harris-Perry, in fact, went so far as to suggest that the movement for school choice stemmed from a collective failure to provide a good education for all children. Harris-Perry noted that in places like Princeton, where she lived at the time, one did not shop for an elementary school for one's children because all the neighborhood schools were excellent. But in places like New Orleans, where she said she would soon be moving to take a job at Tulane University, one had to shop hard because the school system had never been sufficiently funded. This was in essence the argument made two decades earlier by the political scientist Jeffrey Henig against the case for school choice articulated by John Chubb and Terry Moe.[65]

■

When asked about such candor during a follow-up interview at Edison-Learning headquarters in February 2011, Wahl said that he had hoped West,

Dyson, and Harris-Perry might broaden awareness and stimulate productive debate.[66] While the three keynote speakers might have done so, and while Wahl's efforts to streamline the company might have generated more profit, EdisonLearning continued to lose ground.

Wahl was right about RTTT. It indeed vindicated the company's mission. The Edison Project—or Edison Schools or EdisonLearning—did not ulti-mately have to flourish to have an impact. Whittle and Schmidt played a major role in transforming the discussion of public education by emphasizing competition, choice, and results. As allies in this campaign, TFA, KIPP, the New Teacher Project, and New Leaders for New Schools—all nonprofit organizations with a shared dedication to business principles—would flourish. But EdisonLearning would not.

The company's most prominent loss came in Philadelphia. When Wahl joined Edison Schools in 2006 as the company's COO, Edison was managing 101 schools across the country and 22 in Philadelphia alone. Amid dueling accusations of poor collaboration, Edison and Chester Upland had parted ways the previous year. But the company was at the same time awarded two more schools in Philadelphia on top of the twenty it had been assigned in 2002.[67] In 2007 that number dropped back to twenty, the per-pupil premium fell from $750 to $500, and Paul Vallas left Philadelphia to run the school system of New Orleans. In 2008 the number of Edison schools in Philadel-phia dropped to sixteen.[68] In 2009 the number fell to four.[69] And by 2011, much as the *Philadelphia Public School Notebook* had predicted in 2009 the day after the Baltimore School Board's decision to terminate two of three contracts with Edison, the company was out of Philadelphia.[70]

While Edison's entry into Philadelphia had generated nonstop news cov-erage, its exit nine years later went unreported. The same held for Edison's exit two years later as the manager of its one remaining school in Baltimore, Montebello, even though Sarah Horsey, the principal celebrated for turning the school around a decade earlier, had returned to give the commencement speech.[71] By 2013, in total, Edison was managing eleven schools—not eighty-nine, as Wahl had forecasted in 2010—and four cyber charter schools—as opposed to the ten Wahl had predicted that same year.

The eleven remaining schools comprised two conventional district schools—a high school in Gary, Indiana, and an elementary school in

Davenport, Iowa—and nine charter elementary/middle schools—one in Bronx, New York, three in Atlanta, one in nearby College Park, two in Duluth, Minnesota, one in Colorado Springs, and one in Denver. In addition to the two cyber charter schools EdisonLearning had launched in South Carolina in 2009 and Colorado in 2010, the company now had cyber charters in Georgia and Ohio. The partnership with Magic Johnson in running credit-recovery centers did get off the ground, as Wahl had projected, but growth was slow. Called Magic Johnson Bridgescape, this new division had thirteen centers by 2013: eight in Ohio, two in Illinois, and one each in Georgia, New Jersey, and North Carolina. Company officials had forecasted opening fifty more centers during the summer of 2013 across four states—California, Florida, Texas, and Virginia—but closed no deals.[72]

The one bright spot for the company was its Alliance division, helping schools align their curricula with state-mandated exams and assess the progress of their students through the course of the year. By 2013 Edison-Learning had eighty-one client schools, each paying about $350,000 a year: fifty-five in Hawaii; eleven in Virginia; seven in Nevada; three in Indiana; two in Delaware; two in Pennsylvania; and one in California.[73]

According to Wahl, EdisonLearning had to retreat from the business of managing schools because the margins were dropping year after year. Wahl attributed this development to budget cuts. During the interview in February 2011, Wahl shared a chart documenting cutbacks in education budgets across the country: Ohio short $1.7 billion; Clark County, Nevada, $300 million; South Carolina, $800 million; and Missouri, $500 million.[74]

Much as Edison expected a per-pupil premium of $1,500 upon entering Philadelphia in 2002 and instead received $881, only to see that drop to $750 in 2003 and then $500 in 2007, the company's sales staff could no longer find worthwhile opportunities. This was true for cyber charter schools, Wahl said, as well as brick-and-mortar schools, whether run by districts or charter boards.

"When we first met with a governor in the southeast," Wahl said with reference to a potential contract for a cyber charter school, "we were looking at receiving $6,500 in total per student. By the end of his administration, that was down to $2,400. If we don't receive nearly twice that much, we lose money."[75]

To Todd McIntire, who had risen within the company from school principal in 2001 to senior vice president for operations for the eastern half of the country in 2011, the diminishing margins constituted an undeniable hurdle. But in the case of running district schools, in particular, the more fundamental problem, in McIntire's opinion, was the difficulty of adhering to internal methods and goals while answering to district authorities, especially when there was significant turnover in local leadership, as was the case in Philadelphia. Moreover, McIntire said, the pressure on an EMO to bring about achievement gains in specific subjects could divert it from its mission of delivering a well-rounded education and thus engender distrust.

Much as Janice Solkov resigned as principal of Edison's Morton McMichael Elementary School in 2002 after four months on the job because of the challenge of reporting to both company supervisors and district officials, McIntire found that the persistent fluctuation in protocol and personnel in Philadelphia undermined the company's capacity to do its job. "From 2003 to 2008, our partnership has been with five different district managers," McIntire recalled in January 2009. "Plus, the structure of the relationship has changed three times over this period. In 2003, all schools were assigned to one of six different geographical managers; in 2004, this was changed to one manager for each EMO; in 2005, a new person was appointed to this position; the following year, another person was appointed to this position; in 2008, we were back to six different geographical regions. It's tough to build trust this way."[76] Months later, the relationship would change again, with Edison designated a strategic partner rather than a school manager, meaning another shift in responsibilities and reporting structure.[77]

This issue of changing protocol and personnel and Solkov's problem of reporting to two different bosses were both in evidence during a visit to Edison's Ludlow Elementary School in Northeast Philadelphia in February 2009. The fifteen-minute walk from the subway stop at West Girard Avenue and North Broad Street brought to mind West Baltimore. Abandoned lots and vacant buildings covered in graffiti marred one block after another. The sidewalks were littered but lifeless. Amid such blight, Ludlow, a four-story brick building constructed in 1927 with Gothic touches, including an arched entrance in gray stone, conjured an era of long-gone prosperity.

Munching on a signature Philadelphia soft pretzel at her desk at the beginning of the day, Charlotte Buonassisi, in her thirty-first year as a Philadelphia educator and in her fourth as Ludlow's principal, said she was exhausted. Buonassisi explained that in her time in charge of Ludlow, she had worked with four different regional superintendents and had to attend district as well as Edison administrative meetings and fill out paperwork for both. "There's no time to process all this information," said Buonassisi. In her office at the time, in fact, were an Edison regional vice president for educational services and two officials from the district for a weekly meeting to coordinate efforts for differentiated instruction (so that teachers reach a range of students) and to discuss outcomes.[78]

The measurement of outcomes at Ludlow, as at every Edison school I visited, occurred in a designated data room, indistinguishable from other data rooms except for the colors chosen to identify levels of achievement. Also, there was more color in Pennsylvania than in Maryland. Whereas there are three levels of achievement in Maryland (Advanced, Proficient, and Basic), there are four in Pennsylvania (Advanced, Proficient, Basic, and Below Basic).

Despite all the color, as in Baltimore, so in Philadelphia, the mood in the data room was grim. This was true at Edison's Shaw Middle School, which I had visited the previous day, and at Waring Elementary School, which I would visit the following week, as well as at Ludlow. At Shaw, the atmosphere was, in fact, menacing, with the principal and another Edison regional vice president for educational services interrogating a middle-aged math teacher as to why his students repeatedly posted low scores on the benchmark assessments, monthly standardized tests designed to prepare students for the annual state exam, the Pennsylvania School System of Assessment (PSSA).

"You can't look to the benchmarks," the math teacher fought back in a thick Balkan accent, "because the students don't take them seriously." Shaw's principal, Kwand Lang, thirty-six and with Edison for thirteen years, shook his head and explained that it was the teacher's responsibility to make sure his students took the benchmark assessments *very* seriously. The teacher, George Prifti, fifty-nine and in his tenth year as a math teacher at Shaw following twenty-five years as a math and physics teacher in his native Albania, said he would do his best.[79]

In conversation with two Ludlow teachers, I heard concern that the focus on reading and math scores on the PSSA had pushed science and social studies aside. "We barely teach science and social studies anymore," one teacher said. Making AYP had become the school's fixation. To remind her students and perhaps herself of the targeted proficiency levels in reading and math for the year, a seventh-grade teacher whose class I observed had a poster on the wall above her desk: "AYP: Reading, 63%; Math, 56%." In covering fractions that day, she used PSSA model questions. A third-grade teacher whose class I observed drilled students in reading exercises built around the PSSA. Upon shifting from one set of questions to another, she led a routine fill-in-the blank chant: "We must work as a . . . *TEAM* . . . in order to make . . . *AYP!*" Her students obliged in well-rehearsed unison. I afterward witnessed variations of the same methods while observing a fourth-grade reading class and a fifth-grade math class.[80]

The one space in Ludlow free of the stress evident in Buonassisi's office, the data room, and the reading and math classes was an immaculate art studio, located on the top floor and filled with natural light from windows facing east and north. The aproned teacher, an artist who lived in the neighborhood with her husband and young children, moved patiently between students immersed in making papier-mâché creations of their choice, from airplanes to dream houses.[81]

■

Standing two days later in the middle of the two-story octagonal atrium of Edison's Lincoln Charter School in York, one hundred miles west of Philadelphia, I found myself surrounded by posters listing the proficiency rates of each class on monthly benchmark assessments in reading and math. I asked McIntire, with whom I had hitched a ride from Philadelphia early that morning, about this concentration on reading and math scores. McIntire said it was regrettable. He was, after all, at heart a science teacher, he said. After earning a bachelor's degree in physics from Grinnell College, in his native Iowa, McIntire taught science for nine years: two years as a Peace Corps volunteer in Belize, two years at the American Embassy School in the Gambia, two years at Richard R. Green High School in New York, while simultaneously earning a master's degree in education at Teachers College as a Peace Corps Fellow, and three years at the Beacon School, the same New York high school where this book began several years after McIntire had left (while McIntire and I did not overlap at Beacon, we got to know each other through Beacon staff we knew in common). Following Beacon, Mc-Intire served four years as director of technology for the White Plains City School District. Convinced the business model could rationalize the management of schools, McIntire in 2000 left White Plains to become director of technology for LearnNow, the EMO acquired by Edison in 2001 soon after it had won a contract to run one of the ten schools in Chester Upland.

McIntire explained that the pressure on Edison to post competitive results in reading and math had grown so intense with the introduction of NCLB in 2003 that the company concluded that the holistic approach it had developed and proudly advertised would have to be curtailed. "Reading and math scores became the company's currency," he said. Not only would foreign languages, art, and music get less attention, McIntire said, but also science, social studies, and even writing. Edison had, in fact, developed a comprehensive writing curriculum, McIntire said, and once administered monthly benchmark assessments in science and social studies, too. But the writing program and benchmark assessments in science and social studies, he said, got shelved.[82]

McIntire said he found this compromise disappointing and conceded that it opened up Edison to criticism for focusing on only what got measured, which in turn may have hindered the company's growth. But McIntire countered that reading and math nevertheless constituted the subjects most fundamental to boosting the overall academic performance of underprivileged children. McIntire added that Edison had developed systematic methods for teaching reading and math and for monitoring student progress. But implementing these methods, he reiterated, was often complicated by working with protean and controlling districts such as Philadelphia.[83] Implementing these methods at a charter school was far easier, as I would see in observing classes that day in York, but making money by managing a charter school could still be hard, as I would learn over lasagna and tossed salad that night in attending the monthly meeting of Lincoln's board and hearing members press Edison to achieve more for less.[84]

Despite the organizational challenges in Philadelphia, McIntire contended that Edison had brought about significant gains in reading and math. This was the opinion of two scholars at Harvard as well: Paul E. Peterson and Matthew M. Chingos, who coauthored studies in 2007 and 2009, both funded in part by Edison.[85]

The issue of Edison's impact on achievement had for several years been the subject of rigorous assessment. Following the critical analysis by Gary Miron and Brooks Applegate of Western Michigan University issued in 2000, cited earlier, the RAND Corporation published a 250-page study in 2005 called *Inspiration, Perspiration, and Time: Operations and Achievement in Edison Schools.* RAND's exhaustive study, involving visits to Edison schools across the country and sophisticated statistical treatment, was commissioned by Edison in 2000 and cost $1.4 million to complete.[86]

In comparing Edison schools to non-Edison schools with similar student populations, the RAND authors concluded, first, that it took Edison schools four years to post as good or better results in reading and math; and, second, that after five years, Edison schools matched comparison schools in reading and surpassed comparison schools in math, though the achievement gains in math were not deemed statistically significant.[87]

The matter of statistical significance called for qualification and would repeatedly with the subsequent publication of competing academic claims. The RAND authors found that the Edison gains in math were statistically significant if the baseline for comparison constituted results posted on state exams given in the spring of the first year (Y1) the schools were under new management.[88] In promoting Edison, Whittle cited this conclusion.[89] However, the RAND authors also found that if, as is common practice for such investigation, the baseline for comparison constituted results from the year prior to the change in management (Y0)—and thus captured the impact of year one, which for many Edison schools was negative—the statistical significance disappeared.[90]

The RAND authors cautioned, though, that while this latter approach was chronologically sound, it did not account for two potentially significant factors: an abrupt change in student population when Edison took over schools; and the nonexistence of Y0 data for Edison schools (characteristically charters) that were brand new.[91] A study of teacher retention published the same year by the Philadelphia think tank Research for Action (RFA) pointed to another potentially significant factor: an abrupt change in faculty population when Edison as well as other EMOs took over schools.[92] Indeed, according to a 2003 story published by the *Philadelphia Public School Notebook*, teacher turnover from Y0 to Y1 at schools taken over by Edison and Victory spiked from 19 percent to 40 percent and from 17 percent to 40 percent, respectively.[93]

All these clarifications aside, the RAND authors conceded the point repeatedly made by McIntire: "Local constraints, sometimes resulting from compromises required by local contracts, undermine the implementation of Edison's preferred professional environment in some schools."[94] In this regard, John Chubb, Edison's chief education officer, took the RAND study to mean that in the right circumstances, Edison delivered.[95]

In 2006 Douglas J. MacIver and Martha Abele MacIver, researchers at Johns Hopkins University, published another comparative study. Yet their study, funded by the National Science Foundation, was limited to Philadelphia. Comparing district-run schools to those run by outside groups in Philadelphia and using test data from Y0 and earlier, the MacIvers concluded that Edison's schools, on average, posted unimpressive results: specifically, while Edison's K–8 schools exhibited higher achievement gains in reading and math, Edison's middle schools performed no better in math than peer schools and worse in reading.[96]

In 2007 RAND, in collaboration with RFA, published a similar study, funded by local foundations.[97] But this time, researchers compared results from the forty-five schools in Philadelphia managed by all seven private managers as one group, on the one hand, to results from three district cohorts, on the other: twenty-one troubled schools that were restructured and provided intensive professional development as well as an additional $550 per pupil; sixteen underperforming schools that were deemed on their way up and were provided an additional $550 per pupil; and the remaining public schools in the city.[98] All schools in the latter three groups employed a new K–8 curriculum comprising reading, writing, math, science, and social studies, with benchmark assessments every six weeks in all subjects but social studies.[99]

In examining reading and math scores for fifth- and eighth-grade students over six years (from 2000–2001 as Y0 through 2005–2006 as Y5) for schools in these four groups, the researchers found no justification for the city's so-called diverse provider model: while all cohorts exhibited improvement, only the twenty-one restructured schools posted significantly positive effects. In addition, the researchers concluded that there was no evidence that competition from outside school managers had a catalyzing influence on the district as a whole.[100]

Taking issue with the methodology employed by RAND-RFA, Peterson and Chingos used a different approach. They disaggregated results for schools run by for-profit and nonprofit outside operators in Philadelphia, compared these results only to other low-performing schools from the pre-intervention period, and controlled for student movement in and out of schools. Using the same time frame as the RAND-RFA researchers, they concluded in a study published later in 2007 that nonprofit school managers had a largely negative effect on student results in both reading and math, while for-profit operators had a positive impact, with strong statistical significance in math.[101] Peterson and Chingos drew the same conclusion two years later in a follow-up study building on subsequent test results.[102]

But the debate continued. Responding to the initial paper by Peterson and Chingos, Vaughan Byrnes, a researcher at Johns Hopkins, countered in an article published in 2009 that five years of pre-intervention baseline test data, rather than one, should be used to guard against selection maturation or regression to the mean. Byrnes moreover contended that comparing schools managed by EMOs only to other low-performing schools from the pre-intervention period sidestepped the reality that some of the highest-performing schools post-intervention belonged to the cohort of twenty-one troubled schools provided intensive professional development as well as an additional $550 per student.[103]

◼

Whether Peterson and Chingos or RAND, RFA, the MacIvers, and Byrnes were correct, all parties looked at school effectiveness within the narrow confines of reading and math scores. Until 2006 reading and math scores were all that was available as test data. But in 2006 Pennsylvania started administering an annual test in writing to students in fifth and eighth grades. And in 2008 the state began administering an annual test in science to students in fourth and eighth grades. As Edison was running sixteen schools in Philadelphia through 2009 and four of those schools through 2011, there are six years of writing scores to factor into an analysis of the company's effectiveness. And such an analysis provides much more than straight scores. It pulls the curtain on the operation of a company driven to deliver what gets measured and little more.

Reading and math scores determined AYP, the federal standard for school effectiveness since the enactment of NCLB, and thus contract renewals for a company like Edison. Results in subjects such as writing or science did not matter. They did not determine a school's assessment. They rarely, if ever, made it into the press. Writing and science scores were accordingly measures that did not get measured. And for precisely that reason, they are measures that measure a great deal.

If reading scores exceeded writing scores—and math scores exceeded science scores—for Edison's schools in Philadelphia to a greater degree than they did for other schools in the district with similar student demographics, then it is fair to consider the distinction as evidence of the implicit danger of privatizing a complex service like education: the provider has every reason to concentrate on prominent metrics and otherwise shortchange the consumer. Low scores in writing and science should in this regard convey not only little attention to writing and science but also little attention to any subject—from social studies and foreign language to art, music, and physical education—that does not get formally assessed.

As testing in science did not commence in Pennsylvania until 2008 and as proper science instruction requires lab equipment that inadequately funded schools can ill afford, it makes sense for analytical purposes to focus on writing scores, given the six years of data and the low cost of instruction in writing. As Edison worked with Philadelphia's poorest students, and as Pennsylvania disaggregates scores for students in many categories, including those economically disadvantaged, scores for students in this category at Edison's schools may be compared to scores for students in the same category across the district. While a significant majority of students in Philadelphia at this time were classified as economically disadvantaged, even more students in Edison's schools belonged to this category. In 2006, for example, 86 percent of fifth-graders and 82 percent of eighth-graders across the district were defined as economically disadvantaged, while 100 percent of fifth-graders and eighth-graders in Edison's schools in the district were thus classified; five years later, the percentages were nearly unchanged.[104]

What emerges from this analysis is twofold: a classic illustration across the district of Campbell's Law and a classroom illustration in Edison's schools of market failure. Much as Donald Campbell famously contended that the "more any quantitative social indicator is used for social decision-making, the more subject it will be to corruption pressures,"[105] reading scores, which mattered for AYP, far exceeded writing scores, which did not; this finding comports with the conclusion of Brian Jacob in his study of the impact of high-stakes testing in the Chicago Public Schools in the 1990s.[106] And much as the profit motive naturally accentuates the emphasis on results, this difference between reading and writing scores was even greater at schools managed by Edison.

The profit motive did not have to generate such pressure, however. In fact, the one other for-profit school operator in Philadelphia at that time, Victory Schools, did not succumb. Victory had been awarded contracts by the SRC in 2002 to run five schools and did so through 2010; as at Edison's schools in Philadelphia, all fifth- and eighth-graders at Victory's schools were classified as economically disadvantaged. Victory, the authors of the 2007 RAND-RFA report noted, was the only outside provider hired by the SRC—nonprofit or for-profit—to incorporate a comprehensive writing curriculum.[107] The impact of this unlikely resistance to focus on reading and math alone was evident: the gap between reading and writing scores for Victory students was far tighter than for Edison students (see Table 7.1).[108]

Reading and writing scores for Philadelphia as a whole—minus schools run by Edison and Victory—were tight in 2006 and 2007 and then spread. In addition, the divide was wider for eighth-graders than for fifth-graders, suggesting a cumulative effect of focusing on reading at the expense of writing. For 2008 through 2010, the divergence in proficiency for eighth-graders was striking, especially for Edison (see Figure 7.1). The average proficiency rates in reading over these three years for these cohorts were close, especially for Edison and the rest of the district: 56 percent for Edison, 49 percent for Victory, and 59 percent for the rest of the district. But the average proficiency rates in writing for this time period produced a different

Table 7.1 Percentage of students graded proficient on the PSSA reading and writing
exams, and differences in proficiency in these subjects

	2006	2007	2008	2009	2010	2011	Mean
Grade 5							
Edison reading	17.2	14.7	34.0	27.3	21.4	37.1	25.3
Edison writing	16.8	14.2	12.8	21.1	17.9	25.7	18.1
Reading – writing	0.4	0.5	21.2	6.2	3.5	11.4	7.2
Victory reading	14.3	13.3	17.8	20.9	22.4	n/a	17.7
Victory writing	21.6	16.9	17.9	24.9	24.8	n/a	21.2
Reading – writing	−7.3	−3.6	−0.1	−4.0	−2.4	n/a	−3.5
Philadelphia reading	30.0	30.2	33.3	38.1	38.4	43.0	35.5
Philadelphia writing	30.7	24.0	26.0	30.0	33.0	37.1	30.1
Reading – writing	−0.7	6.2	7.3	8.1	5.4	5.9	5.4
Grade 8							
Edison reading	32.5	35.0	48.8	53.1	65.5	51.0	47.7
Edison writing	28.5	34.4	26.1	30.2	36.6	32.1	31.3
Reading – writing	4.0	0.6	22.7	22.9	28.9	18.9	16.4
Victory reading	27.6	31.5	43.6	47.7	56.0	n/a	41.3
Victory writing	34.4	33.1	35.5	37.4	42.5	n/a	36.6
Reading – writing	−6.8	−1.6	8.1	10.3	13.5	n/a	4.7
Philadelphia reading	41.8	47.4	54.1	60.0	64.2	59.2	54.5
Philadelphia writing	39.1	44.2	39.4	44.6	50.1	46.9	44.1
Reading – writing	2.7	3.2	14.7	15.4	14.1	12.3	10.4

Data source: Pennsylvania Department of Education, 2005–2006 through 2010–2011 PSSA and
AYP Results, http://www.portal.state.pa.us/portal/server.pt/community/school_assessments/7442.
Note: Students in all cohorts are classified as economically disadvantaged.

picture: 31 percent for Edison, 39 percent for Victory, and 45 percent for the
rest of the district.

At the heart of resistance to for-profit management of schools has been
suspicion of corner-cutting to boost earnings. While this pattern of reading
and writing scores for Edison does not qualify as explicit proof of such activity,
it does imply a bottom-line approach to education so many opponents

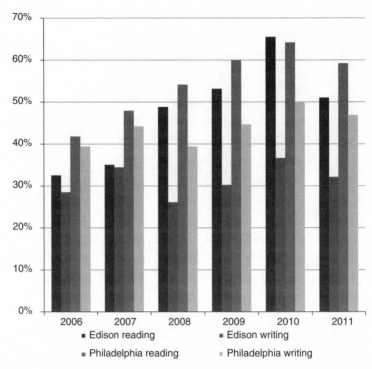

Figure 7.1 Percentage of eighth-grade students scoring proficient in reading and writing on the PSSA. Students in all cohorts are classified as economically disadvantaged. *Data source:* Pennsylvania Department of Education, 2005–2006 through 2010–2011 PSSA and AYP Results, http://www.portal.state.pa.us/portal/server.pt/community/school_assessments/7442.

rejected. Atop shrinking margins, local territorial jealousy, and bureaucratic barriers, distrust of a for-profit company focused on reading and math scores—as McIntire conceded in the lobby of Lincoln Charter School in York—constituted a significant obstacle. What role distrust played in defeating Edison and the for-profit school management sector in general is difficult, if not impossible, to quantify, but the defeat was decisive.

Whittle and the array of aforementioned Wall Street analysts had vastly misjudged the appeal of for-profit management of schools. Whittle's prediction in 1991 that Edison would run 1,000 schools with 2 million students by 2010 appeared in retrospect surreal.[109] Among Wall Street analysts bullish on EMOs, Michael T. Moe of Merrill Lynch stood out. Moe predicted in 1999 that in ten years, for-profit firms would be managing 10 percent of the nation's K–12 schools.[110] Had Moe been right, EMOs would have been running 10,000 schools in total in 2009. They were running 774.[111]

By September 2013, EdisonLearning had relocated its headquarters from New York to Knoxville, the company's initial home two decades earlier, with Jeff Wahl working alone with the assistance of a secretary in an office park in Canton, Ohio. And the company was on the block. Liberty Partners, the private equity group that bought Edison in 2003, was winding down.

Liberty hired the Bank of Montreal (BMO) to find a buyer for Edison-Learning. Liberty sold its $37.5 million stake in Avenues, as noted earlier, to John Fisher. That sale closed in November.[112] In December, BMO sold the bulk of EdisonLearning to a supplementary educational services company based in Camden, New Jersey, called Catapult Learning.[113]

BMO failed to find a buyer for all of EdisonLearning. Catapult, according to a company executive, was not interested in taking over the eleven school management contracts, the four online academies, or the thirteen credit-recovery centers run in partnership with Magic Johnson. Nor was anyone else interested. Catapult wanted only Alliance, the division helping school districts align curricula with state standards; eValuate, software used for benchmark assessments; Learning Force, an intervention program for students struggling in reading and math; and contracts to run summer school programs in Missouri and Illinois.

The price of the sale was not made public, and for good reason. The cost to Liberty of Edison in 2003 was $91 million, 90 percent below its initial valuation in 1999. Ten years later, Liberty, in turn, booked a loss of 85 percent on its investment. According to a banker with direct knowledge of the deal, Liberty received $18 million from Catapult for the lion's share of EdisonLearning and gave $3 million to Thom Jackson, EdisonLearning's COO, to take over the remainder of the company and keep it going in order to honor prior commitments and thus avoid liability for breach of contract. While this latter arrangement might sound implausible, it bears a close resemblance to what for-profit Corinthian Colleges did in 2013: on its way to bankruptcy, Corinthian paid another company to take over four campuses in California.[114]

Much like KKR, which paid $240 million in 1994 for Channel One and all but gave it away to Alloy Inc. in 2007 for nothing more than assumption of liabilities,[115] Liberty would have served its client—the pension fund for Florida's policemen, teachers, and state and county employees—far better by putting its money in an S&P 500 index fund; that investment a decade later would have been worth nearly $200 million. While Liberty may have retained earnings from 2003 through 2013, what is nevertheless clear is that the private equity group paid much more for Edison than it got for the company a decade later.[116] Like Wahl and Stecz before him, Jackson moved from COO to CEO and president.[117] McIntire and many others, including Matt Given, EdisonLearning's chief development officer, who had previously been vice president for development and government relations for Kaplan Virtual Education, moved over to Catapult.

The trajectory of high hopes and dashed dreams of Behavioral Research Labs, taken public in 1971 and shuttered in 1974, and Educational Alternatives Inc., taken public in 1991 and shuttered in 2000, was repeated. Edison's journey lasted longer but traced the same arc. And just as the company's exit from Philadelphia in 2011 and from Baltimore in 2013 went unreported, the sale of the once-celebrated company garnered no media coverage. In its press release, entitled "Combination Creates Largest Intervention Services and Professional Development Provider," Catapult did not even mention Edison-Learning. Catapult merely stated that it had acquired Newton Alliance Inc., comprising Alliance, eValuate, Learning Force, and Summer Journey.[118] In its press release announcing the ascendancy of Jackson, EdisonLearning made no mention of the sale.[119]

The past repeated itself in Philadelphia too. Despite the efforts a decade earlier of such legislators in Harrisburg as Wallace Nunn, James Rhoades, Mario Civera, and Nicholas Micozzie to level school funding across the state,[120] Philadelphia continued to struggle with much less funding. The contrast, for example, between per-pupil spending in Philadelphia and in the five neighboring school districts along the Main Line commuter rail (Great Valley, Haverford, Lower Merion, Radnor, and Tredyffrin-Easttown) remained nearly unchanged (see Figures 5.1 and 7.2). When Edison entered Philadelphia in 2002, the school district had 71 percent as much to spend per pupil as the Main Line school districts. When Edison left Philadelphia in 2011, the school district had 76 percent as much to spend per pupil. The

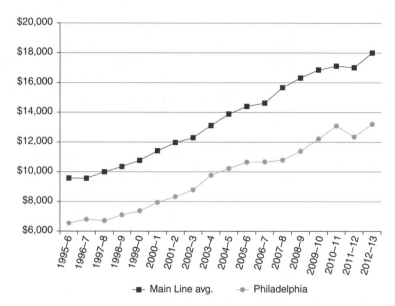

Figure 7.2 Per-pupil expenditure for the school districts of Philadelphia and the Main Line suburbs. The averages for the five school districts of the Main Line are weighted. All information comes from the Pennsylvania Department of Education, Expenditure Data for All LEAs, accessed at http://www.portal.state.pa.us.

next year, that amount dropped to 73 percent and remained there the following year.[121]

Much as the state called in Edison in 2001 to study the Philadelphia School District and paid the company $2.7 million for its analysis, the Philadelphia School Reform Commission hired the Boston Consulting Group (BCG) in 2012 to study the school district and paid the company $4.4 million, all of which came from private sources, for its advice.[122] The title of BCG's report, "Transforming Philadelphia's Public Schools," echoed Edison's, "Strengthening the Performance of the Philadelphia School District." And much as Edison criticized the district for underperformance and recommended turning over its central office to a private firm, contracting with outside operators to run sixty to eighty struggling schools, consolidating curricula, conferring on principals more autonomy to hire and manage, and outsourcing transportation and maintenance,[123] BCG faulted the district for underperformance and recommended streamlining the central office, closing between twenty-nine and fifty-seven underutilized schools, segmenting the district by region into so-called portfolios of eight to ten "Achievement Networks" of charter and district schools, conferring on principals more autonomy to hire and manage, and outsourcing more transportation and maintenance.[124]

Yet BCG's report differed from Edison's in one critical respect. BCG stipulated, in italics, that involvement in the Achievement Networks be off limits to one group: *"For-profit organizations would not be eligible."*[125]

8

MARKET FAILURE

In more numerous respects than are commonly appreciated, the substitution of internal organization for market exchange is attractive less on account of technological economies associated with production but [*sic*] because of what may be referred to broadly as "transactional failures" in the operation of markets for intermediate goods.

Oliver E. Williamson, "The Vertical Integration of Production: Market Failure Considerations," *American Economic Review* 61 (May 1971)

IN STIPULATING in its 2012 report that no for-profit organizations—that is, EMOs—would be eligible to run schools as part of its plan for Philadelphia, BCG did not provide an explanation. Disappointment with the decade-long experiment with Edison figures to have been the reason. The italicized proscription quoted at the end of Chapter 7 conveys a commitment not to repeat the past. The New York State legislature two years earlier had, in fact, amended its education law to read, underlined and in boldface, that applications from EMOs to manage charter schools would no longer be considered.[1] What was nevertheless clear from Edison's travails in Philadelphia as well as Baltimore, Chester, and several other cities is that businesspeople had both underestimated the challenge of turning around schools in underprivileged communities and engendered significant distrust because of their commercial purpose.

Renovated facilities, established administrators, research-based curricula, and cutting-edge data systems would accomplish only so much in these communities. As described earlier, accomplished principals hired by Edison to run schools in Baltimore and Philadelphia confessed bewilderment. Some could not retain staff or maintain student discipline or both. Others who did failed to produce consistently better results on state exams. In Chester, Edison resorted to student suspensions at alarming rates to maintain order and thus provoked the ire of not only the chair of the district's state-appointed control board but also a columnist for the *New York Times*.[2]

Even when allocated more money per pupil, Edison struggled. As explained at the outset of this book, because students themselves, technically speaking, constitute an input in the production function of education, schooling, like health care, differs substantially from conventional business. Much as doctors struggle to achieve the same results for patients from low-income neighborhoods that they achieve for patients from middle- or upper-income neighborhoods, educators struggle in this context too. With little if any control over enrollment, Edison was tasked with compensating for deficits at home and counteracting peer group effects. Making matters worse, with high overhead for marketing, sales, and executive pay, funding for teacher aides to monitor student behavior was frequently cut. Edison's calamitous start in Philadelphia in 2002 constitutes a salient illustration of such cost-cutting.

Research into peer group effects indeed makes clear that troubled students distract classmates from their academic work and get them in trouble. Scott Carrell and Mark Hoekstra, for example, estimated in a 2010 study that "adding one more troubled boy peer to a classroom of 20 students reduces boys' test scores by nearly 2 percentile points (one-fifteenth of a standard deviation), and increases the number of disciplinary infractions boys commit by 40 percent."[3] Carrell and Hoekstra did not have sufficient data to estimate the compounding effect of two or more troubled boys, which stands to be nonlinear: that is, the impact on a classroom of three troubled boys could be much greater than three times the impact of one troubled boy.[4] It is nevertheless evident that the negative externalities of bad behavior can be substantial for any school manager.

Running schools like efficient businesses cannot solve this problem because efficient management is beside the problem. Apart from decades of significant disparity in per-pupil funding between, for example, Philadelphia and neighboring suburbs, as documented earlier, children from low-income neighborhoods start school at a steep disadvantage.[5] The nonprofit charter school networks that have succeeded in underprivileged communities have done so with greater control over enrollment and more money per pupil because of philanthropic largesse. In addition, as nonprofits, they can operate with lower overhead. Moreover, they have been spared the distrust and pushback generated by EMOs.

For precisely these reasons, there was talk in 2003 of Edison becoming a nonprofit rather than transitioning from a publicly traded company to a holding of the private equity group Liberty Partners. Reflecting on the company's demise at Edison headquarters in 2009, Tung Le, senior vice president for research and accountability, said he wished Edison had become a nonprofit. "It would have made our life much, much easier," said Le, who had joined Edison in 1996 straight out of Harvard, where he had majored in government, as a teacher at the Boston Renaissance Charter School. According to Le, who remained with the company until 2012 before becoming the principal of the Heritage Christian School, a K–12 in Indianapolis, Edison executives were too wedded to their commercial ambitions to cut their losses and refashion their goals. As a nonprofit, Edison, in Le's opinion, could have retained executives with substantial though fixed salaries and would have prospered without distrust at every turn about its purpose.[6]

■

Distrust greeted Edison in Baltimore and Philadelphia, as previously detailed, and never faded. In this regard, long before Edison as well as Educational Alternatives Inc. (EAI) failed to flourish as forecasted, theory had established what practice would confirm. In studying information asymmetry, transaction costs, and mission alignment as well as obsolescing usefulness and territorial jealousy, one economist after another had revealed clear boundaries to the business model.

In an article published in 1963 in the *American Economic Review* on the economics of medical care, Kenneth J. Arrow contended that on account of the asymmetry of information between doctor and patient, "the behavior expected of sellers of medical care is different from that of businessmen in general."[7] Arrow elaborated: "Because medical knowledge is so complicated, the information possessed by the physician as to the consequences and possibilities of treatment is necessarily very much greater than that of the patient, or at least so it is believed by both parties." By contrast, Arrow wrote, the gap in information about "production methods" of conventional commodities is much tighter.[8]

Citing a term coined by the sociologist Talcott Parsons, Arrow wrote that there is accordingly a "collectivity-orientation" to medicine that distinguishes it, along with other professions, from standard business, "where self-interest on the part of the participants is the accepted norm."[9] In illustration of this difference between the conduct of doctors and typical businesspeople, Arrow continued:

(1) Advertising and overt price competition are virtually eliminated among physicians. (2) Advice given by physicians as to further treatment by himself or others is supposed to be completely divorced from self-interest. (3) It is at least claimed that treatment is dictated by the objective needs of the case and not limited by financial considerations. While the ethical compulsion is surely not as absolute in fact as it is in theory, we can hardly suppose that it has no influence over resource allocation in this area. Charity treatment in one form or another does exist because of this tradition about human rights to adequate medical care. (4) The physician is relied on as an expert in certifying to the existence of illnesses and injuries for various legal and other purposes. It is socially expected that his concern for the correct conveying of information will, when appropriate, outweigh his desire to please his customers.[10]

Times have obviously changed since Arrow's article was published. Cancer centers, dermatology clinics, and orthopedic hospitals advertise their services today much like hotels, spas, and ski resorts. And hospitals across the country have been recently exposed for charging whatever they can get away with.[11] Arrow's central contention nevertheless stands that because of the asymmetry of information between doctor and patient, doctors are not expected to act like conventional businesspeople; Arrow's argument indeed helps to explain the recent outrage directed at such hospital billing practices.

For everyday goods and services, as Arrow noted, the divide between provider and purchaser is not so wide, though it surely exists. George Akerlof made this and its consequences clear in his 1970 article in the *Quarterly Journal of Economics* entitled "The Market for 'Lemons': Quality Uncertainty and the Market Mechanism."[12] The recent revelation that eight restaurants in New Jersey belonging to the multinational chain T.G.I. Friday's were found by the state's Division of Alcoholic Beverage Control to be pouring bottom-shelf liquor in place of premium spirits ordered by customers provides a specific illustration of the gulf between provider and purchaser.[13] While Akerlof's used-car dealer might sell lemons, a brand-name restaurant might pass off well gin as Bombay Sapphire or Hendrick's.

Because of such information asymmetry, government agencies, like New Jersey's Division of Alcoholic Beverage Control, as well as consumer groups step in to level transactions. The Food and Drug Administration is dedicated to ascertaining that what we eat, drink, and take for medicine is safe and properly labeled; local health departments likewise regularly inspect restaurant kitchens. The Securities and Exchange Commission aims to protect investors by requiring timely, detailed reports from publicly traded companies and by investigating anomalous trading activity. The National Highway Traffic Safety Administration works to make sure that cars are soundly engineered. Furthermore, private publications like *Consumer Reports* issue comprehensive assessments of cars and countless other products to tell buyers what's good, what's not, and why.

While schools are monitored by state and local authorities, ranked by newspapers, magazines, and Web sites, and visited on occasion by parents, the information these parties obtain is necessarily limited. Moreover, just as there is an urgency to the diagnosis and treatment of an illness, there is likewise an urgency to the identification and remediation of a learning disability, lest a cognitive deficit evolve and in the process generate emotional difficulties. There is no such urgency to the purchase of a stock or bond, a car, a dishwasher, or a lawn mower; all such transactions afford the consumer the opportunity to shop around. The difference between educator and student is, accordingly, much akin to the difference between Arrow's doctor and patient. The chasm in knowledge is similar, and the time element crucial.

It was because of my awareness of this asymmetry of information in education that I was from the start skeptical about the potential of for-profit educational management. Setting aside resistance from teachers to curricula imposed by an outside manager and animosity from civic leaders opposed to surrendering control of their schools—on display as early as the 1970s in

Gary, Indiana, in response to the managerial role of Behavioral Research Labs (BRL)—the fundamental reason I found such outsourcing problematic when I began studying this subject a decade ago is that I knew too well as a teacher that the process of education lacks the transparency necessary for proper contract enforcement. In the language of principal-agent theory, there is too much incentive and freedom for the school operator as agent to act selfishly, defying the interests of the taxpayer as principal.

The immediate consumer is, after all, a child or adolescent who is in little position, like Arrow's medical patient, to judge the quality of service rendered, as noted in Chapter 2. Even if the consumer is an adult, as is the case in the controversial for-profit tertiary sector defined by the likes of Career Education, Corinthian, DeVry, Education Management, Grand Canyon, ITT, Strayer, and the University of Phoenix, the gap between instructor and student does not afford sufficient transparency.

This for-profit tertiary sector took off and for some time flourished in a way that EMO founders and analysts had forecasted for the K–12 sector. The difference in trajectories made sense. First, the consumer at the tertiary level is an adult, perhaps taking classes in the evening on the way home from work or perhaps online at home. Second, these institutions met a need unfilled by community colleges and universities that had failed to add capacity or flexible scheduling. In this regard, the federal government had, in essence, outsourced a substantial portion of higher education to private operators, funding instruction with federal student loans and leaving administration to entrepreneurs rather than building more community colleges and universities.

As the U.S. Department of Education has allowed for-profit tertiary institutions to collect up to 90 percent of tuition in the form of federal student loans (and up to 100 percent in the case of veterans, service members, and spouses),[14] this sector differs little in financial terms from EMOs receiving approximately 90 percent of district per-pupil funding to educate students in primary and secondary schools. The means of payment and the jurisdictions differ, but not the math, except that students at the tertiary level are taking out loans they must repay. However, as many students do not make it to graduation at these for-profit tertiary institutions, and as many of those who do so fail to find gainful employment, they default on their loans at more than twice the rate of their counterparts who attended public or private nonprofit schools.[15] The adult student is accordingly not the only consumer in the equation at the tertiary level. The taxpayer too is a party to the transaction and necessarily as an outsider knows much less about the quality of service rendered.

The high dropout and default rates ultimately led to a backlash. By 2014 attorneys general in thirty-seven states were conducting fraud investigations of for-profit colleges.[16] By 2015 only DeVry and Grand Canyon of the eight aforementioned companies stood strong. Corinthian, a darling of Wall Street a decade earlier, was out of business.[17] Education Management was trading for pennies a share. Career Education was trading 88 percent lower than in 2010; ITT, 98 percent lower; Strayer, 81 percent lower; and the University of Phoenix, 75 percent lower.[18]

■

In a long article in the *Yale Law Journal* in 1980 on the economics of nonprofit organizations, Henry Hansmann built on Arrow's argument and placed the disparity between provider and recipient at the heart of his analysis.[19] Hansmann argued that schools, nursing homes, hospitals, and relief agencies like the American Red Cross or CARE (Cooperative for Assistance and Relief Everywhere) do not fit the commercial model because of a particular type of "market failure."[20]

In the case of schools and relief agencies, the recipient is not the purchaser. Much as one would not give money to a for-profit version of CARE because one would be hard pressed to know if the refugee or famine victim benefited as promised, one should be averse, Hansmann wrote, to using a for-profit provider of schooling for one's children because one would likewise be hard pressed to know if services have been provided as promised (Hansmann's analysis predated significant development of the for-profit tertiary sector). In the case of nursing homes and hospitals, the recipient may, in fact, be the purchaser but is regardless ill equipped to evaluate his or her own needs.[21] The result in all cases, Hansmann concluded, is "contract failure," as producers or providers cannot be policed "by ordinary contractual devices."[22]

Hospitals and nursing homes are nevertheless widely run as for-profit enterprises. The same holds for prisons, which companies started managing soon after the publication of Hansmann's article. Management of nursing homes in the United States has, in fact, long been proprietary. According to a 1974 survey, 76 percent of nursing homes were run by for-profit entities; by 2013 the latest year for which data are available, the proportion had slipped but stood strong at 68 percent.[23] Since the publication of Hansmann's article, the share of the nation's community hospitals run by for-profit organizations has climbed significantly, from 13 percent in 1980 to 19 percent in 2013, the latest year for which data are available.[24] Corporate management of prisons came into existence in 1983 with the founding of Corrections Corporation of America (CCA). By 1990 CCA and its competitors were running 5 percent of the nation's state and federal prisons; by 1995, 8 percent; by 2000, 16 percent; and by 2005, the latest year for which data are available, 23 percent.[25]

In all three domains, insufficient transparency has hindered proper contract enforcement and thus opened the way to substantial breaches of protocol. Newspapers, magazines, academic journals, and watchdog organizations have consistently documented such violations.[26] Several studies concern elder care. While nonprofit management of nursing homes has hardly been blameless,[27] the incidence of deficiencies in care at for-profit nursing homes has been significantly higher. This has been documented by the U.S. Department of Health and Human Services as well as many scholars.[28] In a rigorously constructed study published in 2002 in the *Journal of Health Economics,* the economist Shin-Yi Chou, for example, determined that residents of for-profit nursing homes who were not monitored by kin (defined as a visit by a spouse or child within the first month of admission) were more likely to suffer from dehydration and urinary tract infections than their counterparts in the same circumstances at nonprofit nursing homes; Chou found that this was all the more true if these residents were "cognitively unaware."[29]

While for-profit hospitals, nursing homes, and prisons cannot be regulated by conventional contractual means, their financial success should not be a mystery. It derives not from contractual soundness but, rather, inadequate scrutiny and countervailing force. For precisely the reasons Arrow proffered, for-profit hospitals, like all hospitals, are hard to monitor and challenge. As for nursing homes and prisons, Hansmann's critique abides. Yet the feeble elderly represent a marginalized population, and the incarcerated a condemned one. Neither group inspires the sympathy necessary for effective advocacy. Concern for prisoners' rights is especially muted. As a case in point, a hedge fund chief cited a fundamental advantage to the prison management sector in explaining his bullish bet on CCA before an audience at an investor conference at New York's Marriott Marquis in 2009: if your customers try to leave, you can shoot them.[30]

■

While it is true in the case of education, as I learned as Beacon's programmer, that high school students may consistently identify certain teachers as lacking, it is also true that they're apt to complain about certain teachers who are good but demanding and that they're insufficiently informed about subject matter to know whether instructional corners are being cut in, say, a chemistry or language lab; elementary school students make for an even more vulnerable audience. I was reminded of this problem at Beacon's twentieth-anniversary celebration in June 2013 when a 2008 graduate thanked me for having long before encouraged him to stick with a teacher whose class he repeatedly tried to switch out of in the first months of his junior year. This alumnus said that he not only in time came to like this teacher a lot, as I had figured he would, but also learned from the experience how to adapt to classes in college as well as work situations that he initially found frustrating.

As for the parent, taxpayer, and policy maker, he or she can know only so much about what is taking place inside schools. Parent-teacher nights are shows and at that infrequent, brief shows. The schools get spruced up: custodians wax the floors; art teachers and their students redecorate bulletin boards in the lobby and corridors; and teachers cover the walls of their classrooms with student projects. When the curtain goes up, administrators and teachers alike are dressed their best and radiate an uncommon warmth. In the course of the evening, parents rarely spend more than five minutes speaking with individual teachers, and within two hours the curtain falls, not to rise again for another four or five months.

Tests likewise provide a murky picture of what's going on. The infamous incident in Texarkana, Arkansas, in 1970 described in the Prologue—where an experiment in performance-based contracting found that a company hired by the district to run its remediation program had allowed students to preview exam questions—illustrated one dimension of the perverse consequences of testing. The brazen correction of answer sheets by teachers or principals detected by forensic firms hired to do erasure studies and documented by Brian Jacob and Steven Levitt in their 2003 study of cheating in the Chicago Public Schools illustrates another.[31] Discovery in 2011 of pervasive test tampering by teachers or principals in Atlanta, New York, Philadelphia, and Washington, D.C., gives greater weight to this concern.[32]

However, far more widespread than outright disclosure of questions in advance or fixing of responses afterward is the pedestrian practice of teaching to the test, described earlier in Baltimore and Philadelphia. This approach may lead to higher scores that parents, taxpayers, and policy makers can point to in the newspaper but typically constricts curricula, stifles imaginations, and denies classrooms their vitality.

■

In technical terms, the issue of outsourcing school management is a make-buy decision that boils down to transaction costs. If the costs of pricing, negotiation, transportation, and quality inspection involved in purchasing a good or service from an outside provider are deemed too high, as Ronald Coase argued in his seminal 1937 article in *Economica* entitled "The Nature of the Firm," the buyer should internalize production of that good or service.[33]

In the case of especially complex services or manufacturing processes, it is often too difficult and costly to write contracts with sufficient specificity. In elaborating on the work of Coase, Oliver E. Williamson made this clear in a 1971 article in the *American Economic Review* on the vertical integration of production and clearer still in a 1985 book entitled *The Economic Institutions of Capitalism*.[34] "In more numerous respects than are commonly appreciated," Williamson wrote, "the substitution of internal organization for market exchange is attractive less on account of technological economies associated with production but [*sic*] because of what may be referred to broadly as 'transactional failures' in the operation of markets for intermediate goods."[35]

Competition between providers, in other words, looks great in theory but often involves costly inefficiencies in practice. As John D. Donahue subsequently put it in his book *The Privatization Decision,* "Eternally hopeful calls for competition spring from the powerful intellectual aesthetic of economic theory, from a deep and almost mythic American faith in the benign effects of the competitive rough-and-tumble. . . . Yet the healthy conviction that competition is desirable is too often linked with the unwarranted inference that it is easy to arrange."[36]

Fundamental to such difficulty is distrust. On account of relationships cultivated between firms over generations in Japan, Williamson put forth as an example Japanese businessmen, who engage in more subcontracting than their American counterparts: "cultural and institutional checks on opportunism" diminish "the hazards of trading."[37] When such trust can't be mustered, the market mechanism must be rejected in favor of in-house production of the good or service, a decision that often results in the acquisition of the subcontractor, as classically illustrated by General Motors' absorption of Fisher Body in 1926.[38]

It is moreover not merely the cost of padded expenditures that can make subcontracting so expensive but also the price of writing and monitoring contracts to prevent and expose such padding. What applies to businesses applies equally to municipal, state, and federal governments. In assessing the privatization campaign waged in the 1990s by the World Bank, Rafiq Ahmed and Louis T. Wells turned the argument on its head. "The core assumption of privatization enthusiasts—that the scarcity of government skills means that privatizing is easier than improving infrastructure in state hands—has been proved too simple," they wrote in a book on governments in developing countries contracting with multinational corporations. "Even more government skill may be required to privatize and to govern privatized infrastructure than is needed for the difficult task of running state-owned enterprises well."[39] The determinants of market failure indeed transcend sectors, from manufacturing to medical care, corrections, education, and foreign direct investment.

Given the complexity and opacity of the educational process, trust takes on paramount significance when a district outsources school management. Buying, rather than making, discrete goods like scheduling software and textbooks or distinct services like busing and meal preparation involves straightforward contracting and can hence prove highly cost-effective. The same holds for a range of specific tasks commonly outsourced by municipalities across the country. In a rigorous analysis commissioned by the Department of Housing and Urban Development under President Ronald Reagan, the economist Barbara J. Stevens compared the costs of ten cities in Southern California using contractors for eight basic functions to the costs of ten cities in the same region using municipal agencies for the same functions, which comprised payroll preparation, tree maintenance, turf maintenance, trash collection, street cleaning, traffic signal maintenance, janitorial service, and street paving. Controlling for quality, Stevens found that while there was no difference in the cost of payroll preparation, cities spent significantly less in using contractors for the seven other services, from 27 percent less on tree maintenance to 49 percent less on road paving.[40] The high fixed costs for equipment explain this difference. It makes little sense, of course, for a small city to buy asphalt distributor trucks and paving machines that it will not put to everyday use.

Yet outsourcing the management of a city's schools does not entail such straightforward contracting. Both the process and purpose of education are far less subject to objective assessment than trash collection and road paving.[41] Albert Shanker, the president of the American Federation of Teachers, made precisely this point in 1994 in objecting to Edison's model in his weekly column in the *New York Times* sponsored by his union: "When a school district contracts with a for-profit company to build a new gymnasium, it's relatively easy to make sure the district gets what it pays for. But when it considers hiring a for-profit company to manage schools, as a number are now doing, it's a different story. Assessing the quality of this kind of service is very tough, especially since there is little experience to go on."[42]

For Edison and its EMO competitors, this difference in contracting added one more hurdle to the business of running schools as an outsider. In addition to the substantial costs of marketing, contract negotiation, travel, investor relations, and professional development, Edison and its peers faced the persistent challenge of winning trust in a realm of necessarily incomplete contracts.

Making matters worse, even if EMOs win such trust, they may not be able to maintain their contracts for long. Many multinational corporations, explained Ahmed and Wells, enter into so-called obsolescing bargains when investing in foreign mining operations or infrastructure projects (such as telecommunication networks, water filtration systems, energy plants, or utility grids), knowing full well that client countries in time will gain the know-how and desire to assume control.[43] As Raymond Vernon put it in a 1967 lecture entitled "Long-Run Trends in Concession Contracts," both the client government and the foreign concessionaire have understood that "once a bargain had been struck, once capital had been sunk by the foreign concessionaire, his bargaining position was bound to be weakened precipitately."[44]

The evolution of Indosat, an Indonesian subsidiary of International Telephone and Telegraph (ITT), provides a salient illustration of a concessionaire's attenuating leverage, according to Ahmed and Wells. When Indosat rejected a request in 1979 by President Suharto to lay a submarine cable across the Strait of Malacca, on the grounds that it would be a bad investment, the government nationalized the company, nullifying a twenty-year lease seven years early.[45] After thirteen years, Indonesian engineers had developed the skills to run the network on their own, and the government could accordingly exit its agreement with ITT and spare its citizens the cost of a premium to a foreign company.[46]

EMOs have likewise had to concede the ephemeral nature of their appeal. Client districts or charter boards stand to conclude after several years that they can sever ties with EMOs, preserve the best practices, and thus save money without sacrificing quality. When Winston Brooks explained as the superintendent of schools in Wichita, Kansas, in 2002 why the city's school board terminated its agreement with Edison to run two of four of schools under contract, he gave voice precisely to this line of reasoning. Brooks noted that after seven years of working with Edison, Wichita had learned several important pedagogical strategies from the company and could continue to implement them independently without paying a premium. Brooks said that the district expected as a result to save $500,000 a year.[47] Dudley Blodget, the head of the Boston Renaissance Charter School, another of Edison's four initial clients in 1995, likewise contended after ending his relationship with Edison in 2002 that the company's help was no longer needed. "We've now got the internal strength to be more independent," said Blodget. "Edison is a great start-up model. We could never have gotten off the ground without them. But now we want to run the school ourselves."[48] In both cases, Brooks and Blodget, in keeping with arguments made by Coase, Williamson, Vernon, and Ahmed and Wells, internalized production.

■

Obsolescing appeal, asymmetry of information, transaction costs, and territoriality constitute four patent obstacles to for-profit educational management. Less obvious but equally powerful is the "collectivity-orientation" of education that Arrow ascribed to medicine. This orientation underlies the difficulty for EMOS of winning buy-in from teachers. The service identification of teachers runs counter to the commercial purpose of EMOs.[49]

Much as model military personnel work for honor rather than financial compensation and are accordingly driven by their identity as soldiers, good teachers likewise work for civic distinction and are driven by their identity as educators.[50] This conclusion comports with the seminal work of the British sociologist Richard M. Titmuss on blood donation. To Titmuss, monetary compensation for blood donation appeared to nullify the reward of helping one's community and thus diminish or, as economists would later put it, "crowd out" the intrinsic desire to donate blood.[51] Building on Titmuss, the French economists Roland Bénabou and Jean Tirole explained how in many contexts, individuals opt for altruistic behavior over financial gain to win social esteem.[52] Building on Bénabou and Tirole, the Swedish economists Carl Mellström and Magnus Johannesson returned to Titmuss, subjected his case to the rigor of empirical analysis, and concluded that financial incentives can indeed crowd out altruistic behavior.[53]

Workers who identify with the mission of their leaders dedicate themselves selflessly to their work, whereas their opposites do the bare minimum of what is required and typically look elsewhere for employment.[54] It is in this framework that the challenge of EMOs to attract and retain gifted teachers becomes unmistakably clear. This service identification or collectivity orientation, in addition, explains in part the difficulty for EMOs of achieving economies of scale. All labor-intensive sectors are constrained by Baumol's Law, as explained in Chapters 1 and 2.[55] And yet several labor-intensive sectors without such service identification or collectivity orientation—from advertising and consulting to insurance and law—do achieve economies of scale.

According to the National Center for Education Statistics, for fiscal year 2009, the latest year for which data are available, school districts across the country devoted, on average, 81 percent of their budgets to salaries and benefits (see Table 2.1).[56] That same year, the advertising agency IPG devoted 70 percent of its operating expenses to salaries and benefits; the consulting firm Accenture, 80 percent; the insurance company Aon, 70 percent; and the nation's major law firms, 78 percent.[57] However, in adding copy editors, analysts, actuaries, and associates to robust divisions or practices, advertising agencies, consultancies, insurance companies, and law firms realize outsize returns for executives, partners, and shareholders. While these returns are not exponential, as they can be in manufacturing, where unit costs of mass production are dwarfed by set-up or fixed costs, they are indeed sharply linear.

Major law firms, for example, stand to make $141,000 in annual profit off the work of each first-year associate, according to a 2012 study. Firms, in this scenario, gross $468,000 on $327,000 spent on salary, benefits, training, recruiting, computers, office space, and secretarial assistance, amounting, in sum, to a 43 percent return for firm partners.[58] But in this and similar fields, in contrast to education, there is no discomfort with outsize returns, for two reasons. First, there is no collectivity orientation or service identification to the work done. Second, there is sufficient transparency for proper contract enforcement, as the purchaser of the good or service is the recipient.

When Accenture develops a new distribution strategy for Boeing, Kraft Foods, or Pfizer, it specifically serves the interests of company executives and shareholders, not the general public, though the general public is surely served indirectly through better service. Accenture likewise delivers its services to the executives with whom it negotiated contracts. There is no third party, as there is in education, child care, or relief work.

The service identification or collectivity orientation of education is all the more clear in the context of public versus private goods. While quality schooling and medical care serve private ends, they simultaneously serve essential public purposes as well. In contrast to private goods, such as wristwatches or concert tickets, which cannot be enjoyed by anyone if enjoyed by everyone, public goods, like clean air and water, cannot benefit anyone without benefiting everyone.[59] As an educated citizenry is widely understood to lead to a more interesting, productive, and safer society, education in the general sense is much akin to clean air and water. The shared results accordingly call for shared investment, which in turn calls for careful accounting and personal sacrifice. For schools, such careful accounting means trim budgets, with surpluses, when they occur, plowed back into institutional development. And such personal sacrifice means an ethos defying commercial interests.

Catholic schools, in particular, exemplify institutions driven by a collective mission. Their leaders pride themselves on minimal overhead and depend on the selfless dedication of teachers, who until recently were in large part priests, brothers, and nuns. While less specifically mission-driven, public as well as independent schools likewise bear the impress of this same orientation and struggle to make budgets. In fact, this orientation is so strong among American independent schools that its charter organization, the National Association for Independent Schools (NAIS), bars for-profit operators from membership.[60] What applies to schools in this regard applies to police and fire departments as well as the armed forces. Here, too, the shared results of public safety call for shared investment and thus careful accounting and personal sacrifice.

■

The issue of educational management and distrust may be vividly viewed in the context of optics, or appearances, by the kind of car an academic leader drives—or in which he or she is driven.[61] As a fractal, like a grain of sand under a microscope reflecting the contours of a coastline, the car is a powerful image, conveying not only the self-regard of the user but also his or her disposable wealth. In the loose sense of Benoit Mandelbrot's exposition of embedded resemblance, the self-similarity of car and user is often distinct.[62]

If an academic leader has the disposable wealth for a luxury car, or if an academic institution budgets the money to provide its leader with a luxury car, pinched parents, faculty members, taxpayers, and students have cause to question the institution's allocation of resources. Because of the service identification or collectivity orientation of education and because of the information asymmetry inherent to schooling, academic leaders must reassure their constituents that dollars are being well spent. A luxury car consequently sows doubt. By contrast, for the reasons given earlier, few people if any would raise an eyebrow if an executive at Accenture, Boeing, Kraft Foods, or Pfizer drove—or was driven in—a luxury car.

As the president of Harvard University in the early aughts, the economist Larry Summers was derided by faculty and students for being chauffeured in a Cadillac limousine, whereas a predecessor, the legal scholar Derek Bok, was lauded for driving an old Volkswagen Bug, parking it in a university garage, and walking across campus to his office.[63] While strict cost-benefit analysis may have justified Summers's decision to be driven rather than drive (as he could get important work done in the back seat rather than spend time behind the wheel), a loose assessment leads to a different conclusion, especially in the case of a Cadillac limousine rather than a conventional sedan. In this regard, Henry Rosovsky, a Harvard economist from an earlier era and the dean of the university's Faculty of Arts and Sciences for many years as well as the university's acting president for two, articulated a different view of costs and benefits in his 1990 book on university governance. Acknowledging at once the issue of optics and fiduciary responsibility, Rosovsky cautioned that university leaders must be acutely aware of expenses and appearances. Rosovsky noted, in particular, that the luxury of first-class plane travel for Harvard administrators in his day was prohibited by university policy "and rightly so."[64]

Much like Summers, an affable, gregarious headmaster of an independent K–12 school where I taught in the 1990s was ribbed relentlessly for driving a Porsche 911 Carrera convertible, given to him as a fiftieth birthday present by his wife, so much so that he decided to keep the car at his weekend home. Though a private purchase, the Porsche conveyed an unsettling, carefree message to parents struggling to pay tuition and to faculty on tight budgets.

The headmaster, after all, was paid far more than teachers and provided free housing in a large, elegant residence on campus.

A classic scene in the 1992 film *Scent of a Woman* underscores the mismatch of educational management and executive ease. When students at a tony prep school decide to humiliate their imperious headmaster, they target his brand-new dark Jaguar XJS. Putting their scientific and artistic skills to malicious use, they employ a remote-control device to inflate a massive balloon suspended from a lamppost by the headmaster's designated parking spot in the heart of the campus just as he steps out of his car at the beginning of the day. A blasphemous illustration spreads across the expanding balloon depicting the headmaster truckling to trustees. Before a growing crowd of puzzled onlookers, the indignant headmaster pulls out his car key and lunges to puncture the balloon. Both the headmaster and his car end up covered in white paint.[65]

This fictional headmaster, the real headmaster, and Summers all missed the subtext, the subliminal message, much as EMO chiefs have failed to grasp the general implication of for-profit school management. Chris Whittle, in fact, insisted on having his own car and driver. This was true when he was publisher of *Esquire* in the 1980s, to the consternation of Phillip Moffitt, a college friend with whom he had bought the magazine, and when he ran Edison. Moffitt, who served as *Esquire*'s editor, complained that such an expense was extravagant, especially in a city streaming with taxis; an Edison staff lawyer made the same observation two decades later.[66]

Right or wrong, constituents took style to be substance. This psychological effect applies to the previously mentioned matter of teacher buy-in in particular. The financial focus of EMOs crowds out the altruistic spirit basic to teaching. This is not to say that teachers do not care about money; higher salaries have been documented to attract people to teaching.[67] But it is to say that big salaries and bonuses for EMO executives alienate teachers driven by civic ideals. No EMO, in this regard, has generated among its teachers or administrators the enthusiasm of such nonprofits as Teach for America (TFA) or the Knowledge is Power Program (KIPP).

While TFA may anger policy makers as well as career educators for mandating only a two-year commitment to the profession, and while TFA's Summer Institutes for new teachers may be inadequate as preparation for the classroom, more than 50,000 college students vied for 5,000 spots in 2011, and those who succeeded put in long days for five summer weeks studying pedagogical theory and practice without pay.[68] While TFA has recently slipped in its popularity, it is still a top recruiter on campuses across the country.[69] Moreover, thousands of TFA participants and alumni meet regularly without pay at regional conferences to discuss educational policy.[70] While KIPP suffers from high teacher burnout and attrition, more than 3,000 KIPP teachers and administrators year after year attend the organization's annual School Summit at the end of July for four days of professional development without pay.[71] And while these nonprofit organizations compensate their leaders with big salaries, as will be detailed in Chapter 9, the salaries are fixed, in keeping with nonprofit practice. EMOs, by contrast, pay significant bonuses to executives on top of hefty salaries. Some EMO executives earn far more, in fact, than superintendents of school districts far greater in size and complexity.

In 2003, for instance, Edison operated 133 schools (with a total enrollment of 80,000 students) as well as its Educational Services Group, comprising Newton Learning (providing after-school and summer-school programs), Tungsten Learning (providing professional development and assessment software), and Edison U.K. (an educational consultancy serving British school districts). By contrast, the New York City Department of Education in 2003 operated 1,429 schools (with a total enrollment of 1.1 million students) as well as myriad supplementary programs.[72]

As chancellor of the New York City Department of Education in 2003, Joel Klein earned a fixed salary of $245,000.[73] Setting aside profits that may have been made from early allocations of shares in the company, Edison executives made considerable sums. As CEO of Edison, Chris Whittle earned a base salary of $207,000 and a bonus of $625,000; as president and COO, Christopher Cerf earned a base salary of $293,269 and a bonus of $425,000; as chief education officer and executive vice president, John Chubb earned a base salary of $286,539 and a bonus of $285,000; and as vice chairman for business and finance, Charles J. Delaney earned a base salary of $288,192, a bonus of $450,000, and, as a newcomer, a restricted stock award valued at $330,000.[74] In sum, while Klein ran a school system fourteen times bigger than Edison, he did not make half as much as any of the company's four most highly paid executives, and he did not make a quarter as much as the company's vice chairman for business and finance.

To many teachers at schools managed by Edison, the high salaries and bonuses for executives could not be squared with their everyday pedagogical needs. Megan Zor, who taught social studies from 2004 to 2006 at Gillespie Middle School in North Philadelphia, one of the twenty schools in Philadelphia turned over by the state to Edison in 2002, bristled at the contrast between executive pay and the condition of Gillespie. "How could people at the top be making lots of money," Zor wondered three years later, "when we didn't have soap in the bathrooms? How could people at the top be making lots of money when we had six principals in two years, when we had no reading specialist, when we had no resources for the lowest-performing students, except the bubble kids [those students on the cusp of passing state exams]?"[75]

Zor had been placed at Gillespie through TFA upon graduating from the University of Missouri. After completing her two-year TFA commitment at Gillespie, Zor took a teaching position across town at the Shoemaker Campus of Mastery Charter Schools. The principal of Shoemaker, Sharif El-Mekki, had been the principal of nearby Shaw Middle School, another of the twenty schools in Philadelphia turned over by the state to Edison in 2002; Shoemaker likewise had been one of five Philadelphia schools turned over by the state in 2002 to another for-profit firm, Chancellor Beacon Academies. Preceding both Zor and El-Mekki in moving from Edison to the nonprofit realm of charter schools was Richard Barth, who left the company in January 2006 as head of operations for its schools in Philadelphia and president of its District Partnerships Division to become CEO of KIPP.[76]

Preceding Barth in the move from Edison to KIPP was Gap founder and chairman Donald Fisher, who had donated $1.8 million in 1998 to fund the startup of an Edison charter school in San Francisco and pledged $25 million more to California school districts that signed on with Edison.[77] Soon after viewing a *60 Minutes* segment in 1999 about KIPP's two middle schools, one in Houston and the other in the Bronx, the denim magnate and his wife, Doris, wrote a check for $15 million to fund the replication of the charter school.[78] By 2013, thanks to that initial donation and more support from Fisher and other philanthropists, KIPP numbered 141 schools across twenty states and the District of Columbia.[79] Along with Doris and Donald Fisher came their aforementioned son John, a major investor in Edison who would become the chairman of KIPP's board of directors. Preceding the Fishers was Scott Hamilton, an executive at the Edison Project from its first days who then became associate commissioner of education for charter schools in Massachusetts and after that the managing director of the Fisher family's foundation. It was Hamilton who convinced Fisher to watch a video-tape of the *60 Minutes* story.

9

THE FOURTH WAY

In managing a school, you can dance to only one beat. You can't think
about both profits and academic results. Our sole concern is student
performance.

Dave Levin, cofounder, KIPP, November 16, 2008

■ EDISON AND KIPP were conceived and born at the same time. As educational concepts, they could be termed fraternal twins, offspring of the same
movement to challenge conventional public education but distinct in appearance and behavior.

While Chris Whittle was planning his network of schools from 1992 to
1994 with Benno Schmidt, John Chubb, Chester Finn, Dominique Browning,
Sylvia Peters, Daniel Biederman, and Nancy Hechinger at the corporate
headquarters of Whittle Communications in Knoxville, Mike Feinberg and
Dave Levin were teaching at elementary schools in Houston as young members of Teach for America and brainstorming at night as housemates about
how to better serve their students. While Whittle and Schmidt were raising
millions of dollars from Time Warner, Philips Electronics, and Associated
Newspapers, Feinberg and Levin were securing thousands of dollars from
the likes of Jim "Mattress Mack" McIngvale, the owner of a bustling furni-
ture store on the north side of Houston. When Feinberg and Levin opened
KIPP in Houston in 1994 with forty-seven fifth-graders in one classroom
at Garcia Elementary School, Whittle was one year behind, opening four
elementary schools in 1995—one each in Massachusetts, Michigan, Kansas,
and Texas—with a total enrollment of 2,250 students. By 1999, KIPP comprised two schools, the inaugural campus in Houston and a second in the
Bronx, with a total enrollment just shy of 500. Edison, by contrast, comprised

sixty-one schools across seventeen states and the District of Columbia with a total enrollment of 37,500 students.[1]

Although Edison and KIPP were never in official competition with one another, had there been such a competition Edison would have ended up the proverbial hare, and KIPP the tortoise. By 2014 Edison was managing ten schools, down from eleven the previous year, along with four virtual schools and thirteen credit-recovery centers.[2] KIPP meanwhile was managing 162 schools, up from 141 the previous year (see Figure 9.1). Until 2004 KIPP operated only middle schools. By 2014 the organization was running sixty elementary schools and twenty-two high schools as well as eighty middle schools.[3]

KIPP had moreover spawned a multitude of lookalike nonprofit organizations aimed at closing the achievement gap between privileged and

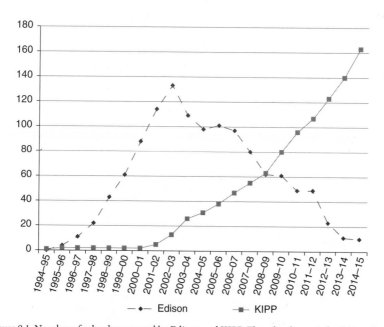

Figure 9.1 Number of schools managed by Edison and KIPP. The school counts for Edison from 1995 to 2003 come from Brian Gill et al., *Inspiration, Perspiration, and Time: Operations and Achievement in Edison Schools* (Santa Monica: RAND, 2005), 13; numbers for subsequent years come from correspondence with Edison officials. The school counts for KIPP through 2011 come from correspondence with KIPP officials; the numbers for 2012 through 2014 come from the organization's Web site.

underprivileged children through longer school days, strict codes of conduct, intense concentration on standardized tests, and contracts with parents to check homework, support school rules, and attend parent-teacher conferences. These organizations, commonly called charter management organizations (CMOs), to be distinguished from for-profit educational management organizations (EMOs), moreover set college as the goal for all students. Finally, in keeping with Myron Lieberman's opposition to unionized teachers as obstacles to collaboration and efficiency, these CMOS, like Edison and its EMO competitors managing charter schools, used at-will contracts, retaining the right to dismiss teachers if and when administrators decided to do so. By 2014, ten such CMOs shared the spotlight with KIPP and together, in sum, managed another 242 schools (see Table 9.1).

Table 9.1　Ten CMOs sharing KIPP's pedagogical philosophy

CMO	Origin	Schools and locations, 2014	Total
Achievement First	New Haven, CT, 1999	17 in Brooklyn; 11 in CT (5 in New Haven, 4 in Hartford, 2 in Bridgeport); 1 in Providence, RI	29
Aspire Public Schools	Oakland, 1999	35 across CA; 3 in Memphis	38
Democracy Prep	Manhattan, 2006	8 in Manhattan; 2 in the Bronx; 2 in Camden, NJ; 1 in Washington, DC	13
IDEA Public Schools	Donna, TX, 2000	30 across Texas	30
Mastery Charter Schools	Philadelphia, 2001	15 in Philadelphia; 2 in Camden, NJ	17
Noble Network of Charter Schools	Chicago, 1999	17 in Chicago	17
Rocketship Public Schools	San Jose, 2007	9 in San Jose; 1 in Milwaukee; 1 in Nashville	11
Success Academy	Manhattan, 2006	15 in Manhattan; 9 in Brooklyn; 6 in the Bronx; 2 in Queens	32
Uncommon Schools	Newark, 1997	21 in Brooklyn; 10 in Newark; 4 in Rochester; 3 in Boston; 2 in Troy, NY; 2 in Camden, NJ	42
YES Prep	Houston, 1998	13 in Houston	13

Data source: Data collected from Web sites of each charter network in September 2014.

While none of Edison's chief EMO competitors suffered Edison's fate, none experienced growth close to KIPP's. In addition, EMOs as a whole steadily lost ground to CMOs. The three EMOs rivaling Edison in 2001 were the Leona Group, with thirty-three schools (fourteen in Arizona and nineteen in Michigan); Mosaica, with twenty-two schools across eleven states, from Massachusetts to Arizona; and National Heritage Academies (NHA), with twenty-eight schools (twenty-three in Michigan, four in North Carolina, and one in Rochester, New York). By 2014 the Leona Group was running sixty-five schools across five states; Mosaica, twenty-eight schools across seven states as well as several online academies; and NHA, eighty-two schools across nine states.[4]

Only EMOs focused on online education—such as K12 and Connections Academy—exhibited the exponential growth posted by KIPP. As explained in Chapter 7, this virtual sector posed little if any threat to local school boards intent on retaining day-to-day managerial authority over their schools. For a school board to turn over school buildings as well as per-pupil expenditures to an EMO is one thing. It is quite another to allocate funds to an EMO for online education of either home-schooled students or students interested in courses like Chinese, Russian, or advanced math that a typical school might not be able to provide. Moreover, as labor-light enterprises, virtual EMOs can grow at much less cost than conventional brick-and-mortar EMOs.

This far less visible and slimmer form of educational outsourcing has accordingly taken off. The number of virtual schools is deceptively small, as several enroll thousands of students: Insight Schools of Portland, Oregon, for example, counted 3,200 students in its Washington State virtual high school in 2011–2012; Altair Learning of Columbus, Ohio, that same year counted 12,304 students in its K–12 Ohio program.[5] But the number of students in virtual schools run by EMOs is patently significant. While amounting to only 10,325 in 2003–2004, the number had climbed to 142,386 by 2011–2012 (see Figures 9.2 and 9.3).[6]

In sum, by 2011–2012, the latest academic year for which cumulative data are available, nearly one-third of students in schools managed by EMOs were online students; the number of CMO schools had far surpassed that of EMO schools; and the number of students in CMO schools had far exceeded the number of students in EMO brick-and-mortar schools. If this trend persists,

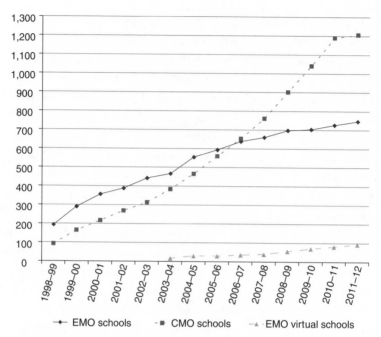

Figure 9.2 Number of EMO and CMO brick-and-mortar schools and of EMO virtual schools. *Data source:* Gary Miron and Charisse Gulosino, *Profiles of For-Profit and Nonprofit Education Management Organizations: Fourteenth Edition, 2011–2012* (Boulder, CO: National Education Policy Center, 2013), http://nepc.colorado.edu/publication/EMO-profiles-11–12.

enrollment in EMO virtual schools stands to break 500,000 by 2020;[7] enrollment in CMO schools stands to surpass 700,000;[8] and the number of KIPP schools stands to exceed 275, with its total enrollment, which now averages 360 students per school, exceeding 90,000.[9]

What is nevertheless clear is that what hurt Edison and stymied its competitors enabled KIPP and its siblings. The result was a fourth way of providing public education. The traditional neighborhood public school constituted the archetype to be reformed. The schools of choice within the public school system developed from the 1970s onward by the likes of Seymour Fliegel, Deborah Meier, and Ted Sizer constituted a second way: principals got waivers from local and state authorities to provide a more flexible curriculum to better address the academic and emotional needs and interests of students, and teachers remained unionized but consented to work outside the boundaries of contract regulations to this end.

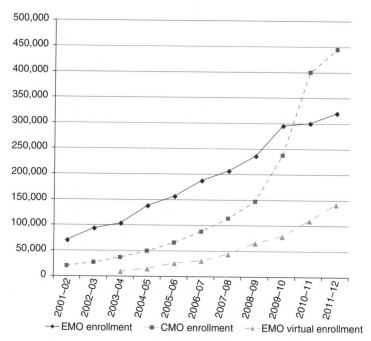

Figure 9.3 Number of students in EMO and CMO brick-and-mortar schools and in EMO virtual schools. *Data source:* Gary Miron and Charisse Gulosino, *Profiles of For-Profit and Nonprofit Education Management Organizations: Fourteenth Edition, 2011–2012* (Boulder, CO: National Education Policy Center, 2013), http://nepc.colorado.edu/publication/EMO-profiles-11-12.

Beacon, the school where this book began, was founded in 1993 as part of that movement for choice within the system. Aiming to amplify such choice and run schools with even greater freedom from central offices, EMOs introduced a third way: with the managerial and marketing tools of big business, external operators like Edison used at-will employment contracts where possible and sought to provide richer curricula, boost test results, and, in the process, make a profit. KIPP and its fellow CMOs introduced a fourth way, using the same managerial and marketing tools of big business, utilizing the same at-will employment contracts, seeking the same goals as EMOs, but substituting for the pursuit of profit a zeal for improvement defined by a shared credo of "no excuses."

In the case of KIPP, in particular, the organization's ubiquitous motto, "Work Hard. Be Nice," and its five so-called pillars conveyed this intensity:

first, "high expectations"; second, "choice and commitment" (by students, parents, and teachers alike to be affiliated with KIPP and to adhere to its high expectations); third, "more time" (meaning a longer school day and year); fourth, "power to lead" (meaning autonomy of school leaders to manage personnel and budgets as necessary); and fifth, "focus on results."[10]

The language used in KIPP's charter to describe parental obligations in their "Commitment to Excellence" is unequivocal: "We will make sure our child arrives at KIPP every day by 7:25 a.m. (Monday–Friday) or boards a KIPP bus at the scheduled time. . . . We will check our child's homework every night, let him/her call the teacher if there is a problem with the homework, and try to read with him/her every night. We will always make ourselves available to our children and the school, and address any concerns they might have." The language used to describe the emphasis on results is likewise blunt: "KIPP schools relentlessly focus on high student performance on standardized tests and other objective measures. Just as there are no shortcuts, there are no excuses. Students are expected to achieve at a level of academic performance that will enable them to succeed at the nation's best high schools and colleges."[11]

This emphasis by KIPP on results is no less businesslike than Edison's, which helps to explain the migration of key Edison people to KIPP, from Scott Hamilton, Donald Fisher, and John Fisher as backers to Richard Barth as an executive. This emphasis on results by CMOs in general helps to explain the significant support and direction they receive from leaders in the financial and business communities. Bankers, fund managers, and corporate executives live by numbers. And these people steer the boards of CMOs like KIPP.

The board of KIPP in 2014, for example, was chaired by John Fisher, head of an investment group called Sansome Partners, and comprised, among others, the CEOs of Netflix and Viacom as well as a senior managing director of Bain Capital. The board of Success Academy the same year was chaired by the maverick hedge fund CEO Daniel Loeb and included, among others, nine investment executives. And the board of Mastery Charter Schools in Philadelphia was chaired by the senior vice president for finance and business operations at Comcast and included, among others, two private equity executives and a partner at Ernst & Young. For their philanthropic efforts, these benefactors are naturally inclined to judge progress in the same numerical terms they employ for assessing success in the workplace. They are likewise inclined to endorse the philosophy of "no excuses" given the competitive ethos of their everyday lives.

The organizational resemblance of CMOs to major corporations may also be explained by this close relationship. The leaders of KIPP and similar CMOs all bear corporate titles, from CEO, CFO, COO, and managing director to positions tailored to education, such as chief learning officer, chief academic officer, and chief research, design, and innovation officer. The New York headquarters of the KIPP Foundation, located on the twentieth floor of an office building on Eighth Avenue two blocks north of Madison Square Garden, feels, in fact, corporate, except that the colors are brighter and conference rooms go by such names as Grit, Optimism, and Zest, in accordance with the organization's can-do spirit and its adoption of eight traits central to an initiative begun in 2011 focused on character education (which also include academic self-control, interpersonal self-control, gratitude, social intelligence, and curiosity).[12]

The compensation of CMO executives likewise reflects corporate pay. For the 2012–2013 school year, Barth, for example, earned $381,819 as CEO of KIPP; Eva Moskowitz earned $567,500 as CEO of Success Academy; Brett Peiser earned $267,396 as CEO of Uncommon Schools; Thomas E. Torkelson earned $326,890 as CEO of IDEA Public Schools; Douglas S. McCurry and Dacia Toll earned $222,979 and $234,565, respectively, as co-CEOs of Achievement First; and James R. Willcox earned $266,587 as CEO of Aspire Public Schools.[13] However, this pay, in contrast to that of EMO executives, is generally fixed. If CMO executives do earn bonuses, they are marginal.[14] CMO executives accordingly cannot benefit from cutting corners in the way EMO executives might.

This distinction explains in part the rise and resilience of Moskowitz in particular. While Moskowitz has provoked ire for her compensation,[15] she has regardless become a folk hero of charter school parents, leading them in a protest march across the Brooklyn Bridge and in rallies in Foley Square and from the steps of City Hall and the State Capitol.[16] By contrast, parents in

New York a decade earlier did not allow Edison a chance to run even one public school. The leaders of Edison were disparaged and dismissed as profiteers.

Another difference between Edison and Success Academy, along with KIPP and most CMOs, is that the former was primarily in the business of taking over public schools, while the latter engage almost exclusively in start-ups, opening new schools and adding one grade at a time. Success Academy, KIPP, and similar CMOs occupy space in public schools, but they rarely take over the operation of public schools, as Edison proposed doing in New York and as it did in cities across the country.

Though corporate in nature, CMOs for these reasons provoke neither the distrust nor the pushback engendered by EMOs. Their nonprofit identification and nimble development strategy have largely spared them public grief; garnered praise from network broadcasters, talk show hosts, op-ed columnists, radio commentators, and scholars; inspired significant philanthropic support; aligned idealistic teachers with management; and allowed executives to focus on pedagogical rather than financial matters. Steady growth has followed. And yet what fuels this growth necessarily limits it, as there's a limited quantity of philanthropic dollars to fund development, a limited quantity of selfless teachers capable of working so hard, and, finally, a limited number of students for whom the "no excuses" environment of long school days, rigid discipline, and academic rigor is suitable.

One person with a rare perspective on the differences between CMOs and EMOs is Richard Barth, the CEO of KIPP since 2006 and an executive at Edison for the seven preceding years. To Barth, the challenge of running an EMO was not so much balancing commercial and academic agendas but doing so under regular political fire. Barth, in this light, was frequently accompanied by an armed bodyguard at the outset of running Edison's schools in Philadelphia.[17] "If KIPP were a for-profit organization, it would be much more difficult for us to grow," Barth said six months into his new job at KIPP. "The for-profit approach adds a layer of politics that can be utterly distracting to the work that must be done."[18]

In the opinion of Dave Levin, the distinction is deeper: it is not merely perceptual but operational, which ultimately explains the difference in public response. The everyday objectives of EMOs and CMOs, Levin said during an interview in 2008 at a middle school in West Harlem called KIPP Infinity, are inherently irreconcilable. "In managing a school, you can dance to only one beat," Levin said. "You can't think about both profits and academic results. Our sole concern is student performance. And it has been from the start. KIPP grew out of the efforts of teachers. We are not businessmen."[19]

Another person with a rare perspective on the differences between CMOs and EMOs is Sharif El-Mekki, the principal of Edison's Shaw Middle School in West Philadelphia from 2003 to 2008 and since then the principal of the nearby Shoemaker Campus of Mastery Charter Schools, a CMO network founded in Philadelphia in 2001 that by 2014 comprised fifteen schools in the city and two more across the Delaware River in Camden, New Jersey. Shoemaker runs from grade seven through twelve. Before Shoemaker was taken over in 2006, it was a middle school managed by the district, then by Miami-based EMO Chancellor Beacon Academies in 2002–2003 as part of the School Reform Commission's experiment with privatization, and after that by the district again.[20]

Like KIPP, Mastery started out with older students. The organization's first four schools, opened from 2001 through 2007, began in sixth or seventh grade. In 2010 Mastery opened its first elementary schools. Of Mastery's fifteen schools in Philadelphia in the 2014–2015 academic year, eight were elementary schools and seven were middle or high schools or some combination. Mastery's two schools in Camden, opened in 2014, were elementary schools.[21] Unlike KIPP and most CMOs, Mastery has not, with the exception of its first school, built from scratch but has rather taken over struggling district schools and tried to turn them around.[22] In all cases but one, these takeovers have been authorized by school officials without a parental vote; on the one occasion such a vote was required, at Steel Elementary in May 2014, parents rebuffed Mastery by a significant margin to keep the school in the district.[23] Like KIPP, Mastery embraces high expectations; stipulates choice by students, parents, and teachers; requires more instructional time; confers considerable latitude on school leaders; and focuses on results. The network motto is "Excellence. No Excuses."

El-Mekki, a Philadelphia native, graduated in 1988 from Overbrook High School, several blocks up Lancaster Avenue from Shoemaker. He lettered in football at Overbrook as a defensive back and led the track team to a city championship as a sprinter. Two decades later, El-Mekki looked like he could still compete in either sport. Only a full beard and a receding hairline gave away his age. After earning his bachelor's degree in criminal justice from Indiana University of Pennsylvania, where he also ran track, El-Mekki returned home unclear about his next steps. He worked as a courier, hung out with friends, and played pickup tackle football on Sunday afternoons on the field of John Bartram High School in Southwest Philadelphia.[24]

El-Mekki nearly lost his life on that field. After he took an opponent down hard in a game in October 1992 and then got into a scuffle with him about it, four friends of the ball carrier sprang from the stands pointing guns.[25] El-Mekki was hit twice in his left leg and once in his right. One bullet pierced an artery. He spent six weeks in the nearby Hospital of the University of Pennsylvania and underwent seventeen operations.[26]

Following his recovery, he worked as a tutor of juvenile delinquents at the city's Youth Study Center and found his calling. Upon learning a year later of a drive to recruit African American men into teaching, El-Mekki became a teacher at Turner Middle School, also in West Philadelphia. He worked at Turner for seven years as a teacher and three as an assistant principal. It was Barth who recruited El-Mekki to become the principal of notoriously troubled Shaw. El-Mekki said he was attracted to Edison by the quality of its professional development and its coordination of curricula with benchmark assessments pegged to state tests.[27]

His primary concern at Shaw, El-Mekki said, was to restore order. El-Mekki took over Shaw in January of the first year of Edison's management of the school. He recalled several years later that he was astounded to learn in September 2002 that Edison had laid off its nonteaching assistants (NTAs). "I remember reading that in the paper when I was at Turner," El-Mekki said, "and I thought these people at Edison are crazy. They have made a big mistake."[28]

In one of his first moves as Shaw's principal, El-Mekki got the school district to send Shaw three police officers in addition to the NTAs Vallas had required Edison to rehire. El-Mekki succeeded in bringing peace to Shaw and implementing the Edison model. He said that the quality of Edison's professional development and curricula had lived up to his expectations. And as Shaw was designated by the district as a hard-to-staff school in the summer of 2004 and thus given "full site select" status, El-Mekki was given authority to hire all staff directly, rather than work with placements made by the central office, per convention. However, despite this advantage and his satisfaction with Edison's professional development and curricula, El-Mekki said he never got the faculty commitment or the control over resources he needed to make Shaw the school he thought it could be.[29]

With Mastery, El-Mekki said he found what he was looking for. "Mastery is what Edison was supposed to be," El-Mekki said during his first year in charge of Shoemaker in 2009 while giving a tour of the spotless, serene school, its floors gleaming and its corridors and classrooms decorated with neat posters both proclaiming the number of days until statewide exams and invoking the words of Maya Angelou, Frederick Douglass, Albert Einstein, and Eleanor Roosevelt on hard work and its rewards. Students looked sharp in school-issue gray shirts with Mastery logos and navy slacks. "We have full mission alignment here with the faculty," El-Mekki said, "and we have total control over our budget."[30]

El-Mekki did not identify with corporate interests. Like Feinberg and Levin, he was not a businessman and did not think of himself as one. He rather identified with the political radicalism of his parents, Hamid Khalid and Aisha El-Mekki, who joined the Black Panthers in the 1960s to protest police brutality in Philadelphia and to cultivate community pride. El-Mekki was, in fact, arrested in 2005 for defying a police officer while attending an antiwar rally with his mother, brother, and son outside a downtown convention hall where President George W. Bush was delivering a speech. El-Mekki was soon after cleared of any wrongdoing, but his politics were made plain in articles about the arrest in the local press.[31] "I tell our teachers that we must work as freedom fighters, as nation builders," El-Mekki said several years later in reflecting on his politics as well as his vocation.[32]

El-Mekki nevertheless sided with many in the business community in contending that teachers' unions have put job protection ahead of instructional quality and school climate. El-Mekki conceded that inner-city schools like Overbrook, Turner, Shaw, and Shoemaker need more funding, but he contended that commitment from faculty is an equally pressing matter and accordingly endorsed at-will teacher contracts.[33] To Joseph Ferguson, Mastery's COO since 2009, mission alignment with the faculty constituted the fundamental difference between the CMO and the Philadelphia School District, where he had worked the four previous years in operations at the central office. School leaders, Ferguson said following his fifth year with Mastery, need autonomy. "I get collective bargaining," he said. "I'm all for collective bargaining. But you can't run a school without the freedom to staff it."[34]

Along with El-Mekki, many teachers at schools managed by Edison in Philadelphia moved to schools run by Mastery. There were eight such teachers at El-Mekki's school alone in the 2013–2014 school year. Across town in North Philadelphia at Mastery's Simon Gratz High School were two more that year, including George Prifti, the veteran math teacher from Albania who had tangled with El-Mekki's successor at Shaw four years earlier over the value of monthly benchmark assessments.[35]

Shaw itself became a Mastery school in 2014 and in the process buttressed El-Mekki's point that Mastery fulfilled the Edison vision: formerly drab hallways and stairwells sparkled; students and staff worked with comparative ease.[36] In a dizzying and equally telling twist, Shaw did not merely become another Mastery school. It became the Hardy Williams campus of the Mastery network as home to the former Hardy Williams Academy Charter School. Mastery in 2011 took over the charter school, which was founded in 1999 by onetime Edison advocate State Senator Anthony Hardy Williams as the Renaissance Advantage Charter School.[37] The school had started out under the management of Advantage Schools Inc., an EMO based in Boston. When New York–based Mosaica Education Inc. bought Advantage in 2001, Renaissance Advantage became another Mosaica school. In 2004 Renaissance Advantage left Mosaica for Edison. Five years later, Senator Williams stepped down as the school's chairman of the board, the school severed its relationship with Edison, and the school's name was changed to honor the senator's father, the late State Senator Hardy Williams.[38]

■

According to a four-page survey—consisting of fixed and open-ended questions—on the differences between working at Edison and Mastery,

Table 9.2 Results, on a scale of 1 to 10, along with standard deviations, from a survey in 2014 of twelve Mastery Charter School staff members who had previously worked at schools in Philadelphia managed by Edison

Category	Edison		Mastery	
	Mean	S.D.	Mean	S.D.
Access to resources	4.5	2.9	7.6	1.2
Commitment of administrators	3.8	1.9	8.9	1.0
Commitment of colleagues	5.7	1.4	8.9	0.7
Commitment of students	5.0	1.5	7.8	1.2
Personal commitment	7.9	1.4	9.1	0.8
Professional development	4.6	2.5	8.0	1.0
Quality of leadership	3.8	2.4	8.8	0.7
Quality of working environment	4.6	2.4	7.9	1.2
Sense of achievement	5.2	2.1	8.0	1.0
Composite	5.0	2.1	8.3	1.0

filled out anonymously in 2014 by twelve staff members at Shoemaker, Simon Gratz, and a third Mastery school (Thomas, located in South Philadelphia), mission alignment constituted a salient distinction. These respondents defined their experience at Mastery as far more collaborative, effective, and rewarding.[39] While this sample is tiny, it is tightly defined, and the results are themselves tight and clear. On a scale of 1 to 10, for example, respondents, in sum, rated the quality of the working environment 4.6 at Edison and 7.9 at Mastery (see Table 9.2).

In answering the open-ended questions, respondents made the following observations:

- "Edison felt like a corporation. . . . I did not have a sense of Edison's mission; that is the tremendous difference between Edison and Mastery. Our mission statement is reinforced by the type of culture we aim to create."
- "There was no effort to work hard under Edison, to reach a goal together."

- "Edison didn't build a culture, didn't seem to have a presence, besides infrequent professional development. . . . Mastery has educators who are more dedicated, who put lots of hours into their work."
- "My experiences at Edison and Mastery have been drastically different. I attribute this to a one-team mentality of all the adults at Mastery, high expectations for students and educators, and the prioritization of student achievement."
- "We had no supplies at Edison: no books, no copy paper, no writing paper, no pencils. There were some teachers' guides that we were expected to plan from, but none of the connected materials [for students]."
- "It appeared on the surface level [under Edison] that all curricula were valued, but in terms of exhaustive effort and support, math/reading scores were where heavy support and follow-through occurred. . . . With Mastery, there's support across various subject areas, not just math and reading."
- "Teams at Mastery very deliberately focus on overall questions, like 'Are we doing what's best for students?' At Edison, this question came up between colleagues, but it was never at the forefront."

Beyond faculty buy-in, administrative autonomy, and school climate at Shoemaker and other schools run by Mastery, the results for Mastery students on the annual state exam, the Pennsylvania School System of Assessment (PSSA), supported El-Mekki's conclusion that Mastery fulfilled the expectations that he and many others had of Edison. It was not merely that Mastery students did far better on the reading and math exams than their peers at schools run by Edison or the city as a whole. Far more striking and telling were their results on the writing exams.

As explained in Chapter 7, on top of the exams in reading and math for students in grades three through eight mandated by No Child Left Behind (NCLB) in 2002, Pennsylvania started administering annual exams in writing to students in fifth and eighth grades in 2006 as well as in science to students in fourth and eighth grades in 2008. Because only scores on the reading and math exams determined a school's Adequate Yearly Progress (AYP), the NCLB standard for school effectiveness, scores on the science and writing exams barely, if ever, got mentioned. As measures that did not get measured, scores on the science and writing exams stood to measure a great deal and thus afford a rare window into how schools in Pennsylvania operated: what a school does when nobody is paying attention stands to say much more than when everybody is looking.

In this regard, schools run by KIPP and Mastery in Philadelphia appear to have provided a far more well-rounded education than Edison, in particular, and Philadelphia's public schools, in general. An amplification of the table of PSSA results in Chapter 7 reveals a conspicuous pattern from 2008 to 2012. For comparative purposes, only the scores of students classified as economically disadvantaged are addressed in this analysis. A significant majority of students in all groups were classified as economically disadvantaged over this time period. For the Philadelphia School District as a whole, 82 percent of eighth-graders in 2008–2009, for example, were classified as economically disadvantaged. For Edison in Philadelphia that year, 99 percent of students belonged to this category; for KIPP, 79 percent; and for Mastery, 79 percent.[40]

The proficiency rates in reading for fifth-graders at schools run by KIPP and Mastery were low and either lower than the proficiency rates in writing or slightly above. For fifth-graders at schools run by Edison and Philadelphia, the proficiency rates in reading were also low but consistently above the proficiency rates in writing. For eighth-graders at schools run by KIPP and Mastery, the proficiency rates in reading were much higher and at the same time close to the proficiency rates in writing. The results for eighth-graders at schools run by Edison and Philadelphia were utterly different: proficiency rates in reading also climbed, but proficiency rates in writing lagged significantly (see Table 9.3 and Figure 9.4).[41]

Results on the science exams appear to provide an equally telling story but of a very different nature. KIPP and Mastery schools along with Edison and the district as a whole posted results on the science exams far below results on the math exams, which seems to convey a disturbing lesson: no matter how committed, staff at schools run by the likes of KIPP and Mastery may struggle to teach subjects that are not adequately funded. As with reading and writing, scores on math and science exams should be similar. But good instruction in science requires much more funding than good instruction in

Table 9.3   Percentage of students in Philadelphia graded proficient on the PSSA
reading and writing exams, and differences in proficiency in these subjects

	2008	2009	2010	2011	2012	Mean
Grade 5						
Edison reading	34.0	27.3	21.4	37.1	n/a	30.0
Edison writing	12.8	21.1	17.9	25.7	n/a	19.4
Reading–writing	21.2	6.2	3.5	11.4	n/a	10.6
Philadelphia reading	33.3	38.1	38.4	43.0	31.1	36.8
Philadelphia writing	26.0	30.0	33.0	37.1	28.3	30.9
Reading–writing	7.3	8.1	5.4	5.9	2.8	5.9
KIPP reading	26.9	36.5	30.3	38.7	25.0	31.5
KIPP writing	27.7	34.4	30.1	37.5	29.8	31.9
Reading–writing	−0.8	2.1	0.2	1.2	−4.8	−0.4
Mastery reading	n/a	n/a	n/a	29.5	33.3	31.4
Mastery writing	n/a	n/a	n/a	42.4	48.7	45.6
Reading–writing	n/a	n/a	n/a	−12.9	−15.4	−14.2
Grade 8						
Edison reading	48.8	53.1	65.5	51.0	n/a	54.6
Edison writing	26.1	30.2	36.6	32.1	n/a	31.3
Reading–writing	22.7	22.9	28.9	18.9	n/a	23.4
Philadelphia reading	54.1	60.0	64.2	59.2	53.2	58.1
Philadelphia writing	39.4	44.6	50.1	46.9	42.2	44.6
Reading–writing	14.7	15.4	14.1	12.3	11.0	13.5
KIPP reading	73.8	79.3	78.2	73.3	74.5	75.8
KIPP writing	83.7	67.2	83.6	82.8	70.4	77.5
Reading–writing	−9.9	12.1	−5.4	−9.5	4.1	−1.7
Mastery reading	65.6	78.8	78.2	66.8	72.6	72.4
Mastery writing	72.9	76.0	80.6	71.3	77.2	75.6
Reading–writing	−7.3	2.8	−2.4	−4.5	−4.6	−3.2

Data source: Pennsylvania Department of Education, 2007–2008 through 2010–2011 PSSA and
AYP Results, http://www.portal.state.pa.us/portal/server.pt/community/school_assessments/7442.
Note: Students in all cohorts are classified as economically disadvantaged.

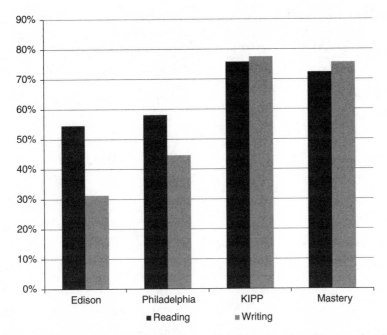

Figure 9.4 Mean percentage of eighth-graders in Philadelphia rated proficient on the PSSA reading and writing exams from 2008 to 2012 (in the case of Edison, from 2008 to 2011). Students in all cohorts are classified as economically disadvantaged. *Data source:* Pennsylvania Department of Education, 2007–2008 through 2010–2011 PSSA and AYP Results, http://www.portal .state.pa.us/portal/server.pt/community/school_assessments/7442.

writing: up-to-date science textbooks are expensive; and science is hard to teach effectively without regular labs, which require designated space, significant equipment, and careful supervision, which, in turn, means smaller classes.

In the well-funded five school districts along the iconic Main Line outside of Philadelphia (Great Valley, Haverford, Lower Merion, Radnor, and Tredyffrin-Easttown), scores on the PSSA math and science exams taken by eighth-graders are indeed tightly grouped. In 2009, for example, the combined rates of proficiency for those five school districts on the eighth-grade PSSA math and science exams were 86 percent and 79 percent, respectively. For comparative purposes, only the results for the economically disadvantaged students in these five districts bear real relevance to the scores of students in

Table 9.4   Percentage of economically disadvantaged eighth-grade students in
Philadelphia and the Main Line school districts rated proficient on the PSSA
math and science exams, and differences in proficiency in these subjects

	2008	2009	2010	2011	2012	Mean
Edison math	47.4	47.3	54.8	48.2	NA	49.4
Edison science	13.5	9.9	18.8	14.7	NA	14.2
Math – science	33.9	37.4	36.0	33.5	NA	35.2
Philadelphia math	46.2	47.6	57.6	53.5	48.7	50.7
Philadelphia science	18.8	18.7	21.4	21.7	19.4	20.0
Math – science	27.4	28.9	36.2	31.8	29.3	30.7
KIPP math	64.3	74.6	72.4	71.7	78.0	72.2
KIPP science	17.1	20.3	26.8	25.0	27.5	23.3
Math – science	47.2	54.3	45.6	46.7	50.5	48.9
Mastery math	62.9	81.6	73.7	71.2	80.0	73.9
Mastery science	11.1	31.5	30.1	24.9	30.6	25.6
Math – science	51.8	50.1	43.6	46.3	49.4	48.2
Main Line math	63.2	61.2	72.3	64.9	74.7	67.3
Main Line science	43.1	49.2	57.2	50.4	58.7	51.7
Math – science	20.1	12.0	15.1	14.5	16.0	15.5

Data source: Pennsylvania Department of Education, 2007–2008 through 2010–2011 PSSA and
AYP Results, http://www.portal.state.pa.us/portal/server.pt/community/school_assessments/7442.

Philadelphia. In the 2008–2009 school year, 6 percent of the students in these
five districts belonged to this category.[42]

Results for these economically disadvantaged students in the Main Line
districts were, in fact, much lower than those of their classmates from middle-
and upper-income homes, but their math and science scores were far *tighter*
than those of the economically disadvantaged students in schools run by
Edison, KIPP, Mastery, or Philadelphia. This was true for all five years for
which PSSA data for science exams are available. Yet in each of these five
years, the economically disadvantaged students at KIPP and Mastery posted
higher math scores than their economically disadvantaged peers in the Main
Line districts (see Table 9.4 and Figure 9.5).[43]

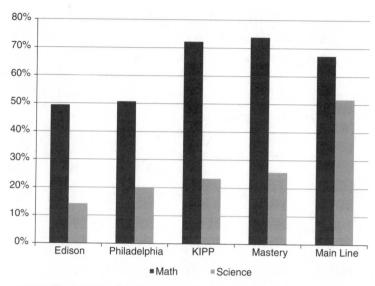

Figure 9.5 Mean percentage of eighth-graders rated proficient on the PSSA math and science exams from 2008 to 2012 (in the case of Edison, from 2008 to 2011). Students in all cohorts are classified as economically disadvantaged. *Data source:* Pennsylvania Department of Education, 2007–2008 through 2010–2011 PSSA and AYP Results, http://www.portal.state.pa.us/portal /server.pt/community/school_assessments/7442.

To what degree smaller classes, more experienced teachers, better and more frequent labs, or more advantaged or motivated classmates explain the far higher science scores posted year after year by economically disadvantaged Main Line students is hard to know. But the difference in resources necessary for smaller classes, more experienced teachers, and better and more frequent labs has certainly been pronounced. The Main Line school districts in 2008–2009, for example, spent 43 percent (or $4,926) more per pupil than Philadelphia (see Figure 7.2).[44]

Outside of exam results, the everyday differences in operations between an EMO and a CMO comport with the contrast in public perceptions of the two models remarked on by Barth and Levin. The consequent advantage for CMOs, and KIPP in particular, has been patent. It has disarmed if not enticed those inclined to oppose outside management of a school, Barth said.[45]

Levin agreed and recalled that right after the laudatory segment about KIPP on *60 Minutes* in 1999 that won over Gap cofounders Doris and Donald Fisher, "Mike [Feinberg] got a call from a school district official who said, 'We'd like to order twenty KIPPs.'" Unlike Edison, KIPP accordingly did not need to employ a team of sales executives or run a series of ads pitching its model. News coverage alone did the job. Smart branding, lucid, detailed annual reports, and sharp, interactive Web sites for the national organization and each region would in time follow but merely served to amplify the message conveyed by TV, radio, and print journalists.

News coverage of KIPP's early years was, in fact, unanimous in its approval. In addition to the 1999 segment on *60 Minutes,* a glowing follow-up piece aired by the CBS program in 2000, and an adulatory essay in between by David Grann in the *New Republic,* newspaper articles year after year hailed KIPP.[46] A Nexis search of KIPP in major newspapers during its first year of expansion, from September 2001 through June 2002, produced seventeen articles, all of them with a positive tenor; by contrast, a Nexis search of Edison during its first year of operation, from September 1995 through June 1996, produced forty-seven articles, twenty-seven of which had a negative tenor. Furthermore, a Nexis search of KIPP four years later, from September 2005 through June 2006, produced twenty-two articles, again all of a positive tenor; a Nexis search of Edison four years after its first year of operation, from September 1999 through June 2000, produced twenty-six articles, six of which had a negative tenor.[47]

Beyond impressive music programs at many KIPP schools, high scores on standardized tests in reading and math for KIPP students, as well as impressive rates of college matriculation for KIPP graduates, the selfless commitment of KIPP teachers and principals inspired much of this positive coverage and continued to capture attention. KIPP staff typically started their day at 7 a.m., finished at 5 p.m., remained available to their students afterward by a KIPP-issued cell phone for homework help, and taught every other Saturday morning as well as three weeks over the summer.

KIPP was in this vein featured on *ABC World News, CBS Evening News, NBC Nightly News,* several National Public Radio programs, *PBS Frontline, The Oprah Winfrey Show,* and even *The Colbert Report.*[48] Bob Herbert and

Thomas Friedman hailed KIPP for its ideals and ethos in op-ed columns for the *New York Times;* Stanley Crouch and Leonard Pitts did the same in op-ed columns for the *New York Daily News* and the *Miami Herald,* respectively; and Jay Mathews, education columnist for the *Washington Post,* wrote a series of articles about the dedication of KIPP staff and built on those articles with a book about the organization's unlikely evolution.[49] The husband-wife team of historian Stephan Thernstrom and political scientist Abigail Thernstrom used the shared CMO credo of "no excuses" as the title of their 2003 book on closing the achievement gap and punctuated their analysis with praise of KIPP for its vision and resolve. Malcolm Gladwell devoted the penultimate chapter of his 2008 book, *Outliers,* to KIPP's exceptional results and linked them to the exceptional hours demanded of teachers and students alike. And Paul Tough likewise celebrated KIPP in his 2012 book on character development, *How Children Succeed: Grit, Curiosity, and the Hidden Power of Character,* for the organization's relentless commitment to nurturing better behavioral as well as improved academic outcomes.[50]

This publicity cleared the way for KIPP's expansion and kindled the philanthropic funding to make it happen. On top of the $15 million the Doris and Donald Fisher Fund gave KIPP in 2000 to start replicating, the foundation has since given the organization another $85 million.[51] Through 2013 the Walton Family Foundation had given KIPP $58.7 million;[52] the Bill and Melinda Gates Foundation, $25.4 million;[53] the Robin Hood Foundation, $21.3 million;[54] and the Tiger Foundation, $3.1 million.[55] Atlantic Philanthropies made a one-time contribution to KIPP in 2006 of $14.6 million.[56] And in recognition of KIPP's distinctive methods, the U.S. Department of Education made a one-time Investing in Innovation grant to KIPP in 2010 of $50 million to fund the organization's expansion.[57]

The impact of this support—as well as the degree of achievement of KIPP students—has been the subject of intense debate. According to a study of KIPP achievement published in 2011 by researchers at Western Michigan University (WMU), a sample of twenty-eight KIPP schools across the country in 2007–2008 received, on average, 50 percent—or $6,500—more in funding per pupil than their neighboring district schools. The WMU researchers, led by Gary Miron, the coauthor of the aforementioned critique of Edison

Schools in 2000, attributed $5,760 of that difference to philanthropic giving. In total, according to this study, these twenty-eight schools, with a combined enrollment of 6,461 students, collected $37.2 million in donations.[58]

In arriving at this advantage of $6,500 per pupil, the WMU researchers tallied only contributions made to the regional offices of KIPP to which these twenty-eight schools belonged, leaving out contributions made to the KIPP Foundation, the organization's national office, which is based in San Francisco and provides professional development and monitors quality across the network. Philanthropic giving to the KIPP Foundation in 2007–2008 amounted to $15.3 million, the researchers noted. Citing the KIPP Foundation's annual report, the researchers pointed out that the foundation estimated it had spent $1,175 per student that year on professional development, school start-up costs, and school support.[59]

Responding for KIPP to the report, spokesperson Steve Mancini fired back with a press release. Sidestepping the role played by the KIPP Foundation, Mancini argued that the WMU researchers would have arrived at a far lower sum had they collected data for all fifty-eight schools in operation in 2007–2008. "This sample of twenty-eight schools included seventy-one percent of the network's private revenue but only forty-five percent of students served in 2007–08," Mancini wrote. In addition, Mancini maintained that the WMU researchers had failed to explain that charter schools customarily use a significant portion of revenue to build or lease facilities, while district schools have no such costs in their budgets; that they had overlooked that KIPP has higher administrative expenses because it must cover the fixed costs of creating and running schools that grow one grade level a year; and, finally, that through no fault of their own, the researchers had factored in $6.6 million of public money misclassified as private revenue by KIPP Newark. In sum, Mancini concluded, philanthropic funding amounted to $2,500 per student in 2007–2008.[60]

The battle continued in the pages of the *New York Times*, with Mancini, Miron, and scholars at the Brookings Institution and the University of California at Berkeley weighing in with their opposing views. What was regardless clear is that KIPP depended heavily on philanthropic dollars, whether it was $2,500 per student or far more. After all, as Mancini explained in the *Times*, KIPP's extended day, Saturday classes, and three-week summer programs cost the organization between $1,200 and $1,600 per student.[61] Covering that cost alone demands significant philanthropic help. And that continues to be true.

In fiscal year 2011—running from July 2011 through June 2012, and the latest period for which data are available—the KIPP Foundation, for example, took in $33.9 million in philanthropic contributions, excluding government grants. In addition, regional KIPP offices took in another $102.1 million in philanthropic contributions, excluding government grants. After cumulative fund-raising expenses of $6.6 million, KIPP in sum brought in $129.4 million of funding to supplement federal, state, and local allocations. With 34,074 students in KIPP schools across the country in 2011–2012, this additional money meant—with several qualifications—an extra $3,796 per student (see Table 9.5).[62]

One qualification about this additional funding concerns location. While all regions receive funding from the KIPP Foundation, each region has its own board of directors responsible for raising money for its schools. Much as some divisions within a university raise much more money from alumni and outside benefactors than others, some KIPP regions raise much more money than other KIPP regions. The range in effectiveness of these boards is wide. The KIPP New York City board, along with boards for the individual schools within the region, for example, raised $21.7 million net in the 2010–2011 school year, with a total enrollment of 1,736 students, and $8.8 million net in the 2011–2012 school year, with a total enrollment of 2,301.[63] By contrast, the KIPP Albany board raised no money in 2010–2011, with a total enrollment of 286, and $52,500 net in 2011–2012, with a total enrollment of 283 (see Table 9.5).

In the case of large amounts raised, such as the sum collected by KIPP New York City in 2010–2011, much of the money may come from major one-time gifts for capital projects or endowments for future spending. The money is certainly not all for annual operational purposes. The difference in the effectiveness of boards just the same exposes the limits of any CMO. Raising money in Albany, Gary, Indiana, or Gaston, North Carolina, is far more difficult than doing so in New York, Houston, or Los Angeles. Even KIPP San Diego has had trouble raising money.

Table 9.5 Enrollment, funding, occupancy costs, and district charter allocations for KIPP schools by region for the school years 2010–2011 and 2011–2012

Region	Pupils	Net regional giving per pupil	KIPP Foundation net giving per pupil	Total net giving per pupil	Occupancy cost per pupil	District charter allocation per pupil
Albany, 10–11	286	$0	$1,208	$1,208	n/a	$11,712
Albany, 11–12	283	$186	$954	$1,140	$1,731	$14,072
Arkansas, 10–11	646	$1,541	$1,208	$2,749	$448	$7,031*
Arkansas, 11–12	860	$1,615	$954	$2,569	$528	$6,665*
Atlanta, 10–11	905	$4,348	$1,208	$5,556	$278	$9,275*
Atlanta, 11–12	1,231	$14,113	$954	$15,067	$735	$8,608*
Austin, 10–11	992	$2,728	$1,208	$3,936	$1,700	$8,761
Austin, 11–12	1,480	$1,475	$954	$2,429	$1,658	$8,033
Baltimore, 10–11	631	$1,328	$1,208	$2,536	$507	$9,425
Baltimore, 11–12	816	$2,729	$954	$3,683	$605	$9,264
Charlotte, 10–11	343	$1,661	$1,208	$2,869	$470	$6,700
Charlotte, 11–12	355	$1,380	$954	$2,334	$309	$4,361
Chicago, 10–11	425	$2,262	$1,208	$3,470	$809	$7,447
Chicago, 11–12	543	$3,313	$954	$4,267	$711	$7,183
Colorado, 10–11	594	$1,599	$1,208	$2,807	$487	$7,260*
Colorado, 11–12	826	$1,629	$954	$2,583	$404	$6,904*

Columbus, 10–11	210	$2,523	$1,208	$3,731	$1,142	$6,100
Columbus, 11–12	306	$625	$954	$1,579	$800	$6,200
Dallas, 10–11	307	$1,961	$1,208	$3,169	$1,596	$8,560
Dallas, 11–12	332	$5,260	$954	$6,214	$1,743	$5,929
Gary, IN, 10–11	297	$0	$1,208	$1,208	n/a	$8,195
Gaston, NC, 10–11	701	$0	$1,208	$1,208	n/a	$8,042
Gaston, NC, 11–12	709	$0	$954	$954	n/a	$7,579
Houston, 10–11	6,448	$1,299	$1,208	$2,507	$468	$9,090
Houston, 11–12	7,884	$797	$954	$1,751	$371	$8,303*
Indianapolis, 10–11	238	$0	$1,208	$1,208	$162	$7,000
Indianapolis, 11–12	265	$9,865	$954	$10,819	$689	$7,368
Jacksonville, 10–11	92	$27,660	$1,208	$28,868	n/a	n/a
Jacksonville, 11–12	176	$4,631	$954	$5,585	n/a	$5,200
Kansas City, 10–11	252	$348	$1,208	$1,556	$1,696	$7,115
Kansas City, 11–12	180	$1,842	$954	$2,796	$2,489	$9,510
Los Angeles, 10–11	1,266	$3,496	$1,208	$4,704	$1,152	$6,102*
Los Angeles, 11–12	1,671	$3,117	$954	$4,071	$1,207	$5,264*
Lynn, MA, 10–11	373	$7,159	$1,208	$8,367	n/a	$11,297
Lynn, MA, 11–12	471	$5,183	$954	$6,137	n/a	$11,517
Memphis, 10–11	398	$5,195	$1,208	$6,403	$1,190	$7,782
Memphis, 10–11	516	$1,943	$954	$2,897	$696	$7,721

(continued)

Table 9.5 (continued)

Region	Pupils	Net regional giving per pupil	KIPP Foundation net giving per pupil	Total net giving per pupil	Occupancy cost per pupil	District charter allocation per pupil
Minneapolis, 10–11	153	$4,740	$1,208	$5,948	$3,182	$11,580
Minneapolis, 10–11	158	$3,298	$954	$4,252	$3,172	$12,575
Nashville, 10–11	293	$2,499	$1,208	$3,707	$782	$8,013
Nashville, 11–12	313	$2,587	$954	$3,541	$1,004	$8,100
Newark, 10–11	1,281	$2,572	$1,208	$3,780	$1,670	$14,609
Newark, 11–12	1,497	$5,810	$954	$6,764	$1,546	$15,406
New Orleans, 10–11	1,792	$1,501	$1,208	$2,709	n/a	$7,148
New Orleans, 11–12	2,462	$971	$954	$1,925	n/a	$7,895
NYC, 10–11	1,736	$12,514	$1,208	$13,722	None	$12,443
NYC, 11–12	2,301	$3,846	$954	$4,800	None	$13,527
Okla. City, 10–11	277	$1,511	$1,208	$2,719	n/a	$5,384
Okla. City, 11–12	272	$1,683	$954	$2,637	n/a	$4,680
Philadelphia, 10–11	697	$2,535	$1,208	$3,743	$1,879	$9,634*
Philadelphia, 11–12	947	$1,839	$954	$2,793	$1,631	$10,273*
San Antonio, 10–11	731	$4,118	$1,208	$5,326	$504	$8,614*
San Antonio, 11–12	883	$362	$954	$1,316	$252	$7,771*
San Diego, 10–11	364	$93	$1,208	$1,301	$863	$6,500
San Diego, 11–12	361	$195	$954	$1,149	$875	$6,500
SF Bay Area, 10–11	2,288	$2,713	$1,208	$3,921	$458	$6,016*
SF Bay Area, 11–12	2,459	$7,398	$954	$8,352	$367	$5,936*

St. Louis, 10–11	156	$8,108	$1,208	$9,316	$1,287	$7,119
St. Louis, 11–12	254	$5,843	$954	$6,797	$1,982	$8,900
So. Fulton, GA, 10–11	321	$6,170	$1,208	$7,378	n/a	$7,956
So. Fulton, GA, 11–12	320	$2,884	$1,040	$3,924	$763	$8,016
Tulsa, 10–11	338	$3,210	$1,208	$4,418	None	$3,400
Tulsa, 11–12	317	$3,977	$954	$4,931	None	$4,092
Washington, 10–11	2,078	$2,269	$1,208	$3,477	$2,598	$13,600
Washington, 11–12	2,626	$1,344	$954	$2,298	$2,163	$14,391
2010–11 Mean	846	$2,935*	$1,208	$4,142*	$1,101	$8,403
2010–11 Total	27,909	$81,909,159	$33,702,615	$115,611,774	n/a	n/a
2010–11 Mean	1,065	$2,843*	$954	$3,796*	$1,137	$8,367
2011–12 Total	34,074	$96,858,230	$32,503,704	$129,361,934	n/a	$305,262,521

Data sources: Philanthropic figures and occupancy costs come from Form 990s filed by KIPP. Enrollment figures and basic district charter allocations by region come from KIPP's annual report cards. These figures were confirmed as correct during a meeting at KIPP headquarters on September 30, 2014, with the organization's COO, Jack Chorowsky, and managing director of finance and accounting for KIPP NYC, Charizma T. Williams.

Notes: The district charter allocations do not necessarily include supplementary funding from districts for such goods and services as textbooks, classroom supplies, transportation, and special education evaluation. The total is not listed for 2010–2011, as KIPP did not list the allocation received from Jacksonville for that year. If Jacksonville allocated the same amount per pupil to students in charter schools that it did the following year, the total would be $251 million for 2010–2011. Total occupancy costs are not available, as several regions do not list charges. Gary, Indiana, is listed only for 2010–2011, as KIPP Gary folded after that school year. Amounts followed by an asterisk are weighted averages: for KIPP regions with several schools receiving different amounts per pupil; and for net giving per pupil by region and in total. Net giving amounts exclude fund-raising expenditures and reflect annual contributions, *not* expenditures. The unweighted average for net giving per pupil by region was $3,626 in 2010–2011 and $3,147 in 2011–2012. For three regions, contributions came through more than one local KIPP authority: KIPP schools in Chicago received funds from both a nonprofit organization overseeing the schools and a nonprofit organization responsible for the region as a whole; KIPP Newark (known formally as TEAM Academy Charter Schools) received additional funds from the Friends of TEAM Academy Charter Schools; and KIPP NYC benefited to a small degree from funds raised by boards of individual schools in the local network.

A second qualification about this additional funding concerns costs of occupancy that district schools do not bear. In 2011–2012, only in New York City and Tulsa did KIPP, for example, benefit from free co-location within district buildings. In every other city in which KIPP operated, the organization built or bought buildings, or it leased space from school districts, commercial realtors, or, in eight cases across the country, local archdioceses.[64] The cost in 2011–2012, according to reports filed with the IRS by KIPP regional offices, averaged $1,137 per student and ranged from $252 per student in San Antonio to $3,172 in Minneapolis, the latter of which illustrated Mancini's point about high overhead (while KIPP Minneapolis was already in its fourth year, enrollment had grown to only 158 students, falling far short of expectations). As with philanthropic contributions, the occupancy costs the previous year were also nearly identical. The costs in 2010–2011 averaged $1,101 per student and ranged from $162 per student in Indianapolis to $3,182 in Minneapolis.[65]

More recently, according to KIPP COO Jack Chorowsky, the organization has trimmed its occupancy costs by leasing space at nominal rates in buildings constructed or owned by philanthropies. The aforementioned Robin Hood Foundation, for instance, largely funded the construction of a new home in the South Bronx for KIPP's College Prep High School. The building opened in 2013 and costs KIPP only $1 a year. The high school had outgrown its space in West Harlem allocated by the city, Chorowsky explained, and nothing appropriate was available elsewhere in the system despite years of intense efforts to find space. Robin Hood came to the rescue, he said, and similar philanthropies have negotiated similar leases with KIPP in Newark, Philadelphia, Washington, DC, Atlanta, Houston, and Los Angeles.[66] This development constitutes an invisible and welcome form of support for the organization. Yet like the philanthropic dollars it mimics, it can exist to only a finite degree, as there are only so many foundations with such capacity.

Occupancy costs accordingly consume a substantial portion of philanthropic dollars and amount to a major barrier to growth for KIPP and all charter networks. The Achievement First network, for example, had to raise from philanthropists $12 million of the $36 million needed to construct a new high school in New Haven, Connecticut, in 2014. "There's all this talk about philanthropic advantage for charter networks," said Ken Paul, Achievement First's vice president for development, upon conducting a tour of the new school in 2015. "But philanthropy just gets us to sea level."[67]

Where KIPP, Achievement First, and other networks do not have such occupancy or construction costs, its schools can operate on about the same footing as neighboring district schools. The degree to which this holds depends on the region, as some school districts are more generous to charters than others. In New York City, much as previously described in Baltimore, charter schools with free co-location got more money per pupil than district schools, according to studies in 2010 and 2011 by the New York City Independent Budget Office (IBO). This contradicted widespread claims, such as the contention by one *Wall Street Journal* columnist amid the 2013 New York City mayoral race, that charter schools in the city receive "several thousand dollars less" per pupil than neighboring traditional public schools.[68]

With Bill de Blasio vowing as a mayoral candidate to end free co-location for charter schools, charter advocates, like the columnist for the *Wall Street Journal,* fought back that charter schools already received far less funding. Basic to the case of one charter advocacy group making this argument was the complex matter of pension obligations: as teachers at traditional public schools participate in retirement programs with payments pegged to income and with guaranteed health-care benefits, future costs could far exceed current contributions and must accordingly be accounted for in determining per-pupil expenditures; by contrast, teachers in charter schools typically participate in defined-contribution retirement programs, which cannot, by their very nature, suffer from underfunding.[69]

According to officials at the IBO, the purpose of their studies was to assess "*actual* public spending in support of charters and traditional schools in a given school year, as presented in the Bloomberg Administration's financial plan." In this regard, they countered in their defense that estimates of future obligations varied too much to factor into their analysis.[70]

In the opinion of the IBO, charter schools without free co-location were indeed at a disadvantage. Using figures from the New York City Department of Education (DOE) budget for 2008–2009, the IBO explained in its 2010 report, with qualifications a year later, that charters without free co-location failed to benefit from money allocated for facilities, utilities, upkeep, and security as well as for debt service for construction of DOE buildings. The resulting contrast was $15,672 per student in traditional public schools, which comprised $2,215 in pension costs for staff as well as $2,712 spent on facilities, utilities, upkeep, security, and debt service, and $13,661 per student—or 12.8 percent less—in charter schools without free co-location.[71]

However, charter schools in 2008–2009 with free co-location received 4.5 percent—or $701—more per student, the IBO reported, for a total of $16,373. This sum comprised three parts: $12,444 per student for general education spending, which covered pension costs for staff; $1,217 in pass-through money for everything from textbooks and health-care services to classroom supplies and library materials; and the $2,712 spent on facilities, utilities, security, upkeep, and debt service.[72]

The IBO moreover implied that because charter schools without unionized staff—and most charter schools operate without union presence—are at liberty to offer less-generous pension plans, they stand to have more money for general operating purposes.[73] The IBO made a similar case about the 2009–2010 budget, with charter schools with free co-location receiving 4 percent—or $649—more per student than district schools.[74]

In a meeting to review charter school finances at the central office of the New York City DOE several months after de Blasio had taken office, Ola Duru, the DOE's director of operations for the division of charter school accountability, confirmed the IBO's assessment as accurate. Like Laura Weeldreyer, the deputy chief of staff for Baltimore's public schools, Duru is a charter advocate; she was, in fact, the founding chief of operations for a charter network in Brooklyn. And like Weeldreyer, Duru said that charters with free co-location experienced no financial disadvantage.[75]

By this point, the very issue of occupancy costs for charter schools in New York City had become moot: siding with charter advocates, Governor Andrew Cuomo had circumvented Mayor de Blasio in March and sealed a deal with Republican legislators in Albany to guarantee charter schools in New York City the most generous terms in the country: the DOE was required to make space available for free to charter schools; if the DOE could not find such space, it had to provide up to $40 million a year in funding for rental of private space.[76] By 2015, the IBO reported, funding for charter and district schools was essentially the same: charter schools with free co-location received $29 less per pupil, whereas charter schools in private space were compensated with mandated rental assistance that covered all but $139 of the difference per pupil.[77]

Philanthropic contributions to KIPP and networks like it can consequently go far in New York City. The needs are nevertheless many. In this regard, a third qualification concerning the advantage conferred KIPP by philanthropic contributions relates to KIPP Through College (KTC). For students who graduate from KIPP middle schools but don't attend one of the organization's twenty-two high schools, KTC provides college guidance, administers test prep, conducts financial aid workshops, and coordinates campus tours. Moreover, KTC provides mentoring to all former KIPP students while they're in college to help them make it through college. Funding for KTC comes from the KIPP Foundation as well as the KIPP regions. In some regions, such as New York, KTC accounts for approximately 30 percent of money raised. KTC in New York in 2014 had seventeen people on staff helping 1,036 KIPP alumni. The annual budget was $2.9 million, or $2,800 per student.[78] While KTC thus implicitly benefits KIPP schools in conveying to students that they are on the road to college, it is an alumni program and accordingly not an operational expenditure.

In sum, once the costs of occupancy and KTC are deducted from philanthropic contributions, there is little more, on average, than the $1,200 to $1,600 necessary to fund the longer school day, Saturday classes, and three-week summer programs. According to Mancini, most KIPP regions as of 2014 had, in fact, eliminated Saturday classes and cut the school day from 9.5 hours to 8.5. Mancini said that KIPP cofounder Mike Feinberg, a passionate advocate of more time in school, fought this change but relented in the face of mounting complaints from teachers about the need for more manageable schedules.[79]

10

LIMITS

They call it the KIPP burn.

Ky Adderley, founding principal, KIPP AMP,
Brooklyn, June 6, 2011, upon stepping down
after six years at the helm

■ ALONG WITH ELIMINATING or, at least, driving down occupancy costs, making the schedules of teachers more manageable is critical to the future of KIPP and similar CMOs. Much as there is a finite supply of philanthropic dollars to support KIPP's extra efforts, there is a finite supply of teachers capable, year after year, of putting in ten-hour days at school and remaining available to students in the evening and over the weekend by cell phone, as required, for homework help.[1] On top of stamina, KIPP teachers, like all teachers in underprivileged communities, need rare patience and acumen to connect with and guide students combating economic disadvantage. Of KIPP's 50,221 students in 2013–2014, 88 percent qualified for free or reduced-price lunch.[2]

Teacher retention has accordingly been a central challenge for KIPP as well as similar CMOs. The price is not merely time, energy, and money lost to recruitment and training of replacements but also quality of instruction. In a study published in 2008 of KIPP's five middle schools in the San Francisco Bay region, SRI International elucidated the degree of the problem: only 51 percent of eighty-four teachers in 2006–2007 returned in 2007–2008; 69 percent did so the year before; and 60 percent did so two years earlier.[3] By contrast, the rate of teacher retention at charter schools and at urban public schools across the country in 2008–2009, according to the National Center for Education Statistics (NCES), was 76 percent and 84 percent, respectively.[4]

The study, authorized by KIPP and funded by the William and Flora Hewlett Foundation, moreover reported that of the 121 teachers hired in total by the schools since 2003–2004, only forty-three, or 36 percent, were still in the classroom by 2007–2008, though twenty-three, or 30 percent, had continued to work for KIPP in different capacities. To KIPP administrators and teachers alike at these five schools, according to SRI, this turnover distracted staff from instructional responsibilities and undermined collaboration and innovation.[5]

Acknowledging the problem in their 2009 annual report, KIPP's national officials declared teacher retention a central priority and conceded that those KIPP schools with lower teacher turnover rates perform better.[6] This conclusion, along with the observations about teacher turnover reported by SRI, comports with abundant research. A recent example of such research is a 2013 article in the *American Educational Research Journal* entitled "How Teacher Turnover Harms Student Achievement" by Matthew Ronfeldt, Susanna Loeb, and James Wyckoff.

In studying the effect of teacher turnover on 850,000 fourth- and fifth-grade students in New York City schools over eight years, Ronfeldt and his coauthors found that teacher turnover had a significantly negative impact on student performance in both math and reading and, moreover, proved especially harmful in schools with higher proportions of low-achieving students. According to the authors of this study and many other scholars whose work they cite, the explanation for the negative impact of high teacher turnover appears to derive not only from insufficient experience of new teachers but also from inadequate institutional stability, in turn fundamental to fostering cooperation among colleagues, nurturing new faculty, and developing trust with students. Whether teachers individually peak in their effectiveness after seven or eight years as classroom instructors, as some scholars have claimed, is beside the point, according to Ronfeldt and his coauthors: students and young teachers alike benefit from the guidance of veteran faculty.[7]

KIPP officials in their 2009 annual report noted progress since 2006–2007, with an increase of teacher retention from 62 percent to 69 percent across the country, and pointed out that an additional 6 percent of teachers in 2009 stayed within the KIPP network, some taking teaching positions at different

KIPP schools and others taking on administrative responsibilities.[8] To KIPP's great credit, the organization has been forthcoming about this problem. Since the publication of the SRI study in 2008, KIPP has documented in its annual reports the teacher retention rate for nearly every region. Yet the commitment of KIPP officials to improve retention has run up against the stubborn reality of how hard it is to keep teachers on staff while demanding so much of them. According to data drawn from its annual reports, the weighted teacher retention rate for KIPP schools was 73 percent in 2010–2011; 69 percent in 2011–2012; 69 percent again in 2012–2013; and 68 percent in 2013–2014 (see Table 10.1).[9]

KIPP's struggle appears to mirror that of other ambitious CMOs set on radically improving the lives of underprivileged children. While no other CMO has reported teacher retention data in such detail,[10] the New York City Charter School Center (NYCCSC) reported numbers for charter schools in the city for 2006–2007 through 2010–2011 that reflect those of KIPP: 69 percent in 2006–2007; 73 percent in 2007–2008; 67 percent in 2008–2009; 74 percent in 2009–2010; and 70 percent in 2010–2011. For comparative purposes, the NYCCSC also reported teacher retention rates for the city's district schools for the same years: 84 percent in both 2006–2007 and 2007–2008; 86 percent in 2008–2009; and 87 percent in both 2009–2010 and 2010–2011.[11] For the nation as a whole, according to NCES, teacher retention in 2012–2013 was 82 percent at both charter schools and urban public schools.[12]

Though Achievement First has not published teacher retention data, the CMO did upon request provide numbers for its schools for 2012–2014 (see Table 10.2). Like KIPP, Achievement First employs the "no excuses" model, placing great demands on its teachers as well as students. However, unlike KIPP and much like Mastery, Achievement First grew far more gradually, comprises a much smaller number of schools (twenty-nine in 2014–2015 in contrast to 162 for KIPP), is concentrated in one region (spreading from Brooklyn to Providence, Rhode Island), and utilizes a significantly tighter administrative and curricular philosophy, with member schools functioning as subdivisions rather than relatively autonomous affiliates, as in the case of KIPP. Achievement First's slightly better numbers appear to reflect both these advantages and limitations.

Table 10.1 Number of teachers by KIPP region and the percentage of those who returned to the classroom at the same school the following year

Region	2009–10		2010–11		2011–12		2012–13		2013–14	
	Teachers	Retained	Teachers	Retained	Teachers	Retained	Teachers	Retained	Teachers	Retained
Arkansas	41	71%	42	70%	61	69%	78	57%	80	59%
Bay Area, CA	122	71%	127	66%	134	74%	133	71%	150	69%
Los Angeles, CA	58	77%	79	80%	97	72%	129	85%	163	73%
Colorado	31	64%	42	64%	56	70%	67	43%	72	67%
Washington, DC	129	58%	166	64%	222	64%	253	67%	311	70%
Jacksonville, FL	n/a	n/a	n/a	n/a	12	71%	n/a	n/a	43	63%
Atlanta, GA	47	69%	62	77%	77	72%	110	78%	140	67%
Chicago, IL	37	57%	28	68%	35	58%	45	67%	61	82%
New Orleans, LA	84	86%	159	78%	186	75%	245	66%	252	65%
Baltimore, MD	30	54%	48	84%	62	86%	74	73%	86	73%
Massachusetts	n/a	n/a	28	73%	40	78%	61	80%	81	83%
St. Louis, MO	n/a	n/a	12	100%	16	64%	n/a	n/a	n/a	n/a
Newark, NJ	93	79%	118	84%	130	84%	168	81%	195	85%
New York, NY	106	70%	148	85%	186	74%	243	81%	286	73%
Gaston, NC	n/a	n/a	n/a	n/a	47	54%	53	61%	58	70%
Philadelphia, PA	27	43%	47	68%	72	75%	83	59%	99	72%

(continued)

Table 10.1 (continued)

Region	2009–10		2010–11		2011–12		2012–13		2013–14	
	Teachers	Retained	Teachers	Retained	Teachers	Retained	Teachers	Retained	Teachers	Retained
Memphis, TN	27	71%	28	65%	31	48%	49	39%	79	42%
Nashville, TN	n/a	n/a	n/a	n/a	22	42%	n/a	n/a	n/a	n/a
Austin, TX	43	69%	63	77%	85	74%	124	60%	180	63%
Dallas, TX	n/a	n/a	17	61%	16	78%	n/a	n/a	n/a	n/a
Houston, TX	293	71%	366	68%	428	62%	507	65%	567	60%
San Antonio, TX	33	67%	46	59%	58	47%	82	76%	98	60%
Teacher total	1,201		1,626		2,073		2,504		3,001	
Returnees	836		1,183		1,429		1,727		2,032	
Mean retention by region		67.4%		73.2%		67.8%		67.2%		68.2%
Weighted retention		69.6%		72.8%		68.9%		69.0%		67.7%

Data source: All data were derived from KIPP's annual report cards, accessed at http://www.kipp.org/reportcard.

Notes: Mean retention is defined by region. Rates of retention of staff within the organization as teachers at different schools or in non-instructional capacities were significantly higher. For 2012–2014, only regions with two or more schools reported retention data. The weighted rates of within-network retention were 75.4 percent in 2009–2010, 79.7 percent in 2010–2011, 74.8 percent in 2011–2012, 74.9 percent in 2012–2013, and 74.4 percent in 2013–2014.

Table 10.2 Number of teachers by Achievement First region and the percentage of
those who returned to the classroom at the same school the following year

Region	2012–13		2013–14	
	Teachers	Retained	Teachers	Retained
Bridgeport, CT	52	83%	62	68%
Hartford, CT	69	75%	78	69%
New Haven, CT	125	74%	135	74%
Brooklyn, NY	346	77%	417	75%
Providence, RI	n/a	n/a	14	100%
Teacher total	592		706	
Returnees	454		522	
Mean retention by school	76.1%		75.4%	
Weighted retention	76.7%		73.9%	

Data source: Data obtained from Tracey Geller, director, human capital, Achievement First,
by e-mail, July 9, 2015.

Notes: Mean retention is defined by school rather than region because of the small number
of regions (Achievement First comprised twenty-two schools in 2012–2013 and twenty-five
schools in 2013–2014). Rates of retention of staff within the organization as teachers at different
schools or in noninstructional capacities were marginally higher. The weighted rates of
within-network retention were 77% percent in 2012–2013 and 76.6% percent in 2013–2014.

Yet the numbers for Achievement First were still low. For 2013–2014, for
example, the average retention rate for the CMO's twenty-five schools was
75.4 percent. At that rate, only 32.3 percent of teachers would be working at
the same school four years later. For KIPP, with a retention rate of 68.2 percent
per school in 2013–2014, the portion four years later would be 21.6 percent.[13]

■

For KIPP, the struggle with teacher retention has varied both by region and
by year for each region. Moreover, KIPP's struggle varies within region by
school, something KIPP's annual report cards do not capture, yet something
made clear through school visits and interviews. In New York City, for
example, the organization's four middle schools exhibited significantly
different rates of teacher retention from 2005–2006 to 2008–2009. KIPP
Academy, located in the Bronx and founded by Dave Levin in 1995 as the

network's second school, experienced hardly any teacher turnover over these three years: only two of twenty-one teachers moved on.[14] Likewise, at KIPP Infinity, located in West Harlem and founded in 2005, only two of twenty teachers over the same three years departed.[15] However, at KIPP STAR (which stands for Success Through Achievement and Responsibility), located in nearby Morningside Heights and founded in 2003, ten of twenty-one teachers left after both the 2006–2007 and 2007–2008 school years.[16] And at KIPP AMP (an acronym for Always Mentally Prepared), located in the Crown Heights section of Brooklyn and founded in 2005, teacher turnover was also repeatedly high. By 2010–2011, only two of the twenty-six teachers on staff, along with the principal, remained from the founding faculty six years earlier.

Both teachers—Fabiano Pinheiro and Nicole Lavonne Smith—taught a combination of Portuguese and capoeira, the Brazilian martial art blending music, dance, acrobatics, and combat. Following the final day of summer school in July 2011 while overseeing dismissal from the sidewalk, Smith said that she would not have lasted as a strictly academic teacher. She explained that the pressure involved in prepping for academic classes, grading assignments, helping students by phone at night with their homework, and getting them ready for annual state exams in reading and math would have in time worn her out. By contrast, in teaching capoeira, Smith said, she got to help students let go and exhale; and in teaching Portuguese, she got to broaden their understanding of language and culture without regard to year-end standardized exams.[17]

For its focus as well as its location, KIPP AMP at that time stood out among KIPP schools. KIPP AMP was defined by capoeira. All students had to study capoeira. Pinheiro, a Brazilian native and capoeira master, and Smith, a native New Yorker who learned Portuguese while doing graduate work in Brazil, were accordingly core members of the faculty. And the school used capoeira not only as a form of physical education but also as a prism for understanding history, anthropology, and aesthetics.

After the 2011–2012 school year, however, capoeira was history. And Pinheiro and Smith were no longer on staff. The dance studio was converted into an additional classroom, and Portuguese was cut from the curriculum. The purpose of this change was to focus on math and reading and at the same time boost results on the state-mandated tests in those subjects. KIPP AMP became another "no excuses" charter school, leaving many students, according to several teachers, without an athletic and aesthetic outlet they craved.[18]

Anastasia Michals, a math teacher at KIPP AMP from 2009 through 2013, recalled a year after leaving the school that shutting down the capoeira program hurt, in particular, students who struggled in the classroom. "Capoeira was far more than physical education," said Michals, who has a keen appreciation for sports. She played both soccer and lacrosse at Bryn Mawr College, where she majored in economics and minored in mathematics before heading into teaching through Teach for America (TFA) in 2005. "Capoeira built cultural awareness," she said, "with trips to dance events across the city, and instilled self-confidence, especially in students having troubles academically. Capoeira got these students excited about school."[19]

Much like capoeira, the neighborhood around KIPP AMP is a rare mix. KIPP AMP is situated on the top floor of a four-story building it shares with two district middle schools, M.S. 334 and M.S. 354. Across Park Place to the north is Albany Houses, a project comprising nine identical red-brick highrise apartment buildings symmetrically placed amid two blocks of lawns and trees. Across Sterling Place to the south stretches a neighborhood of Caribbean restaurants, beauty salons, corner markets, brownstones both renovated and weathered, and myriad churches, from the stately neo-Gothic Bethany Methodist Church on St. Johns Place to such humble storefront congregations as the Mount Olive Primitive Baptist Church, the Open Door Church of God in Christ, and Jordan's Holy Temple Pentecostal Church. Three blocks to the west is a bustling Hasidic Jewish community anchored by yeshivas and synagogues.

Cultural texture nevertheless did not mean safety. The streets could be dangerous. A fourteen-year-old boy was shot dead in front of a bodega around the corner from the school early on the evening of June 1, 2011.[20] Because the murder was gang related and because several students in M.S. 334 and M.S. 354 either belonged to rival gangs or had siblings in rival gangs, police stood in the lobby and on every stairwell landing for the next week.[21]

■

KIPP AMP was the vision of Ky Adderley, the founding principal, who stepped down after six years at the helm in June 2011. His successor, Debon

Lewis, who cut the capoeira program, would step down three years later amid a swirl of uncertainty.[22] "They call it the KIPP burn," Adderley said.[23] The burn for Adderley did not merely concern exhaustion. The burn was also personal.

Adderley, an All-American middle-distance runner at Georgetown University with broad shoulders and an infectious smile, had poured himself into his job. As a principal, he continued to radiate the poise and determination of an athlete driven to win. That drive was in his family. His father, Nelson Adderley, played halfback at Ohio State and then for the Toronto Argonauts of the Canadian Football League; his uncle Herb Adderley played halfback at Michigan State and then became a Hall of Fame cornerback for the Green Bay Packers and the Dallas Cowboys. Ky played youth football but opted for track as a teenager at Central High School in his native Philadelphia. He loved the freedom of running, he said.[24]

After earning a bachelor's degree in psychology in 1998, Adderley stayed at Georgetown to train for the 2000 Olympic trials while working part-time as a research assistant for Jens Ludwig, a professor of economics and an expert on urban affairs, and studying for a master's degree in education and social policy. A strained Achilles tendon kept Adderley from competing in the Olympic trials. He completed his master's in 2001 and then went into teaching through TFA, the path taken by Mike Feinberg, Levin, and countless KIPP leaders. Adderley taught eighth grade for three years in Washington, D.C., before winning a fellowship funded by the Fisher family to become a KIPP principal. As a Fisher Fellow, Adderley developed the capoeira-based curriculum that distinguished KIPP AMP. He bought an apartment three blocks from the school and made KIPP AMP his life.[25]

Monday through Friday, Adderley dressed in a suit and tie, circled the neighborhood on his orange mountain bike every morning between 7:00 and 7:20 to herd students to school on time and every afternoon following dismissal to supervise their return home, and worked late afterward in his office. To ensure the punctuality of his students, he negotiated a deal with the proprietors of the corner markets in the neighborhood not to sell to them in the morning. Adderley's only break came in the middle of the day when he returned home briefly to walk his Rhodesian ridgeback, named Shango after an African deity.[26]

Adderley had expected everyone on staff to work as hard and obediently follow his lead. Teachers were expected to be in the building from 7:00 a.m., thirty minutes before the arrival of students, to 5:00 p.m., and to adhere without question to school practice.[27] In a revolt that made the pages of the *New York Daily News* and the *New York Times,* teachers protested in January 2009, in the school's fourth year, that they were overworked, unheard, and ready to unionize. While KIPP teachers are paid approximately 20 percent more than their district counterparts for the extra hours they must put in,[28] teachers at KIPP AMP alleged that the expectations were nevertheless unrealistic and their lack of administrative input unacceptable. "We're looking to promote the kind of teaching environment that people can stay in," Kashi Nelson, a social studies teacher, said in the *Daily News.*[29] Her colleague Luisa Bonifacio, a reading teacher, made the same case the same day in the *Times:* "It's a matter of sustainability for teachers."[30] The breaking point for the teachers came with the dismissal of two colleagues without explanation to the staff.[31] According to Bonifacio, the *Times* reported, fifteen of the school's twenty-two teachers had signed cards for unionization.[32] Three months later, in April, the KIPP AMP staff joined the United Federation of Teachers (UFT).[33]

Much of 2008–2009, Adderley was helping run the KIPP regional office while two junior colleagues managed day-to-day affairs at KIPP AMP. In September 2009, Adderley returned to KIPP AMP full time. The teachers ultimately voted in April 2010 to opt out of the UFT;[34] a court-ordered revote of this decertification in November 2010 generated the same result.[35] Adderley just the same felt bitter, he recalled in his final month at the school, and decided to move on. He considered offers to start a new KIPP school in Philadelphia or Dallas but declined. "Starting a KIPP is consuming," Adderley said. "It takes one year to plan and three years to get going." He instead took a job in Rio de Janeiro as an education consultant advising foundations dedicated to helping underprivileged Brazilian children.[36]

Among those who left KIPP AMP in 2009 following the turmoil that led to the campaign for unionization was Yabome Kabia, a charismatic math teacher who had grown up in East Lansing, Michigan, and earned a bachelor's degree at Boston College with majors in economics and sociology. Through the New York City Teaching Fellows program, an alternate route to certification for public school teachers, Kabia taught math for three years at the Theater Arts Production Company School, known as Tapco, in the Bronx and simultaneously earned a master's degree in math instruction at City College of New York. Kabia then taught for two years at KIPP San Francisco Bay Academy before joining the KIPP AMP faculty in September 2008. Within six weeks at KIPP AMP, Kabia expressed concern about burnout. "I certainly would not be able to do this job with a family," she said after teaching algebra to a class of twenty-six eighth-graders and urging students to call her in the evening if they needed any help with their homework.[37] Several months later, Kabia was one of the KIPP AMP teachers to vote for UFT affiliation.[38]

The following year, Kabia was teaching at the Berkeley Carroll School, a private school with smaller classes and a more manageable schedule in Park Slope, two miles and several income brackets away. Reflecting five years after her departure from KIPP AMP during a free period at Berkeley Carroll in October 2014, Kabia, who had since married and now had a seventeen-month-old girl, said the difference with teaching at Berkeley Carroll was not merely the workload. Kabia said the environment was far more harmonious, but the same was true, she added, of KIPP San Francisco Bay Academy. "KIPP is not one entity," Kabia said.[39] This is true of finances, as previously explained. It is also true of climate as well as academic results.

Like separate units in any large organization, some KIPP schools work better than others. And some fold. Although KIPP's growth has been impressive, scaling up the organization has involved strife and failure as well as success and thus exposed the difficulty of expanding such a demanding model of schooling. Of the forty-three KIPP middle schools opened between 2002 and 2006, eight had closed by 2010 and two broke away because of philosophical differences. Those ten schools were located in cities large and small across the country: Annapolis, Maryland; Asheville, North Carolina; Atlanta; Buffalo; Camden, New Jersey; Chicago; Fresno; Gary, Indiana; and Sacramento.[40]

While KIPP AMP marched on, teacher turnover indicated trouble. Michals, who went on to become the dean of students at an Ascend Learning charter school in the Canarsie section of Brooklyn, said the churn undermined the development of curricula as well as school culture. "Every year, we felt like we were starting over," she said. "We couldn't build momentum."[41]

In particular, there were few veteran teachers to provide guidance to young faculty. When asked during the summer session of 2011 what kind of support he received from senior colleagues in his department, a social studies teacher in his second year at KIPP AMP, who was struggling to reach some reluctant students, said he had no senior colleagues in his department.[42]

■

Some turnover was the necessary price of KIPP's expansion, as the organization needs talented KIPP teachers to take on administrative roles at new schools. Among those who joined Adderley in leaving in 2011, in this light, was Emily Carroll, a firm but gentle fifth-grade teacher. Carroll had grown up in Chicago attending the highly regarded progressive University of Chicago Laboratory Schools, studied political science at Washington University in St. Louis, taught for two years in a public school in the Bronx through TFA, taught for two more years at an Achievement First charter school in the Bedford-Stuyvesant section of Brooklyn, and then earned a master's in education policy at Harvard before joining the staff of KIPP AMP. It was Carroll's second year at the school. On the final day of the school year, Carroll explained to her students that she would be leaving to train at New York University as a Fisher Fellow, like Adderley before her, to become a KIPP principal. A visibly disappointed girl shot her hand up and waited to be acknowledged. "You said at the beginning of the year you were going to stay with us." Carroll winced: "Yes, but this opportunity came up." Unappeased, another student chimed in without waiting to be called on: "You're leaving already, after only two years?" While Carroll would be back a year later as the founding principal of the KIPP AMP Elementary School, the middle school at a time of transition and instability had in the process lost a fine teacher whose competence would be hard to match and whose relationships developed over two years with students and colleagues could not be matched.[43]

Another teacher leaving in 2011, Antonia Phillip, would be neither returning as a teacher nor staying within the organization in a different capacity. Phillip was a science teacher who had grown up in Trinidad attending a Catholic school for girls. She earned a bachelor's degree in biology from Howard University, taught for one year at the Match Public Charter School in Boston, and joined the staff of KIPP AMP in 2010. It was Phillip's only year at a KIPP school and, she said, it would be her last. Phillip said she knew by January that the fit was not right. "You have to have a warrior spirit to teach at KIPP," Phillip said as she packed her belongings in June. "I don't have a warrior spirit."[44]

It was not merely the long hours but also the intensity of KIPP's mission, Phillip explained, that required this warrior spirit.[45] The ubiquitous posters exhorting good behavior at KIPP AMP as well as at KIPP Academy, KIPP Infinity, KIPP STAR, and KIPP schools visited in Baltimore, Los Angeles, and San Diego provided an obvious but superficial indication of this intensity. The silent single-file lines of students between classes, the stern mien of many teachers, the rigid pedagogy in many classrooms, the relentless focus on test results, and the strict codes of conduct echoing the ubiquitous exhortatory posters gave everyday form to this intensity.

In hallways, classrooms, and stairwells, these posters articulate an array of moral reminders and morale boosters:

- DREAM IT! DO IT!
- All of US WILL LEARN!!!
- Climb the MOUNTAIN to and through COLLEGE!
- KIPPsters DO THE RIGHT thing because it's the RIGHT thing to do!
- Find a way or make one.
- KIPPsters leave a place cleaner than they found it.
- Know self. Be proud.
- KIPP CREDO
  If there is a problem, we look for a solution.
  If there is a better way, we try to find it.
  If we need help, we ask.
  If a teammate needs help, we give.
- Be Nice. Work Hard. [This inversion of the KIPP motto echoes the original formulation conceived by Rafe Esquith, a legendary elementary school teacher in Los Angeles who mentored Feinberg and Levin; Levin preferred the original sequence, but Feinberg liked the inversion and prevailed in making it the motto for the organization as a whole, except in New York, Levin's domain.][46]

- There are <u>NO SHORTCUTS!!</u> [This was Esquith's trademark slogan and became the title of his memoir.][47]

Dovetailing with these posters at KIPP AMP was "The AMP 6," the school's core principles for behavior:

1. SSLANT. (This is an acronym shared by all KIPP schools as a code of conduct for students in class: Smile, Sit up, Listen, Ask and answer questions, Nod your head [if you understand], and Track the speaker [that is, follow the speaker with your eyes].)
2. PETSY. (This acronym is widely shared by KIPP schools and covers the basic words for proper dialogue: Please, Excuse me, Thank you, Sorry, and Yes, not yeah or huh [though some at KIPP consider Y to stand for You're welcome].)
3. Dress code: belt; shirt tucked in; no jewelry.
4. Follow directions the first time.
5. SHUT UP is a curse word.
6. Questions require respectful responses: no sucking teeth or heavy sighs; no rolling eyes or turning away.

Similar posters appear in the hallways, stairwells, and classrooms of schools run by Mastery. Mastery's mission statement and code of conduct are complementary lobby fixtures.[48]

Our Mission:
All Students Learn The Academic
And Personal Skills They Need
To Succeed In Higher Education,
Compete In The Global Economy,
And Pursue Their Dreams.

Code of Conduct:
I choose to be here!
I am here to Learn and Achieve!
I am responsible for my Actions!
I contribute to a Safe, Respectful, Cooperative
    Community!

I come with a clear mind and a healthy body!
This is OUR school, WE make it Shine!

In Achievement First schools, signage affirming the network's mission is pervasive.[49] The network's core values, similar to KIPP's five pillars, are captured with the acronym REACH: Respect, Enthusiasm, Achievement, Citizenship, and Hard Work. As in KIPP schools, posters everywhere reinforce the core values with a range of adages, prescriptions, and vows:

- If you want it, you can have it. SUCCESS STARTS HERE AND NOW!
- WHATEVER IT TAKES
- TEAM Always Beats Individual
- Many Minds, One Mission
- EDUCATION = FREEDOM
- Sweat the Small Stuff
- TEAM WORK MAKES THE DREAM WORK
- FOCUS. DRIVE. SUCCEED.
- Give Back
- Envision Success
- OWN IT. FIX IT. LEARN FROM IT.
- Read, Baby, Read.—Harriett Ball [a legendary veteran teacher in Houston's Bastian Elementary School who inspired Levin as a novice instructor across the hall in 1992 to set high expectations, prepare diligently, and integrate chants as devices for bonding as well as learning][50]
- Education is not received. It is ACHIEVED.
- The HARDER I work, the luckier I get.—Samuel Goldwyn
- Excellence is a Habit.
- I am happy for knowledge to get me to college!
- If my mind can conceive it, and my heart can believe it, then I can achieve it.—Muhammad Ali
- We are the change we seek.—Barack Obama
- Until we get equality in education, we won't have an equal society.—Justice Sonia Sotomayor
- ¡Si Se Puede!—Cesar Chavez

- Be Nice. Work Hard. [As at KIPP AMP, this sequence echoed Rafe Esquith's formulation.]
- If There's A Problem, WE SOLVE IT.
  If There's A Wrong, WE RIGHT IT.
  If There's A Hurt, WE HEAL IT.
  If There's A Mountain, WE CLIMB IT.[51]

On top of the long hours, the task of imposing an exacting code of conduct can be exhausting. Teachers at KIPP, Mastery, and CMOs like it are far more than conventional academic instructors. They are also coaches responsible for relentlessly modeling and molding behavior. More to Phillip's point, they are soldiers on the front lines of the war on poverty, carrying on the war launched in 1964 by President Lyndon B. Johnson in the name of his so-called Great Society.[52] But this is a war steered as much by philanthropists as government officials and seen primarily through a cultural rather than structural or economic prism. Resources clearly matter to make KIPP and similar CMOs work. The longer day, strong music programs, heavy professional development, and three weeks of summer school would not otherwise exist. But what drives and defines these CMOs is a "no excuses" philosophy of hard work and probity.

Much as many teachers struggle to enforce these expectations, many students chafe under them. In discussing all the rules during a break at Simon Gratz High, a notoriously troubled school in North Philadelphia taken over by Mastery in 2011, three junior boys in the spring of 2014 gave voice to different perspectives. One complained about the strict dress code and the lanyard all students had to wear with an attached card to record attendance, homework completion, and any demerits for misconduct or tardiness. "I am so tired of all the rules, all the demerits," he said. Another countered in defense of Mastery: "They're trying to prepare you for life. You can't be late in real life. You can't show up to work with your shirt untucked in real life. You have to be right, look right." The third, a 6'1" tight end on the school football team who had transferred the year before from John Bartram High School in Southwest Philadelphia, found common ground with his classmates: "I don't like the rules either, but I feel safe here. You can focus on your learning. At Bartram, you had to worry about your safety." The second student concurred: "True, true. There's no drama here, no violence."[53]

For this philosophy of "no excuses," KIPP, Mastery, and similar CMOs constitute, in essence, a cultural response to the Coleman Report of 1966, which famously concluded that the achievement gap was explained more by differences at home than at school.[54] With its longer day and steep behavioral expectations in particular, these CMOs strive zealously to compensate at school for what is not taking place at home and in the community at large. LuQuan Graham, a guidance counselor at KIPP Infinity in West Harlem, made this purpose plain. "The day has to be long to keep kids off the street and away from TV," he said. "I saw *Family Guy* [a satirical animated sitcom on Fox] the other night and was horrified. Our students need to be too busy to watch that stuff."[55]

Graham's conviction comports with a signature story in KIPP lore. In KIPP's second year, Mike Feinberg could not get a fifth-grade student in Houston named Abby to do her homework. Feinberg went to Abby's home and learned from her mother that Abby spent all her time watching TV. Feinberg urged the mother to keep the TV off until Abby completed her homework. The mother agreed. When Abby showed up the next day without her homework, Feinberg returned to the home and proposed he take the family TV and keep it at school until Abby consistently did her homework. The mother protested that it was the family's only TV. Feinberg replied that if she would not give him the TV, Abby was out of KIPP. The mother consented, Abby cried, and Feinberg took the TV. Feinberg returned it three weeks later following Abby's consistent completion of her homework.[56]

Such extreme effort is the exception among KIPP teachers, but it captures the mission of the organization and what Phillip identified as the warrior spirit. The same spirit is required of teachers to enforce KIPP's rules day after day as well as work such long hours. When Auriel Watson, an eighth-grade English teacher at KIPP STAR, ten blocks south of KIPP Infinity, heard students talking while walking in single file behind her up three flights of stairs from the cafeteria to class following lunch, she marched them back to the cafeteria and sternly lectured the group that not a peep should be uttered during such transitions. When someone in line giggled several minutes later just as the group was about to exit the stairwell, Watson again marched them back to the cafeteria. The process took ten minutes, but Watson later said it was time necessarily spent.[57]

Teachers in class likewise typically make methodical use of the organization's trademark acronym, SSLANT. They habitually pepper their lessons with behavioral reminders, telling students to smile, sit up, listen, nod in acknowledgment of something understood, and track the eyes of the speaker, all while breaking down a quadratic equation, explaining mitosis, or diagramming a sentence.

Not all KIPP teachers adhere to this routine. Frank Corcoran, a math teacher at KIPP Academy in the Bronx from the beginning, in 1995, and the school's principal since 2011, used none of it in the course of two ninety-minute classes observed in 2008. Corcoran did not need it. He is a master teacher with the presence of a grounded veteran.[58] Like Feinberg and Levin, with whom he lived in Houston as a fellow novice teacher, Corcoran came into education through TFA. He grew up in Rhode Island and majored in history, with a concentration in peace studies, at the University of Notre Dame. With a passion for social justice, he considered entering the priesthood but chose instead to go into public education.[59] Yet, while Corcoran could teach without concern for behavioral issues because of his magical command of the classroom, the long day alone proved challenging.[60]

As KIPP was Adderley's life, so it has been Corcoran's. Single and without children, he lived two blocks from KIPP Academy, had an extra bedroom in his apartment for former students in need of a place to stay, and arrived at school at 6:30 a.m. and stayed till 6:30 p.m. By 2007, Corcoran said, he had concluded that the workload was too much. "I'm struggling with sustainability," he said following the two observed math classes. "I pay former students who are now in high school to grade tests. They stop by on Friday afternoon. I treat them to dinner, pay them $25 or $50 for the grading help. I started doing this last year. I can't do the grading anymore. And I pay some former students to tutor, as well."[61]

Corcoran figured out a way to cope and stayed. But he is an outlier among outliers, profiled, in fact, as an exceptional teacher in Malcolm Gladwell's chapter on KIPP in his book *Outliers*.[62] For the vast majority of KIPP teachers, especially those with families, the long day and rigorous disciplinary code they must enforce are together too much. Some KIPP principals have devised flexible schedules to give teachers more freedom and thus make their jobs more manageable. As principal, Corcoran stuck to tradition, contending that he could not require students to be in school for nine and a half hours a day while not demanding the same of teachers.[63] However, Joseph Negron, the principal of KIPP Infinity, for example, constructed a schedule allowing teachers one late start (at 9 a.m. rather than 7 a.m.) and one early departure (at 3 p.m. rather than 5 p.m.) per week.[64] To accomplish more than that, KIPP would need more money to hire more teachers so they could work staggered schedules.

The day at Mastery schools is likewise long but not as long as at KIPP schools. The school day runs from 8 a.m. to 3 p.m., with office hours and tutorials running until 4 p.m., though many teachers arrive early and stay late to prepare for classes and meet with colleagues. Furthermore, unlike KIPP teachers, Mastery teachers are not expected to be available by cell phone for homework help in the evening. In addition, teaching on Saturday mornings has from the beginning been optional and comes with extra pay. The same holds for the three-week summer session. At KIPP, the summer session is mandatory for all students and teachers. At Mastery, it is only for students who failed a course; and, as with classes on Saturday mornings, teaching in the summer is optional and comes with extra pay.[65]

"We've learned a lot from KIPP," said Scott Gordon, Mastery's CEO and founder. "But we're quite different. We're concentrated in one area and operate like a small school district. And we've designed our model with a long-term plan in mind. A central question for us is, 'Can people continue to work here ten years from now with families of their own?'"[66]

Mastery does not issue official data on teacher retention. According to Joseph Ferguson, Mastery's COO, the annual retention rate from 2009 through 2014 has been approximately 85 percent: about 8 percent of teachers are not invited back; and about 7 percent decide not to return.[67] Nevertheless, of nineteen Mastery teachers who filled out anonymous questionnaires in May 2014 regarding the duties, challenges, and rewards of their jobs, eleven wrote that they struggled to make time for their personal lives. (The question read: "What are your chief challenges at Mastery?")[68]

"There is NO work-life balance," wrote a teacher in his or her fifth year of teaching and third with Mastery. This teacher explained that he or she taught four fifty-five-minute literature classes a day with more than thirty students in each class and could not keep up with grading papers. "One of the areas students consistently need drastic help in," this teacher wrote, "is with their written expression, and I cannot read all of their writing with the turnaround time that is also necessary." A fellow teacher in his or her sixth year of teaching and third with Mastery explained that he or she loved his or her work but could not foresee remaining in the position for long: "Ultimately, this [work] is not sustainable. For any real and significant change to happen, society needs to change."[69] A third teacher, in his or her tenth year of teaching and eighth with Mastery, expressed similar concern about work-life balance and explained, "The fight against poverty and its impact on our community is daunting."[70]

Six teachers cited the strain of enforcing the code of conduct as a chief challenge. At Mastery, this task involves not only the conventional regulation of behavior but also the marking of the aforementioned merit cards of each student each period to document deportment as well as attendance, punctuality, and homework completion. In a characteristic exchange at the end of a period, a ninth-grade English teacher at Shoemaker named Christopher Hilpl looked a student square in the eye upon returning her card with a demerit for chatting in class and said, "I know you know how to be. You need to get some grit."[71]

In focusing on grit, Hilpl and his Mastery colleagues have adopted the language of KIPP. Alongside KIPP's five pillars—high expectations, choice and commitment, more time, power to lead, and focus on results—grit had become an unofficial sixth pillar and perhaps its most controversial.

Upon seeing year after year that many academically gifted KIPP middle school alumni did not fare as well in high school and college as less talented but more diligent and socially competent classmates, Dave Levin in 2005 consulted Martin Seligman, a professor of psychology at the University of Pennsylvania and a prolific analyst of character, and then immersed himself in studies of mindset and perseverance. KIPP's goal for all of its students was that they graduate from college. A student entering fifth grade at a middle school in 1999, for instance, was accordingly not considered a member of the class of 2003 of that middle school but rather of 2011 of some college to be determined. It was already clear to Levin by 2005, however, that many KIPP alumni would not graduate from college.[72]

In 2011 KIPP issued a report entitled "The Promise of College Completion: KIPP's Early Successes and Challenges." The report stated that only 33 percent of students who had finished KIPP middle school ten or more years earlier went on to graduate from college. Although this surpassed the national average of 31 percent for all students across the country who had earned a bachelor's degree by the age of twenty-nine and far exceeded the average of 8 percent for twenty-nine-year-olds coming from the same cohort of low-income families as KIPP students, it fell far short of what Levin and Feinberg had envisioned.[73]

"Nearly two decades ago, KIPP was built on a promise: helping 47 fifth-graders from low-income families climb the mountain to and through college," the two cofounders wrote in the report's foreword, coauthored with Richard Barth, KIPP's CEO. "Reaching this challenging goal has proved even more difficult than we originally thought." While acknowledging that KIPP students had outperformed students across the country and especially students from the same background, Feinberg, Levin, and Barth concluded that KIPP alumni should graduate from college at the same rate as students from the top economic quartile. That rate was 75 percent. Anything less, they maintained, was unfair to the disadvantaged children KIPP served.[74]

To that end, Levin worked with Seligman's junior colleague Angela Duckworth to develop a "character growth" report card with eight categories, in turn broken down into twenty-four subcategories, all graded on a scale of 1 to 5: grit, zest, academic self-control, interpersonal self-control, optimism, curiosity, gratitude, and social intelligence.[75]

Grit on the initial iteration of this report card,[76] for example, was computed as the average of scores for three criteria:

- Finishes whatever he or she begins
- Tries very hard even after experiencing failure
- Works independently with focus

Academic self-control was computed as the average of scores for four criteria:

- Comes to class prepared
- Pays attention and resists distractions
- Remembers and follows directions
- Gets to work right away rather than procrastinating

Interpersonal self-control was computed as the average of scores for another four criteria:

- Remains calm even when criticized or otherwise provoked
- Allows others to speak without interruption
- Is polite to adults and peers
- Keeps his/her temper in check

With this report card and a conventional report card, students in some KIPP schools started in 2012 to earn a character point average (CPA) each quarter as well as a standard grade point average (GPA). Moreover, Levin instructed teachers not only to address student conduct in these terms (just as Hilpl did at Mastery's Shoemaker campus) but also to integrate messages about character into their lesson plans, from word problems in math classes to plot analyses in literature classes.[77]

To several observers, Duckworth and Levin had made too much of grit in particular, and of formal character assessment in general. To researchers at the University of Texas and Yale who independently studied the relationship between grit and creativity, there was no correlation: grit might help a student win a spelling bee or get to and through college, these researchers concluded separately, but it did not lead to thoughtfulness or innovation.[78] To an education historian writing in the *New Republic* in 2014, the mechanical quantification of conduct involved in keeping character report cards promoted an instrumentalist or careerist conception of advancement anathema to healthy moral development.[79] To discussants on a panel about grit at an education conference (called EduCon) in Philadelphia in 2015, Duckworth and Levin were ultimately tilting at windmills: disadvantaged students did not fail to make it to and through college because of insufficient character, these critics argued, but because of insufficient social and financial resources taken for granted by middle- and upper-class students.[80]

These important matters aside, KIPP teachers were now tasked with keeping close tabs on each student in eight areas of behavior, on top of working long hours and vigilantly imposing a strict code of conduct. KIPP as well as Mastery and similar networks may nevertheless be on their way to becoming less stressful places for teachers. As previously noted, until 2004 KIPP operated only middle schools; until 2010 the same was true for Mastery. This meant that KIPP and Mastery have had to acculturate students accustomed to less demanding academic and behavioral expectations. As KIPP by 2014 had sixty elementary schools feeding eighty middle schools, and as Mastery had eight elementary schools feeding seven middle schools in Philadelphia (as well as two elementary schools that may lead to middle schools in Camden), that task of acculturation is naturally less arduous. As of 2014, only KIPP middle schools in Houston, Newark, and New York had fifth-graders who transitioned from KIPP elementary schools. Reports from those middle schools so far, according to KIPP officials, indicate that starting students in KIPP in elementary school may be far more effective than doing so in middle school.[81]

Levin, in fact, said during an interview in 2008 that he and Feinberg wanted to do this from the start, but they were middle-school teachers and could not imagine convincing parents to enroll their children in a new school run by people with no background in elementary education. Moreover, Levin said, parents had to experience their neighborhood schools first before opting for something different. "Now that KIPP has a reputation," Levin said, "we can open elementary schools and are eagerly doing so."[82]

■

Beyond the challenges of retaining teachers and raising necessary supplementary funding from philanthropists, KIPP, Mastery, and similar CMOs face the more fundamental problem of suitability for a broad range of students, even if they begin in kindergarten rather than fifth grade. KIPP, in particular, has worked well for a segment of the student population, but it has been a small segment and appears necessarily limited in size because of the long day, the strict code of conduct, the obligation of parents to abide by the organization's "Commitment to Excellence," and the relentless emphasis on academic results. The termination of capoeira at KIPP AMP is one illustration of this emphasis on academic results.

To many scholars, KIPP's results accordingly do not mean what they seem to mean. KIPP, in keeping with charter school law, does employ a lottery for admission if oversubscribed. While several scholars have shown that KIPP's lottery winners post better reading and math scores on state exams than KIPP's lottery losers,[83] those students ill suited for KIPP's high demands may not enter KIPP lotteries or may not do so in proportionate numbers. In this regard, some scholars have cited higher levels of academic achievement of matriculating students at KIPP schools than at neighboring schools; disproportionately high enrollment of girls (who on average perform better in middle school and cause fewer disciplinary problems); and disproportionately low enrollment of English-language learners as well as students with special needs. Scholars in this same camp have also cited much higher levels of grade retention at KIPP schools for students in fifth grade. Such retention both affords weaker students additional time in school before they are assessed as eighth-graders and conveys to fifth-graders as well as potential applicants that KIPP schools are especially demanding.[84]

Of matriculating fifth-graders at KIPP Academy in the Bronx in 2002, for example, one group of scholars found that 42 percent had passed the state reading test in fourth grade and not one was an English-language learner. Meanwhile, 28 percent of their peers in the thirty-one area elementary schools had passed the same reading test and 17 percent were English-language learners.[85] In a study of KIPP schools across the country from 2005 to 2009, another group of scholars found that, on average, over these four years 8 percent of KIPP students were English-language learners in comparison to 15 percent for the host districts, while 6 percent of KIPP students were diagnosed with learning disabilities in comparison to 12 percent for the host districts.[86]

Moreover, attrition and replacement patterns further distinguish KIPP students. Of those students who do gain admission to KIPP but do not prove a good fit, a significant number drop out after one or two years, return to their neighborhood district schools, and either get replaced by higher-performing transfers or do not get replaced at all, leading to smaller, more academic cohorts in seventh and eighth grades. In studying thirty KIPP middle schools across the country from 2007 to 2009, this second group of scholars found that enrollment from sixth grade to eighth grade dropped 30 percent, whereas the decline for schools in host districts was 6 percent.[87] For this cohort of KIPP schools, attrition was especially pronounced for black boys, amounting to 40 percent in two years. The attrition rate for black girls was, by contrast, 28 percent; for Hispanic boys and girls, 30 and 12 percent, respectively; and for white boys and girls, 25 and 26 percent, respectively.[88]

In a subsequent study of nineteen KIPP middle schools across the country from 2001 to 2009, a third group of scholars concluded that "late entrants" who transfer into KIPP in sixth grade or later (though relatively few students transfer into KIPP middle schools after sixth grade) to replace exiting students tend to comprise fewer male students, fewer students with learning disabilities, and more students with higher baseline scores on fourth-grade reading and math exams.[89] This third group of scholars, researchers at Mathematica commissioned by KIPP, found that the shift in these baseline scores was significant: from the 46th percentile on the fourth-grade reading and math exams for KIPP students in the fifth grade to the 53rd and 55th percentiles in reading and math, respectively, on those same exams for KIPP students in the eighth grade.[90]

Mathematica researchers likewise found significant differences in grade retention of students in fifth grade at KIPP schools and host district schools. In a 2010 survey of twenty-two KIPP schools across the country, Mathematica found that 11 percent of fifth-graders at KIPP schools were held back in contrast to 2 percent of their counterparts in host district schools. The difference for sixth-graders was 5 percent and 2 percent, respectively.[91] In a follow-up study in 2013 of forty-three KIPP schools across the country, Mathematica found grade retention rates of 9 percent and 2 percent for fifth-graders in KIPP and host district schools, respectively, and 4 percent and 2 percent for sixth-graders, respectively.[92]

■

Rates of improvement of KIPP students must therefore be qualified, as entry and exiting cohorts can be far different groups and as the message of high grade retention of fifth-graders is unmistakable. Even if the rates of improvement are confined to specific students who stay from fifth grade through eighth in the case of middle school, the advantage conferred on such students of being in classes with similarly motivated peers can be significant, particularly as the late entrants enrolling in KIPP schools comprise students with higher baseline scores in reading and math. Much as runners typically benefit from racing against faster runners, students do better in classrooms with better students. The researchers at Mathematica made precisely this point.[93]

While the gains for KIPP students who stayed from fifth through eighth grades significantly exceeded those of students in the lottery who did not get into KIPP, peer group effects may explain a good deal of that superior performance, the Mathematica researchers maintained. If so, they conceded, "the scalability of the KIPP model" comes into serious question: "If KIPP's impacts are produced primarily by an improvement in the peer environment that derives from selective replacement of departing students, then it might be difficult to replicate KIPP's success in schools that have a different mix of students."[94] Without accounting for unobserved factors (such as parental expectations or student conduct) that might attract students to KIPP rather than district schools, Mathematica researchers concluded that the gains of KIPP students over four years were so significant that peer group effects would at best explain 29 percent of the total KIPP impact in reading and 21 percent of the total KIPP impact in math. If such unobserved factors, however, were somehow acknowledged, the Mathematica researchers cautioned, the peer group effects stood to be greater.[95]

The negative impact of troubled students on classmates can be substantial, as noted with reference to research by Scott Carrell and Mark Hoekstra.[96] What this means for a school with significant control over student enrollment is telling and thus goes a long way in differentiating the record of an organization like KIPP from a company like Edison or any public school district. As a school takeover rather than start-up organization, Mastery has had less control over enrollment than KIPP. But once established, Mastery too has an admission process that discourages students uncomfortable with a "no excuses" environment from enrolling. Like KIPP, Mastery can also make life uncomfortable for enrolled students who don't conform.

Working with the Houston Independent School District, the economist Roland Fryer put the KIPP model to the test in conventional district schools with no admission process in an experiment called Apollo 20. Beginning with nine high schools in 2010 and adding eleven elementary schools in 2011, Fryer applied two of KIPP's pillars verbatim, implemented two variations, and substituted a fifth: a culture of high expectations; more instructional time (with ten more days in the school year and an extra hour of classes Monday through Thursday); more effective principals and teachers through more rigorous selection; data-driven instruction based on benchmark assessments given three times a year; and supplementary tutoring for an hour a day in math for students in fourth, sixth, and ninth grades. The additional cost at the secondary level was $1,837 per pupil (no sum was provided for the additional cost at the primary level). As of August 2014, Fryer reported significant annual gains in math but little impact in reading. "Perhaps the most worrisome hurdle of implementation," Fryer wrote in a study of this experiment, "is the labor supply of talent available to teach in inner-city schools."[97]

With Apollo 20, Fryer's team did have the freedom to hire its own teachers. The Houston Independent School District had spent $5 million to buy out teacher contracts so that Apollo 20 could begin anew.[98] But that freedom, Fryer concluded, was still not enough to get the staff Apollo 20 needed.[99] Implementing the KIPP model in twenty schools at once clearly proved daunting, especially without the buy-in KIPP obtained from parents and students alike before students even applied. While schools in Apollo 20, Fryer wrote, were instructed to put into effect "school-parent-student contracts" akin to KIPP's "Commitment to Excellence" contracts, parents and students did not know about these contracts prior to the start of the school year. To derive critical lessons from Apollo 20, Fryer was, of course, set on barring any self-selection from taking place.[100] Absent this buy-in of students as well as parents, peer group effects as well as individual motivation stand to be significantly different.

At traditional public schools, such contracts have no place at all. And that proscription constitutes the most stubborn of conceptual constraints for KIPP and similar CMOs. As with Catholic schools, which have been lauded for their analogous impact on student outcomes,[101] the very existence of KIPP and other CMOs embracing the philosophy of "no excuses" depends on the presence of a fallback system of schooling, where students can go if KIPP, Mastery, or Achievement First does not prove a good fit. But there is no alternative system of schooling to the traditional system of public schooling, except in the rare cases of juvenile offenders.

Catholic schools, independent schools, and KIPP as well as similar CMOs thus work, in part, because they don't have to work. Administrators at traditional public schools cannot, for example, do what Mike Feinberg did in Houston in telling the mother of a KIPP student that her daughter will no longer have a place at the school unless she stops watching TV and completes her homework.

This qualification is critical. As an Achievement First executive conceded, "The 'no excuses' environment does not work for all students, and it doesn't work for all families."[102] For his part, Dave Levin does not view KIPP as a panacea. It is rather one response to a system that he and Feinberg found falling far short. When asked at a forum on school improvement at Teachers College, Columbia University, in 2010 about what should be done to improve education in New York in particular, Levin did not hesitate: "The only way to really improve New York's schools is if there were a giant lottery, with no parents knowing where their kids would go to school. That way everyone would be in the same boat, and all schools would get the support they needed."[103]

This giant lottery—much akin to the process advocated by John Rawls of making all societal decisions from behind a "veil of ignorance" as to personal outcomes—is clearly not something, however, Levin was waiting for early in his career or later.[104] As a young, idealistic, indignant educator, Levin, along with Feinberg, set about building demanding charter schools that worked for some students and stood to bear lessons for many more. As such, KIPP and similar CMOs have at once made great strides and exhibited significant limits.

■

To New York's Mayor Bill de Blasio and his allies, the necessarily restricted reach of KIPP and similar CMOs amounted to the chief problem with charter schools in general. In his ill-fated effort to block the expansion of charter schools in New York City in 2013 by demanding that their operators pay rent for use of public school buildings, de Blasio gave clear expression to the case made two decades earlier by the political scientist Jeffrey Henig that the movement for school choice sidestepped central challenges.[105] "We have a crisis when it comes to education," de Blasio said in advance of the aforementioned charter school rally in Foley Square. "The answer is not to find an escape route that some can follow and others can't. The answer is to fix the entire system."[106]

In dissenting against the Supreme Court majority opinion in *Zelman v. Simmons-Harris* in 2002 supporting vouchers for a small fraction of students in Cleveland, Justice John Paul Stevens had made a similar argument. "The solution to the disastrous conditions that prevented over 90 percent of the student body from meeting basic proficiency standards," Stevens wrote, "obviously required massive improvements unrelated to the voucher program."[107]

In defense of charter schools as well as vouchers, Marc Sternberg, director of K–12 education reform at the Walton Family Foundation and former deputy chancellor for new school development in the New York City Department of Education, fired back in a 2014 interview with the *New York Times* that it is the critics who are in denial of pressing realities. "What's the argument there?" Sternberg said. "Don't help anybody until you can help everybody?"[108]

With this interrogative rebuttal, Sternberg captured the defiant spirit of many charter school advocates and defined their pragmatic perspective. Scalability, particularly for those CMOs employing the "no excuses" model, nevertheless remained an undeniably daunting challenge.

11

A DISTANT MIRROR

A majority of Swedish schools will in time be run for profit, as there will
be pressure for greater efficiency. There's too much slack in the current
system.

Peje Emilsson, chairman and founder, Kunskapsskolan Education Sweden AB,
Stockholm, May 11, 2009

▦ THE ONE PART OF THE WORLD that comes closest to employing the
giant lottery imagined by Dave Levin for determining school enrollment
(or to making educational policy from behind a "veil of ignorance" as to
personal outcomes, in the language of John Rawls) is the Nordic region.
Denmark, Finland, Iceland, Norway, and Sweden fund their schools
fairly, grant parents paid maternity/paternity leaves lasting approximately
one year to nurture solid starts for all infants, provide excellent health care
to everyone, heavily subsidize preschool, and levy steeply progressive taxes
to make all this possible and at the same time contain income inequality.[1]

This Nordic conception of equality is deeply ingrained. The idea of the
nation as family or "people's home" (*folkhem*) took hold in Sweden, in
particular, with the endorsement of Social Democratic leader Per Albin
Hansson in the 1920s.[2] In a storied speech before fellow legislators in the
Riksdag in 1928, Hansson invoked *folkhem* in laying the groundwork for
the Nordic welfare state: "The foundation of the home is community and
solidarity. The good home knows no privilege or neglect, no favorites
and no stepchildren. . . . Applied to the great people's and citizens' home,
this would mean the breakdown of all social and economic barriers that
now divide citizens into privileged and deprived, into the rulers and the
ruled, into rich and poor, the propertied and the destitute, the robbers and
the robbed."[3]

Akin to *folkhem* is the widespread Nordic belief in humility or, more specifically, nonexceptionalism, captured by the Danish-Norwegian novelist Aksel Sandemose, a Hansson contemporary, as the Law of Jante. In describing the behavioral strictures of a mythical Danish town called Jante in his 1933 novel, *A Fugitive Crosses His Tracks* (*En flyktning krysser sitt spor*), Sandemose explained in the form of ten commandments how nobody should think he or she is better than anyone else.[4] Known as *Janteloven* in Danish and Norwegian, the ubiquitous Law of Jante is called *Jantelagen* in Swedish and *Janten laki* in Finnish.

This shared reverence for equality aside, the Nordic countries differ substantially in how they run schools. For its significant privatization of school management, Sweden stands out as utterly distinct from its Nordic neighbors. In 1991 Sweden embarked on a path reflecting Chilean practice and U.S. ambitions. In the same year that Chris Whittle announced his Edison Project and Minnesota passed legislation for charter schools,[5] Sweden approved the first of two bills paving the way to the introduction of vouchers the following year to be used at independent schools run by either nonprofit or for-profit organizations (*friskolor*).[6] Denmark, Finland, and Norway have all barred for-profit operation of schools, though the Norwegian government proposed in its legislative agenda in 2013 introducing a variation on Sweden's model.[7]

■

The same laissez-faire triumphalism in the wake of the fall of the Berlin Wall that animated Whittle, Benno Schmidt, and many of their allies in the United States inspired legislators and entrepreneurs behind the transformation of Swedish schooling. This embrace of the free market, in fact, swept Sweden's conservative Moderate Coalition Party (Moderaterna) into power in 1991, bringing an end to nearly six decades of rule by the Social Democratic Party molded by Per Albin Hansson. Since 1932 Sweden had been run by the Social Democrats but for a break between 1976 and 1982.

While the conservatives did not threaten the free provision of basic services defining Sweden as *folkhem*, they did call for a radical transformation of the delivery of those services. To the conservatives, Sweden under the Social Democrats had become an iconically inefficient, stale welfare state. Privatization, they claimed, would rejuvenate Sweden through competition and choice. Soon after becoming prime minister, Carl Bildt, leader of the Moderaterna, made this plain: "The time for the Nordic model has passed. . . . It created societies that were too monopolized, too expensive and didn't give people the freedom of choice that they wanted; societies that lacked flexibility and dynamism."[8]

For Bildt and his party, educational choice was of paramount importance. There were few independent schools in Sweden at the time and mounting discontent with municipal schools. In the 1991–1992 school year, all but 1 percent of the country's 1.2 million students at the primary and secondary levels attended municipal schools.[9] Of the independent schools, many were small Montessori, Waldorf, or religious schools enrolling under one hundred students; six were international schools with English, French, or German as the primary language of instruction; and three were exclusive boarding schools (Gränna, Lundsberg, and Sigtuna) for the children of the country's thin layer of affluent elite. The government covered approximately 50 percent of tuition at the Waldorf, Montessori, and religious schools and approximately 35 percent of tuition at the international schools.[10] Tuition at the boarding schools was far beyond the means of the average family.[11]

Much of the discontent with municipal schools proceeded from reforms implemented in the 1960s. In the name of social integration, Sweden in 1962 did away with tracking by level of academic proficiency for students in grades one through six and placed all students in the same comprehensive school (*grundskola*), comprising grades one through nine.[12] In 1968 Sweden went a step further, nullifying what remained of streaming students by level of academic proficiency in the upper grades of these new comprehensive schools.[13] Yet this transformation never fulfilled what the reformers had envisioned, writes the Norwegian social historian Francis Sejersted, because it came without the necessary modifications in pedagogy to accommodate the changes in classroom composition. "It had been a precondition that teacher education would be overhauled," writes Sejersted, "but this was never done."[14]

The most obvious indication of this failure, according to Sejersted, was demotion of the teacher: "The teacher was no longer the learned knowledge broker but, at best, an organizer. He or she was placed on the sidelines."[15] In protest arose "the knowledge movement,"[16] much in sync with E. D. Hirsch's campaign in the United States for "core knowledge," mandating mastery of specific content at each grade level.[17] While this countermovement was led by conservatives, it had advocates among Social Democrats as well. In recognition of the decline in academic rigor at schools, Bengt Göransson, the education minister for the Social Democrats in the 1980s, worked to make intellectual, not social, development the chief goal of schools.[18]

Through the educational choice program put forth by Carl Bildt, parents could make their own decisions about what kind of curricula they wanted for their children. The voucher legislation proposed in 1991 and passed in 1992 entitled parents to vouchers worth 85 percent of the per-pupil expenditure in neighboring public schools. When the Social Democrats returned to power in 1994, they reduced this allocation to 75 percent. But the Social Democrats two years later increased coverage to 100 percent, with the stipulation that independent schools could not charge any additional fees.[19] This provision at once shielded parents from extra costs and ultimately pulled Sweden's few expensive international and boarding schools into participation in the voucher program, with the qualification that boarding costs had to be covered independently (vouchers cover the full cost of attendance for day students from the community who live at home).[20]

■

The growth in voucher use proved slow but consistent. Five years after implementation, in the 1997–1998 academic year, 2.7 percent of students attending *grundskolor* used vouchers to go to independent schools (or *friskolor*), and 3.1 percent of students attending *gymnasieskolor* (the equivalent of grades ten through twelve) did the same. Ten years after implementation, the proportions grew to 5.5 percent of students attending *grundskolor* and 8.2 percent of students attending *gymnasieskolor*. By 2010 the proportions grew to 11.9 percent of students attending *grundskolor* and 23.8 percent of students attending *gymnasieskolor*. Because independent schools in Sweden, as in the United States, tend to be smaller than municipal schools, the proportion of independent schools exceeded the proportion of students attending them (see Figure 11.1). By 2010, 1,230, or 21.8 percent, of the country's 5,641 *grundskolor* and *gymnasieskolor* combined were independent schools: 741 of 4,626 *grundskolor*, and 489 of 1,015 *gymnasieskolor*. Of that combined number, nearly 930—75.6 percent of independent schools and

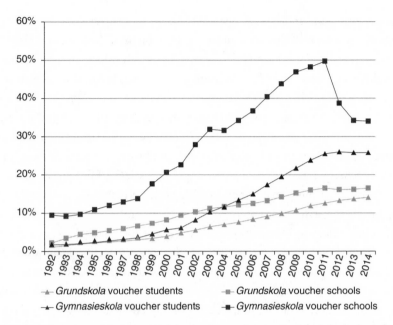

Figure 11.1 Percentage of students at each level using vouchers to attend *friskolor* (independent schools) and percentage of schools at each level that are *friskolor*. *Data source:* Swedish School Agency, http://www.skolverket.se/. Approximately 75 percent of *friskolor* are run for profit.

16.5 percent of all schools—were run by for-profit operators, or, more specifically, limited companies, defined in Swedish by AB, for *aktiebolag*.[21]

This growth surpassed what Wall Street analysts like Michael T. Moe of Merrill Lynch had predicted in 1999 for for-profit operators of publicly funded primary and secondary schools in the United States. Moe, as described, had forecasted that 10 percent of the nation's approximately 100,000 K–12 public schools would be managed by companies like Edison within a decade.[22] The reality, again, was under 1 percent.[23] Swedish for-profit school operators, by contrast, benefited from several telling advantages.

Most critically, in Sweden from 1996 onward, for-profit school operators received the same per-pupil allocation as neighboring municipal schools. In the United States, such parity was the rare exception. In Baltimore and Philadelphia, as described, Edison earned per-pupil premiums for overhead costs and did not have to pay for space. However, Edison and its competitors typically earned marginal if any premiums for overhead costs and almost always paid significant amounts for space in managing charter schools. Charter schools in New York City without free co-location in 2008–2009, as explained by the Independent Budget Office, received 12.8 percent less in funding than neighboring public schools.[24] According to Peje Emilsson, the founder and chairman of Kunskapsskolan AB, one of Sweden's largest for-profit school operators, parity in funding was essential to his involvement in education. Like Whittle, Emilsson was a precocious businessman with a strong commitment to privatization. At twenty-four, soon after graduating from Stockholm University, where he studied economics and political science, Emilsson cofounded a communications consultancy in 1970 called Kreab AB; in 2009 Kreab merged with Gavin Anderson of New York to become Kreab Gavin Anderson AB, with offices in twenty-five countries across four continents. In 1989, a year after completing Harvard Business School's Owner/President Management (OPM) program, a midcareer executive training course spread over three summers, Emilsson started Demoskop AB, a marketing firm. In 1995 he created the Magnora Group AB, a holding company comprising Kreab and Demoskop as well as other interests and counting Carl Bildt as a board member. Four years later, Emilsson launched Kunskapsskolan as another part of the Magnora portfolio. A decade afterward, Emilsson established Silver Life AB, a company operating elder homes, as yet another part of the Magnora portfolio.[25]

Meaning "knowledge schools," Kunskapsskolan represented a formal continuation of the knowledge movement in refutation of the education reforms introduced by the Social Democrats in 1962. Basic to the identity of Kunskapsskolan was personalized learning, with students spending significant portions of the day working on their own and at their own pace. In a 2009 interview, Emilsson faulted, in particular, Olof Palme for lowering academic standards and stifling individual development in Swedish schools. Palme had served as education minister from 1967 to 1969 and then as prime minister from 1969 to 1976 and from 1982 until his stunning death in 1986, wrought by a lone gunman while Palme was strolling home with his wife without any security detail after seeing a late movie in central Stockholm. In Emilsson's opinion, Palme had elevated equity over excellence as education minister and preserved that emphasis as leader of the Social Democrats. "Palme turned teaching into social work," Emilsson said, "and thereby drove people serious about content away from the profession. The focus of school had become fair play, not learning."[26]

Also like Whittle, Emilsson was immersed in politics and ambitious on an international scale. While getting Kreab off the ground, he served from 1970 to 1972 as chairman of the Confederation of Swedish Conservative and Liberal Students (Fria Moderata Studentförbundet), affiliated with Britain's Federation of Conservative Students and the United States' College Republicans. Bildt served under Emilsson as vice chairman and then succeeded him. In this capacity, Emilsson befriended Karl Rove and Jeb Bush and has remained close since. Emilsson subsequently served as *chef de cabinet* of the International Chamber of Commerce from 1973 to 1981.[27] In sync with Whittle's celebration of the fall of communism in Eastern Europe, Emilsson took particular pride in buying the former Czechoslovakian embassy, a ten-story brutalist composition of cement, red brick, and glass in the stately Östermalm section of Stockholm, and making it his corporate headquarters in 2000. Emilsson kept a massive antenna on the roof from the Cold War era as a trophy.[28]

As with Kreab, so with Kunskapsskolan, Emilsson had global aspirations. His plan was to grow the education company gradually in Sweden and then open schools in Britain and the United States. Like many Swedish for-profit school entrepreneurs, Emilsson waited until 1996 before entering the education business. The vouchers, he said, had to be worth the same as per-pupil allocations in neighboring schools before he or his competitors could implement sound business plans. Emilsson nevertheless met in 1992 with Schmidt and Whittle to discuss strategy and potential opportunities for collaboration. Nothing came of that meeting, Emilsson said, other than sharpened hopes of someday operating charter schools in the United States.[29]

In a telling episode of Swedish-American engagement, however, a Kreab client, Investor AB, a publicly traded holding company in Stockholm run by the legendary Wallenberg banking family, took a 9 percent stake in Edison for $20 million in 1997 and with it a seat on the company's board. Representing Investor on Edison's board was Klas Hillström.[30] In a 2009 interview, Hillström said Investor managed to make a sizable profit on its investment in Edison because it reduced its stake to 1 percent in 2001 and exited in 2002. Hillström could not recall the precise return on investment. But it is easy enough to estimate from an average of the daily closing prices of Edison's stock in 2001 and 2002: $21.56 and $5.38, respectively. Investor indeed made a sizable profit. With a 9 percent stake worth roughly 4.5 million shares, Investor got approximately $86.7 million for the sale of 4 million shares in 2001 and $2.7 million for the sale of 500,000 shares in 2002, for a total profit of about $69 million on an investment of $20 million, amounting to an approximate return of 345 percent in five years.[31]

Hillström, who moved on in 2003 to the Stockholm office of the London-based private equity group 3i, explained over coffee in a conference room at 3i's office on Birger Jarlsgatan, a ten-minute walk through Humlegården from Magnora headquarters, that Investor got out because the Edison model ultimately did not make sense: charter schools required significant capital infusions for building or leasing facilities; district schools required similar infusions for site renovations; contracts with charter boards and host districts meanwhile lasted only five years; and per-pupil allocations typically ran 15 percent below those for neighboring district schools.[32]

In Sweden, for-profit school operators benefited from not only funding parity but also administrative sovereignty. Kunskapsskolan, like Edison, would have to invest considerable sums to build, lease, and renovate facilities. Yet Kunskapsskolan and its Swedish counterparts were freestanding entities without contract obligations to charter boards or district offices. Swedish school companies would flourish or fade according to demand from parents and students. The politics of charter and school boards that dogged EMOs in the United States did not exist in Sweden.

■

Following a period of planning from 1998 to 2000, Emilsson opened five Kunskapsskolan sites: four lower-secondary schools (comprising grades six through nine) and one upper-secondary school (comprising grades ten through twelve) along with a craft center shared by all schools on a rotating basis where students would board in a dormitory for two weeks at a time and work on woodshop and art projects. The upper-secondary school was located in the Stockholm suburb of Nacka. Three of the lower-secondary schools were located in the Stockholm suburbs of Skärholmen, Täby, and Tyresö; the fourth was located in the small city of Norrköping, 100 miles southwest of the capital. The craft center was located in the small city of Falun, 140 miles northwest.

The planning committee was chaired by Birgitta Ericson, a career educator from Norrköping who had taught history and religion at the upper-secondary level for fifteen years before becoming the head of a progressive *grundskola* in Norrköping called Navestadsskolan. Emilsson had heard of Ericson's work through Per Unckel, the minister of education from 1991 to 1994, and Anders Hultin, Unckel's assistant responsible for drafting Sweden's voucher plan. Unckel was on Kunskapsskolan's board, and Hultin was the company's CEO; both came from the Norrköping area. Much as Whittle was close to Secretary of Education Lamar Alexander, Emilsson was close to Unckel.[33]

Ericson developed a curriculum with the assistance of a longtime colleague, Torbjörn Bindekrans, a veteran teacher of math and science. Their brand of progressive pedagogy at once meshed with the knowledge movement embraced by Emilsson and with Emilsson's desire for a return on capital to build, market, and staff schools: the curriculum was defined by mastery of content, and the staffing model was labor light, with 5.4 teachers per 100 students in contrast to the Swedish national average of 8.3 per 100.[34] Emilsson's Magnora Group provided initial financing and sold a 30 percent stake to Investor in 2002, soon after Investor's exit from Edison, and allocated a 6 percent stake to management.[35]

The curriculum called for students demonstrating competence through achievement of specific goals in each subject on their own and at their own pace. Schooling would be broken into two divisions: lower-secondary and upper-secondary; operating a primary division was out of the question, as younger students could not be expected to spend so much time working independently. Teachers would serve both as classroom instructors leading three forty-five-minute classes a day and as tutors monitoring the progress of twenty students under their supervision via a twenty-minute one-on-one meeting with each student per week. During those weekly sessions, tutors would review company-issued logbooks kept by students to see precisely what they had accomplished; parents, as well, would be expected to review these logbooks with their children on a regular basis. To facilitate teacher engagement with students, a company Web site, called the Knowledge Portal, with lesson plans shared by teachers in all subjects, would cut down on prep time.[36]

Students would start the day at 8:30 with a thirty-minute homeroom meeting run by their tutor and end the day with a ten-minute homeroom meeting at 2:20. The morning meeting would include watching a portion of Swedish network news on a classroom monitor and discussing major stories. In keeping with Ericson's model of learning as an upward journey, homeroom would be called "base camp," and the base camp would stay together with the same tutor year after year through each division. Students would attend only one class per subject per week and otherwise work on their own or with classmates. To promote independent and collaborative work, the school buildings, to be designed by the architect Kenneth Gärdestad, would have light-filled common areas anchored by cafés and airy computer labs as well as seminar rooms and small lecture halls. No bells would punctuate the day.[37]

Ericson put this curriculum into motion as the inaugural head of Kunskapsskolan's lower-secondary school in Norrköping in 2000. A year later she became the company's full-time director of education and development, splitting her time between company headquarters in Stockholm and an office for curriculum and IT in Norrköping. In a 2009 interview in the company's Stockholm office, Ericson said that Kunskapsskolan was initially derided by critics as "another Summerhill," referring to the child-centered British boarding school founded by A. S. Neill in 1921. "But our students have done well on the national exams administered in ninth grade," Ericson said. "Municipalities now follow us in using logbooks, tutorials, and Web portals with shared lesson plans."[38]

Tord Hallberg, the founding principal of the company's upper-secondary school in Uppsala, echoed Ericson. Hallberg had been a teacher for seventeen years and a principal for ten in conventional municipal Swedish schools. Frustrated with his inability to implement change, Hallberg joined Kunskapsskolan in 2007. "After two years with Kunskapsskolan, I think I've had a greater impact on conventional schools, as they're taking lessons from us," he said. "When I see my old boss, he tells me, 'We're learning from you. We're now using the Web in innovative ways, getting our students to take more responsibility, having our teachers work more one-one-one with students.'"[39]

Of students interviewed at six Kunskapsskolan sites, nearly all considered their freedom both a gift and a burden. "The good thing about Kunskapsskolan is that you can go at your own speed," said a ninth-grader at a school in Enskede, a district in the south of Stockholm. "The bad thing is you can easily fall behind."[40] Several ninth-graders echoed this sentiment in a group interview during morning base camp at a Kunskapsskolan four miles east in the suburb of Nacka. In the background, a Swedish network news story played on the classroom monitor about rioting young men setting cars and dumpsters ablaze in the heavily immigrant Rosengård district of the southern city of Malmö. The base camp leader, an English and French teacher named Pernilla Brorsson, afterward asked her students what they thought about the turmoil in Malmö. One student mentioned feelings of discrimination among immigrant youth as a cause for anger. Brorsson nodded and cited three satellite communities northwest of Stockholm (Husby, Rinkeby, and Tensta) as smaller versions of Rosengård.[41]

Of teachers interviewed at these same schools, nearly all called the tutorial system effective and the Knowledge Portal useful. Several, though, said classes, especially in mathematics, should meet more than once a week. Several more voiced concern about the stress generated by the company's method for teacher evaluation and compensation: raises were determined by (1) the academic progress of one's students as both a tutor (with twenty students to supervise) and a subject teacher (with approximately sixty students to instruct and assess); and (2) one's rankings by students on a five-point scale (from strongly disagree to strongly agree) regarding helpfulness, organization, and content.[42]

According to several Kunskapsskolan administrators, the company used student results on national exams administered in grade nine as a check against grade inflation. However, this policy was porous. As at schools across the country, the national exams were not graded by external readers or even colleagues within the same building. Rather, teachers graded the national exams of their own students. In grade three, all students are tested in Swedish and math; in grade six, in Swedish, math, and English; in grade nine, in those three subjects as well as science; and at the upper-secondary level, in Swedish, math, and English.[43]

Suspicions of grade inflation were thus substantial. This was true for Kunskapsskolan and all schools in Sweden, whether public or independent. According to a 2009 op-ed in *Dagens Nyheter,* the nation's most widely read paper, by two Swedish economists, Magnus Henrekson and Jonas Vlachos, grades spiked for upper-secondary students from 1997 to 2007, while performance on international assessments dropped and diagnostic examinations at the college level showed no improvement. Henrekson and Vlachos concluded that the pressure placed by the free-market enrollment system on both municipal and independent schools to attract students and retain them as satisfied customers constituted the only compelling explanation for the grade inflation and urged education authorities to implement both external assessment of national exams and something akin to France's baccalaureate at the end of upper-secondary school.[44]

Annual reports from 2011 through 2014 by Skolinspektionen (the Swedish Schools Inspectorate), in fact, found that independent readers grading national exams gave much lower marks than teachers grading national exams taken by their own students.[45] Yet the policy of having teachers grade their own students remained in place.[46]

■

By 2009 Kunskapsskolan had thirty-two schools across Sweden, with twenty-two lower-secondary schools and ten upper-secondary schools. The company also had a second craft center, located in Gamleby, a small town 160 miles south of Stockholm, and a science center, with an adjoining dormitory, located in a former observatory atop a sylvan hill in the seaside Stockholm suburb of Saltsjöbaden, to be used, like the craft centers, on a rotating basis. With growth came the profits that eluded Edison. Losses in the first three years were substantial, but Kunskapsskolan broke even its fourth year and went on to post a profit its fifth year and steadily increasing profits over the four ensuing years (see Table 11.1).[47]

To Emilsson, the trend was unmistakable for Kunskapsskolan and for the for-profit school sector in Sweden as a whole. "A majority of Swedish schools will in time be run for profit, as there will be pressure for greater efficiency," Emilsson said in a 2009 discussion of American and Swedish educational policy over dinner with his board and guests at his headquarters in Östermalm. "There's too much slack in the current system. Sweden can be the role model for other countries in being egalitarian while using corporate management. Interest from abroad certainly leads us to think we have something

Table 11.1   Kunskapsskolan schools, estimated enrollment and financial data (in
millions of Swedish kronor; the Swedish krona fluctuated over this time
period from 5.9 to 10.9 kronor to the U.S. dollar)

Fiscal year	Schools	Estimated enrollment	Revenue	Earnings	Earnings/ revenue
2001	5	880	48 m. kr	(25.8 m. kr)	(53.8%)
2002	12	2,767	159 m. kr	(26.7 m. kr)	(16.8%)
2003	20	5,148	266 m. kr	(30 m. kr)	(11.3%)
2004	22	6,060	367 m. kr	0	0.0%
2005	22	6,397	436 m. kr	7.8 m. kr	1.8%
2006	23	7,020	485 m. kr	11 m. kr	2.3%
2007	26	8,155	571 m. kr	19.5 m. kr	3.4%
2008	30	9,161	657 m. kr	25 m. kr	3.8%
2009	32	9,663	726 m. kr	36 m. kr	5.0%

Data source: Kunskapsskolan Education Sweden AB, Årsredovisning och koncernredovisning för räkenskapsåret 2014, Bolagsverket, http://www.bolagsverket.se.

special." Emilsson predicted that within five years, Kunskapsskolan would
be running at least ten schools abroad and ten more in Sweden.[48]

Emilsson mentioned Rahul Gandhi as one foreign leader, in particular,
interested in replicating Kunskapsskolan. After touring several Kunskapsskolan sites during a visit to Sweden as head of the Indian Youth Congress in
2008, Gandhi told Emilsson that Kunskapsskolan would flourish in India.
Emilsson soon after flew to Chennai and met with government officials and
potential investment partners.[49] Kunskapsskolan opened its inaugural Indian campus in Gurgaon in 2013.[50]

By 2014 Kunskapsskolan was also running four schools in Great Britain,
though on a nonprofit basis, per British regulations, one charter school in
New York, also on a nonprofit basis, per New York regulations, and a second
school in Gurgaon. Because Kunskapsskolan as a trademarked commercial
brand could not be used in its nonprofit capacity in Great Britain and the
United States, the four schools in Great Britain were called Learning Schools
and the one school in New York, Innovate Manhattan Charter. The school
in Gurgaon, however, retained the company name and functions as a fee-
based for-profit private school (fees for middle school students for the 2014

academic year amounted to 214,000 rupees, or approximately $3,400).[51] Though Kunskapsskolan did not have ten schools abroad by 2014, as Emilsson had forecasted, seven nevertheless represented a solid accomplishment.

Among U.S. visitors to Kunskapsskolan sites in Sweden, Jeb Bush toured the company's school in the Kista district of Stockholm in 2008 while in the city for business (following his second term as governor of Florida) and concluded that Kunskapsskolan would have great potential in Florida. John White the following year visited the Kunskapsskolan in Nacka as deputy chancellor of the New York City Department of Education. White, who went on to become Louisiana's superintendent of schools in 2012, encouraged Emilsson to open a school in New York, helped him establish the school, which would be Innovate Manhattan Charter, and saw to it that space would be provided for the school its first year, 2011–2012, in Tweed Courthouse, the central office of the Department of Education.[52] In 2011 Rupert Murdoch toured the Kunskapsskolan in Enskede together with Joel Klein, soon after Klein had stepped down as chancellor of the New York City Department of Education to become head of the education division of Murdoch's News Corp.[53] To be rebranded Amplify in 2012, the education division of News Corp. grew out of Murdoch's purchase of Brooklyn-based Wireless Generation in 2010 for $360 million. Murdoch and Klein's mission with Amplify was to put curricula on wireless computer tablets and thus enable students to work like Kunskapsskolan students: on their own and at their own pace with minimal assistance from teachers.[54]

■

Because of Ericson's innovative curriculum and Emilsson's political and marketing savvy, Kunskapsskolan is perhaps the best known of for-profit school operators in Sweden. The company garnered praise in six articles in *The Economist* alone from 2007 to 2010.[55] But it is one company among many and not close to the largest. AcadeMedia AB is one major competitor. Founded in 1996 as an adult education company, listed on the Swedish Stock Exchange in 2001, and in the business of running *friskolor* by 2007, AcadeMedia would mushroom through mergers and acquisitions. Internationella Engelska Skolan AB (IES) is a second major competitor. Founded in 1993 by an American science teacher of Swedish origin, IES provided a traditional secondary curriculum defined by "tough love" and dedicated to fluency in English. IES operated twenty-two schools with 15,500 students by 2012, when it was taken over by TA Associates, a private equity group based in Boston. Pysslingen AB is a fourth major commercial school operator, with more than eighty preschools and primary schools by 2009, when it was taken over by Polaris, a private equity group based in Copenhagen.[56]

John Bauer Gymnasiet AB is a fifth such company, though focused on job training. John Bauer, named after the celebrated turn-of-the-century Swedish painter, started out in 2000 as one vocational upper-secondary school in the southern city of Jönköping. Through a series of acquisitions of competitors, the company grew to become the country's largest chain of vocational schools, with twenty-nine sites and 10,000 students by 2008, when it was acquired by Axcel, another private equity group based in Copenhagen, and renamed JB Education. Baggium AB was also a chain of vocational upper-secondary schools. Started as one school in the southwestern city of Kungsbacka in 1999, Baggium evolved over a decade into a chain of forty-one schools with 4,700 students as well as a network of care and treatment centers for immigrant and refugee children with psychological problems. In 2010 FSN Capital, a private equity group based in Oslo, took a 70 percent stake in Baggium and a year later sold the care and treatment division to Humana AB, a Swedish health-care company.[57]

Bure Equity AB, a Stockholm-based publicly traded holding company similar to Investor, took a major stake in AcadeMedia in 2007, purchasing all outstanding shares. Bure already owned Anew Learning AB, an education conglomerate comprising five separate school companies: Didaktus AB, a chain of adult education programs and upper-secondary vocational schools focused on child-care and health professions; Vittra AB, a chain of primary and lower-secondary schools employing the Montessori method; IT-Gymnasiet AB, a chain of upper-secondary schools focused on technology; Framtidsygymansiet AB, a chain of upper-secondary vocational schools dedicated to building and mechanical trades; and Rytmus AB, an upper-secondary music school in Stockholm that would soon evolve into a chain.[58]

In 2008 AcadeMedia merged with Anew Learning, retaining only the first company's name. Two years later, EQT Partners AB, a Stockholm-based private equity group created by the Wallenberg family in 1994, took Acade-Media private; Investor, already holding a 30 percent stake in Kunskaps-skolan, was, in turn, an anchor investor in EQT with a 19 percent stake.[59] In 2011 EQT purchased Pysslingen from Polaris and added it to its AcadeMedia holdings. By 2014 AcadeMedia was managing 285 preschools and schools across Sweden as well as 130 adult education programs. The company's revenue from the Swedish government for the fiscal year was 5.1 billion kronor (or approximately $730 million), making it the nation's largest school operator behind the municipality of Stockholm.[60]

This profusion of commercial school operators and dizzying movement of investment organizations in and out of the sector baffled many Swedes.[61] Among them, Bengt Westerberg, deputy prime minister under Carl Bildt from 1991 to 1994 and leader of the Liberal People's Party from 1983 to 1995, confessed bewilderment. Westerberg, who had moved on to become chairman of Finansinspektionen (the Swedish Financial Supervisory Authority), said during a 2012 interview at the Finansinspektionen headquarters in central Stockholm that he was a supporter of the voucher legislation as deputy prime minister but never envisioned schools becoming businesses and could not have imagined the contemporary role of private equity in education.[62]

In Westerberg's opinion, private equity groups, especially, should be barred from education because they typically take only a short-term interest, aiming to reshape school companies and sell them within a few years for significant gains. Westerberg, in addition, disagreed with Emilsson about the future for commercial operation of schooling in Sweden, predicting decline rather than growth: "If you have an inefficient public sector, then it's easy for the for-profits to come in and make money. But over time, the municipal operators will become more efficient."[63]

Of equal concern to Westerberg was segregation. He said he had recently visited his high school alma mater in his native Södertälje, a midsized city twenty miles southwest of Stockholm with a significant immigrant population. It was his first return to his alma mater in many years. To his surprise, he said, nearly all the students were immigrants or children of immigrants. Westerberg said he asked the school principal about the rest of the children in Södertälje. Westerberg quoted the principal's response: "They almost all now go to *friskolor.*"[64]

▪

Beyond funding parity with municipal schools for independent school operators, administrative sovereignty for their leaders, and desire among many Swedes for school choice after decades of limited options, an interconnected, vigorous Nordic investment community played a substantial role in boosting educational privatization. The coordination of Swedish banks and businesses, in particular, has a long history. Called the "Wallenberg system" by Francis Sejersted, ownership groups with controlling interests in Swedish companies also hold major stakes in banks, which they, in turn, use to facilitate loans. Among the so-called fifteen families operating in this manner, the Wallenbergs have stood out, holding, for example, controlling interests through EQT and Investor in such companies as Alfa Laval, Atlas Copco, Electrolux, Scania-Vabis, and SKF as well as AcadeMedia while also maintaining a major stake in Skandinaviska Enskilda Banken (better known as SEB).[65] In conformity with the concept of *Jantelagen,* in fact, the Wallenberg motto, chiseled into a black granite wall at SEB headquarters, captures this quiet ubiquity: *Esse non videri* (To be yet not seen).[66]

But for EQT and Investor of the Wallenbergs, along with Bure Equity and Magnora, Kunskapsskolan and several of its competitors would never have evolved into sprawling enterprises. These school companies benefited, as well, from two additional advantages denied Edison and many other EMOs: first, much lower perceptions of corruption, or, as Transparency International puts it, "abuse of entrusted power for private gain"; and second, far less childhood poverty, meaning children come to school better prepared to learn as well as much less likely to cause trouble for classmates (or, in technical terms, generate negative peer group effects).[67]

According to Transparency International, a think tank based in Berlin dedicated to measuring trust in government and corporate officials in countries around the world, Sweden, like its Nordic neighbors, has year after year been a model nation. Over the course of two decades of annual surveys, from 1995 to 2014, Sweden averaged a ranking of fourth most transparent (or least corrupt) country, ranging from most transparent to sixth most. By contrast, the United States has averaged a ranking of eighteenth, ranging from fifteenth to twenty-fourth.[68]

In everyday circumstances, such trust can be seen in parents leaving infants in carriages outside cafés while meeting friends inside for coffee or in café proprietors leaving woolen blankets on outdoor chairs to keep customers warm. By extension, parents, union leaders, and journalists in the 1990s and early aughts accorded for-profit school operators ample trust that student interests would be paramount.

In fact, both teachers' unions—Lärarförbundet (representing preschool and elementary teachers) and Lärarnas Riksförbund (representing secondary teachers)—welcomed the free school movement and continued to support it. According to Anna Jändel-Holst, a senior policy adviser at Lärarnas Riksförbund, teachers welcomed the opportunity to work at different schools and expected additional competition between schools to drive up salaries. Speaking in 2009 at her office in central Stockholm, Jändel-Holst, who was previously a lower-secondary social studies teacher for seven years, explained that many members of her union taught in commercially operated schools and that she had no objection herself to the concept. Her son, after all, was a ninth-grader at a Kunskapsskolan, she said, and was challenged and happy.[69]

Jändel-Holst said the only problem with the voucher legislation was that it did not stipulate that teachers in *friskolor* had to be certified. Some schools consequently hired unqualified teachers, she said, and this exemption moreover put downward pressure on teacher salaries.[70] Salaries for Swedish teachers did, in fact, sink from 2000 to 2009. In 2000 teacher pay equaled per capita GDP for primary and lower-secondary teachers and amounted to 1.07 as much for upper-secondary teachers. By 2009 primary teachers earned 0.93 as much as per capita GDP; lower-secondary teachers, 0.96; and upper-secondary teachers, 1.01. The trend in Norway was the same, whereas the opposite was true in Denmark and Finland.[71]

Along with her colleague Olof Lundberg, another senior policy adviser, Jändel-Holst agreed that both unions had erred in failing to anticipate the consequences of this exemption for *friskolor*. But both were quick to point out that legislation was passed in 2006 to mandate that teachers in all schools be certified, though uncertified teachers already employed at *friskolor* were grandfathered in.[72]

Per Ledin, Anders Hultin's successor as CEO of Kunskapsskolan and leader of the company from 2007 to 2012, attributed this trust to Swedish modesty and cited *Jantelagen* as a pervasive, tempering influence. Ledin, who had previously served as Kunskapsskolan's marketing director from 2002 to 2007, knew Emilsson as a fellow member of the Confederation of Swedish Conservative and Liberal Students in the early 1970s. Ever since, Ledin had worked for Emilsson, first at Kreab and then at Kunskapsskolan. Like Emilsson, Ledin also participated in Harvard Business School's OPM program, completing the three-summer course a year after Emilsson. Ledin pointed out that the company's target for earnings was itself modest: 5 to 7 percent a year, not the 20 percent envisioned by leaders of both EAI and Edison.[73] The culture of Kunskapsskolan moreover exhibited the impress of *Jantelagen*. The company headquarters was located in the nondescript Hammarbyhamnen district of Stockholm, four miles and three bridges south of the city center. Ledin said that Emilsson had suggested he relocate to the Magnora headquarters in tony Östermalm, but Ledin declined, contending that the address would convey the wrong impression to legislators, journalists, and parents. At this headquarters for a company with 800 employees and thirty-two schools in 2009, Ledin worked without a secretary, answered the phone himself, and saved printouts for scrap paper. To get from school to school, Ledin did not have a driver or a company car. He drove his family's station wagon, a 1999 silver Audi with a bag of soccer balls in the rear for his daughter's team, which he helped manage. Ledin was driving the same car when I made a return visit three years later.[74]

In his station wagon, Ledin regularly crisscrossed the country visiting schools in the Kunskapsskolan network and attending headmaster meetings held at a different school each month, from Borlänge in the north to Helsingbor, Landskrona, and Trelleborg in the south.[75] While Kunskapsskolan did not have any schools in the aforementioned heavily immigrant communities of Husby, Rinkeby, Rosengård, or Tensta, the company did have schools nearby enrolling students from these communities, especially in the case of Rosengård.[76] In addition, Landskrona is one such community, as is Botkyrka, where the company has run schools since 2001 and 2003, respectively. The same is true of Skärholmen and Kista, where the company ran schools from 2000 to 2010 and from 2002 to 2015, respectively, before a combination of inadequate space and intense competition from other *friskola* companies led Kunskapsskolan to close its schools in these communities.[77] Moreover, beyond running schools in affluent suburbs like Nacka and Täby or university towns like Lund and Uppsala, the company has been running schools in a range of working-class cities and towns. Borlänge and Trelleborg fall into this category, as do Enköping, Katrineholm, Norrköping, and Örebro.[78]

The hurdles children face in disadvantaged communities in Sweden, however, do not compare to the hurdles confronting children in disadvantaged communities in the United States. Disadvantage itself means something quite different in the two countries. Of European nations, Sweden ranks second, behind Iceland, for child welfare.[79] Of the thirty OECD countries ranked in descending order by UNICEF for "relative child poverty" (determined as "the percentage of children [ages 0 to 17] who are living . . . in a household in which disposable income, when adjusted for family size and composition, is less than 50% of the national median income"), Sweden ranks seventh, with 7.3 percent of children in this cohort, while the United States ranks last, with 23.1 percent.[80]

Moreover, Stieg Larsson's depictions aside, there is no comparable degree of violence. In 2012, in all of Sweden, with a population of 9.6 million, there were sixty-eight cases of murder or manslaughter (or 0.7 cases for every 100,000 residents); in Stockholm County, with a population of 2.1 million, there were eighteen cases (or 0.9 cases for every 100,000 residents); in the communities of Husby, Kista, Rinkeby, and Tensta, there were none.[81] That same year in Baltimore alone, with a population of 625,000, there were 218 cases of murder or manslaughter (or 35 cases for every 100,000 residents). For the United States as a whole, with a population of 314 million, there were 14,827 cases of murder or manslaughter (or 4.7 cases for every 100,000 residents).[82]

While Husby, Kista, Rinkeby, and Tensta, as examples of marginalized communities in Stockholm County, house many immigrants and post high rates of unemployment,[83] these communities bear no physical resemblance to East Harlem, North Philadelphia, West Baltimore, or South Central Los Angeles. The reputation of these Swedish communities was certainly tarnished by angry young men torching cars and public buildings in May 2013 in reaction to the deadly police shooting of a local man brandishing a knife in Husby.[84] Yet visits four years earlier revealed no dilapidated buildings or boarded-up storefronts or overgrown abandoned lots or broken sidewalks speckled with discarded crack vials.[85]

Cultural separation in these communities was indeed obvious from attire, restaurant fare, and newsstand offerings as well as satellite dishes mounted to every third balcony of apartment buildings for TV programs from the residents' native countries. The metro stations, however, were spotless but for some graffiti excoriating the police or celebrating the eponymous artist. The public squares were litterless and orderly; the playgrounds, parks, and soccer fields well maintained.[86] For all parents in these communities, as in all of Sweden, there is generous maternity/paternity leave and heavily subsidized day care. Likewise, as for all Swedes, there is first-rate free medical care no matter the diagnosis.[87]

Although children from Kista or neighboring Husby do not start school with the same benefits as their counterparts in the upscale suburbs of Nacka or Täby, the difference pales in comparison to the chasm between children in North Philadelphia and nearby Lower Merion or between West Baltimore and nearby Pikesville. The challenge for Kunskapsskolan and other *friskola* companies was accordingly not the challenge encountered by Edison and other EMOs. In contrast to EMOs, *friskola* companies thus not only had far more opportunity to open schools because of the virtual absence of independent schools in the early 1990s but also far greater reason to expect children to come to school ready to learn.

■

Despite all these advantages *friskola* companies had over EMOs, they hit a wall in 2011. AcadeMedia would continue to grow because of mergers and acquisitions, but other companies, including Kunskapsskolan, would slow down or, in one prominent case, shut down.

While the teachers' unions continued to back the *friskola* movement, many legislators, scholars, and journalists turned on it. The trouble began with a change in government policy at the beginning of the year regarding enrollment in upper-secondary schools, heated up in September with a report from a prestigious centrist think tank critiquing the nation's free-market makeover, and then intensified, first, with a series of muckraking articles in the press in October about for-profit mismanagement of nursing homes and, second, with a muckraking documentary in December on for-profit mismanagement of schools broadcast on national television.

Widely referred to as GY11, for *Gymnasieskola* 2011, the new curriculum for upper-secondary schools, as part of the Swedish Education Act of 2011, was tightened, in the name of better quality control, to give all schools across the country concrete common goals and thus better prepare students for jobs or further study. In particular, GY11 specified that the country's plethora of vocational programs had to be limited to twelve carefully defined areas of study (from child care, culinary arts, and business administration to auto repair, building construction, and HVAC maintenance). Moreover, GY11 made vocational education a far more direct path to the job market. With GY11, once students began vocational programs following graduation from lower-secondary school, they were no longer in much of a position to attend universities, as admission requirements to universities were simultaneously tightened to mandate certain academic coursework.[88] Though the government had made clear the purpose of GY11 as early as 2009, for-profit vocational school operators struggled to retrofit their schools to meet the new standards.[89]

In addition, no amount of retrofitting would compensate for the new limits on options for students in vocational schools. Much as corporations engaged in foreign direct investment risk losing contracts because of local ambitions to take control of operations and thus increase autonomy and cut costs, they also assume political risk that local policies will remain favorable to their business model. For the Danish private equity group Axcel, owner since 2008 of JB Education, GY11 meant a collapse in revenue. From 2008 to 2011, enrollment in year one (the equivalent of tenth grade) at JB Education's vocational schools plummeted 62 percent. In municipalities where JB Education operated vocational schools, applications to vocational schools in general dropped from 40 percent of students in the final grade of lower-secondary school in 2010 to 28 percent in 2011.[90]

Affecting all *friskola* companies was a detailed report published in September on the impact of privatization on the provision of education, individual and family welfare services, health care, and elder care. The report was published by the highly regarded Studieförbundet Näringsliv och Samhälle (SNS), known in English as the Center for Business and Policy Studies, and presented at a forum at the SNS headquarters in Stockholm broadcast by SVT, the Swedish Public Service Television Company.[91] At the forum and in an op-ed published the same day in *Dagens Nyheter,* Laura Hartman, the SNS research director and editor of the 279-page report, concluded that there was no evidence competition had improved delivery of services.[92]

In the chapter on education in particular, the aforementioned economist Jonas Vlachos contended that the process of education is inherently too opaque for competition between schools to necessarily benefit parents and students.[93] Vlachos, in this regard, refined his contention that free-market reforms had generated grade inflation, pointing out that students from lower-secondary *friskolor* recorded lower grades at upper-secondary municipal schools, whereas those students from lower-secondary municipal schools posted grades at the upper-secondary level consistent with their lower-secondary grades. Vlachos argued, as well, that the free-market reforms had driven up costs, increased student segregation, and created an uneven playing field in allowing leaders of *friskolor* significant control over enrollment while leaders of municipal schools had to take all students.[94]

A ruckus followed Hartman's introduction at the forum and later in the press. Peje Emilsson afterward took the floor and called the report the worst piece of research published by SNS in twenty years. Emilsson took issue with several conclusions, especially Vlachos's claim that leaders of *friskolor* had significant control over enrollment. "It was like nothing I had ever seen," said Per Ledin, who attended the forum. "There was blood on the walls."[95] Hartman maintained her cool but not her job. Asked after the forum by the head of SNS to refrain from publicly commenting on the report, Hartman decided to step down, a move that, in turn, brought the report more attention in the press.[96]

In an interview eight months later at her office at Försäkringskassan, the Swedish Social Insurance Agency, in central Stockholm, where she had taken the position of director of analysis and forecasting, Hartman stood by every conclusion in the report, particularly Vlachos's claim that leaders of *friskolor* have considerable control over enrollment. "They can develop curricula suitable only for students who are easy to work with," she said. "They can establish admission preferences for siblings. They can limit enrollment when they choose. Municipal schools cannot do any of these things."[97]

Providing a school administrator's perspective on the report that same week, Einar Fransson, the director of education for the municipality of Nacka, where 20 percent of students attend *friskolor,* said that the determinations about enrollment, grade inflation, and segregation were all correct. Fransson said he liked the variety of options provided by *friskolor* and was particularly fond of Kunskapsskolan, where he had been a principal for seven years before assuming his position in Nacka in 2010. Yet the *friskola* movement, Fransson said, created as many problems as it solved.[98]

Fransson knew the Swedish system thoroughly. Before joining Kunskapsskolan, he had been the principal of a municipal school for fifteen years and prior to that a secondary teacher of history for four years. Fransson confirmed Vlachos's conclusion that leaders of *friskolor* have ways of controlling enrollment and that grade inflation at lower-secondary *friskolor* is a serious matter, noting a clear pattern at Nacka's two municipal upper-secondary schools of students earning lower grades than they had achieved at lower-secondary *friskolor.* Regarding segregation, Fransson said savvy parents search aggressively for the best fit for their children, that their children and the children of their friends and neighbors exit municipal schools together for that best fit, and that the children without such parents stay behind.[99]

To Fransson, however, the most troubling aspect of the *friskola* movement was that it deflected attention from two fundamental problems that competition between schools did not address: inadequate preparation and pay for teachers. Fransson said that low teacher pay was a long-standing issue and recalled that when he and his wife, also an educator, went to a bank for a loan to buy a bigger apartment in the Stockholm area in the 1980s, the banker was appalled at their combined income: "He said we had three options: move north, leave teaching, or go abroad."[100]

■

While the SNS report had a jarring effect, it amounted to a gentle prelude to a media storm generated by a series of stories in October in *Dagens Nyheter* on abuses discovered at a chain of for-profit nursing homes called Carema,[101] a subsidiary of a Swedish health-care company called Ambea, jointly owned by the private equity groups KKR, based in New York, and Triton, based in Frankfurt. KKR (previously described as the owner of Channel One from 1994 to 2007) and Triton had bought Ambea from 3i, the London-based private equity group, in 2010.[102]

According to *Dagens Nyheter,* poor care in the name of cutting costs at Carema led to significant malnourishment of residents, unnecessary amputations, contusions and fractures suffered from falls, and extended use of diapers. Following its initial series in October, *Dagens Nyheter* ran more than 120 stories about Carema over the next twelve months. Soon known as *Caremaskandalen,* the revelations led to numerous articles in competing papers, broadcasts on Swedish television, and parliamentary debate.[103] While Carema officials and independent commentators would dispute key findings reported in *Dagens Nyheter,* there was no remedy for the damage done by the relentless coverage.[104] In time, Ambea changed the name of Carema to Vardaga, equivalent, roughly, to "Everyday Living."[105]

To Ledin, the impact of the scandal was profound, igniting distrust of all privatized delivery of services, especially education.[106] A harsh illustration of this distrust came in December in the form of a documentary on UR, the Swedish Educational Broadcasting Company, deriding *friskola* companies as driven by greed. Entitled *Vinstmaskinerna* (meaning "Profit Machines"), the documentary was one episode in a four-part series crudely entitled *Världens bästa skitskola* (loosely, and more politely, translating as "The World's Worst Schools").[107] Much as many Chileans at the same time were protesting their nation's long-standing system of for-profit school management, initiated in 1981, Swedish critics started to raise their voices in opposition.[108] The Chilean adversaries would soon prevail, with President Michele Bachelet declaring in January 2015 that her government would phase out for-profit school management.[109]

Basic to the UR series was a crisis of faith in Swedish education known as "PISA shock." Of all OECD nations, only Sweden had seen scores on the triennial Program for International Student Assessment (PISA) successively drop with each administration of the exam since its introduction in 2000.[110] Each episode was narrated by Nathaneal Derwinger in the manner of Michael Moore.[111]

In *Vinstmaskinerna,* Derwinger reported that Ola Sälsten, the founder and owner of Baggium, the chain of vocational schools launched in Kungsbacka in 1999, had personally retained 43 million kronor (approximately $5.5 million) in earnings since founding the company and was moreover paying himself a salary of 1 million kronor per year (approximately $150,000).[112] Derwinger went to Kungsbacka, where Sälsten lived and served as a Social Democratic member of the city council, seeking an interview with Sälsten to learn how he justified making such money. After being repeatedly rebuffed in the course of roaming about Kungsbacka and simultaneously telling the story of Baggium, Derwinger went north to Sundsvall to interview students and teachers at a vocational school run by JB Education. One student reported spending much of the day playing video games, several others admitted receiving higher grades than they deserved, teachers spoke of being told by administrators to give students higher grades to make the school look better, and one former teacher contended that he was pressured by administrators to mark absent students as present to qualify the company for per-pupil allocations from the local government.[113] Like defenders of Carema responding to allegations of negligence, defenders of JB Education described the coverage as a hatchet job based on limited evidence, yet the damage was irreversible for the company in particular, and the for-profit school management sector in general.[114]

In an interview at his office in May 2012, Ledin confessed anxiety about Kunskapsskolan's fate. He said applications to the company's upper-secondary schools in February for the following academic year were down sharply and added that applications to upper-secondary *friskolor* across the country were down 25 percent. The company was not on course to fulfill Emilsson's prediction in 2009 that it would be running forty-two schools in Sweden, up from thirty-two, by 2014. The company's school count in 2011–2012 was thirty-three, with four schools added since 2009 (in Jönköping, Kroskslätt, Örebro, and Uppsala, all at the lower-secondary level) and three lost (one lower-secondary school in Skärholmen and two upper-secondary schools, one in Kista and the other in Nacka). In addition, total enrollment from 2008–2009 to 2011–2012 was flat, going from 9,663 students to 9,658. While revenue was up from 726 million kronor to 794 million, earnings were down from 36 million kronor to 24 million.[115]

Three weeks later, Cecilia Carnefeldt, Emilsson's daughter, who had succeeded her father as chairman of the Kunskapsskolan board in 2010, asked Ledin to step down as CEO and become quality manager for international operations. Ledin declined, and Carnefeldt took over as CEO.[116]

For JB Education, the numbers were far grimmer. Axcel, the Danish private equity group that took over the company in 2008, fired the CEO in 2012 and replaced him with Anders Hultin, the founding CEO of Kunskapsskolan, who had been working in London since 2007, first for GEMS Education, Sunny Varkey's school management company based in Dubai, and then for Pearson, the education and publishing conglomerate. Hultin brought on Ledin as chief of staff. Within a year, however, Vilhelm Sundström, the partner at Axcel overseeing the group's investment in JB Education, decided that it was too late to turn the company around. Applications in February 2013 for the upcoming academic year were down 31 percent.[117]

JB Education declared bankruptcy in June. Eight of the company's thirty-four vocational schools were closed. The remaining twenty-six were taken over by either companies or municipalities (AcadeMedia absorbed five; Hultin took over four and started a new company, Fria Läroverken, with Ledin as his executive vice president). In addition, of the five primary schools the company had acquired since 2008, four were taken over by AcadeMedia and one was closed; and of the company's three adult education programs acquired since 2008, two were taken over by AcadeMedia and one by a competitor, ThorenGruppen AB.[118]

Using a marker to jot stakeholders, sums, circles, and arrows on a flipboard in a conference room at Axcel's headquarters in Copenhagen in January 2014, Sundström explained during an interview the valuation of John Bauer in 2008, how much money Axcel and other stakeholders had invested, and how much was ultimately lost. Most impressive about John Bauer, Sundström said at the outset, was the company's enrollment growth rate of 7 percent each year from 2006 through 2008.[119]

Following six months of due diligence, Sundström said, Axcel valued the company at 675 million Swedish kronor (approximately $95 million), invested 133 million kronor of the group's own money, took over John Bauer's bank loan of 318 million kronor (initially made by Fortis, a Benelux bank, and then assumed by FIH, a Danish bank), secured a vendor loan of

200 million kronor from John Bauer's founder, Rune Tedfors, valued Tedfors's remaining stake at 14 million kronor (which Axcel bought out in 2011), and raised another 10 million kronor from unidentified investors. From 2008 to 2012, Axcel invested an additional 240 million kronor in acquisitions and improvements, without retaining any earnings. In 2013 Axcel invested another 100 million kronor to keep schools open through the end of the academic year. In total, JB Education's collapse cost 1.015 billion kronor (approximately $150 million): Axcel lost 487 million kronor; FIH, 318 million kronor; Tedfors, 200 million kronor; and unidentified investors, 10 million kronor.[120] There were virtually no assets to offset this loss.[121]

Gracious, understated, frank, and multilingual, Sundström personified Nordic high finance. A Swedish-speaking Finn who grew up on the Åland Islands, Sundström studied business at the Swedish School of Economics in Helsinki and worked for several years for Morgan Stanley in Stockholm and then for Merrill Lynch in London before joining Axcel in 2006. He split his time between offices in Stockholm and Copenhagen.[122]

Sundström conceded that turning around schools was far more challenging than he and his partners had expected. He said one-third of the schools they took over in 2008 were good, one-third middling, and one-third subpar. "It was particularly difficult to get the school leaders and teachers necessary to get the job done at the subpar schools," he said. Sundström added that Axcel had attempted, as well, to grow too fast in 2010 in moving into management of primary schools. And, most crucially, Sundström explained that Axcel failed to respond adequately to the GY11 reforms announced in 2009. Axcel had no reason to anticipate those reforms in 2008, he said, but could and should have responded more aggressively in 2009.[123]

Kunskapsskolan meanwhile turned around under Carnefeldt, growing to thirty-six schools by 2014–2015 and posting earnings of 41 million kronor on revenue of 1.002 billion kronor, for a profit margin of 4.1 percent. While the school count had grown only 12.5 percent since 2008–2009, rather than 31 percent, as Emilsson had forecasted, enrollment figures told a more promising story. This boost in enrollment resulted from Carnefeldt's decision to respond to the recalibration of schooling divisions by the Swedish Education Act of 2011. With this legislation, elementary education went from grades one through five to one through three (students in Sweden start grade one at age seven); lower-secondary education went from grades six through nine to seven through nine; and a new middle division, comprising grades four through six, was created. Carnefeldt decided to add grades four and five to the company's lower-secondary schools and increase the teacher-to-student ratio in these new grades to provide more structure. Largely on this account, enrollment had grown from 2008–2009 to 2014–2015 by 17 percent, from 9,663 to 11,329.[124]

Yet in a telling sidebar, Kunskapsskolan failed in New York. In the fourth year of its five-year charter, the board of Innovate Manhattan Charter School decided in March 2015 to shut the school down in June. A middle school, with grades six through eight, located in private space on the Lower East Side (following its first year in Tweed Courthouse), Innovate Manhattan had seats in 2014–2015 for 225 students but enrolled only 145, of whom only 29 were sixth-graders.[125] Results on New York State exams in reading and math were low. For the 2013–2014 academic year, 15 percent of the school's students were rated proficient in reading, compared to a district average of 38 percent; and 6 percent were rated proficient in math, compared to a district average of 37 percent.[126] Of its students, 66 percent qualified for free or reduced-price lunch, a proxy for economic disadvantage, compared to 65 percent across the district.[127] In this one instance, Kunskapsskolan struggled much like Edison and other EMOs to boost the academic performance of underprivileged children.

When asked about Innovate Manhattan Charter two months after the school closed, Carnefeldt said she wished she could start the school over again. "I am certain our approach can work for all students," she said. "But we didn't adapt appropriately. We underestimated how much structure the students needed. We figured this out by the 2013–2014 school year and got the right leadership in place by January 2014, but it was too late."[128]

12

ACROSS THE GULF

In my career [twelve years as a teacher and twenty as a principal], I met one school inspector. He stood in the back of my class, spent a few minutes surveying the room, and left. It was a new building, and we were having problems with the pipes. I thought he was the plumber.

Eeva Penttilä, Director of International Relations, Helsinki Department of Education, April 20, 2009

■ SWEDISH EDUCATIONAL AUTHORITIES introduced the comprehensive *grundskola* (comprising grades one through nine) in 1962 but never followed through, as planned, in reforming teacher education so that teachers would be better prepared to differentiate instruction in classrooms with students exhibiting a range of aptitudes.[1] Across the Gulf of Bothnia, Finnish educational authorities introduced their own version of *grundskola*, called *peruskoulu*, ten years later and did follow through in making such reforms. Like the Swedes, the Finns postponed the tracking of students until seventh grade on the grounds that judgments about aptitude any earlier occurred too soon to be accurate and denied less precocious students the benefit of learning from gifted peers (the Swedes postponed tracking from fourth grade to seventh; the Finns, from fifth grade to seventh). Unlike the Swedes, the Finns stipulated that from 1979 onward, all students studying to become teachers go through a five-year program, combining a bachelor's and master's degree and concluding with a research-based thesis.[2]

This set Finland apart from not only Sweden but also Denmark and Norway as the only Nordic nation requiring all teachers to have a master's degree before taking over a classroom. This distinction remains true thirty-seven years later. Furthermore, Finnish authorities agreed in the 1970s to boost teacher pay in acknowledgment of the additional mandated study. Upon phasing out tracking of students by aptitude in grades seven through

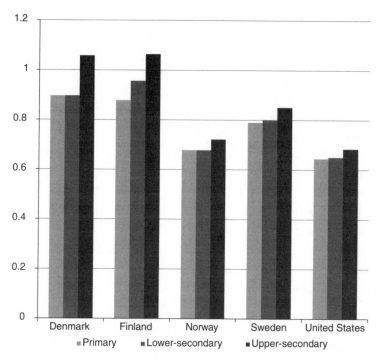

Figure 12.1 Pay ratio of teachers at each level of instruction for each country following fifteen years of experience relative to pay of fellow citizens with tertiary degrees, aged twenty-five to sixty-four. Year of reference for Denmark, Finland, and the United States is 2009; for Norway, 2007; and for Sweden, 2008. For Denmark, pay is defined by official government salary schedules; for the remaining countries, pay is defined by actual salaries. *Data source:* OECD, *Education at a Glance 2011* (Paris: OECD, 2011), table D3.1, 417.

nine in 1985, much as the Swedes had done in 1968, the Finns both reduced class size to make teaching in this new environment more manageable and boosted teacher pay again, this time in recognition of the additional challenge of leading heterogeneously grouped classes in the upper grades.[3]

A comparative picture of teacher pay a generation later is revealing. Norwegian and Swedish teachers, much like U.S. teachers, earn considerably less than fellow citizens with tertiary degrees, while Danish and Finnish teachers earn competitive salaries, slightly less at the primary and lower-secondary levels, about the same at the upper-secondary level (see Figure 12.1).

"We had no choice," reflected Matti Saarinen, a Social Democratic member of Parliament from the city of Lohja and a former school administrator, in a

2010 interview. "In Finland, we have our timber and we have our brains. That is all. To become an economically modern nation, we had to have very good schools, which meant we had to have very good teachers."[4]

In contrast to Finland's dearth of valuable natural resources, Sweden is home to great mineral wealth, hydroelectric power, and long-established banks and industries; Norway has been the beneficiary of vast oil and gas reserves discovered under the North Sea in 1969 as well as abundant fisheries and hydroelectric power; and Denmark, like Sweden, is home to long-established banks and industries as well as strong agricultural sectors.

Finland is not only resource-poor. It is also a young nation following centuries as a subject state (under Sweden from 1323 to 1809 and then under Russia until 1917). Finland was accordingly struggling to catch up with its Nordic neighbors. While Denmark, for example, led the world in introducing compulsory elementary education in 1814, and Norway and Sweden followed suit in 1827 and 1842, respectively, Finland did not mandate elementary education until 1921.[5] While Denmark, Norway, and Sweden had comprehensive social insurance systems in place by the 1930s, Finland had nothing but workers' accident insurance until 1963.[6]

In addition, soon after declaring its independence in 1917, Finland suffered through a brutal civil war, claiming 37,000 lives in three months. World War II brought more death and destruction. In battling the Soviets, Finland lost 90,000 lives and 10 percent of its territory. Peace meant resettling 450,000 citizens (12 percent of its population) and reparations to the Soviets of $300 million in goods (at 1938 prices) to be paid by 1952.[7] As a neutral country, Sweden emerged from World War II relatively unscathed and thus poised to prosper in the aftermath. Much the same held for Denmark as an occupied nation; although Norway suffered significant hardship as an occupied nation, it came out in far better shape than Finland.

For nation building as well as economic development, schools would play a critical role. This would be true for South Korea, too, another young nation without valuable natural resources emerging from occupation and war in the same era. However, South Korea, in the grip of Confucian tradition, would impose a heavy testing regimen utterly contrary to the progressive philosophy of Nordic educators.[8]

The school in Finland as a community centerpiece and vehicle for instilling patriotism was on prominent display when I visited the Kallahti Comprehensive School on the eastern edge of Helsinki in December 2010. For forty-five minutes, some 450 students and staff stood in the school courtyard under light snow at the start of the day to witness a ceremony honoring Finnish Independence Day, a rite solemnly observed at schools across the country the day before the national holiday, when schools and businesses are closed. It was −9 degrees Celsius (16 degrees Fahrenheit). Timo Heikkinen, the principal, spoke briefly. A recording of the national anthem played on portable speakers while students slowly raised the Finnish flag, white as the surrounding snow, segmented by a blue cross. Heikkinen then introduced two veterans, both in their upper eighties, in uniform, stern, and decorated with medals. Each spoke, the first about the terror wrought by Soviet planes repeatedly bombing Helsinki in World War II, the second about his combat experience as a teenager in the forest against invading Soviet troops and the shrapnel he has carried in his body since.[9]

The Finnish conception of education as an instrument for nation building may be seen as well in the stately, hushed atmosphere of the offices of the Finnish Ministry of Education and Culture, the Finnish National Board of Education (FNBE), the Finnish Education Evaluation Center (FINEEC), the Helsinki Department of Education, and the Finnish teachers' union, Opetusalan Ammattijärjestö (OAJ). Lobbies are elegant. Receptionists are sharply dressed, with men wearing jackets and ties. For their formality and attire, senior officials could be mistaken for personnel at the Ministry of Foreign Affairs. In all cases, interviews began with a uniformed staff member wheeling in cinnamon rolls and coffee on a trolley.[10] At schools across the country, faculty lounges are likewise striking for their style, comfort, and amenities, conveying high regard for teachers.[11]

On a more rudimentary level, the conception of education as an instrument for nation building may be seen in the country's provision of a free hot balanced lunch for all students in primary, lower-secondary, and upper-secondary schools. This has served a social as well as nutritional purpose, guaranteeing that students from all corners of the community eat together and eat well. The Finns introduced this policy in 1948.[12] A typical Finnish school lunch today consists of thick salmon soup, dark bread, cucumber salad, and lingonberry porridge.[13] By contrast, students bring or buy lunch in Denmark and Norway.[14] From 1946 onward, many municipalities in Sweden provided a free lunch to all students in primary and lower-secondary schools, but only in 1997 did the national government mandate that muncipalities provide a free lunch to all students in primary and lower-secondary schools, though not at the upper-secondary level.[15]

A look at historical economic data indeed confirms Saarinen's contention that Finland had to develop its human capital. In 1950 Finland's GDP per capita was 63 percent of Sweden's, the same as in 1930; in 1960 it was 72 percent of Sweden's. Over the next two generations, the Finnish economy grew. By 1975 Finland's GDP per capita was 81 percent of Sweden's; by 1995, 91 percent; by 2005, 95 percent.[16]

While correlation is not causation, the high-tech sector, necessarily dependent on good schooling, along with improved terms of international trade following the end of the Cold War fueled a significant portion of this growth. The same was true for South Korea. Representing this sector in Finland have been Kone in elevators and escalators; Orion in medical diagnostics and pharmaceuticals; Polar in heart-rate monitors; Vaisala in meteorological and environmental measurement; Murata in accelerometers and pressure sensors; Suunto in navigational and timekeeping devices; and the ill-fated Nokia in telecommunications (long dominant but, in the end, too slow in responding to challenges from Apple as well as South Korea's Samsung in developing smartphones).

■

Finnish education has won much attention because Finnish students have consistently posted top scores on the Program for International Student Assessment (PISA), the OECD's exam in reading, math, and science given every three years since 2000 to a random sample of approximately 5,100 fifteen-year-olds in each member nation. What has generated little attention, however, is how much better Finnish students have done than their Nordic counterparts. All four countries are small, egalitarian, and homogeneous (with the exception of growing immigrant populations in and around such cities as Oslo, Gothenburg, Malmö, Stockholm, Copenhagen, and Helsinki).

As with its Nordic neighbors, so with Finland, child welfare is of paramount importance. Of European nations, Finland ranks fourth for child welfare, just below Iceland, Sweden, and Norway, and just above Denmark.[17] Of the thirty OECD countries ranked in descending order by UNICEF for "relative child poverty," Finland ranks second, with 5.3 percent of children in this cohort (again, the United States ranks last, with 23.1 percent).[18] Finnish educational policies, however, are substantially different. Much as Sweden stands out for privatization and choice, Finland stands out for shared pedagogical strategy, seasoned but light management, and innovative student assessment as well as solid teacher preparation and pay.

Some cynics of Finland's success on PISA have countered that Finnish students have an advantage because Finnish is phonetic and thus less of a challenge to young readers.[19] While this is true, Finnish grammar is exacting and the cause for much special education intervention in early grades, particularly for boys.[20] As with Latin, so with Finnish, the final syllable of a noun determines its grammatical case. Latin has six cases (nominative, vocative, accusative, genitive, dative, and ablative); Finnish has fifteen.

Setting aside whether Finnish students have an advantage over their Nordic counterparts in reading on PISA (and given the complexity of Finnish grammar, it is far from clear that they do), what is clear is that they do far better in math and science as well, both of which require no more than basic proficiency in reading. The difference in science scores may be most telling because Finnish teachers, as explained, must have master's degrees, whereas their counterparts in Denmark, Norway, and Sweden do not. In addition, as a result of decent pay, fine training, good working conditions, and consequently high status, teaching is an esteemed profession in Finland. There is accordingly no shortage of science teachers. By contrast, teaching is not esteemed in Denmark, Norway, and Sweden. In all three countries, there is a shortage of science teachers in particular.[21]

Denmark, Norway, and Sweden have, in fact, all recently introduced programs associated with Teach for America to provide fast alternate routes to teacher certification. Danish authorities not only introduced Teach First Denmark in 2015 to provide a fast track into teaching but also ran an advertising campaign to attract students to teaching in 2010 costing 5.7 million

Danish kroner (approximately $1 million).[22] Norwegian authorities not only introduced Teach First Norway in collaboration with Statoil in 2010 to attract science students specifically, but also ran an advertising campaign that year similar to Denmark's costing 22 million Norwegian kroner (approximately $3.3 million).[23] Swedish authorities not only introduced Teach for Sweden in 2013 but also revealed that the shortage of certified chemistry teachers in 2012 was so great that there were only ten new university graduates across the country qualified to teach the subject and only one in Stockholm.[24]

Finally, science is taught through doing labs in Finnish schools. This is especially true at the lower-secondary level. Furthermore, in keeping with the rule that any class using machinery for crafts (from woodshop and textiles to culinary arts) be capped at sixteen students, principals typically adhere to that limit in programming science classes in order to facilitate student engagement and faculty supervision.[25] There is no such commitment or expectation in science classes in Danish, Norwegian, or Swedish schools and certainly not in U.S. schools.[26] In Norway, for example, science classes often involve demonstration labs done by teachers in front of the class. When I asked a Teach First Norway lower-secondary science teacher about this practice after observing two of her classes for eighth-graders at a school in Oslo as well as science classes in several other Norwegian lower-secondary schools, she said labs were the exception, not the rule. This teacher noted that classes were either too large or equipment inadequate to run labs properly. When asked about her own experience as a student a decade earlier in Bergen, she said she could not recall doing any labs.[27]

The differences in investment in facilities and smaller classes as well as teacher preparation and pay are patent. The same holds for the differences in PISA results. In the course of five administrations of the exam, Finnish students averaged a 550 in science, while their Nordic counterparts recorded nearly indistinguishable scores and posted a combined average of 494 (see Figure 12.2). With 100 points constituting one standard deviation, this difference is profound, indicating that what distinguishes Finnish pedagogical practice from Danish, Norwegian, and Swedish pedagogical practice must be substantial. This difference is all the more telling in that U.S. students over this same period posted an average of 496.

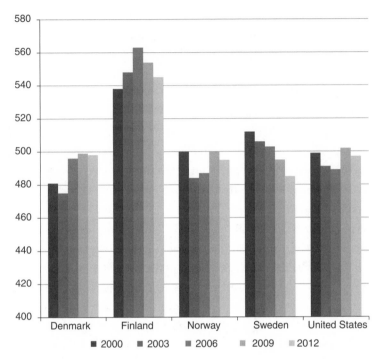

Figure 12.2 PISA scores in science. *Data source:* OECD, PISA 2000, 2003, 2006, and 2009, http://www.oecd.org/pisa/.

The similarity of U.S. scores to Danish, Norwegian, and Swedish scores buttresses the arguments made by critics of *A Nation at Risk* a generation ago that U.S. schools in general did a fine job but fell short in serving poor children. After all, while PISA results have recently caused concern in Denmark, Norway, and Sweden, schools in these three countries are by most accounts considered decent. Moreover, nothing akin to *A Nation at Risk* has been published in these three countries.[28] That Finnish schools appear much stronger is simply a testament to policies and practices that can and should be replicated.

■

Beyond investing in more science labs, reducing class size so these labs may be properly run, and improving teacher education and pay, Finnish educational authorities have taken several distinctive steps. While Swedish educational authorities distinguished themselves as commercially minded in introducing vouchers in 1992 and allowing for-profit operators to run schools, their Finnish counterparts have, ironically, done a better job of implementing core business strategies.

Improving teacher training and raising teacher pay are two obvious applications of signature lessons from the business world. In cultivating leaders and policy makers from within the ranks of teachers—rather than appointing lawyers and businessmen—the Finns have likewise applied a central business strategy of building product expertise over time and enfranchising employees with significant opportunities for professional advancement.

Less obvious manifestations of business strategy include the decisions by Finnish authorities to abolish their school inspectorate in 1991 and never follow their Nordic neighbors and much of the rest of the world in administering standardized exams to all students.[29] In this regard, the Finns applied a far more subtle business lesson. In administering exams to small samples of students rather than employing universal assessments, Finnish authorities conferred on principals and teachers more autonomy and thus ownership. At the same, they exhibited admirable efficiency, sparing students, teachers, administrators, and parents alike much stress, protecting instructional time from test prep as well as test administration, and saving money on test creation, proctoring, and grading. In the process, with minimal disruption, the Finns derived excellent information about student progress by employing fine exams and using external readers as graders.

These methods constitute the ultimate paradox of Finnish education. It is not merely that the Finns have produced an excellent school system without deploying heavy accountability measures or outsourcing school management. The Finns have achieved their success by being savvier in their understanding and implementation of business strategies.

The decision to boost teacher income, to start, is a textbook illustration of efficiency wages: it costs less to pay more. Henry Ford famously proved this in 1914 when he doubled the wage of assembly line workers from $2.50 a day to $5 while reducing the workday from nine hours to eight. Ford thus brought in better hires, increased the quality of production, and drove down the costs of both supervision and turnover.[30] In a different domain, this is precisely what the Finns have accomplished: teachers make close to what their college classmates make, as explained, and they typically teach four periods a day in contrast to the U.S. average of five.[31] In addition, in rejecting merit pay, the Finns echo the legendary managerial theorist W. Edwards Deming, who contended that merit ratings as well as merit pay generate fear, undermine teamwork, and reward only individuals who know how to succeed in the system but not the system itself.[32]

In choosing principals, superintendents, and policy makers internally rather than looking outside, Finnish authorities have likewise taken a page from the corporate playbook: great organizations, as the business historian Alfred Chandler documented, groom talent from within; this is especially true of sports dynasties, though that revealing subject was beyond the scope of Chandler's analysis.[33] Of the many officials I interviewed at the Finnish Ministry of Education and Culture, the FNBE, FINEEC, and the Helsinki Department of Education, all had been teachers for at least four years and several had taught for more than ten. In fact, two of the three authors of a landmark study of Finnish schooling published by the World Bank in 2006 are former teachers: Erkki Aho, who taught primary school for five years, then worked as a school psychologist, and eventually served from 1973 to 1991 as director general of the National Board of General Education, which merged in 1991 with the National Board of Vocational Education to form the FNBE; and Pasi Sahlberg, who taught math and science at the lower-secondary level for seven years and went on to earn a doctorate in pedagogy and serve as a policy analyst at the Education Ministry and the World Bank.[34] There is no comparable representation of teachers at administrative or policy-making levels in the neighboring Nordic nations or, for that matter, in the United States.[35]

The Finnish approach to school supervision and student assessment comport, in particular, with Deming's emphasis on leadership rather than scrutiny, and on high-quality sampling rather than universal examination.[36] Deming argued that quality should best be determined before production, not after. "Cease dependence on inspection to achieve quality," he wrote as the third of his fourteen points for management. "Eliminate the need for inspection on a mass basis by building quality into the product in the first place."[37] In elaborating, Deming wrote, "Routine inspection becomes unreliable through boredom and fatigue." Deming urged instead careful study of small samples.[38]

National school inspectors had never played a significant role in Finnish educational culture. By 1991 they had no role. The FNBE shut the division down, in part because of budgetary constraints brought on by a deep recession, in part because authorities concluded that schools ran perfectly well without central monitoring. Going forward, municipal officials would be responsible for overseeing schools and submitting occasional reports to the FNBE.[39]

In the opinion of Eeva Penttilä, who was a teacher from 1965 to 1977 and thereafter a principal until 1997, there was so much trust in Finnish society that the school inspectorate was never necessary. In this respect, Finland is much like Sweden. Over the course of two decades of annual surveys conducted by Transparency International, from 1995 to 2014, Finland averaged a ranking of second most transparent (or least corrupt) country, ranging from most transparent to sixth most.[40]

"In my career," Penttilä recalled in a 2009 interview as director of international relations for the Helsinki Department of Education, "I met one school inspector. He stood in the back of my class, spent a few minutes surveying the room, and left. It was a new building, and we were having problems with the pipes. I thought he was the plumber. At the end of the day, my principal introduced me."[41]

Trust, according to Sahlberg, goes a long way in explaining the Finnish employment of sampling rather than universal testing as well. Much as the United States tests all students in reading and math in grades three through eight and one year in high school,[42] Denmark tests all students in Danish in grades two, four, six, and eight; in math in grades three and six; in English in grade seven; and in science in grade eight.[43] Norway tests all students in Norwegian, math, and English in grades five, eight, and nine.[44] Sweden, as explained in Chapter 11, tests all students in Swedish and math in grade three; in Swedish, math, and English in grade six; in Swedish, math, English, and science in grade nine; and in Swedish, math, and English at the upper-secondary level.[45]

The Finns not only restrict their testing to micro samples but also test a far broader spectrum of subjects. Their practice is to cover every subject in the school curriculum (from math and reading to music, visual arts, wood-shop, home economics, and physical education) over a ten-year cycle while testing a randomly chosen sample of approximately 10 percent of students in two or three subjects every year in grade nine. In addition, for longitudinal purposes, one cohort of approximately 6,000 students is tested in math every three years starting in grade three. FINEEC administers and grades the exams, except for the culinary component of home economics. In the case of music, visual arts, and woodshop, videos are made and centrally assessed. In all cases, students do not receive grades, nor do teachers. Only the principals find out from FINEEC how their students performed.[46] Had Deming ever designed a system for assessing schools, it would most probably have looked like the Finnish system (see Table 12.1).

To Sahlberg, the Finnish approach is both revealing and efficient. He likens his country's method of educational assessment to medical protocol. "When your doctor needs to check your blood," Sahlberg said at a 2014 symposium on Finnish education in New York, "he or she takes three or four vials, not five liters. We feel the same way in Finnish schools about standardized testing. Careful sampling gets us all the information we need to know how schools are doing without any stress."[47]

This method is all the more practical for two reasons. First, the Finns administer a matriculation examination in the final year of upper-secondary school to all students wishing to attend university. Much like France's baccalaureate, the Finnish matriculation exam comprises a battery of tests. In the case of Finland, it's a battery of tests in four to seven subjects (with Finnish, Swedish, math, and either humanities or natural sciences as mandatory).[48] The matriculation exam thus guides students as well as teachers years in advance.

Second, the Finnish method of sampling works because teacher training is of such high quality. In this regard, Deming's words apply again: mass inspection is unnecessary if quality is built into the product from the beginning. In attracting solid students to teaching and in preparing them carefully for the profession, the Finns indeed "build quality" at the outset. Several days of observations of teacher instruction at the University of Helsinki and the University of Jyväskylä made clear the rigor and depth of these programs. For earth science at the University of Helsinki, for example, students each

Table 12.1 National exam program for Finnish students from 2010 to 2015

Year	Grade	Subject	Sample	Duration
2010	9	Finnish, as native tongue Swedish, as native tongue	10% 30%	Three 60-minute sessions covering reading comprehension, grammar, writing
2010	9	Sports, visual arts, music, crafts	5%	Two 45-minute sets of drills in physical fitness and agility plus a 60-minute written exam; or four 45-minute written exams covering visual arts, music, and crafts plus either 2 hours to produce a drawing; 2 hours to compose and perform a short piece of music; or 4 hours to craft a product in woodshop
2010	9	Civics	100%	All students take a 60-minute written exam in one of the following fields: human development; cultural identity; communications; environmental responsibility; public safety; society and technology
2011	9	Science	10%	Half take two 45-minute exams in biology and geography; half take two 45-minute exams in physics and chemistry
2011	9	History and social studies	10%	Three 45-minute written exams
2012	9	Math	10%	One 30-minute and two 45-minute exams
2012	9	Math follow-up	Cohort from grades 3 and 6	One 30-minute and two 45-minute exams

Year	Grade	Subject	Percentage	Description
2013	9	Health	10%	Two 45-minute written exams
2013	9	Foreign language	10% for English and Swedish; 100% for German and Russian	One 30-minute written exam; 45-minute exams in both reading and listening comprehension; 5-minute oral exam
2014	9	Finnish/Swedish as native tongue	10%	One 70-minute exam in grammar; two 45-minute exams in writing
2014	9	Home economics	10%	One 20-minute background questionnaire; 75-minute written exam; two 45-minute cooking/baking tasks
2015	9	Minority languages: Romani, Sami	100%	60-minute exams in grammar and writing; 75-minute exams in reading and listening; 15-minute exam in speaking
2015	9	Sign language	100%	One 30-minute visual exam; two 60-minute exams in reading and writing
2015	9	Math	10%	One 20-minute background questionnaire; two 45-minute exams
2015	12	Math follow-up	Cohort from grades 3, 6, and 9	One 15-minute background questionnaire; two 45-minute exams

Data source: Finnish Education Evaluation Center, June 2015.

week attend a lecture and then one four-hour lab, where they work in groups of four on intricately developed lessons designed for elementary school students. A professor circulates and provides input when asked. For math at the University of Helsinki, students each week attend a lecture and two ninety-minute labs of a similar nature. All students also take adult versions of courses in crafts and physical education they took as children, even if they will never teach crafts or physical education. Through carving in woodshop or playing volleyball, students in teacher education programs learn the pedagogical philosophy and techniques behind the courses they all took as children so that they can better relate to their students.[49]

■

Much has been made of the selectivity of Finnish programs for teacher education (designed for teachers at the *peruskoulu* level, grades one through nine).[50] It is indeed hard to get into these programs, but the degree of selectivity calls for qualification. The widespread claim that only 10 percent of applicants are accepted and that all successful applicants come from the top academic decile or quintile of upper-secondary school graduates both need amending. The correct portion, as will be explained, is 16 percent of applicants, which is still daunting but must be understood in the context of Finland's system of numerus clausus, meaning a fixed number of seats in university programs. Moreover, successful applicants represent a cross section of upper-secondary graduates, not the top decile or quintile. These applicants are judged as much for personality and versatility as academic excellence (though these students in turn represent half their age cohort, as approximately 51 percent of Finnish lower-secondary graduates attend academic upper-secondary schools while approximately 41 percent attend vocational upper-secondary schools and the rest go directly into the job market).[51]

The application process requires clarification for a better understanding of this selectivity and its implications for policy makers in other countries. First, students who sign up to take the national teacher admission exam—a two-hour multiple-choice test based on several articles about pedagogy available online six weeks in advance—don't all follow through in taking it and consequently should not be counted as applicants. Second, applicants have been able to apply to only three programs and be considered for admission at only one.[52] Third, the rate of acceptance should be calculated according to offers of admission, not spots.

Accordingly, in 2010, for example, 1,037 students signed up to take the admission exam for entrance to the University of Eastern Finland at Joensuu, 869 students followed through in taking the exam, 365 listed the university as their first choice (meaning they couldn't be considered by another program if granted an interview by Joensuu), 241 were interviewed, 79 were admitted, 17 of those admitted declined, and 17 came off the waiting list to take their places, meaning 96 were admitted out of 365 applicants. This is clearly selective, but 96 out of 365 (or 26 percent) paints a different picture than 79 out of 1,037 (or 8 percent). In total, there were 5,162 applicants to all teacher education programs in 2010, 752 spots, and 873 offers of admission, with 124 students coming off waiting lists, meaning an overall acceptance rate of 17 percent and a mean institutional acceptance rate of 23 percent (see Table 12.2). These numbers reflect data gathered from 2001 to 2013. The acceptance rate over this time period averaged 16 percent and ranged from 15 percent to 19 percent.[53]

At base, however, it is the Finnish employment of a system of numerus clausus that makes the admission process especially tight. The number of seats is set by the Ministry of Education and Culture to improve job prospects for graduates as well as control quality and contain costs.[54] Denmark, Norway, and Sweden do not use numerus clausus systems for their education programs. In Denmark, all students earning a grade point average of 7 or above on a scale of −3 to 12 are admitted; half of those applicants whose grade point average is below 7 are admitted through an interview process.[55] In 2011 Norwegian teacher education programs admitted 82 percent of applicants, and Swedish teacher education programs admitted 81 percent.[56] The United States likewise does not employ a numerus clausus system.

For policy-making purposes, the trouble with the numerus clausus system for teacher education in Finland is that it gives the impression that only a small portion of applicants are qualified when, in fact, according to several professors who interview applicants, many qualified candidates don't gain admission simply because there are not enough spots.[57] The numerus clausus system in turn sends the message that the excellence of Finnish schooling derives more from the selectivity of the admission process to teacher education

Table 12.2   Applicants to teacher education programs at Finnish universities in 2010

University	Exam registrants	Applicants	Ranking first	Interviewed	Spots	Waiting list admits	Admission rate
Eastern Finland–Joensuu	1,037	869	365	241	79	17	26%
Eastern Finland–Savonlinna	619	521	109	120	40	15	50%
Helsinki	2,069	1,531	1,129	360	120	8	11%
Jyväskylä	1,893	1,494	848	240	76	20	11%
Lapland	831	688	262	69	64	5	26%
Oulu	1,091	844	494	80	20	1	4%
Oulu-Kajaani	734	619	238	180	73	14	37%
Tampere	1,909	1,507	553	321	67	3	13%
Turku	1,602	1,283	584	205	74	12	15%
Turku-Rauma	1,073	898	339	180	65	19	25%
Vaasa	323	241	241	n/a	74	10	35%
Total	13,181	10,495	5,162	1,996	752	124	17%

Data sources: National Selection Cooperation Network in the Field of Education, Valtakunnallinen kasvatusalan valintayhteistyöverkosto (VAKAVA), http://www.helsinki.fi/vakava/hakijamaarat%20ja%20pisterajat_2010.pdf; University Application Registry, Yliopistojen hakija- ja opinto-oikeusrekisteri (HAREK), October 5, 2010, obtained by e-mail from the Finnish National Board of Education, January 23, 2014; Tuuli Asunmaa, admission coordinator, teacher education, University of Helsinki, January 27, 2014.

Notes: Admission rate is determined by offers (spots plus waiting list admits) over unique applicants (those ranking universities as their first choice). The teacher education program at the University of Vaasa is for Swedish-speaking Finns.

programs than from the strength of these programs or many other contributing factors. For cultural reasons, policy makers in other countries may not be able to make teaching as popular a profession as it is in Finland. But they can certainly follow in Finland's path in improving their teacher education programs as well as teacher working conditions and pay, all of which should also boost the popularity of the profession.

The Finns stand to keep the numerus clausus system,[58] but they can and should simplify the application process. This holds for many fields of study in Finland. Aspiring doctors, for example, can apply to only one of five medical schools; aspiring lawyers, only one of five law schools. If students don't get in, they can apply again the following year or study in another country.[59] Students should be able to apply to several programs, as they do in many other countries (Denmark, Norway, Sweden, and the United States among them), and let the application process sort itself out. The current system forces students to play a stressful guessing game about where to apply and ultimately keeps them from knowing where they might have been accepted, a serious consequence for those who don't gain admission to their selected program but might have been admitted elsewhere. That 17 percent of successful applicants to teacher education programs in 2010 (that is, 124 of 749 initial admits) chose to go in a different direction indicates that many students hedge their bets and apply to programs in different fields.

This would be unnecessary if students could be considered for admission by a range of programs in the same field. The market, so to speak, would clear or at least do a far better job of clearing. Worse yet, this application process prevents numerous young people from starting their studies and moving on in their lives. In this regard, the Finns have fallen far short of applying wise business principles to education policy.

Many university students in education and other fields explained in interviews that it took them two or three attempts before gaining admission; some mentioned friends who gave up and enrolled in programs abroad (though studying abroad is not an option for students wishing to become *peruskoulu* teachers). These students also said they would have gladly begun their studies at a second, third, or fourth choice if given the opportunity to apply to several programs in the same field.[60] This matter is all the more pressing for a country with an aging population dependent on a pension system defined, like many pension systems, by transfer of payments from current workers to retirees.

When asked about this issue in a 2014 interview, Krista Kiuru, Finland's minister of education and culture at the time and a former teacher herself, said the application process was unreasonable, unfair, and inefficient. "It's merely the way things have been done for a long time, perhaps because Finland has been a very regional country, perhaps because university leaders don't want to share a uniform process for application," Kiuru said. "Unfortunately, the tradition of government officials in Finland is not to question how universities operate. But we cannot go on this way. The system does not work."[61]

■

Frustrations with the admission process aside, many young Finns want to become teachers and often go through the application process a second or third time before gaining admission to a teacher education program. According to Tuuli Asunmaa, the admission coordinator at the University of Helsinki, who was previously a teacher of crafts, many young people want to become teachers because they liked school so much themselves. The Finnish commitment to art, music, crafts, and play in grades one through nine is indeed uncompromising and makes school enticing for students. While art, music, crafts, and play are also important in Danish, Norwegian, and Swedish schools, there is no commensurately systemic allocation of time and resources.[62]

Finnish authorities consider play so essential, in fact, that they mandate that schools throughout the country schedule fifteen minutes of recess for every forty-five minutes of instruction, for a total of seventy-five minutes of recess per six-hour school day.[63] Finnish authorities also mandate lots of arts and crafts, as the FINEEC assessments conveyed. Students in grades one through nine take from four to eleven periods a week of art, music, cooking, sewing, woodshop, or metalwork.[64]

These courses serve an important pedagogical function. They nurture critical cooperative skills, provide natural venues for learning math and science, and implicitly cultivate respect for people who make their living working with their hands. Yet these courses also represent another ironic lesson from the business world lost on so many advocates of heavy testing and accountability.

In technical terms, as explained at the beginning of this book, students constitute an input in the production function of education, beyond capital investment, labor, and technological innovation. Much like executives at Aetna, Google, and SAS Institute, Finnish authorities have understood that more work at the expense of recreation and relaxation can be counterproductive. Executives at Aetna, Google, and SAS Institute accordingly designed their offices with recreation and relaxation in mind and encouraged employees to take breaks in the middle of the day to run, swim, meditate, or do yoga.[65] Finnish educational authorities have likewise concluded that students who enjoy school will do better in school.

Timo Heikkinen, the principal of the Kallahti Comprehensive School, on the eastern edge of Helsinki, made this eminently clear to me during a visit in April 2009. We were watching recess together after lunch. It was cold. I asked Heikkinen if students go out when it's very cold. He said they do. I then asked Heikkinen if they go out when it's very, very cold. He smiled. "If minus 15 [Celsius] and windy," he said, "maybe not, but otherwise, yes. The children can't learn if they don't play. The children must play."[66]

This commitment stands in sharp contrast to American practice. Since the enactment of No Child Left Behind in the United States in 2002 led to a focus on annual testing in reading and math in grades three through eight, 20 percent of the country's school districts eliminated or reduced recess, driving down time for play to an average of twenty-seven minutes a day, according to a 2007 survey by the Center on Education Policy. Nearly the same portion of the country's school districts over a similar period eliminated or reduced classes in art, music, and drama, according to a 2012 report by the National Center for Education Statistics.[67]

■

There is nothing heretical about a pedagogical commitment to play or a corporate commitment to recreation and relaxation. In addition to conceding the need for a balance of mind and body, in keeping with Juvenal's timeless words about a sound mind in a sound body, such a commitment exhibits a sophisticated understanding of intellectual activity itself.[68]

Academic work, after all, constitutes a particular form of play. The Dutch cultural historian Johan Huizinga made precisely this case in 1938 in *Homo Ludens: A Study of the Play-Element in Culture.* Contrary to the rationalist claims of the Enlightenment, Huizinga contended, humans are guided by more than reason than the term *Homo sapiens* (thinking man) indicates. And contrary to the conventions of the Industrial Revolution, Huizinga argued, humans are defined by more than productivity than the phrase *Homo faber* (making man) allows. As a creature driven as much by the challenge and joy of proving oneself as a teammate or an opponent, Huizinga concluded, a human being is *Homo ludens* (playful man), in fields as diverse as art, poetry, debate, philosophy, law, and commerce.[69]

If a human is as much *Homo ludens* as *Homo sapiens* or *Homo faber,* then surely the child is in essence *Puer ludens* (playful child). In prescribing significant time at school for play as well as art, music, and crafts, the Finns reveal their deep understanding of this conception of human nature and expose a fundamental problem with how U.S. schools are managed.

When I returned to Heikkinen's school in December 2010, I wondered during the morning ceremony honoring Finnish Independence Day whether he would keep his word. It wasn't −15 degrees Celsius. But it was −9, windy, and snowing. Following the first class after the ceremony, sure enough, Heikkinen's students were outside for recess. Much as the storied Italian Renaissance schoolmaster Vittorino da Feltre saw to it six centuries ago that students at his school in Mantua, called La Giocosa (The Pleasant House), played outdoors every day no matter the weather, Heikkinen and principals across Finland do not let low temperatures, wind, and snow get in the way.[70] With joyful abandon, and nearly anonymous in their puffy snowsuits, some played soccer, others played tag, and a gleeful group of girls and boys perched on a small hill took turns sliding down a steep, icy chute they had cleared through the snow.

EPILOGUE

It's not the tables. It's the floor.

Franklin Singleton, Senior,
Beacon School, October 1999

■ IN MY FIRST YEAR as a teacher at the Beacon School, where this book began, I shared a classroom with a French teacher, a senior colleague and inspiring instructor named Nicole Cherry, fluent in Portuguese and Spanish as well as French. It was 1999–2000. The classroom was 104. For four periods of the seven-period schedule, Cherry taught in 104. For the other three, I did; in addition, I taught a fourth class in another classroom. This is how teachers at Beacon shared space.

We had eight round tables in 104, with four chairs at six and five at two. The statutory ceiling for class size for New York City public high schools was thirty-four; hence the additional two chairs. Cherry's desk was at one end of the classroom, mine at the other. The north wall was punctuated with windows behind black steel fencing. The south wall was covered with a whiteboard.

The tables with five chairs were tight, but we made do. The real problem with the tables wasn't their size. The problem was that they wobbled. Over the first few weeks of the school year, students muttered at the beginning of class about the wobbling, folded some paper, and jammed it under the short leg or legs, or they moved previous engineering efforts from one leg to another. As the challenges of prepping for class and learning the names of students dominated my attention, I didn't give much thought to this matter of wobbling tables until one day when a squabble broke out at one table five minutes into class in early October about which leg was short.

It was a class in economics for seniors. In exasperation, a student named Franklin Singleton stood up, dropped to his hands and knees, and pressed one side of his head to the floor for several seconds. The class went silent. I stopped outlining my lesson on the whiteboard about inflation or unemployment or opportunity costs. Singleton popped up and intoned, "We need to stop all this foolishness. It's not the tables. It's the floor." Everyone nodded. They were accustomed to contrarian but sensible comments from Singleton, a gifted math student as well as a sharpshooting forward and powerful rebounder on the school's basketball team. I returned to outlining my lesson.

During a break later in the day, I thought about Singleton's observation. He was certainly right. The building, after all, was previously a warehouse for heavy equipment for ABC Television, whose studios were a few blocks north, east, and south of the school. It made sense that the floors weren't level. But as a metaphor, Singleton's observation was clearly profound. We often mistake symptoms for causes. This has been especially true in the realm of education policy: underperforming schools underperform because of insufficient accountability, the prevailing argument has gone. And we've only made things worse by tightening the screws. That is precisely what has happened since the publication of *A Nation at Risk* in 1983. With the focus on test results pushed by state officials and for-profit school management advocates in the 1990s and reinforced thereafter by No Child Left Behind (NCLB) in 2002 and Race to the Top (RTTT) in 2009, our misguided efforts have intensified.

The purposes of NCLB and RTTT could not have been nobler. Closing the achievement gap between underprivileged and privileged children represents the greatest of democratic ideals. Yet regular testing to identify deficiencies has not accomplished much but identify deficiencies. We must acknowledge the power of child poverty and take the action necessary to eliminate it.[1] Ranking last among thirty OECD nations in a 2012 UNICEF study of child poverty, as noted, should alone make clear the gravity of this problem, as should the cited comparative crime data: in particular, Baltimore as home to forty times the number of cases of murder and manslaughter per capita as Stockholm.[2] While scholars may argue that the degree of child poverty in the United States has been exaggerated,[3] there is no denying that the straits of poor children NCLB and RTTT were meant to help are grim.

Organizations like Achievement First, KIPP, and Mastery do great work despite the force of poverty, but their dependence on a finite supply of generous philanthropists, tireless teachers, and students as well as families capable of abiding by rigid academic and behavioral expectations limits their reach. These organizations have led the way in showing what can be accomplished for a subset of students by granting administrators significant autonomy, extending the school day, providing intensive remedial help, and raising expectations. The next step is to make these strategies work for all students in disadvantaged communities. Such replication would necessitate substantial public investment to hire additional staff. The result would ultimately comport with the community school concept, with afternoon programs in art, music, crafts, sports, and homework help as well as associated medical, dental, and counseling services.

This paradigm would be all the more successful if schools were granted the freedom to broaden their curricula. That could happen if we reversed course and abolished our current accountability system, which we undoubtedly should. In this regard, while addressing exogenous factors, there is much we can do about endogenous factors: that is, while working to level the floor, we can at the same time accomplish a good deal by fixing the tables, as there is now much wrong with the tables, so to speak, because of years of misguided education policy.

Much of our mistaken thinking about education policy derives from our commercial mindset. There is nothing inherently wrong about employing a commercial mindset in making education policy. Schools are necessarily part of any nation's economic infrastructure. The Finns, too, employ a commercial mindset in formulating education policy. The Finns, too, care about results. But they think long term. And they view policy from the perspective of the child. In doing so, they implicitly adhere to yet another of W. Edwards Deming's core principles: "The consumer is the most important part of the production line. Quality should be aimed at the needs of the consumer, present and future."[4] The present and future needs of the child as consumer of education, as odd as that string of words might sound, include art, music, crafts, play, and an array of academic subjects.

In the United States, despite the best of intentions, education policy makers have thought neither long term nor from the perspective of the child. Chris Whittle's contention in advertorials in *Education Week* in 2005 and 2006 that schools should provide parents with data about their children's academic progress much as Federal Express supplies customers with data about their packages is a telling illustration. As noted, Whittle argued that just as Federal Express informs customers exactly when a package shipped and where it is in transit, schools should pinpoint for parents their children's levels of proficiency in reading and math throughout the year.[5] In testing all students in grades three through eight and one year in high school in reading and math, as mandated by NCLB, and in recording data for students on regular benchmark assessments in preparation for these annual tests, schools have come close to fulfilling Whittle's vision. Typifying the embrace of annual testing, the editorial board of the *New York Times* in December 2015 dismissed as absurd a proposal in the Senate concerning reauthorization of NCLB that would have permitted states to end annual testing. Such legislation, the editors contended, "would leave the country no way of knowing whether students were learning anything or not."[6]

Yet we don't need annual testing to know whether students are learning. With sophisticated sampling techniques, school administrators can obtain all the information they need and at the same time preserve time for art, music, crafts, and play as well as academic subjects other than reading and math. School administrators can thus also reclaim valuable time, energy, and resources expended on constructing, proctoring, and grading these tests.

A reader might fault me for this conclusion by pointing out how much data analysis there is in this book. But much of that data analysis concerned the perverse consequences of heavy testing in Baltimore and Philadelphia: tampering in the first case; disregard in the second for subjects (specifically, writing and science) that had no bearing on determining a school's Adequate Yearly Progress, the metric introduced by NCLB to assess schools.[7] The remaining data analysis concerned child welfare, crime, per-pupil expenditure, teacher pay, and the Program for International Student Assessment

(PISA), the exam administered by the OECD every three years since 2000 to a small random sample of fifteen-year-olds in each member nation.

The evidence against the usefulness of all our testing is robust and compelling. Perhaps most damning was a detailed report published in 2011 by the National Research Council drawing on analysis of ten years of test-based accountability systems as well as merit pay programs for teachers and pay-for-performance experiments for students. Entitled *Incentives and Test-Based Accountability in Education,* the report was the work of a blue-ribbon commission made up of seventeen leading professors of business, economics, education, law, psychology, and sociology. The authors found little if any effect on student progress and, in some instances, counterproductive outcomes.[8]

Paul Reville, the secretary of education for Massachusetts, drew a similar conclusion in 2008 upon reflecting on efforts in the state since passage of the Massachusetts Education Reform Act in 1993. Reville, one of the architects of the act, said that despite aggressive efforts at measurement and accountability, the state had failed to alter the strong relationship of socioeconomic status to educational achievement.[9]

Worse yet, our emphasis on testing has led school officials to invest good money after bad in analyzing test results to guard against cheating by principals and teachers worried sick about the impact of student performance on their evaluations and pay. In August 2015, New York City Schools chancellor Carmen Fariña announced the creation of an Academic Integrity Task Force to investigate irregularities in test scores as well as rates of graduation and course credit accumulation. "Principals and guidance counselors will have to attend additional training sessions to help them maintain high standards," reported the Associated Press. Auditors from the accounting firm Ernst & Young will assist the task force in reviewing data. According to the *New York Times,* the task force is expected to cost $5 million a year.[10] Fariña and superintendents like her have little choice. They must comply with federal mandates. But federal lawmakers who draft and ratify education legislation have a choice.

■

Far from all this turbulence, on the other hand, a reassuring illustration against the usefulness of heavy testing, as explained, may be observed in

Finland, which, unlike its Nordic neighbors as well as the United States, administers national exams to only small samples of students and does so in a wide range of subjects. In appraising all the attention garnered by Finland for its impressive PISA results, Kari Louhivuori, the principal of the Kirkkojärvi Comprehensive School in Espoo, said in a 2010 conversation, "PISA showed that occasional testing of samples of students proves regular testing of all students is unnecessary."[11]

With the National Assessment of Educational Progress (NAEP), we already have in place an excellent form of sampling. Introduced in 1969, NAEP has been periodically administered to test small but representative samples of students in reading, writing, math, and science in grades four, eight, and twelve in public schools across the country. Since 2007 NAEP has been administered every two years. The sample size is, on average, 2,500 students in each grade in each state.[12]

We need little more than NAEP. For reading, writing, math, and science, NAEP is sufficient. Beyond these four subjects, states could follow the lead of the Finnish Education Evaluation Center in administering thorough assessments to samples of students in art, music, crafts, culinary arts, history, civics, geography, foreign language, and physical fitness and agility. We would as a result obtain not only far more accurate and holistic information; we would also redirect significant resources from central offices to schools, win back from test prep countless hours for academic instruction and enrichment, and thus make school more enticing for students and teachers alike.

In addition to improving teacher preparation and pay, we have to make the everyday experience of teaching more appealing to attract people to the profession and keep them. Five days after the *New York Times* ran its article about Fariña's Academic Integrity Task Force, the paper devoted its lead story to a dire teacher shortage across the country and in California in particular. In response, five letter writers cited micromanagement, high-stakes testing, low pay, or some combination as key deterrents.[13]

My former student Franklin Singleton is one capable young person who recently told me he would like to become a teacher. He is now an officer in the army based at Fort Bragg, in North Carolina, working in helicopter maintenance and repair. He had come up to New York to see family and contacted me in advance to introduce me to his wife, Aisha, and catch up over dinner. Singleton told me about his tours of duty in Afghanistan, his current work at Fort Bragg, and an upcoming assignment in South Korea. He said he liked the army but would like to get his college degree and become a math teacher. Singleton would make an excellent math teacher. And he would be all the more effective, like teachers across the country, if given the latitude professionals deserve and students need.

NOTES

Abbreviations

AER	American Economic Review	PPSN	Philadelphia Public School Notebook
EW	Education Week	TBS	Baltimore Sun
NYDN	New York Daily News	TPI	Philadelphia Inquirer
NYT	New York Times	WP	Washington Post
PDN	Philadelphia Daily News	WSJ	Wall Street Journal

Prologue

1. For an analysis of the application process and how it was transformed, see Atila Abdulkadiroglu, Parag A. Pathak, and Alvin E. Roth, "The New York City High School Match," *AER* 95 (May 2005): 364–367.

2. Samuel G. Freedman, "Student Rankings? Computers Flunk, and College Plans Are in Chaos," *NYT,* March 16, 2005.

3. Beacon was founded in 1993 as part of an initiative launched by Chancellor Joseph Fernandez in the early 1990s to create small high schools with enrollments topping off at 500. However, according to Steve Stoll, he and Ruth Lacey, cofounders and codirectors of the school, decided, upon moving into their own building in 1995, a former warehouse for ABC Television on West 61st Street, that as they had more space than they needed, they would fill it with more students for fear they would have to share the building with another school and thereby compromise the site's cultural integrity as a school focused on the arts. In addition, Stoll explained, the enrollment formula allowed principals to admit additional students "over the counter." Standard procedure specified that half the

school's students enter via random assignment, with a certain portion scoring in the top, middle, and bottom on citywide tests; the other half, admitted over the counter, had to represent the same distribution of test scores, but school principals could take into account grades, attendance, and input from middle school guidance counselors. To give greater weight to grades, attendance, and such input than to scores on citywide tests, the Beacon administration decided to exercise its right to admit more students over the counter. In 2005, Beacon obtained from the New York City Department of Education the right to admit students according to its own criteria. Beacon thus went on to become a selective school, requiring that all applicants go through an interview, write an essay while waiting for their interview, and submit a portfolio of their best work. Stoll, telephone interview, May 25, 2010.

4. David Rogers, *Can Business Management Save the Cities? The Case of New York* (New York: Free Press, 1978), 23, 73–92.

5. David Tyack and Larry Cuban, *Tinkering toward Utopia: A Century of Public School Reform* (Cambridge, MA: Harvard University Press, 1995), 78. For an analysis of how frustration with such inefficiency paved the way for Mayor Michael Bloomberg's takeover of New York's school system, see David Rogers, *Mayoral Control of the New York City Schools* (New York: Springer, 2009), 21–22.

6. According to a 2009 study of twelve school districts across four states published by the New Teacher Project, "at least half of the districts studied have not dismissed a single nonprobationary teacher for poor performance in the past five years." See Daniel Weisberg et al., "The Widget Effect: Our National Failure to Acknowledge and Act on Differences in Teacher Effectiveness" (New York: New Teacher Project, 2009), 6, http://widgeteffect.org/. See also Steven Brill, "The Rubber Room: The Battle over New York City's Worst Teachers," *New Yorker*, August 31, 2009, 30–36.

7. F. A. von Hayek, "Freedom and the Economic System," *Contemporary Review* 153 (January 1938): 434–442; Hayek, *The Road to Serfdom* (Chicago: University of Chicago Press, 1944), 60–61, 199–200, 218–220; Hayek, *The Constitution of Liberty* (Chicago: University of Chicago Press, 1960), 299–300, 381; Milton Friedman, "The Role of Government in Education," in *Economics and the Public Interest*, ed. Robert A. Solo (New Brunswick, NJ: Rutgers University Press, 1955), 123–144; Friedman, *Capitalism and Freedom* (Chicago: University of Chicago Press, 1962), 2–3, 8–9, 29–31, 85–107, 178–189; George J. Stigler, "The Theory of Economic Regulation," *Bell Journal of Economics and Management Science* 2 (Spring 1971): 3–21; Gary S. Becker and George J. Stigler, "Law Enforcement, Malfeasance, and Compensation of Enforcers," *Journal of Legal Studies* 3 (January 1974): 1–18; Robert W. Poole, *Cutting Back City Hall* (New York: Universe Books, 1980); Myron Lieberman, *Privatization and Educational Choice* (New York: St. Martin's, 1989). For an overview of this transformation, see Joseph Stanislaw and Daniel Yergin, *The Commanding Heights: The Battle between Government*

and the Marketplace That Is Remaking the Modern World (New York: Simon and Schuster, 1998). For critiques of this transformation, see John D. Donahue, *The Privatization Decision: Public Ends, Private Means* (New York: Basic Books, 1989); Robert Kuttner, *Everything for Sale: The Virtues and Limits of Markets* (New York: Knopf, 1998); Elliott D. Sclar, *You Don't Always Get What You Pay For: The Economics of Privatization* (Ithaca, NY: Cornell University Press, 2000); and Richard R. Nelson, ed., *The Limits of Market Organization* (New York: Russell Sage Foundation, 2005).

8. Friedman, "Role of Government in Education," 127; Friedman, *Capitalism and Freedom,* 89.

9. Henry M. Levin, "The Failure of the Public Schools and the Free Market Remedy," *Urban Review* 2 (June 1968): 22–37. See also Dennis Epple and Richard E. Romano, "Competition between Private and Public Schools, Vouchers, and Peer-Group Effects," *AER* 88 (March 1998): 33–62.

10. Amy Stuart Wells, *Time to Choose: America at the Crossroads of School Choice Policy* (New York: Hill and Wang, 1993), 152–153.

11. President's Commission on Privatization, *Privatization: Toward More Effective Government; Report of the President's Commission on Privatization* (Washington, DC: Government Printing Office, 1988), 92–95.

12. Lieberman, *Privatization and Educational Choice,* 4, 268.

13. Paul T. Hill, Lawrence C. Pierce, and James W. Guthrie, *Reinventing Public Education: How Contracting Can Transform America's Schools* (Chicago: University of Chicago Press, 1997), 51–52.

14. National Center on Education and the Economy, *Tough Choices or Tough Times: The Report of the New Commission on the Skills of the American Workforce* (San Francisco: John Wiley and Sons, 2007), 67–78.

15. Lieberman, *Privatization and Educational Choice,* 85–117. See also Edward M. Gramlich and Patricia P. Koshel, *Educational Performance Contracting: An Evaluation of an Experiment* (Washington, DC: Brookings, 1975); Craig E. Richards, Rima Shore, and Max B. Sawicky, *Risky Business: Private Management of Public Schools* (Washington, DC: Economic Policy Institute, 1996), 31–37; and Carol Ascher, "Performance Contracting: A Forgotten Experiment in School Privatization," *Phi Delta Kappan* 77 (May 1996): 615–621.

16. Ascher, "Performance Contracting," 615.

17. Lieberman, *Privatization and Educational Choice,* 100.

18. Joan Cook, "Business-Run Schools: Companies' Profits Linked to Students' Progress," *NYT,* November 29, 1970.

19. David Tyack, "Reinventing Schooling," in *Learning from the Past: What History Teaches Us about School Reform,* ed. Diane Ravitch and Maris A. Vinovskis (Baltimore: Johns Hopkins University Press, 1995), 199–200.

20. Fred M. Hechinger, "Negative Verdict on a Teaching Program," *NYT,* February 6, 1972.

21. Ibid.

22. Andrew H. Malcolm, "Company to Teach Gary, Ind., Pupils," *NYT*, July 26, 1970; Associated Press, "Gary, Ind., Ends Pact with Concern Running School," *NYT*, December 5, 1972; Ascher, "Performance Contracting," 619.

23. Tyack, "Reinventing Schooling," 198–199.

24. Richards, Shore, and Sawicky, *Risky Business*, 54–72.

25. Hill, Pierce, and Guthrie, *Reinventing Public Education*, 5–6.

26. Mark Walsh, "Minneapolis Ends Unique Management Contract," *EW*, June 4, 1997, http://www.edweek.org/ew/articles/1997/06/04/36minn.h16.html.

27. Alex Molnar et al., *Profiles of For-Profit Education Management Companies: Fourth Annual Report, 2001–2002* (Tempe, AZ: Commercialism in Education Research Unit, Education Policy Studies Laboratory, Arizona State University, 2002), 11, http://nepc.colorado.edu/files/EMO102.pdf.

28. As of 2001, only Milwaukee and Cleveland had implemented full-fledged voucher programs. Milwaukee began with a pilot program in 1990 with modestly valued vouchers for children from low-income homes at secular private schools; in 1999, Wisconsin permitted inclusion of religious schools. In 1995, Cleveland followed suit with modestly valued vouchers available to low-income students at religious as well as secular private schools (if more vouchers were allocated than needed by students from low-income homes, the remainder could be used by students from homes of greater means, though the vouchers decreased in value). As of the 1999–2000 academic year, about 7,600 students in Milwaukee employed vouchers at 91 private schools (the maximum value was $5,106); and about 3,400 students in Cleveland used vouchers at 52 private schools (the maximum value was $2,250 for students from low-income homes and $1,875 for students from homes of greater means). See U.S. General Accounting Office, School Vouchers: Publicly Funded Programs in Cleveland and Milwaukee (GAO-01-914), August 2001.

29. Molnar et al., *Profiles of For-Profit Education Management Companies*, 5–6.

30. Jacques Le Goff, *Un Autre Moyen Âge* (Paris: Éditions Gallimard, 1999), 1274–1275. Le Goff cites the following biblical passages as basic to usury laws in medieval Europe: Exodus 22:24, Leviticus 25: 35–37, Deuteronomy 23: 20, Psalm 25, and Ezekiel 18: 13. Glyn Davies explains in *A History of Money: From Ancient Times to the Present Day* (Cardiff: University of Wales Press, 2002), 218–223, that a parliamentary act approving interest on loans passed in 1545 was repealed in 1552 and then reenacted in 1571. Simon Schama explains in *The Embarrassment of Riches: An Interpretation of Dutch Culture in the Golden Age* (New York: Knopf, 1988), 330, that bankers and their families were barred from communion in Holland until 1658.

31. Viviana Zelizer, *Morals and Markets: The Development of Life Insurance in the United States* (New York: Columbia University Press, 1979).

32. See Jamie Robert Vollmer, "The Blueberry Story," *EW,* March 6, 2002, 42; and Larry Cuban, *The Blackboard and the Bottom Line: Why Schools Can't Be Businesses* (Cambridge, MA: Harvard University Press, 2004), 1–5.

33. This has been true from the start. BRL's contract in the early 1970s was to run a school in Gary, Indiana, a struggling former industrial city. EAI's contracts from 1991 to 1996 were to run schools in poor parts of Miami, Baltimore, and Hartford. Edison's contracts likewise from its beginning in 1995 were to run schools in underserved communities. Representative of the company's work were contracts to turn around clusters of schools in such troubled districts as Baltimore; Chester, Pennsylvania; Dallas; Flint and Inkster, Michigan; Philadelphia; and San Antonio. One exception among EMOs is National Heritage Academies, which has built charter schools in many suburban communities in response to demand from parents for an alternative to district schools.

34. See Richard Rothstein, *Class and Schools: Using Social, Economic, and Educational Reform to Close the Black-White Achievement Gap* (Washington, DC: Economic Policy Institute, 2004), 13–59; and David C. Berliner, "Our Impoverished View of Educational Reform," *Teachers College Record* 108 (2006): 949–995.

35. Regarding peer group effects, see Epple and Romano, "Competition between Private and Public Schools"; Richard J. Murnane, "The Role of Markets in K–12 Education," in Nelson, *Limits of Market Organization,* 161–184; and Scott E. Carrell and Mark L. Hoekstra, "Externalities in the Classroom: How Children Exposed to Domestic Violence Affect Everyone's Kids," *American Economic Journal: Applied Economics* 2 (January 2010): 211–228.

36. No Child Left Behind Act of 2001, Pub. L. No. 107-110, January 8, 2002, Section 1001 (3) and Section 1111(b)(3)(C)(v).

37. Ibid., Section 1111(b)(2)(C)(v).

38. Ibid., Section 1116(b) and (e).

39. Ibid., Section 1116(b)(1) regarding School Improvement; 1116(b)(7), Corrective Action; and 1116(b)(8), Restructuring.

40. Ibid., Section 1111 (b)(2)(A)(iii) and Section 2113(c)(12).

41. U.S. Department of Education, "Race to the Top Program, Executive Summary," November 2009, 9: Reform Plan Criteria (D)(2)(ii) and (D)(2)(iv)(b), http://www2.ed.gov/programs/racetothetop/executive-summary.pdf.

42. Center on Education Policy, "NCLB Year 5: Choices, Changes, and Challenges: Curriculum and Instruction in the NCLB Era," July 24, 2007, 5–10, http://www.cep-dc.org/publications/; and Basmat Parsad and Maura Spiegelman, *Arts Education in Public Elementary and Secondary Schools: 1999–2000 and 2009–10,* National Center for Education Statistics, Institute of Education Sciences, U.S. Department of Education, Washington, DC, 2012, http://nces.ed.gov/pubs2012/2012014rev.pdf.

43. Sharon L. Nichols and David C. Berliner, *Collateral Damage: How High-Stakes Testing Corrupts America's Schools* (Cambridge, MA: Harvard Education Press, 2007), 149–168; Linda Perlstein, *Tested: One American School Struggles to Make the Grade* (New York: Holt, 2007), 119–123, 189–199; Rafe Esquith, *Real Talk for Real Teachers* (New York: Viking, 2013), 106–114; "Why Great Teachers Are Fleeing the Profession," *WSJ,* July 17, 2013.

44. Arne Duncan, "A Back-to-School Conversation with Teachers and School Leaders," *Homeroom: The Official Blog of the U.S. Department of Education,* http://www.ed.gov/blog/2014/08/a-back-to-school-conversation-with-teachers-and-school-leaders/.

45. Ruma Kumar, "Schools Push Rigor, Reach for Stars," *TBS,* May 13, 2007; Maureen Downey, "Are Teachers under Too Much Pressure from 'War Rooms' and Constant Scrutiny?," *Atlanta Journal-Constitution,* March 29, 2010; Stephanie McCrummen, "D.C. Principal's Hands-On Tack Transforms Sousa Middle but Ruffles Feathers," *WP,* July 6, 2010; Francisco Vara-Orta, "Schools Going to War—of Sorts," *San Antonio Express-News,* February 5, 2012; Paul Bambrick-Santoyo, *Driven by Data: A Practical Guide to Improve Instruction* (San Francisco: Jossey-Bass, 2010), 4. Also, in visits to schools in Baltimore, New York, and Philadelphia, I heard several administrators refer to their offices dedicated to data analysis as war rooms.

46. Kate Zernike, "Obama Administration Calls for Limits on Testing in Schools," *NYT,* October 24, 2015.

47. Raymond Callahan, *Education and the Cult of Efficiency: A Study of the Social Forces That Have Shaped the Administration of the Public Schools* (Chicago: University of Chicago Press, 1962), 7, 19–25, 67–94. For additional insight into the development of this ethos, see Merle Curti, *The Social Ideas of American Educators* (1935; reprint, Paterson, NJ: Littlefield, Adams, 1959), 203–260; and Samuel Bowles and Herbert Gintis, *Schooling in Capitalist America: Educational Reform and the Contradictions of Economic Life* (New York: Basic Books, 1976), 131–141, 160–163. For insight into contemporary manifestations, see Cuban, *The Black-board and the Bottom Line,* 1–14; and Diane Ravitch, *The Death and Life of the Great American School System: How Testing and Choice Are Undermining Education* (New York: Basic Books, 2010), 69–91. For the impact of business on tertiary education in particular, see David L. Kirp, *Shakespeare, Einstein, and the Bottom Line: The Marketing of Higher Education* (Cambridge, MA: Harvard University Press, 2003), 6–7, 11–12, 259–263.

48. Richard Hofstadter, *Anti-intellectualism in American Life* (New York: Knopf, 1963), 237–252, 299–322.

49. Regarding portfolio management, see Paul Hill, "Put Learning First: A Portfolio Approach to Public Schools," Progressive Policy Institute, February 2006, 2, http://www.crpe.org/publications/put-learning-first-portfolio-approach-public-schools: "Like investors with diversified portfolios of stocks and bonds,

school boards would closely manage their community's portfolio of educational service offerings, divesting less productive schools and adding more promising ones."

50. Gary Miron and Christopher Nelson, *What's Public about Charter Schools? Lessons Learned about Choice and Accountability* (Thousand Oaks, CA: Corwin Press, 2002), 2; National Alliance for Public Charter Schools, http://www.publicchar ters.org.

51. Before Katrina, 9 of the 125 schools in New Orleans (or 7 percent) were charter schools. In 2009–2010, 51 of the city's 88 schools (or 58 percent) were charter schools. These numbers were obtained by phone on February 10, 2009, from Siona LaFrance, director of communications, Louisiana Recovery School District.

52. Howard Blume and Jason Song, "Major Shift for L.A. Schools; Board OKs a Plan That Could Turn Over 250 Campuses to Charter Groups and Other Outsiders," *Los Angeles Times,* August 26, 2009.

53. Jennifer Medina, "Mayor Again Calls for Lifting Cap on Charter Schools," *NYT,* September 30, 2009.

54. National Alliance for Public Charter Schools, *A Growing Movement: America's Largest Charter School Communities* (Washington, DC: National Alliance for Public Charter Schools, November 2015), 3–7, http://www.publiccharters .org/publications/enrollment-share-10/.

55. Gregory Elacqua, "For-Profit Schooling and the Politics of Education Reform in Chile: When Ideology Trumps Evidence," Centro de Políticas Comparadas de Educación, Documento de Tragajo CPCE no. 5, July 2009, 36, http:// www.ncspe.org/publications_files/OP178.pdf.

56. James Tooley, *The Global Education Industry: Lessons from Private Education in Developing Countries* (London: Institute of Economic Affairs, 1999), and *The Beautiful Tree: A Personal Journey into How the World's Poorest People Are Educating Themselves* (Washington, DC: Cato Institute, 2009); Joanna Härmä, "Can Choice Promote Education for All? Evidence from Growth in Private Primary Schooling in India," *Compare* 39 (March 2009): 151–165. See also Riddhi Shah, "Class Difference: Poor Neighborhoods around the World Embrace a Surprising Idea: Incredibly Low-Priced Private Schools," *Boston Globe,* May 9, 2010.

57. In the 2013–2014 academic year, according to Friskolornas riksförbund, the Swedish Association of Independent Schools, 73 percent of students in grades one through nine attending independent schools went to schools run by *aktiebolag* (limited companies); of independent schools for grades one through nine, 69 percent were run by *aktiebolag;* at the upper-secondary level, 85 percent of students attending independent schools went to schools run by *aktiebolag;* and of independent upper-secondary schools, 86 percent were run by *aktiebolag.* These figures come from Friskolornas riksförbund, "Fakta om friskolor," April 2015, 2, http://www.friskola.se/fakta-om-friskolor. The raw numbers of students

and schools were obtained from Skolverket, the Swedish School Agency, http://www .skolverket.se/statistik-och-utvardering/statistik-i-tabeller. In the academic year 2013–2014, there were 920,997 students in grades one through nine, of whom 125,960 attended 792 independent schools, and 330,196 students in upper-secondary school, of whom 85,079 attended 460 independent schools. Given the percentages reported by Friskolornas riksförbund, 164,268 of 1,251,193 students attended 942 schools run by *aktiebolag.*

58. Political Platform for a Government Formed by the Conservative Party and the Progress Party, October 7, 2013, 55, http://www.hoyre.no/filestore/Filer /Politikkdokumenter/politisk_platform_eng.pdf. While the platform stipulated that such schools "will be prohibited from paying dividends to the owners," there was no language restricting schools from being treated as long-term investments that could be sold for profit.

59. "Viva la Revolución: The British Government Must Continue to Push Ahead with Its Bold School Reforms," *The Economist,* October 11, 2014, 18.

60. See, for example, Caroline Brizard, "École: la leçon finlandaise," *Le Nouvel Observateur,* February 17, 2005, 62–64; Pasi Sahlberg, *Finnish Lessons: What Can the World Learn from Educational Change in Finland?* (New York: Teachers College Press, 2011); LynNell Hancock, "A+ for Finland," *Smithsonian,* September 2011, 94– 102; Anu Partanen, "What Americans Keep Ignoring about Finland's School Success," *Atlantic,* December 29, 2011, http://www.theatlantic.com/national/archive /2011/12/what-americans-keep-ignoring-about-finlands-school-success/250564/; Hannele Niemi, Auli Toom, and Arto Kallioniemi, eds., *Miracle of Education: The Principles and Practices of Teaching and Learning in Finnish Schools* (Rotterdam: Sense, 2012); Amanda Ripley, *The Smartest Kids in the World: And How They Got That Way* (New York: Simon and Schuster, 2013); Eduardo Andere, *Teachers' Perspectives on Finnish School Education: Creating Learning Environments* (New York: Springer, 2014); and Hannu Simola, *Historical and Sociological Essays on Schooling in Finland* (New York: Routledge, 2015). In citing the work of Alfred D. Chandler, I addressed this matter, but not in detail, in "The Children Must Play: What the U.S. Could Learn from Finland about Education Reform," *New Republic,* January 28, 2011, http://www.newrepublic.com/article/politics/82329/education -reform-Finland-US.

61. Beacon's enrollment in 2001 was 917. It grew to 1,085 by 2007 and to 1,140 by 2009.

62. Samuel Freedman, "Student Rankings? Computers Flunk," *NYT,* March 16, 2005; Freedman, "The System Is Down. Is That a Problem?," *NYT,* June 8, 2005.

63. United Federation of Teachers, Case Study in Partnership, June 3, 2008, http://www.uft.org/files/attachments/uft-report-2008-06-atrs-and-new-teacher -project.pdf.

64. Arthur M. Okun, *Equality and Efficiency: The Big Tradeoff* (Washington, DC: Brookings, 1975), 119.

1. Fundamental Change

1. Lynn Hirschberg, "Is Chris Whittle the Devil?," *Vanity Fair,* March 1990, 196–197.

2. Chris Whittle, interview, New York, November 8, 2005.

3. Hilary Stout, "Whittle Lays Out Plans to Establish For-Profit Schools," *WSJ,* May 17, 1991; Mark Walsh, "Entrepreneur Whittle Unveils Plans to Create Chain of For-Profit Schools," *EW,* May 22, 1991, 1, 13.

4. Laura Simmons, "Whittle to Build 1,000 Schools: Cost of First 200 to be $2.5 Billion," *Knoxville News Sentinel,* May 15, 1991; Stout, "Whittle Lays Out Plans"; Susan Chira, "Whittle's School Unit Gains Prestige and Pressure," *NYT,* May 27, 1992.

5. Simmons, "Whittle to Build 1,000 Schools"; Walsh, "Entrepreneur Whittle Unveils Plans."

6. Stout, "Whittle Lays Out Plans."

7. Milton Friedman, "Selling School like Groceries: The Voucher Idea," *NYT,* September 23, 1975.

8. Mark Walsh, "Brokers Pitch Education as Hot Investment," *EW,* February 21, 1996, http://www.edweek.org/ew/articles/1996/02/21/22biz.h15.html; Walsh, "All Eyes on Edison as Company Goes Public," *EW,* November 24, 1999, 17. See also Chris Whittle, *Crash Course: Imagining a Better Future for Public Education* (New York: Riverhead, 2005), 25–26.

9. Whittle, *Crash Course,* 26.

10. Alexis de Tocqueville, *Democracy in America,* trans. George Bevan (1835; New York: Penguin Putnam, 2003), 52, 74–77, 80. See also in this vein Robert S. Lynd and Helen Merrell Lynd, *Middletown: A Study in Modern American Culture* (New York: Harcourt, Brace, 1929); Lynd and Lynd, *Middletown in Transition: A Study in Cultural Conflicts* (New York: Harcourt, Brace, 1937); Jane Jacobs, *The Death and Life of Great American Cities* (New York: Random House, 1961); and Thomas Bender, *Community and Social Change in America* (New Brunswick, NJ: Rutgers University Press, 1978).

11. David Tyack, "Reinventing Schooling," in *Learning from the Past: What History Teaches Us about School Reform,* ed. Diane Ravitch and Maris A. Vinovskis (Baltimore: Johns Hopkins University Press, 1995), 198–199.

12. Brian O'Reilly, "Why Edison Doesn't Work," *Fortune,* December 9, 2002, 148–154.

13. Chris Whittle, "An Education Edison," *Tennessee Illustrated,* Winter 1990, cited by Vance H. Trimble, *An Empire Undone: The Wild and Hard Fall of Chris Whittle* (New York: Birch Lane, 1995), 262–263. Whittle wrote: "When Edison invented electric illumination, he didn't tinker with candles to make them burn better. Instead, he created something brilliantly new: the light bulb. In the same fashion, American education needs a fundamental breakthrough, a new dynamic that will light the way to a transformed educational system."

14. Tyack, "Reinventing Schooling," 191.

15. Stout, "Whittle Lays Out Plans."

16. For a similar take on the importance of vouchers to the initial conception of the Edison Project, see Jonathan Kozol, "Whittle and the Privateers," *The Nation*, September 21, 1992, 273–278; and Kenneth J. Saltman, *The Edison Schools: Corporate Schooling and the Assault on Public Education* (New York: Routledge, 2005), 34, 56–57.

17. Dinitia Smith, "Reform School: Benno Schmidt, Chris Whittle, and the Edison Project," *New York*, July 20, 1992, 34–35.

18. Tung Le, vice president for research and accountability, EdisonLearning, interview, New York, August 25, 2009. The advertorials ran on page 2 of *Education Week* in the following issues: September 28 and December 7, 2005; and February 15 and 22 and May 3, 2006.

19. John S. Friedman, "Big Business Goes to School," *The Nation*, February 17, 1992, 190.

20. James Phinney Munroe, *New Demands in Education* (Garden City, NY: Doubleday, 1912), v.

21. Ibid., 106–107.

22. Ibid., 23, 63.

23. Ibid., 20.

24. President George H. W. Bush, Presentation of the National Education Strategy, April 18, 1991, as published in *America 2000: An Education Strategy* (Washington, DC: Department of Education, 1991), 10.

25. Karen De Witt, "Bush Sets Up Foundation to Start Model Schools," *NYT*, July 9, 1991.

26. *America 2000*, 28.

27. National Commission on Excellence in Education, *A Nation at Risk: The Imperative for Educational Reform* (Washington, DC: Government Printing Office, April 1983), 9.

28. Ibid., 11.

29. Ibid., 9.

30. Ibid., 10.

31. Ibid. Recommendations, http://www2.ed.gov/pubs/NatAtRisk/recomm.html.

32. See Robert M. Solow, "A Contribution to the Theory of Economic Growth," *Quarterly Journal of Economics* 70 (February 1956): 65–94; and Solow, "Technical Change and the Aggregate Production Function," *Review of Economics and Statistics* 39 (August 1957): 312–320. See also David Warsh, *Knowledge and the Wealth of Nations* (New York: W. W. Norton, 2006), 140–157.

33. For claims that the decline in SAT scores was entirely the result of a "composition effect," see C. C. Carson, R. M. Huelskamp, and T. D. Woodall, "Perspectives on Education in America," *Journal of Educational Research* 86 (May/June

1993): 259–310; and Gerald W. Bracey, "The First Bracey Report on the Condition of Public Education," *Phi Delta Kappan* 73 (October 1991): 98. For claims that the decline in SAT scores was only partially the result of a "composition effect," see Lawrence C. Stedman, "The Sandia Report and U.S. Achievement: An Assessment," *Journal of Educational Research* 87 (January/February 1994): 133–146. For additional qualifications, see College Entrance Examination Board, *On Further Examination* (New York: College Board, 1977); David C. Berliner and Bruce J. Biddle, *The Manufactured Crisis: Myths, Fraud, and the Attack on America's Public Schools* (Cambridge, MA: Perseus, 1995), 14–23; and Daniel Koretz, *Measuring Up: What Educational Testing Really Tells Us* (Cambridge, MA: Harvard University Press, 2008), 84–90.

34. Lawrence Cremin, *Popular Education and Its Discontents* (New York: Harper and Row, 1989), 103. For a more technical assessment of the shortcomings of attributing U.S. economic competitiveness to the quality of the nation's schools, see Henry M. Levin and Carolyn Kelley, "Can Education Do It Alone?," *Economics of Education Review* 13 (June 1994): 97–108.

35. See Jonathan Kozol, *Savage Inequalities: Children in America's Schools* (New York: Crown, 1991); and Claudia Goldin and Lawrence Katz, *The Race between Education and Technology* (Cambridge, MA: Harvard University Press, 2008), 345–353.

36. For background, see Will Woodward, "The Legacy of Blue Ken," *The Guardian,* March 28, 2008. For legislative clauses by order of mention, see House of Commons, Education Reform Act 1988, I.2; I.14; II.159; I.46; and I.52.

37. De Witt, "Bush Sets Up Foundation"; Margaret Spillane and Bruce Shapiro, "A Small Circle of Friends: Bush's New American Schools," *The Nation,* September 21, 1992, 280.

38. Susan Bodilly, *New American Schools' Concept of Break the Mold Designs: How Designs Evolved and Why* (Santa Monica, CA: RAND, 2001), 11.

39. Ibid., 2, 4.

40. Trimble, *An Empire Undone,* 44.

41. Ibid., 49, 50–56.

42. Ibid., 61–63.

43. Ibid., 73–76.

44. Ibid., 77, 84–85.

45. Ibid., 49, 59, 119.

46. Ibid., 86, 105–109.

47. N. R. Kleinfield, "What Is Chris Whittle Teaching Our Children?," *NYT,* May 19, 1991.

48. Trimble, *An Empire Undone,* 85, 137–140, 193. See also Charlotte Evans, "2 Tennesseans Buy Esquire," *NYT,* May 1, 1979.

49. Trimble, *An Empire Undone,* 210–211.

50. Hirschberg, "Is Chris Whittle the Devil?," 232.

51. Kleinfield, "What Is Chris Whittle Teaching Our Children?"

52. Simmons, "Whittle to Build 1,000 Schools."

53. Trimble, *An Empire Undone*, 209, 229–233. The highly regarded political commentator and editor Michael Kinsley interviewed with Whittle for a top job and later said he would have taken it had it been offered. See James B. Stewart, "Grand Illusion," *New Yorker*, October 31, 1994, 73–74, 80.

54. Kleinfield, "What Is Chris Whittle Teaching Our Children?"

55. Trimble, *An Empire Undone*, 316.

56. Ibid., 317.

57. Hirschberg, "Is Chris Whittle the Devil?," 233–234; Trimble, *An Empire Undone*, 235; Edwin McDowell, "Author Quits Whittle's Book Project," *NYT*, June 13, 1989.

58. Suzanne Alexander, "California Judge Rules against State in Whittle Case," *WSJ*, November 25, 1992.

59. Whittle introduced the design team at a press conference in Washington in February 1992 as well as in full-page ads in several major newspapers. John E. Chubb, "Lessons in School Reform from the Edison Project," in *New Schools for a New Century: The Redesign of Urban Education*, ed. Diane Ravitch and Joseph P. Viteritti (New Haven, CT: Yale University Press, 1997), 88.

60. Ad for Edison Project, *NYT*, March 2, 1992, A16; *WSJ*, March 2, 1992, A7; *EW*, March 4, 1992, 4.

61. Trimble, *An Empire Undone*, 267–268; J. S. Friedman, "Big Business Goes to School," 189; Smith, "Reform School."

62. Whittle, *Crash Course*, 74.

63. Ad for Edison Project, *NYT*, May 28, 1992, A24; and *WSJ*, May 28, 1992, A7.

64. Smith, "Reform School," 38–39.

65. Ibid., 39. Smith noted that when Schmidt informed Vernon Louckes Jr., senior fellow of the Yale Corporation, in May 1992 that he would be stepping down to lead the Edison Project, Louckes urged him to stay.

66. Chubb, "Lessons in School Reform."

67. Deborah Sontag, "Yale President Quitting to Lead National Private-School Venture," *NYT*, May 26, 1992.

68. Benno Schmidt, "Educational Innovation for Profit," *WSJ*, June 5, 1992.

69. National Commission on Excellence in Education, *A Nation at Risk*; Eric Hanushek, "The Economics of Schooling: Production and Efficiency in Public Schools," *Journal of Economic Literature* 24 (September 1986): 1145–1146.

70. Schmidt, "Educational Innovation."

71. Richard Rothstein, "The Myth of Public School Failure," *American Prospect*, Spring 1993, 20–34.

72. Data on national health-care expenditures accessed from the Centers for Medicare and Medicaid Services (CMS) at http://www.cms.gov/Research

-Statistics-Data-and-Systems/Statistics-Trends-and-Reports/NationalHealthEx pendData/NationalHealthAccountsHistorical.html.

73. William J. Baumol, *The Cost Disease: Why Computers Get Cheaper and Health Care Doesn't* (New Haven, CT: Yale University Press, 2012), 20–24.

74. Kurt Vonnegut, *Player Piano* (New York: Random House, 1952), 204–205.

75. Deborah Meier, "Choice Can *Save* Public Education," *The Nation,* March 4, 1991, 253–271; Meier, *The Power of Their Ideas: Lessons for America from a Small School in Harlem* (Boston: Beacon Press, 1995), 37, 67, 93, 104, 180–181.

76. Seymour Fliegel, *Miracle in East Harlem: The Fight for Choice in Public Education* (New York: Manhattan Institute, 1993), 3–4, 7, 9–10, 12, 26–27, 87–96, 106–108, 115–126.

77. Ibid., 11–12, 192; Meier, *Power of Their Ideas,* 100.

78. Jeffrey R. Henig, *Rethinking School Choice: Limits of the Market Metaphor* (Princeton, NJ: Princeton University Press, 1994), 3–12, 101–148.

79. See Martin Carnoy et al., *The Charter School Dust-Up: Examining the Evidence on Enrollment and Achievement* (New York: Teachers College Press and Economic Policy Institute, 2005); Diane Ravitch, *The Death and Life of the Great American School System: How Testing and Choice Are Undermining Education* (New York: Basic Books, 2010); and Ravitch, *Reign of Error: The Hoax of the Privatization Movement and the Danger to America's Schools* (New York: Knopf, 2013). See also Justice John Paul Stevens's dissent in *Zelman v. Simmons-Harris,* 536 U.S. 639 (2002).

80. David Rogers, *110 Livingston Street: Politics and Bureaucracy in the New York City School System* (New York: Random House, 1968), 267.

81. David Rogers and Norman H. Chung, *110 Livingston Street Revisited: Decentralization in Action* (New York: New York University Press, 1983), 216–225.

82. Bel Kaufman, *Up the Down Staircase* (Englewood Cliffs, NJ: Prentice Hall, 1965).

83. Theodore R. Sizer, *Horace's Compromise: The Dilemma of the American High School* (New York: Houghton Mifflin, 1984), 206–221; Sizer, *Horace's School: Redesigning the American High School* (New York: Houghton Mifflin, 1992), 50–64.

84. Albert Shanker, National Press Club speech, March 31, 1988, https://www .reuther.wayne.edu/files/64.43.pdf. Basic to Shanker's proposal was the work of Ray Budde, author of *Education by Charter: Restructuring School Districts* (Andover, MA: Regional Laboratory for Educational Improvement of the Northeast and Islands, 1988).

85. John Chubb and Terry Moe, *Politics, Markets, and America's Schools* (Washington, DC: Brookings, 1990), 183.

86. Edison Project, *The Edison Project: Partnership Schools Make an Affordable, World-Class Education Possible for Every Child* (New York: Edison Project,

1994), 10, 16–17, 26, 34, 38–39, 40, 42, 78, 87. See also Trimble, *An Empire Undone,* 294–298.

87. Chubb, "Lessons in School Reform," 111. For Diane Ravitch's subsequent rejection of market-based reforms and standardization, see Ravitch, *Death and Life* and *Reign of Error.*

88. Edison Project, *The Edison Project,* 7. See also Trimble, *An Empire Undone,* 295, where Schmidt is quoted as saying in an interview, "We will create schools that achieve quantum gains in the academic performance of American students, in the quality of their lives, and in the well-being of our nation."

89. David Ellis, "Knowledge for Sale," *Time,* June 8, 1992, 69.

90. N. R. Kleinfield, "Plan for High-Tech Private Schools Poses Risks and Challenges," *NYT,* May 26, 1992.

91. Ibid. See also Dow Jones News Service, "Philips Electronics to Pay $175 Million for 25% of Whittle," *WSJ,* February 6, 1992.

92. Smith, "Reform School," 34.

93. Patrick M. Reilly, "Whittle Seeks Edison Funding of $750 Million," *WSJ,* May 5, 1993; Patrick M. Reilly and Suzanne Alexander, "Whittle's Plan for Big Growth Runs into Snags," *WSJ,* August 6, 1993; Jolie Solomon, "Mr. Vision, Meet Mr. Reality," *Newsweek,* August 16, 1993, 62; Mark Walsh, "Scaled-Back Edison Plan Focuses on Managing Schools," *EW,* September 8, 1993, http://www.edweek .org/ew/articles/1993/09/08/01whit.h13.html; Steve Stecklow, "Whittle Seeks $50 Million to Replenish Operating Funds of the Edison Project," *WSJ,* July 18, 1994.

94. Myron Lieberman, *Privatization and Educational Choice* (New York: St. Martin's, 1989), 100–105.

95. Whittle, interview, New York, November 8, 2005.

96. Stout, "Whittle Lays Out Plans."

97. Chubb, "Lessons in School Reform," 113.

98. Walsh, "Scaled-Back Edison Plan."

99. Peter Schmidt, "Management Firm Finds Schools a Tough Sell," *EW,* October 14, 1992, http://www.edweek.org/ew/articles/1992/10/14/06eai.h12.html.

100. Gwen Stephens, principal of the Harriet Tubman Charter School in New York, and Marge Hendricks, the school's director of operations, interviews, New York, December 7, 2005. Both noted that Tubman and other Edison schools lacked funding for the arts; furthermore, they noted that in representing a school belonging to a for-profit company, they had trouble raising money for the arts from philanthropic organizations. Benno Schmidt, interview, New York, October 6, 2005. Schmidt explained that as part of Edison's effort to become less "capital-intensive," Edison ended its home computer program in 2002.

101. Craig E. Richards, Rima Shore, and Max B. Sawicky, *Risky Business: Private Management of Public Schools* (Washington, DC: Economic Policy Institute, 1996), 54.

102. See Table 6.1 for school counts. Independent researchers differed with Edison in determining the company's school count, claiming that the company sometimes double-counted by tallying elementary and middle divisions within one building and with one principal as two schools rather than one.

103. "Edison Project Plans to Offer Stock Options to Its Teachers," *WSJ*, October 22, 1998; "Edison Project Raises an Additional $71 Million," *WSJ*, July 30, 1999.

104. Schmidt, interview, New York, October 6, 2005.

105. Stewart, "Grand Illusion," 80.

106. Ibid., 75.

107. Ibid., 64–81.

108. Ibid., 64.

109. Katie Collins, "Federal Courthouse Downtown Holds Hidden History," *Tennessee Journalist*, May 17, 2008. Costing $56 million to build, the corporate headquarters was sold to the federal government for $22 million.

110. Moe left Merrill Lynch in 2001 to cofound ThinkEquity Partners LLC, a boutique investment bank in San Francisco. Glassman left the *Washington Post* in 2004 to become a resident fellow at the American Enterprise Institute in Washington, DC.

111. Michael T. Moe, Kathleen Bailey, and Rhoda Lau, *The Book of Knowledge: Investing in the Growing Education and Training Industry* (New York: Merrill Lynch, April 9, 1999), 74–75.

112. William C. Symonds et al., "For-Profit Schools," *Businessweek*, February 7, 2000, 64.

113. Though investment banks do not publish their fees for individual deals, one may estimate the sums from the difference between the funds raised from public offerings (price of shares multiplied by volume) and the net proceeds listed in 10-Q reports filed by companies with the Securities and Exchange Commission (SEC). In Edison's case, $285.7 million was raised in three offerings, while net proceeds to the company, according to the company's filings with the SEC, amounted to $261.5 million, meaning fees of approximately $24 million to be shared by Merrill Lynch and other underwriters. See Edison Schools Inc., "Securities and Exchange Commission File No. 000-27817 (Form 10-Q)," December 23, 1999, November 14, 2000, and May 14, 2001 (accessed July 1, 2006, at www.sec.gov).

114. James K. Glassman, "It's Elementary: Buy Education Stocks Now," *WP*, July 2, 1995.

115. Evelyn Nussenbaum, "Wall St. Boosters High on 'Privatizer,'" *New York Post*, April 1, 2001. See also "Analyst Interview: Brandon Dobell," *Wall Street Transcript*, March 2002, 6. See also Symonds et al., "For-Profit Schools."

116. Edison Schools Inc., "Securities and Exchange Commission File No. 000-27817 (Form 10-Q)," December 23, 1999.

2. Market Discipline

1. Edison Schools Inc., "Securities and Exchange Commission File No. 000-27817 (Form 10-Q)," December 23, 1999, November 14, 2000, and May 14, 2001, http://www.sec.gov.

2. Mark Walsh, "Edison Project, Now Edison Schools Inc., Plans to Go Public," *EW*, September 8, 1999, 6.

3. Edison Schools Inc., "Securities and Exchange Commission File No. 000-27817 (Form 10-Q)," December 23, 1999, November 14, 2000, and May 14, 2001, http://www.sec.gov. Higher volume for the secondary offerings (5.5 million shares in August 2000 and 6.7 million shares in March 2001) was reported elsewhere. See Diana Henriques and Jacques Steinberg, "Edison Schools in Settlement with SEC," *NYT*, May 15, 2002.

4. "Behavioral Research Labs," *WSJ*, February 5, 1971.

5. "Behavioral Research Reports $111,449 Loss for Fiscal Nine Months," *WSJ*, August 9, 1971; Vincent Marottoli, "The Success of the Private Language Schools: A Lesson to Be Learned," *Foreign Language Annals* 6 (March 1973): 354–358.

6. *National Monthly Stock Summary*, April 1, 1971 (New York: National Quotation Bureau, 1971), 261.

7. "Behavioral Research Suspended by Amex," *WSJ*, March 14, 1974, 20.

8. Peter Schmidt, "Management Firm Finds Schools a Tough Sell," *EW*, October 14, 1992, http://www.edweek.org/ew/articles/1992/10/14/06eai.h12.html.

9. Ibid.

10. Mark Walsh, "For-Profit School Management Company Hits Hard Times," *EW*, February 9, 2000, 5. See also Elizabeth Gleick and Marc Hequet, "Privatized Lives," *Time*, November 13, 1995, 88.

11. Edward Wyatt, Anemona Hartocollis, and Jacques Steinberg, "Bulletin Board: Education Pays Off Royally," *NYT*, November 17, 1999.

12. Louis V. Gerstner et al., *Reinventing Education: Entrepreneurship in America's Public Schools* (New York: Dutton, 1994), 15.

13. Ibid., 21.

14. John E. Chubb, "Lessons in School Reform from the Edison Project," in *New Schools for a New Century: The Redesign of Urban Education*, ed. Diane Ravitch and Joseph P. Viteritti (New Haven, CT: Yale University Press, 1997), 102.

15. Ibid., 113.

16. Jolie Solomon, "Mr. Vision, Meet Mr. Reality," *Newsweek*, August 16, 1993, 62; Chris Whittle, interview, New York, November 11, 2005.

17. Mark Walsh, "Channel One Debut Wins Viewer Plaudits, but School Groups Pan 'Commercialism,'" *EW*, March 15, 1989, http://www.edweek.org/ew/articles/1989/03/15/08210068.h08.html.

18. The cost of installation varied in newspaper accounts. *Education Week* reported a per-school cost of $50,000. See ibid. The *Wall Street Journal* reported a

per-school cost of $20,000 and a total start-up cost of $150 million. See Patrick M. Reilly, "Whittle Signs Up 500 Schools to Get Channel One Show," *WSJ*, October 30, 1989. *Education Week* later put the per-school cost as ranging from $30,000 to $50,000. See Robert Kubey, "Whittling the School Day Away," *EW*, December 1, 1993, http://www.edweek.org/ew/articles/1993/12/01/13kubey.h13.html. Both publications, however, reported the same cost for commercials. According to the ad campaign run by Whittle Communications in the *Times* in March 1989, the cost per school was $50,000.

19. Dow Jones News Service, "Whittle Says It Sold Advertising Totaling $150 Million," *WSJ*, September 1, 1989.

20. Emily Smith, *The Cloris Leachman Handbook* (n.p.: Emereo, 2013), 495–496.

21. Chris Whittle, "Commercials, plus Education: Business Can Aid Starved Schools," *NYT*, March 1, 1989. See also Joanne Lipman, "Criticism of TV Show with Ads for Schools Is Scaring Sponsors," *WSJ*, March 2, 1989.

22. The fourteen ads for Channel One in the *Times* in 1989 appeared as follows: March 1, D28; March 2, A28; March 6, A18; March 7, A26; March 8, D32; March 16, D32; March 17, D20; June 7, A28; June 8, D5; June 9, D28; June 11, E30; June 13, 1989, A28; June 14, D28; and June 15, D32.

23. Ad for Channel One, *NYT*, March 1, 1989, D28.

24. Ad for Channel One, *NYT*, March 2, 1989, A28.

25. Randall Rotherberg, "The Media Business: A Rush Job on Whittle's Fight," *NYT*, March 9, 1989.

26. Ad for Channel One, *NYT*, June 9, D28; June 11, E30; June 14, 1989, D28.

27. Dow Jones News Service, "Whittle Hires Turner Aide as Chairman of New Unit," *WSJ*, May 7, 1990.

28. Dow Jones News Service, Marketing Brief, *WSJ*, April 5, 1991.

29. Mark Walsh, "California Chief Sues District to End Use of 'Channel One,'" *EW*, January 8, 1992, http://www.edweek.org/ew/articles/1992/01/08/16whittl.h11.html.

30. Dow Jones News Service, "Rhode Island Ends Its Ban of Whittle's Channel One Program," *WSJ*, July 24, 1992; Suzanne Alexander, "Education: Whittle Wins California Fight over School TV," *WSJ*, September 10, 1992.

31. "Channel One Gains in New York," *EW*, June 7, 1995, http://www.edweek.org/ew/articles/1995/06/07/37caps.h14.html.

32. Mark Walsh, "Classroom Advertiser to Send Its Message over Television," *EW*, January 25, 1989, http://www.edweek.org/ew/articles/1989/01/25/08140051.h08.html.

33. Mark Walsh, "Conservatives Join Effort to Pull the Plug on Channel One," *EW*, April 7, 1999, 5.

34. John S. Friedman, "Big Business Goes to School," *The Nation*, February 17, 1992, 190; Dinitia Smith, "Reform School: Benno Schmidt, Chris Whittle, and the Edison Project," *New York*, July 20, 1992, 36.

35. Patrick M. Reilly, "Whittle Appoints an Advisory Board for Channel One to Improve Its Image," *WSJ*, August 28, 1989, 1.

36. Mark Walsh, "Whittle to Unveil New Programming for Teachers," *EW*, October 31, 1990, http://www.edweek.org/ew/articles/1990/10/31/10400048.h10 .html; Walsh, "Shanker Quits Channel One Advisory Panel," *EW*, November 21, 1990, http://www.edweek.org/ew/articles/1990/11/21/10050039.h10.html.

37. Robert Goldberg, "TV: Faustian Bargain with the Schools?," *WSJ*, March 13, 1989.

38. David Tyack, "Reinventing Schooling," in *Learning from the Past: What History Teaches Us about School Reform*, ed. Diane Ravitch and Maris A. Vinovskis (Baltimore: Johns Hopkins University Press, 1995), 203.

39. Jerome Johnston, "Channel One: The Dilemma of Teaching and Selling," *Phi Delta Kappan* 76 (February 1995): 436–442.

40. Mark Walsh, "Channel One More Often Used in Poorer Schools, Study Finds," *EW*, October 27, 1993; William Hoynes, "News for a Captive Audience: An Analysis of Channel One," *Fairness and Accuracy in Reporting*, May 1997, http://fair.org/extra-online-articles/news-for-a-captive-audience/; Erica Weintraub Austin et al., "Benefits and Costs of Channel One in a Middle School Setting and the Role of Media-Literacy Training," *Pediatrics* 117 (March 2006): 423–433.

41. Mark Walsh, "California, New York Move to Bar 'Channel 1,'" *EW*, May 31, 1989, http://www.edweek.org/ew/articles/1989/05/31/08320044.h08.html.

42. Meg Cox, "New York Joins California in Opposing Whittle's News Program for Students," *WSJ*, June 19, 1989.

43. Mark Walsh, "Whittle to Ask to Exceed Daily Limit for Ads on Channel One," *EW*, June 2, 1993, http://www.edweek.org/ew/articles/1993/06/02/36whit .h12.html.

44. Walsh, "Channel One Debut Wins Viewer Plaudits"; Mark Walsh, "As Advertising Aimed at Youths Increases, Firm Plans 'Video Kiosks' in High Schools," *EW*, August 1, 1990, http://www.edweek.org/ew/articles/1990/08/01/09460006 .h09.html; Dow Jones News Service, "Group Sets Boycott of Pepsi over Ads on Channel One," *WSJ*, May 5, 1992; "News in Brief: Group Aims to End Commercialism," *EW*, October 7, 1998, 4; Walsh, "Conservatives Join Effort."

45. Mark Walsh, "Nader, Schlafly Lambaste Channel One at Senate Hearing," *EW*, May 26, 1999, 20.

46. William L. Rukeyser, telephone interview, May 26, 2011.

47. Rhea R. Borja, "Channel One Struggling in Shifting Market," *EW*, July 27, 2005, 3, 14.

48. Rhea R. Borja, "Media Conglomerate to Drop Channel One," *EW*, December 22, 2006, http://www.edweek.org/ew/articles/2006/12/22/18channelone_web.h26 .html.

49. Business Wire, "Alloy Broadens Media Offerings; Acquires Channel One," April 23, 2007, http://www.businesswire.com/news/home/20070423005476/en.

50. Had KKR played the tortoise instead of the hare, it could have invested that $240 million in an S&P 500 index fund such as State Street Global Advisors' SPY. On September 30, 1994, when KKR was finalizing its purchase of Channel One, SPY closed at $46.17 a share. On April 23, 2007, when KKR sold Channel One to Alloy Inc. for nothing more than assumption of liabilities, SPY closed at $148.06. With annual dividends of 2 percent reinvested and taxed at the qualified dividend rate of 15 percent conferred on corporations, that $240 million would have grown by April 2007 to approximately $844 million.

51. Alloy Media and Marketing, investor presentation, March 15, 2010, 9, http://www.alloymarketing.com/.

52. GlobalNewswire, "Channel One Network and CBS News to Co-produce Award-Winning Newscast for Teens," July 21, 2009, http://globenewswire.com /news-release/2009/07/21/401096/169374/en/Channel-One-Network-and-CBS -News-to-Co-Produce-Award-Winning-Weekday-Newscast-for-Teens-Begin ning-This-Fall.html.

53. The 10-K filed by Alloy Inc. for fiscal 2007 reports combined revenue for Channel One and FrontLine Marketing (a company selling in-store display board advertising), both properties purchased that year, as $20.5 million (revised downward from the $24.3 million reported in the company's initial 10-K for fiscal 2007). According to the company's 10-K for fiscal 2008, Channel One posted an increase in revenue of $7 million, and FrontLine an increase of $6 million, for their first full years as Alloy subsidiaries. According to the company's 10-K for fiscal 2009, Channel One posted an increase in revenue of $1.6 million, and FrontLine an increase of $2.6 million. The implied combined revenue for these two properties for fiscal 2009 was thus $37.7 million. Even if Channel One accounted for all the revenue reported for both properties in fiscal 2007, it could not account for more than $29.1 million of the combined revenue in fiscal 2009. See Alloy Inc., Form 10-K for fiscal years ended January 31, 2009, and January 31, 2010, http://www.sec.gov.

54. Matt Jarzemsky, "ZelnickMedia to Pay $126.5 Million for Alloy," *WSJ*, June 24, 2010.

55. William J. Baumol, *The Cost Disease: Why Computers Get Cheaper and Health Care Doesn't* (New Haven, CT: Yale University Press, 2012), 20–24.

56. National Center for Education Statistics, Digest of Education Statistics, 2009, table 180: Total Expenditures for Public Elementary and Secondary Education, by Function and Subfunction: Selected Years, 1990–91 through 2006–07, http://nces.ed .gov/programs/digest/d09/tables/dt09_180.asp.

57. Matthew Andrews, William Duncombe, and John Yinger, "Revisiting Economies of Size in American Education: Are We Any Closer to a Consensus?," *Economics of Education Review* 21 (June 2002): 245–262. See also Henry M. Levin,

"Why Is This So Difficult?," in *Educational Entrepreneurship: Realities, Challenges, Possibilities,* ed. Frederick M. Hess (Cambridge, MA: Harvard Education Press, 2006), 165–182.

58. Edison began this sustained advertising campaign in *EW* on March 3, 2004. Ads appeared in nearly every issue through July 18, 2007. From August 31, 2005, onward, Edison advertised on page 2 of every issue.

59. Mark Walsh, "Edison Project Spares No Cost in Wooing Prospective Clients," *EW,* October 14, 1998, 1, 16. Richard O'Neill, senior vice president and general manager of Edison's Partnership Division from 1997 to 2005, said in a telephone interview on November 6, 2006, that he recalled attending at least four such annual retreats at the Broadmoor and remembered them as being expensive events. Ana Tilton, senior vice president of Edison's School Support Division from 1997 to 2002, said in a telephone interview on October 30, 2006, "There was a huge number of people at high salaries selling Edison. Nobody at Edison was considering the scale of marketing and sales costs when assessing the company's budget."

60. O'Neill, telephone interview, November 6, 2006.

61. Ibid.

62. Gary Miron and Brooks Applegate, "An Evaluation of Student Achievement in Edison Schools Opened in 1995 and 1996," December 2000, vii, http://www .wmich.edu/evalctr.

63. Steven F. Wilson, *Learning on the Job: When Business Takes on Public Schools* (Cambridge, MA: Harvard University Press, 2006), 297–299.

64. Edison Schools Inc., "Securities and Exchange Commission File No. 000-27817 (Form 10-K)," September 28, 2000, 16; September 26, 2001, 16; September 30, 2002, 15; and September 30, 2003, 18. In addition to summaries of academic gains in these reports to the SEC, Edison published annual studies with detailed accounts of academic progress.

65. Marge Hendricks, director of operations, Harriet Tubman Charter School, interview, New York, December 7, 2005. SASI, a product of Pearson School Systems, is a truncated acronym for School Administration Student Information System. Hendricks's observation about minimal training provided by the NYC Department of Education to school programmers conforms with my experience as the programmer of a NYC high school from 2001 to 2008 and leader of programming workshops for New Visions for Public Schools, June 2005, and the NYC Department of Education, July 2005.

66. Based on interviews on November 30, 2005, with Camille Bell, principal of Montebello Elementary; Sarah Horsey, former principal of Montebello; Kent Luetke-Stahlman, Baltimore Edison Partnership Schools Community technical services manager; and Tanya Lipscomb, Montebello's special education instructional coordinator; on December 7, 2005, with Gwen Stephens, principal of Harriet Tubman Charter School, and Marge Hendricks, Tubman's director of operations;

and on visits to Edison's headquarters on October 6 and 18, 2005; November 8, 2005; March 16, 2006; January 3, 2007; March 16, 2009; August 25, 2009; April 7, 2010; May 5, 2010; and February 25, 2011; as well as numerous calls to Edison's headquarters.

67. "Edison's Elusive Profits," *Rethinking Schools,* Spring 2002, 17.

68. Edison Schools Inc., "Securities and Exchange Commission File No. 000-27817 (Form 10-K)," September 28, 2000.

69. Peter Applebome, "For-Profit Education Venture to Expand," *NYT,* June 2, 1997.

70. Edison Schools Inc., "Securities and Exchange Commission File No. 000-27817 (Form 10-K)," September 28, 2000.

71. William C. Symonds, "Edison: Pass, Not Fail," *Businessweek,* July 9, 2001, 70.

72. For criticism of Edison in this regard, see Kenneth J. Saltman, *The Edison Schools: Corporate Schooling and the Assault on Public Education* (New York: Routledge, 2005), 54.

73. Ann Grimes, "School Board Seeks to Revoke Edison Charter," *WSJ,* February 20, 2001.

74. Somini Sengupta, "Edison Project Gets Aid to Open New Schools," *NYT,* May 27, 1998.

75. Peter Schrag, "Edison's Red Ink Schoolhouse," *The Nation,* June 25, 2001, 24.

76. Howard M. Smulevitz, "2 Experimental Schools Get Green Light, Funds," *Indianapolis Star,* September 29, 2001.

77. David Evans, "Edison Schools Fails to Deliver $10.5 Million Promise to Las Vegas," *Bloomberg News,* August 12, 2002, http://www.bloomberg.com/, subscription required.

78. Edison Schools Inc., "Securities and Exchange Commission File No. 000-27817 (Form 10-K)," September 26, 2001, 36.

79. Jim Howland, interview, New York, October 18, 2005

80. Ibid.

81. Walsh, "Edison Project Spares No Cost."

82. For information on Inkster in particular, see Darcia Harris Bowman, "Michigan District Hires Edison to Manage Its Schools," *EW,* February 23, 2000, 3; and Mark Walsh, "Edison Schools Joins with IBM in Technology Alliance," *EW,* June 21, 2000, 9.

83. Robert C. Johnston, "Pa. Targets 11 Districts for Takeover," *EW,* May 17, 2000, 1, 26.

84. Liz Bowie and JoAnna Daemmrich, "Two Companies Vying to Manage Troubled Schools Visit Three Sites," *TBS,* February 15, 2000; June Kronholz, "Baltimore Public School Struggles to Improve Its Scores," *WSJ,* June 16, 2000.

85. Myron Lieberman, *Privatization and Educational Choice* (New York: St. Martin's, 1989), 4, 268.

3. On the Wire

1. Visits to Montebello Elementary, November 30, 2005, and March 23, 2009.

2. Sheryl Gay Stolberg, "Baltimore Enlists National Guard and a Curfew to Fight Riots and Looting," *NYT,* April 27, 2015; Stolberg, "After Thousands Rally in Baltimore, Police Make Some Arrests as Curfew Takes Hold," *NYT,* May 2, 2015.

3. Jeff Wahl, interview, New York, February 25, 2011.

4. See Howell S. Baum, *"Brown" in Baltimore: School Desegregation and the Limits of Liberalism* (Ithaca, NY: Cornell University Press, 2010), 208–210, 225 in particular.

5. National Center for Education Statistics, Common Core of Data (CCD), "Public Elementary/Secondary School Universe Survey," 1998–2009, www.nces .gov. For the 2008–2009 school year, 92 percent of Furman Templeton's 556 students qualified for free or reduced-price lunch, as did 93 percent of Gilmor's 469 students and 71 percent of Montebello's 799 students.

6. Visit to Furman Templeton Elementary, March 27, 2009.

7. Jessica Portner, "Plan Tying Increased Aid, State Control of Baltimore Schools Backed," *EW,* April 16, 1997, http://www.edweek.org/ew/articles/1997 /04/16/29md.h16.html.

8. Liz Bowie, "Board Votes to Consider Outside Help," *TBS,* September 22, 1999.

9. Ibid.

10. "Second Chance for Privatization," *TBS,* September 29, 1999.

11. Darcia Harris Bowman, "Private Firms Tapped to Fix Md. Schools," *EW,* February 9, 2000, 1, 22; Howard Libit, "Maryland Assumes Control of Three Baltimore Schools," *TBS,* February 2, 2000. Dunn's appointment in August 1999 is recorded in the *MSDE Bulletin,* August 25, 1999. Neither *Education Week* nor the *Baltimore Sun* reported a response to Dunn's question. See also Maryland State Department of Education, minutes, February 1, 2000, 7, http://www.maryland publicschools.org/stateboard/index.html.

12. Libit, "Maryland Assumes Control"; JoAnna Daemmrich, "Takeover of Three Schools Questioned," *TBS,* February 3, 2000.

13. Daemmrich, "Takeover."

14. Alex Molnar, Jennifer Morales, and Alison Vander Wyst, *Profiles of For-Profit Education Management Companies: Year 1999–2000* (Milwaukee: Center for the Analysis of Commercialism in Education, 2000), 16–17, http://repository .asu.edu/attachments/78986/content/02_1999–00.pdf. See also Steven F. Wilson, *Learning on the Job: When Business Takes on Public Schools* (Cambridge, MA: Harvard University Press, 2006), 62–67.

15. Liz Bowie and JoAnna Daemmrich, "Two Companies Vying to Manage Troubled Schools Visit Three Sites," *TBS,* February 15, 2000; Katie Wang, "Charter Schools Fight to Exist," *Morning Call,* March 12, 2000.

16. Bowie and Daemmrich, "Two Companies."

17. Darcia Harris Bowman, "Md. Picks Edison to Run Three Baltimore Schools," *EW*, March 29, 2000, 3.

18. Eric Siegel, "School Pact Draws Suit," *TBS*, April 21, 2000.

19. "Are City Teachers Ready for Reform?," *TBS*, April 24, 2000.

20. Erika Niedowski, "Judge Backs School Plan," *TBS*, August 23, 2000.

21. Bowie, "Board Votes"; "Second Chance for Privatization."

22. Erika Niedowski, "New School Model Begins," *TBS*, July 30, 2000.

23. Marion Orr, "Baltimore: The Limits of Mayoral Control," in *Mayors in the Middle: Politics, Race, and Mayoral Control of Urban Schools,* ed. Jeffrey R. Henig and Wilbur C. Rich (Princeton, NJ: Princeton University Press, 2004), 44.

24. Gelareh Asayesh, "Baltimore Board Weighs Private School Operation," *TBS*, May 17, 1991; Ann LoLordo, "Mayor Was Convinced Early That Golle Firm Deserved Chance to Run Schools," *TBS*, June 13, 1992; Laura Lippman, "A Private Man Who Sees Profit in Public Schools," *TBS*, June 12, 1992.

25. "Schools in Another Dimension," *TBS*, June 11, 1992.

26. Mark Bomster, "Pastors' Group Balks at Plan to Let Firm Run Nine Schools," *TBS*, July 15, 1992.

27. Michael A. Fletcher, "A Firm Schmoke Limits BUILD's Role at City Hall," *TBS*, July 21, 1992.

28. "Let the Mayor Be Mayor," *TBS*, July 23, 1992. See also Orr, "Baltimore," 45.

29. Mark Bomster, "Contract Passed with Firm to Run City Schools," *TBS*, July 23, 1992; Mike Bowler, "BTU's Two-Woman Team Sees Success and Failure," *TBS*, August 15, 1994.

30. Lippman, "A Private Man"; Frank Roylance, "Company Set to Run 9 City Schools Has Similar Operation in Fla. School," *TBS*, June 10, 1992.

31. Peter Schmidt, "Management Firm Finds Schools a Tough Sell," *EW*, October 14, 1992, http://www.edweek.org/ew/articles/1992/10/14/06eai.h12.html.

32. Ann LoLordo and Laura Lippman, "Firm Calls Rein on Costs Key to Profit on Schools," *TBS*, June 11, 1992; Mark Bomster, "Test Begins for Minn. Firm and 9 City Schools," *TBS*, September 1, 1992.

33. Bomster, "Test Begins."

34. Mark Bomster, "City Teachers Divided on Takeover of Schools," *TBS*, August 26, 1992; Bomster, "Parents Air Frustrations about 'Tesseract' Project," *TBS*, September 18, 1992; Bomster, "9 Schools Start to Mend," *TBS*, November 15, 1992.

35. "Selected Education IPOs: 1991 to Present," *EW*, November 24, 1999, 16; later figures come from Bloomberg LP, http://www.bloomberg.com/, subscription required.

36. Ian Johnson, "Schools Manager EAI Aces Market Test," *TBS*, June 5, 1993.

37. Bomster, "Contract Passed"; Ian Johnson, "EAI Ends Year in the Black," *TBS*, September 21, 1993.

38. Ian Johnson, "EAI Shouldn't Get Schools Contract, City Official Says," *TBS*, November 24, 1993.

39. Ian Johnson, "Critics Say EAI, Manager of Several City Schools, Fools Investors with Accounting," *TBS*, December 19, 1993; Bloomberg LP. See also Craig E. Richards, Rima Shore, and Max B. Sawicky, *Risky Business: Private Management of Public Schools* (Washington, DC: Economic Policy Institute, 1996), 93–95.

40. Kim Clark and Michael Ollove, "EAI Test Revelation May Hurt Credibility," *TBS*, June 8, 1994.

41. Mike Bowler, "Officials Disagree about EAI Violations," *TBS*, August 4, 1994; Bowler, "The City Superintendent Receives His Report Card," *TBS*, April 30, 1997.

42. Gary Gately, "EAI Schools' Test Scores Fall Short," *TBS*, October 18, 1994.

43. Gary Gately, "Amprey Defends Work of EAI," *TBS*, October 20, 1994.

44. Gary Gately, "Amprey Wants EAI to Run More Schools," *TBS*, May 6, 1994.

45. See Richards, Shore, and Sawicky, *Risky Business*, 67, 104–109.

46. "Hartford System Hires EAI," *TBS*, October 4, 1994; Vance H. Trimble, *An Empire Undone: The Wild and Hard Fall of Chris Whittle* (New York: Birch Lane, 1995), 339; June Kronholz, "Desk Sergeants: Tesseract and Others March Briskly ahead in School Privatization," *WSJ*, August 13, 1999.

47. Mark Walsh, "For-Profit School Management Company Hits Hard Times," *EW*, February 9, 2000, 5; Walsh, "Losing Money, Tesseract Sells Charters, College," *EW*, June 7, 2000, 5.

48. Jean Thompson, "Amprey Leaving Schools Post," *TBS*, April 28, 1997; Bowler, "City Superintendent Receives His Report Card."

49. Trimble, *An Empire Undone*, 339.

50. Data derived from NCES Table Generator at https://nces.ed.gov/ccd/elsi/tableGenerator.aspx.

4. Reprise

1. Kalman R. Hettleman, "State Not Being Fair in Schools Takeover," *TBS*, July 12, 2000; Hettleman, "Privatized City Schools Receive Greater Funding," *TBS*, August 8, 2000.

2. Nancy S. Grasmick, "Privatizing Schools Gives Kids a Chance," *TBS*, August 12, 2000; Sharon Blake and Lorretta Johnson, "Privatization Hurts Other City Schools," *TBS*, December 9, 2000.

3. Kalman R. Hettleman, "Edison's 3 Schools Must Reveal Costs," *TBS*, December 1, 2000.

4. Richard O'Neill, "Edison Schools Serves City Well," *TBS*, December 16, 2000; Kalman R. Hettleman, "Edison Schools Do Get Favors from the State," *TBS*, December 29, 2000.

5. Sara Neufeld, "Privately Run City Schools Cost More to Improve," *TBS,* September 9, 2005; Benno Schmidt, interview, New York, October 6, 2005.

6. Jim Howland, interview, New York, October 18, 2005. For insight into the growth in private provision of ancillary services, see Patricia Burch, *Hidden Markets: The New Education Privatization* (New York: Routledge, 2009).

7. Chris Whittle, interview, New York, November 8, 2005.

8. Chris Whittle, *Crash Course: Imagining a Better Future for Public Education* (New York: Riverhead Books, 2005), 5, 158–165.

9. Ibid., 101–133.

10. Henry Levin, "Déjà Vu All Over Again," *Education Next* 6 (Spring 2006): 21–24.

11. Laura Weeldreyer, interview, Baltimore, March 27, 2009.

12. Ibid.

13. William S. Ratchford II, "Going Public with School Privatization," *The Abell Report,* September/October 2005, 2–8. Ratchford's list of schools from 1999 doesn't comport precisely with the ten lowest-performing recorded on the Web site of the Maryland State Department of Education, but his determination nonetheless holds that Edison's three schools were selected from a group of comparable schools.

14. Neufeld, "Privately Run City Schools"; National Center for Education Statistics, http://nces.ed.gov/.

15. MSPAP data obtained by e-mail from the Maryland State Department of Education, July 2012; MSA data come from the Web site of the Maryland State Department of Education, http://www.marylandpublicschools.org/MSDE.

16. The demographic data had hardly budged from 1999. The percentage of students in 2005 entitled to free or reduced-price lunch was as follows: at Bay-Brook, Dr. Martin Luther King, Jr., and William Paca, 90, 88, and 93, respectively; and at Furman Templeton, Gilmor, and Montebello, 91, 88, and 80, respectively. The percentage of nonwhite students at the non-Edison schools was 89, 99, and 95, respectively; and at the Edison schools, it was 99. See National Center for Education Statistics, http://nces.ed.gov/

17. Abell Foundation Web site: http://www.abell.org/.

18. Gary Gately, "Private Firm's Influence May Grow in City Schools," *TBS,* September 1, 1993; Gately, "Education Gospel according to City Schools' Chief Amprey," *TBS,* September 19, 1993.

19. Robert C. Embry Jr., interview, Baltimore, March 27, 2009; "Test Security," unpublished, August 3, 2004, shared by Embry.

20. Robert C. Embry Jr., letter to Nancy Grasmick, September 17, 2004; Jean Thompson, "Baltimore School Test Scores Cut after State Probe," *TBS,* January 8, 1997; Nancy Grasmick, letter to Robert C. Embry Jr., November 23, 2004. Embry forwarded correspondence by e-mail, July 22, 2011. The 1995 math score comes

from Thompson; the 1996 math score comes from the Web site of the Maryland State Department of Education, http://www.marylandpublicschools.org/MSDE.

21. Robert C. Embry Jr., "Catching the Cheaters," *TBS*, March 8, 2005.

22. Robert C. Embry Jr., e-mail to Ben Feldman, March 9, 2005; Ben Feldman, e-mail to Robert C. Embry Jr., March 17, 2005; Embry, letter to Grasmick, March 14, 2005; Grasmick, letter to Embry, March 23, 2005. Embry forwarded correspondence by e-mail, July 22, 2011.

23. Embry, letter to Grasmick, April 29, 2005, citing Associated Press, "Edison Principal Suspended While Cheating Charge Investigated," April 29, 2005; Grasmick, letter to Embry, May 9, 2005. Embry forwarded correspondence by e-mail, July 22, 2011.

24. Associated Press, "Officials at Edison School in Wichita Removed over Testing Fraud Claims," *Topeka-Capital Journal*, December 23, 2001; Dale Mezzacappa, "Edison's Role in City Gets Murky," *TPI*, December 24, 2001. See also Kenneth J. Saltman, *The Edison Schools: Corporate Schooling and the Assault on Public Education* (New York: Routledge, 2005), 73–74.

25. Howard Libit, "The Power of a Strong Principal Leadership: Sarah Horsey Pushes Pimlico Elementary Teachers and Pupils to Be the Best in Baltimore," *TBS*, May 29, 2000.

26. Erika Niedowski, "City MSPAP Scores up for Fifth Straight Year," *TBS*, January 29, 2002.

27. Thompson, "Baltimore School Test Scores Cut"; Web site of the Maryland State Department of Education, http://www.marylandpublicschools.org /MSDE.

28. In addition to Montebello Elementary posting a decline of 13.8 percentage points in third- and fifth-grade reading and math proficiency from 2002 to 2003, Bentalou dropped 6 points; Franklin Square, 4; Frederick, 0.9; and Mount Royal, 18.2. MSPAP and MSA data obtained from the Maryland Department of Education, July 2012.

29. Calls were made to Sarah Horsey's home number on March 13, March 14, March 20, and April 14, 2014, and messages were left each time for comment, but no reply was ever received.

30. Susan Snyder, "In Baltimore, Edison Fixes Schools While Facing Critics," *TPI*, November 5, 2001.

31. Dale Mezzacappa, "Edison's Role in City Gets Murky," *TPI*, December 24, 2001.

32. Menash Dean, "Parents' Trip Sheds Light on Edison," *PDN*, November 9, 2001.

33. PBS *Frontline*, "Public Schools Inc.," July 3, 2003.

34. Peter Sacks, *Standardized Minds: The High Price of America's Testing Culture and What We Can Do to Change It* (New York: Perseus, 2001), 140–151.

35. Ibid.

36. Michael Vaden-Kiernan et al., *Evaluation of the Efficacy Initiative: A Retrospective Look at the Tacoma School District* (Cambridge, MA: Abt Associates, 1997), 5–6.

37. JoAnna Daemmrich, "Three Hired to Head Failing Schools," *TBS,* June 16, 2000; Erika Niedowski, "New School Model Begins," *TBS,* July 30, 2000; Karla Scoon Reid, "Sharing the Load," *EW,* November 16, 2005, 27–30; Liz Bowie, "Edison Fails to Improve Two Schools," *TBS,* January 30, 2002.

38. Erika Niedowski, "Trying for a New Start," *TBS,* October 10, 2010; Camille Bell, interview, Baltimore, March 23, 2009; Laura Weeldreyer, interview, Baltimore, March 27, 2009; Marlaina Palmeri, interview, Baltimore, March 24, 2009.

39. Ken Cherry, interview, Baltimore, March 27, 2009; Sara Neufeld, "School Due More Police Presence," *TBS,* March 22, 2007.

40. Palmeri, interview, Baltimore, March 23, 2009.

41. Camille Bell, interview, Baltimore, November 30, 2005.

42. Bell, interview, Baltimore, March 23, 2009; Sam Stringfield, "Edison Schools Progressed?," *TBS,* June 3, 2001; Weeldreyer, interview, March 27, 2009; Liz Bowie, "City Quashes Expansion for Edison," *TBS,* June 12, 2002.

43. Based on visits to Montebello and Furman Templeton, March 23 and 27, 2009, respectively.

44. Baltimore Edison administrators' meeting, Montebello School, November 30, 2005.

45. Ibid.

46. See David C. Berliner and Bruce J. Biddle, *The Manufactured Crisis: Myths, Fraud, and the Attack on America's Public Schools* (Reading, MA: Addison-Wesley, 1995), 194–202; Sharon L. Nichols and David C. Berliner, *Collateral Damage: How High-Stakes Testing Corrupts America's Schools* (Cambridge, MA: Harvard Education Press, 2007), 122–143; Linda Perlstein, *Tested: One American School Struggles to Make the Grade* (New York: Holt, 2007), 119–123, 189–199.

47. David Simon, Season Four, Episode Seven, "Unto Others," *The Wire,* HBO, 2007. While Pryzbylewski tells his assistant principal he wants to obtain the board games from the school's book room in order to integrate them into his lessons, his intention is to use the dice from the board games to teach his students the basics of probability.

48. Laura Weeldreyer, interview, Baltimore, November 6, 2013.

49. Todd McIntire, interview, New York, October 23, 2013.

50. Liz Bowie, "Edison Schools See Drop in Scores," *TBS,* July 13, 2006. While Table 4.2 exhibits a slight gain for Furman Templeton for 2006, that gain disappears if scores for grades four and six are included. For purposes of consistency with the MSPAP results, only scores for grades three and five are included in these tables.

51. Ibid.

52. "No Magic Bullet," *TBS*, July 14, 2006.

53. "Second Chance for Privatization," *TBS*, September 29, 1999; "Are City Teachers Ready for Reform?," *TBS*, April 24, 2000; "Making Progress a Little at a Time," *TBS*, May 27, 2001.

54. Niedowski, "Trying for New Start," *TBS*, October 10, 2000; Niedowski, "At Troubled City School, Discipline Takes Priority," *TBS*, November 26, 2000; Niedowski, "Welcome Signs of Improvement," *TBS*, January 16, 2001; Niedowski, "Adios, Language Barrier," *TBS*, March 16, 2001; Niedowski, "Troubled City School Still at the Margins," *TBS*, June 2, 2001.

55. "Students or Shareholders?," *TBS*, June 9, 2002.

56. Ian Johnson, "EAI Shouldn't Get Schools Contract, City Official Says," *TBS*, November 24, 1993.

57. David Evans, "Edison Schools Boosts Revenues with Funds Not Received," *Bloomberg News*, February 13, 2002, http://www.bloomberg.com/, subscription required; Queena Sook Kim, "Edison Schools' Quarterly Loss Widened, Stock Falls amid Accounting Questions," *WSJ*, February 14, 2002.

58. Diana Henriques and Jacques Steinberg, "Edison Schools in Settlement with SEC," *NYT*, May 15, 2002.

59. Bloomberg Terminal, subscription required; Carolyn Said, "Balance Sheet Doesn't Back Up Edison's Grand Boasts," *San Francisco Chronicle*, July 9, 2002.

60. "Students or Shareholders?"

61. Liz Bowie and Doug Donovan, "Schools in Spotlight," *TBS*, September 19, 2006; "Taking Over for Edison," *TBS*, April 16, 2007.

62. Weeldreyer, interview, Baltimore, March 27, 2009.

63. Sara Neufeld, "School Board Votes to Let Edison Keep Control of 3 Elementaries," *TBS*, May 9, 2007; Bell, interview, Baltimore, March 23, 2009.

64. Sara Neufeld, "End of Experiment," *TBS*, March 22, 2009.

65. Ann Grimes, "School Board Seeks to Revoke Edison Charter," *WSJ*, February 20, 2001. For more detail on Edison's travails in San Francisco, see Saltman, *The Edison Schools*, 135–140, 142–146.

66. BCPSS board meeting, March 24, 2009.

67. Ibid.

68. Ibid.

69. Ibid.

70. Ibid.

71. Palmeri, interview, Baltimore, April 14, 2010. See also Sam Dillon, "Inexperienced Companies Chase U.S. School Funds," *NYT*, August 9, 2010.

72. CBS Baltimore, "Baltimore Parents and Students Want Charter School Principal Reinstated," June 29, 2011; Camille Bell, telephone interview, July 19, 2011.

73. Peter Hermann, "Boy, 12, Dies of Injuries," *TBS*, May 27, 2011.

5. The Governor's Proposal

1. Helen Gym, "Edison on the Ropes in Baltimore; Is Philly Far Behind?," *PPSN,* March 24, 2009, http://thenotebook.org/blog/091193/edison-schools-rope s-baltimore-philly-far-behind.

2. The determination of contract retention is based on a review of Edison's contracts with the company's general counsel, David Graff, February 16, 2006.

3. Darcia Harris Bowman, "Michigan District Hires Edison to Manage Its Schools," *EW,* February 23, 2000, 3.

4. Dan Hardy, "Chester Upland Chooses Three Firms to Run Schools," *TPI,* March 23, 2001.

5. Dan Hardy, "School-Manager Purchase Worries Chester Upland," *TPI,* June 5, 2001; "Edison Schools to Buy Rival School Manager for $36 Million in Stock," *WSJ,* June 5, 2001; "Edison Completes LearnNow Deal," *WSJ,* July 6, 2001.

6. Anya Kamenetz, "For Profit and People," *NYT,* November 1, 2013.

7. Dan Hardy, "Chester Upland Privatizes 9 Schools," *TPI,* August 24, 2001.

8. Susan Snyder, "Teachers Learn Edison Methods," *TPI,* September 6, 2001; Dan Hardy, "As Schools Open, District Hopeful about a Privatized Chester Upland," *TPI,* September 12, 2001; Dale Mezzacappa, "Pluses, Minuses for Edison," *TPI,* November 29, 2001.

9. Hardy, "Chester Upland Chooses Three Firms"; Dale Mezzacappa, "Big Change at Districts, Less So in Classrooms," *TPI,* November 4, 2001.

10. Ken Dilanian and Susan Snyder, "A Mandate for Change," *TPI,* July 22, 2001; Dale Mezzacappa and Susan Snyder, "Ridge Puts Money behind Belief in For-Profit Schools," *TPI,* August 5, 2001; "Yo, Adrian!," *WSJ,* August 21, 2001; "City of Brotherly Thugs," *WSJ,* December 3, 2001; Dale Mezzacappa, "Political Tension Led to School Takeover," *TPI,* December 23, 2001.

11. Dilanian and Snyder, "Mandate for Change"; Susan Snyder, "Private Firm Hired to Help Save Philadelphia Schools," *TPI,* August 2, 2001.

12. Dilanian and Snyder, "Mandate for Change."

13. Thomas Fitzgerald, "Pennsylvania Proposal Would Raise Income Tax to Aid Schools," *TPI,* November 14, 2001.

14. Ibid.; Anthony R. Wood and Ovetta Wiggins, "House Panel Says Cut Property and Wage Taxes," *TPI,* September 11, 2002.

15. Catherine Gewertz, "Forces Target Pennsylvania School Aid Changes," *EW,* November 28, 2001, 18, 20.

16. Ibid.

17. Ibid.

18. Edison Project, *The Edison Project: Partnership Schools Make an Affordable, World-Class Education Possible for Every Child* (New York: Edison Project,

1994), 10, 16–17, 26, 34, 38–39, 40, 42, 78, 87; Edison Investor Conference, St. Regis Hotel, New York, July 31, 2000.

19. Maryland Department of Education, Selected Financial Data: Ten-Year Summary, 2001–2002, table 15, http://www.marylandpublicschools.org/MSDE /newsroom/special_reports/financial.htm.

20. Catherine Gewertz, "It's Official: State Takes Over Philadelphia Schools," *EW,* January 9, 2002, 1, 14–15.

21. Mezzacappa, "Political Tension"; Gewertz, "It's Official."

22. Ibid.

23. Martha Woodall, "Of Philadelphia Schools or Edison, Who's Really Rescuing Whom?," *TPI,* August 19, 2001.

24. Ibid.

25. William Bunch, "Stock in Edison Schools Rose on News of City Deal," *PDN,* August 3, 2001.

26. Woodall, "Of Philadelphia Schools or Edison."

27. Edward Wyatt, "Floyd Flake to Take Post with Education Company," *NYT,* May 3, 2000, B3.

28. Woodall, "Of Philadelphia Schools or Edison."

29. Eric Siegel, "School Pact Draws Suit," *TBS,* April 21, 2000; "Are City Teachers Ready for Reform?," *TBS,* April 24, 2000.

30. ACORN was famously forced to fold in 2010 after employees in Baltimore, New York, and Washington, D.C., were exposed in undercover videos for providing tax advice to muckraking conservative activists posing as a pimp and a prostitute. See Clark Hoyt, "The ACORN Sting Revisited," *NYT,* March 20, 2010.

31. Susan Snyder, "Groups Vow a Fight if City Schools Seek Privatization," *TPI,* August 3, 2001.

32. Edward Wyatt, "Privatizing of Five Schools Faces a Fight," *NYT,* January 30, 2001; Michael O. Allen and Dave Saltonstall, "Rudy: Give 'Em 20 Schools," *NYDN,* April 1, 2001; Anemona Hartocollis, "As Election on Privatizing Schools Winds Down, Call Goes Out for Plan B," *NYT,* April 1, 2001.

33. Edward Wyatt, "Defeat Aside, Edison Plans to Expand," *NYT,* April 1, 2001. Edison would absorb a charter school in the Bronx—Harriet Tubman—later in the year through its acquisition of LearnNow, but that single-school contract fell far short of Edison's aspirations in New York.

34. Edward Wyatt and Abby Goodnough, "School Privatization Foes Say Chosen Company Unfairly Gets Board's Help with Vote," *NYT,* February 26, 2001.

35. Ibid.

36. Abby Goodnough, "Public Lives: Agitator Turns Charm against School Privatization," *NYT,* March 14, 2001.

37. Abby Goodnough, "Scope of Loss for Privatizing by Edison Stuns Officials," *NYT,* April 3, 2001; Lynette Holloway, "Parents Explain Resounding Rejection of Privatization at 5 Schools," *NYT,* April 13, 2001.

38. Goodnough, "Scope of Loss."

39. Anonymous source, March 29, 2001.

40. Goodnough, "Scope of Loss."

41. Securities prices come from Wharton Research Data Services, Center for Research in Security Prices (CRISP), https://wrds-web.wharton.upenn.edu/wrds/, subscription required.

42. "The Kids Lose Again," *New York Post,* March 31, 2001; "Kids Are Losers in Edison Vote," *NYDN,* April 3, 2001; "And the Schools Sink On," *New York Post,* April 3, 2001.

43. Michael Kramer, "Parents Failed Their Kids," *NYDN,* April 1, 2001; Joyce Purnick, "Metro Matters: Giuliani's Wagnerian Aria," *NYT,* April 2, 2001; John Tierney, "The Big City: Preferring the Devil They Knew," *NYT,* April 3, 2001.

44. Hartocollis, "As Election on Privatizing Schools Winds Down."

45. Ibid. See also Sidney Schwager, "An Analysis of the Evaluation of the More Effective Schools Program Conducted by the Center for Urban Education," United Federation of Teachers, November 14, 1967, http://files.eric.ed.gov/full text/ED014526.pdf; and Richard D. Kahlenberg, *Tough Liberal: Albert Shanker and the Battles over Schools, Unions, Race, and Democracy* (New York: Columbia University Press, 2007), 54–58, 71–81, 198.

46. Seymour Fliegel, interview, New York, November 17, 2015.

47. Susan Snyder, "Groups Fight Delay of Lawsuit against State's School Funding," *TPI,* August 4, 2001.

48. "Will Edison Be Medicine for Fixing Schools?," *PDN,* August 3, 2001.

49. Menash Dean, "Protesters Rail at School Evaluators; Demand to Meet Edison Inc.'s CEO," *PDN,* August 10, 2001; Snyder, "Private Firm Hired to Help Save Philadelphia Schools."

50. Frederick Cusick, "Seeking Comment, Edison Draws Flak," *TPI,* August 31, 2001; Menash Dean, "Edison Schooled on Kids' Needs," *PDN,* August 31, 2001.

51. Larry Eichel, "Edison Isn't the Issue," *TPI,* September 5, 2001.

52. Elmer Smith, "Mark Schweiker: Do You Hear What I Hear?," *PDN,* October 24, 2001.

53. Susan Snyder and Dale Mezzacappa, "Ridge Pleads for Philadelphia Schools," *TPI,* October 3, 2001.

54. Menash Dean, "Guv's Radical School of Thought," *PDN,* October 25, 2001.

55. Ibid.

56. Susan Snyder, Ovetta Wiggins, and Dale Mezzacappa, "Governor to Suggest Three Tiers for Schools," *TPI,* October 31, 2001; Susan Snyder and Dale

Mezzacappa, "Edison Rips District over 'Accountability,'" *TPI*, November 1, 2001; PRNewswire, "Pennsylvania Governor Mark Schweiker Announces a Sweeping Plan for Philadelphia Schools," November 1, 2001; Susan Snyder, "Edison CEO Wants Multiyear Pact," *TPI*, November 2, 2001.

57. Ibid.

58. Catherine Gewertz, "Unprecedented Change Eyed for Phila. Schools," *EW*, November 7, 2001, 3.

59. Snyder, "Edison CEO Wants Multiyear Pact."

6. Waterloo

1. Dale Mezzacappa, Susan Snyder, and Frederick Cusick, "Street: Schools Proposal Is 'Flawed,'" *TPI*, November 1, 2001.

2. Susan Snyder and Dale Mezzacappa, "Pennsylvania Plan: Let Edison Run City District," *TPI*, October 23, 2001.

3. Susan Snyder, "Vowing Defiance, Street Opens Office in District Headquarters," *TPI*, November 10, 2001.

4. Susan Snyder and Dale Mezzacappa, "Deal Reached on Philadelphia Schools," *TPI*, November 21, 2001.

5. Bob Warner, "Protesters Vow to Fight Privatization," *TPI*, November 8, 2001.

6. Susan Snyder and Dale Mezzacappa, "Mayor: Drop Plan to Privatize Schools," *TPI*, November 9, 2001; Dave Davies and Mark McDonald, "Pols Give Edison a Rough Greeting," *PDN*, November 9, 2001.

7. Menash Dean, "They're Lining Up for Chance to Run Schools," *PDN*, October 26, 2001.

8. Susan Snyder, "Private Proposals to Take Over 28 Schools," *TPI*, April 26, 2001; Dean, "They're Lining Up"; Universal Companies Inc., "Voices and Experiences: A Community Outreach Report on Education Reform in Philadelphia 2001," published as an appendix to Edison Schools Inc., *Strengthening the Performance of the Philadelphia School District: Report to the Governor of Pennsylvania* (New York: Edison Schools, October 2001).

9. John Chubb and Terry Moe, *Politics, Markets, and America's Schools* (Washington, DC: Brookings, 1990), 183.

10. Mezzacappa, Snyder, and Cusick, "Street: Schools Proposal."

11. Snyder, "Vowing Defiance."

12. Larry Eichel, "True Flexibility the Key in School-Reform Deal," *TPI*, November 2, 2001.

13. Edison Schools Inc., *Strengthening the Performance of the Philadelphia School District*, 2, 4, 14–17, 25, 28, 34, 45, 48–53, 58–60, 65. While central to the controversy in Philadelphia, this $2.7 million report was difficult to locate a de-

cade later. The company itself did not have a copy, Jeff Wahl, CEO of Edison-Learning, informed me by e-mail on May 16, 2013. The only copy I could find was in the Pennsylvania State Library in Harrisburg.

14. Elmer Smith, "The Battle over the School Takeover," *PDN*, November 2, 2001; Tom Ferrick Jr., "Report by Edison Is Pages of Politics," *TPI*, November 7, 2001; Acel Moore, "Edison Plan for Philadelphia Schools Will Extend History of Failure," *TPI*, November 8, 2001.

15. Susan Snyder, "Edison Rips District over 'Accountability,'" *TPI*, November 6, 2001.

16. Edison Schools Inc., *Strengthening the Performance of the Philadelphia School District*, 2.

17. Ibid., 9.

18. Edison cited NCES data for the 1998–1999 fiscal year in reporting the following expenditures per pupil: Philadelphia, $5,702; Houston, $5,340; Clark County (Las Vegas), $5,108; and Broward County (Fort Lauderdale), $5,453. See ibid., 9. The average for the three other districts was $5,300.

19. Ibid., 9–10.

20. According to the National Center for Education Statistics (NCES), *Digest of Education Statistics*, for 1999–2000, 14 percent of children ages five to seventeen in Broward County lived below the poverty line, as did 13.4 percent in Clark County, 26 percent in Houston, and 23.8 percent in Philadelphia. The weighted average for the three comparison districts is 17.6 percent. See http://nces.ed.gov/programs/digest/d03/tables/dt091.asp: table 91. For the percentage of students qualifying for free or reduced-price lunch and for enrollment figures in major urban districts in 2000, see http://nces.ed.gov/pubs2001/100_largest/table09.asp and http://nces.ed.gov/pubs2001/100_largest/table03.asp. For the school year 1999–2000, the percentage of students in Philadelphia eligible for free or reduced-price lunch was 68.6; in Broward County, 36.9; in Clark County, 36.5; and in Houston, 65.7; for the school year 2008–2009, the percentage of students in Philadelphia eligible for free or reduced-price lunch was 77.3; in Broward County, 41; in Clark County, 47.8; and in Houston, 63.5. See http://nces.ed.gov/pubs2010/100largest0809/tables/table_a09.asp. For spending data, see note 84 of this chapter.

21. Edison's collaborators and payments to them are listed in Robert J. Casey Jr., *A Performance Audit of the Pennsylvania Department of Education's Contract No. SP161120001 with Edison Schools Inc.* (Harrisburg, PA: Pennsylvania Department of the Auditor General, November 20, 2002), 50.

22. NCES, *Digest of Education Statistics*.

23. This calculation is based on comparison of cost-of-living estimates made by the American Chamber of Commerce Researchers Association (ACCRA) for the three quarters in 1998 for which data are available for all four cities (Fort

Lauderdale, Houston, Las Vegas, and Philadelphia). ACCRA did not publish data for Fort Lauderdale for the first quarter of 1998 or for any quarter in 1999. However, data for Q1 and Q2 in 1999 for the three other cities exhibit insignificant variation from the preceding two quarters. With 100 as the national baseline index, the following numbers hold: Fort Lauderdale, 106.4 (Q2, 1998), 107.5 (Q3, 1998), and 107.7 (Q4, 1998); Houston, 94.4 (Q2, 1998), 93.8 (Q3, 1998), 93.6 (Q4, 1998), 94.9 (Q1, 1999), and 95 (Q2, 1999); Las Vegas, 107.9 (Q2, 1998), 105.2 (Q3, 1998), 104.3 (Q4, 1998), 104.6 (Q1, 1999), and 106.6 (Q2, 1999); Philadelphia, 122.1 (Q2, 1998), 121.2 (Q3, 1998), 121.9 (Q4, 1998), 120.5 (Q1, 1999), and 118.7 (Q2, 1999). See ACCRA, *ACCRA Cost of Living Index* (Alexandria, VA, 1998–1999), vols. 31 and 32.

24. With the cost of living in the three other districts being only 84 percent of Philadelphia's, the cost adjustment for the averaged per-pupil expenditure of $5,300 in these three districts calls for multiplying that average by 1/.84, which equals $6,310, which is, in turn, 11 percent above Philadelphia's per-pupil expenditure. Conversely, Philadelphia's per-pupil expenditure of $5,702 is 10 percent less.

25. Michael Casserly, "Company's Report Doesn't Inspire Trust," *TPI*, November 11, 2001; Council of the Great City Schools, "Analysis and Comment on the Edison Schools, Inc. Report on the Philadelphia Public Schools," December 2001, obtained by e-mail from Casserly.

26. Susan Snyder, "Board Cites 'Risk' in Schools Proposal," *TPI*, November 6, 2001; Susan Snyder, Dale Mezzacappa, and James M. O'Neill, "City Schools Takeover Delayed," *TPI*, December 1, 2001; "Figures Don't Add Up," *PDN*, December 3, 2001; Philip R. Goldsmith, "Remarks to the Board of Education: Compromise, Cooperation, and Common Sense," November 5, 2001, http://www.phila.k12.pa.us/executiveoffices/ceo/CEOonEdison.pdf.

27. Snyder, "Board Cites 'Risk'"; Jill Porter, "Looks Like Edison Has a Lot to Learn," *PDN*, November 30, 2001; "Yo, Adrian!," *WSJ*, August 21, 2001; "Philadelphia Story," *WSJ*, November 14, 2001.

28. Snyder and Mezzacappa, "Deal Reached."

29. Ibid.

30. Ken Dilanian, "No Clear Victor in Deal for Schools," *TPI*, November 25, 2001.

31. Susan Snyder, "Hundreds Protest Takeover of Philadelphia Schools," *TPI*, November 29, 2001.

32. Susan Snyder, James M. O'Neill, and Ovetta Wiggins, "No Deal Yet on Takeover of Philadelphia Schools," *TPI*, November 30, 2001.

33. Kathleen Brady Shea, "Ministers Vow to Fight for Schools," *TPI*, December 3, 2001.

34. Menash Dean, "Edison Turns Light on Itself with Ads," *PDN*, December 13, 2001.

35. Susan Snyder, "Street, Schweiker to Go Face-to-Face on Philadelphia Schools," *TPI*, December 18, 2001; Snyder, "City Agrees to Provide More Funds for Schools," *TPI*, December 19, 2001.

36. Menash Dean, "Suit Claims Conflict," *PDN*, December 18, 2001; Barbara Laker, "Judge Denies Request for Injunction on Edison," *PDN*, December 28, 2001.

37. Casey, "Performance Audit."

38. Len Rieser, interview, Philadelphia, February 9, 2009.

39. Susan Snyder and Marc Schogol, "City Agrees to State Takeover," *TPI*, December 22, 2001.

40. Susan Snyder and Marc Schogol, "Now City Schools Are Pennsylvania's Problem," *TPI*, December 23, 2001.

41. Martha Woodall, "Swarthmore Businessman Called Upon to Help Schools," *TPI*, December 23, 2001.

42. Dale Mezzacappa and Susan Snyder, "Edison's Share of City School Deal: $101 Million," *TPI*, December 13, 2001; Dale Mezzacappa, "Edison's Role in City Gets Murky," *TPI*, December 24, 2001.

43. Susan Snyder and Martha Woodall, "Edison Voted In as Manager of Philadelphia Public Schools," *TPI*, March 27, 2002.

44. Susan Snyder and Martha Woodall, "School Assignments," *TPI*, April 18, 2002.

45. Susan Snyder, "School Overhaul List under Review," *TPI*, April 17, 2002; Karla Scoon Reid, "Groups Named to Lead Dozens of Ailing Philadelphia Schools," *EW*, April 24, 2002, 10.

46. Snyder and Woodall, "School Assignments."

47. "Philadelphia's Loss," *WSJ*, April 19, 2002.

48. Chris Brennan, "Stock Pros: Do Your Job, Edison," *PDN*, May 1, 2002; D. C. Denison, "School of Hard Knocks," *Boston Globe*, May 26, 2002; Rebecca Winters, "Trouble for School Inc.," *Time*, May 27, 2002, 53; all stock prices come from Wharton Research Data Services, Center for Research in Security Prices (CRISP), https://wrds-web.wharton.upenn.edu/wrds/, subscription required.

49. Jacques Steinberg, "Panel to Safeguard School Management Contracts," *NYT*, May 16, 2002; Tali Woodward, "Edison's Failing Grade," *CorpWatch*, June 20, 2002; Edison Schools Inc., "Securities and Exchange Commission File No. 000-27817 (Form 10-K)," June 30, 2003, 23.

50. Diana Henriques and Jacques Steinberg, "Edison Schools in Settlement with S.E.C.," *NYT*, May 15, 2002.

51. Queena Sook Kim, "Edison Schools' Quarterly Loss Widened, Stock Falls amid Accounting Questions," *WSJ*, February 14, 2002.

52. Edison Schools Inc., "Securities and Exchange Commission File No. 000-27817 (Form 10-K)," September 29, 2003.

53. Edison Investor Conference, July 31, 2000, St. Regis Hotel, New York. Whittle's figure of 15.5 percent comes from the nine months ending March 31, 2000, when, according to the company's quarterly report to the SEC, Edison spent $28.889 million on central administration out of $192.529 million in total expenditures, which is 15.5 percent. See Edison Schools Inc., "Securities and Exchange Commission File No. 000-27817 (Form 10-Q)," May 15, 2000.

54. For 1996–2000 annual data on expenditures, see "Securities and Exchange Commission File No. 000-27817 (Form 10-K)," September 28, 2000. For 2001–2003 annual data on expenditures, see "Securities and Exchange Commission File No. 000-27817 (Form 10-K)," September 29, 2003. See also William C. Symonds, "Pass, Not Fail," *Businessweek*, July 9, 2001, 70.

55. Daniel Golden, "Boston School Severs Its Ties with Edison," *WSJ*, May 16, 2002; Mike Wowk, "Edison Breaks Mt. Clemens Schools Deal," *Detroit News*, June 19, 2002; CRISP.

56. Susan Snyder and Dale Mezzacappa, "Pa. Hiring of Edison Slammed by Casey," *TPI*, August 2, 2002.

57. Diana Henriques and Jacques Steinberg, "Edison Schools in Settlement with S.E.C.," *NYT* May 15, 2002; Martha Woodall, "Edison's Stock Dive Raises Concerns," *TPI*, May 8, 2002.

58. Mark Walsh, "Edison Gets Financing for Philadelphia Expansion," *EW*, June 12, 2002, 4; Walsh, "Edison Outlines Strategies to Reassure Wall Street," *EW*, August 7, 2002, 19.

59. Ellen Lord, "Bibb School Board Ousts Edison," *Macon Telegraph*, August 16, 2002.

60. Tawnell D. Hobbs, "Dallas School Trustees End Relationship with For-Profit Edison Schools," *Dallas Morning News*, August 23, 2002; Hobbs, "DISD Likely to Cut Edison Ties," *Dallas Morning News*, August 17, 2002.

61. Associated Press, "NASDAQ Warns Edison Schools of Possible Delisting," *NYT*, August 30, 2002; Edison Schools Inc., "Securities and Exchange Commission File No. 000-27817 (Form 10-Q)," November 14, 2002.

62. Chris Brennan, "Casey Is Probing Edison Contract," *PDN*, August 2, 2002.

63. Ibid.

64. Martha Woodall, Susan Snyder, and Dale Mezzacappa, "State Warns It May Hold Back Aid for Schools," *TPI*, July 19, 2002.

65. Susan Snyder, "Vallas: Playing Field Must Be Level," *TPI*, July 20, 2002; Chris Brennan, "State School Money Challenged," *PDN*, July 23, 2002; Elmer Smith, "It's 'Legislators Anonymous' on School Funding," *PDN*, July 24, 2002.

66. Smith, "It's 'Legislators Anonymous.'"

67. Snyder, "Vallas"; Brennan, "State School Money Challenged."

68. Susan Snyder, Martha Woodall, and Dale Mezzacappa, "Seven Groups to Get $120 Million to Run Schools," *TPI*, August 1, 2002.

69. Chris Brennan, "Unable to Pay, Edison Returns Supplies," *PDN*, August 30, 2002.

70. Dale Mezzacappa, "Aides, Secretaries Get Layoff Notices," *TPI*, August 28, 2002; Menash Dean, "More Than 200 Nonteaching Aides Fired," *PDN*, August 23, 2002. Neither of Philadelphia's daily newspapers reported an exact number of nonteaching personnel laid off by Edison, but both reported that the bulk of 211 layoffs in the district were made by Edison. In addition, if the reported dismissal of four NTAs at Shaw and five at another Edison school—Penn Treaty Middle School—was typical, then the total number of NTAs laid off for twenty schools would have been about ninety; regarding Penn Treaty Middle School, see Dale Mezzacappa, "The Philadelphia Experiment," *TPI*, June 6, 2003. If there were as many SSAs as NTAs at each school and if at least one secretary at each school was laid off, the total of nonteaching personnel laid off by Edison approximated 200.

71. Mezzacappa, "Aides, Secretaries Get Layoff Notices."

72. Menash Dean, "More Than 200 Nonteaching Aides Fired," August 23, 2002.

73. Anonymous, March 5, 2006.

74. Paul Socolar, "CEO Vallas Commits to a Fresh Start," *PPSN*, Fall 2002, http://thenotebook.org/fall-2002/021480/ceo-vallas-commits-fresh-start.

75. Dale Mezzacappa, "Edison Gets a Warning on Finances," *TPI*, August 31, 2002.

76. Chris Brennan, "Violence Erupts at Shaw Middle School," *PDN*, September 18, 2002; Menash Dean, "District to Begin Intense Scrutiny of Schools," *PDN*, September 19, 2002; Sharif El-Mekki, interview, Philadelphia, May 5, 2014.

77. Chris Brennan, "Probe Begun after Principal Fails to Report Violent Fight," *PDN*, September 27, 2002.

78. Martha Woodall and Dale Mezzacappa, "District Delays Edison's Pay; Police, Aides Sent to School," *TPI*, October 5, 2002.

79. Mezzacappa, "The Philadelphia Experiment."

80. Sara Rimer, "Philadelphia School's Woes Defeat Veteran Principal," *NYT*, December 15, 2002; Janice I. Solkov, "Privatizing Schools Just Shouldn't Be This Hard," *WP*, February 2, 2003.

81. Rimer, "Philadelphia School's Woes." See also William C. Symonds, "Edison: An 'F' in Finance," *Businessweek*, November 3, 2002, 52, for an explanation of Edison's decision to phase out its practice of providing home computers for all students in third grade and above.

82. Rimer, "Philadelphia School's Woes."

83. Menash Dean, "Edison Schools Loses Top Official," *PDN*, January 17, 2006.

84. Todd McIntire, telephone interview, March 5, 2014; see also Valerie Russ, "Teachers Union Questions Safety of Schools That Lost Monitors," *PDN*, June 11, 2008.

85. Menash Dean, "Vallas: Edison's Contract in Jeopardy," *PDN*, August 31, 2002; Chris Brennan, "Schools to Pay Money Owed to Edison Firm Awaiting $5.3 Million in Payments," *PDN*, October 28, 2002.

86. Chris Brennan, "Edison Finally Gets Its First Paycheck from Philly Schools, 8 Weeks Late," *PDN*, October 29, 2002.

87. Menash Dean, "Vallas Rips Edison for 300G Junket," *PDN*, October 11, 2002.

88. Chris Whittle, *Crash Course: Imagining a Better Future for Public Education* (New York: Riverhead, 2005), 101–133.

89. Dale Mezzacappa and Martha Woodall, "Edison Founder Has Work-Study Idea," *TPI*, October 11, 2002.

90. Ibid.

91. Dan Hardy, "Edison Gains a Richer Deal in Chester," *TPI*, November 15, 2002.

92. Brent Staples, "Editorial Observer: Fighting Poverty in a Worst-Case School," *NYT*, March 4, 2002.

93. Dan Hardy, "Chester Upland May End Edison's Contract," *TPI*, October 11, 2002.

94. Dan Hardy, "Edison's Scores Drop in Chester Upland," *TPI*, October 16, 2002. The one exception to the bad news for Edison in Chester Upland was the proficiency rate of eighth-graders in reading at Showalter Middle School, which climbed by 15.7 percent from 2001 to 2002; however, the proficiency rates of fifth- and eighth-graders in math at the same school declined over this time period by 45.3 percent and 21.9 percent, respectively. See test data for 2001 and 2002 at http://www.portal.state.pa.us/portal/server.pt/community/data_and_statistics /7202.

95. Ad for Edison Schools, *NYT*, October 28, 2002, A9; November 7, 2002, C7; and November 4, 2002, C5.

96. Stock prices come from CRISP. On Tuesday, October 15, 2002, EDSN closed at 34 cents; four weeks later, on Tuesday, November 12, it closed at 97 cents.

97. EDSN failed to close above $1.00 from July 16, 2002, to November 13, 2002. The stock afterward closed above $1.00 until it was taken private on October 31, 2003, except for a stretch running from March 31 to April 17 when the stock closed below $1.00 on eleven of fourteen trading days. Source: CRISP.

98. "High on the High School Plan Vallas Strikes a Blow for Public Education," *PDN*, March 3, 2003.

99. Susan Snyder, "Vallas Seeks Less Funding for Edison," *TPI*, May 22, 2003.

100. Dale Mezzacappa, "Vallas Assents to More Time for Schools' Outside Managers," *TPI*, May 30, 2003; Susan Snyder, "Philadelphia District Sets 2003–04 Fees for School Managers," *TPI*, June 12, 2003.

101. Susan Snyder and Martha Woodall, "Schools to Make Modest Changes," *TPI*, April 17, 2003; Tania Deluzuriaga, "1+1=1 as School Companies Merge," *Orlando Sentinel*, June 11, 2004.

102. Diana Henriques, "Edison Stays Afloat by Altering Course," *NYT*, July 3, 2003.

103. While *Forbes* reported the buyout as worth $174 million, the sum of $95 million comports with the company's final 10-K, which states that the company's Class A and Class B shares totaled 54,128,252. With the buyout at $1.76 a share, the company's total value accordingly amounted to $95 million. See Edison Schools Inc., "Securities and Exchange Commission File No. 000-27817 (Form 10-K)," September 30, 2003, 2; and Nelson D. Schwartz, "The Nine Lives of Chris Whittle," *Fortune*, October 27, 2003, 103–104. Regarding Liberty Partners and the Florida Retirement System in particular, see Kenneth J. Saltman, *The Edison Schools: Corporate Schooling and the Assault on Public Education* (New York: Routledge, 2005), 58–64, and Sydney P. Freedberg, "Florida's Pension Administrator Touts Transparency . . . with Exceptions," *Tampa Bay Times*, April 23, 2011.

104. Schwartz, "The Nine Lives."

7. Redefinition

1. Edison Schools Inc., "Securities and Exchange Commission File No. 000-27817 (Form 10-K)," September 28, 2000, 4; September 30, 2002, 16, 27; and September 30, 2003, 17, 28.

2. Alan Richard, "Edison Alliance Hired to Help Struggling S.C. District," *EW*, August 11, 2004, 5.

3. Ibid.; Dan Martin, "Edison Schools Are Only Average," *Honolulu Star-Bulletin*, October 13, 2005. The number of Alliance schools in South Carolina comes from Alex Molnar, Gary Miron, and Jessica Urschel, *Profiles of For-Profit Educational Management Organizations: Tenth Annual Report, July 2008*, 55, http://nepc.colorado.edu/files/EMO0708.pdf.

4. Alan Desoff, "Trouble in Paradise," *District Administration Magazine*, January 2010, http://www.districtadministration.com/article/trouble-paradise.

5. Interview, anonymous Edison Alliance administrator, July 7, 2010.

6. Richard Barth, telephone interview, July 19, 2006.

7. Ibid.

8. Jim Howland, interview, New York, October 18, 2005.

9. No Child Left Behind Act of 2001, Pub. L. No. 107-110, January 8, 2002, Section 1116 (e)(12)(C).

10. Karla Scoon Reid, "Districts Spar with Ed. Dept. over Tutoring," *EW*, November 2, 2004, 3.

11. Catherine Gewertz, "Chicago Resisting Federal Directive on NCLB Tutoring," *EW*, January 4, 2005, 1, 15.

12. Catherine Gewertz, "Chicago, Ed. Dept. Settle Tutoring Dispute," *EW*, February 9, 2005, 3, 11.

13. Rhea R. Borja, "Market for NCLB Tutoring Falls Short of Expectations," *EW*, December 20, 2006, 5, 13.

14. Todd McIntire, interview, New York, October 23, 2013.

15. Howland, interview, New York, October 18, 2005.

16. McIntire, interview, New York, October 23, 2013.

17. Catherine Gewertz, "Edison Moves into Online-Learning Market," *EW*, July 1, 2008, http://www.edweek.org/ew/articles/2008/07/01/43edison_web.h27.html; Gewertz, "Edison Schools Retools Itself as Online-Learning Provider," *EW*, July 15, 2008, 7.

18. NCES, "Issue Brief: 1.5 Million Homeschooled Students in the United States in 2007," December 2008, http://nces.ed.gov/pubs2009/2009030.pdf.

19. NCES, *Digest of Education Statistics: 2013*, Table 206.10, https://nces.ed.gov/programs/digest/d13/tables/dt13_206.10.asp.

20. While the average per-pupil expenditure at a brick-and-mortar school in Florida in 2010, for example, was $8,500, the cost at the state's Florida Virtual School was $5,490. See Paul E. Peterson, *Saving Schools: From Horace Mann to Virtual Learning* (Cambridge, MA: Harvard University Press, 2010), 250.

21. David K. Randall, "Virtual Schools, Real Businesses," *Forbes*, July 24, 2008, http://www.forbes.com/forbes/2008/0811/084.html. For enrollment data, see Molnar, Miron, and Urschel, *Profiles of For-Profit Educational Management Organizations: Tenth Annual Report*, 14; and Alex Molnar, Gary Miron, and Jessica Urschel, *Profiles of For-Profit Educational Management Organizations: Eleventh Annual Report*, September 2009, 15, http://nepc.colorado.edu/publication/profiles-profit-emos-2008-09.

22. Gary Miron and Charisse Gulosino, *Profiles of For-Profit and Nonprofit Educational Management Organizations, Fourteenth Edition*, November 2013, 23, 37–38, http://nepc.colorado.edu/publication/EMO-profiles-11-12; Katherine Rushton, "Pearson Buys US 'Virtual School Academies' for $400 M," *Daily Telegraph*, September 16, 2011.

23. Shelly Banjo, "Whittle Starts a City School," *WSJ*, January 31, 2011.

24. Ibid.

25. Julian Guthrie, "The Fisher King," *San Francisco Chronicle*, October 18, 1998; Chris Whittle, Fourth Annual Avenues New Year Letter, January 7, 2014, 9, http://www.avenues.org/New-Year-Letter/Avenues_New_Year_Letter_2014.pdf.

26. Jenny Anderson, "The Best School $75 Million Can Buy," *NYT*, July 8, 2011.

27. For advertisements, see *NYT,* February 1, 2011, A28; February 10, 2011, B20; February 16, 2011, A26; February 23, 2011, A24; and March 1, 2011, A21.

28. See, for example, *WSJ,* February 1, 2011, A30; February 8, 2011, A26; and February 28, A30; *Downtown Express,* February 1, 2012, 16; *West Side Spirit,* February 2, 2012, 3; *Our Town,* February 23, 2012, 4; *New York Times Magazine,* September 16, 2002, 7; and *New Yorker,* September 24, 2012, 25.

29. Data come from adspender.kantarmediana.com. The cost may have been lower than $3 million because of discounts issued by publications for volume. Ad$pender listed 605 Internet ads.

30. The essays ran as a series under the heading "Open Thinking: On a New School of Thought." For the first in the series, "Can Success Be Taught?," see *Downtown Express,* February 1, 2012, 16; for the second, "Can Children Learn Language Like Music?," *West Side Spirit,* February 2, 2012, 3; for the third, "Time to Reinvent the Class Schedule?," *NYT,* February 26, 2012, SR2; and for the fourth, "Is the Sky the Limit for Technology in School?," *NYT,* March 4, 2012, SR2.

31. For the mission statement of Avenues, see http://www.avenues.org/avenues-school-mission.

32. Anderson, "The Best School"; Amanda M. Fairbanks, "Chris Whittle Seeks Global Reach in Private School Venture," *EW,* September 26, 2012, 10–11.

33. Anderson, "The Best School."

34. Gardner P. Dunnan, interview, New York, February 23, 2012.

35. Advertisement, "The First First Day," *NYT,* September 10, 2012, A26; *WSJ,* September 10, 2012, A20; *New Yorker,* September 24, 2012, 25; *New York Times Magazine,* September 16, 2012, 8.

36. *Avenues: The World School* (brochure), 2011, 28, http://www.avenues.org/wp-content/uploads/2011/01/Master_Brochure.pdf; Robin Pogrebin, "Renovated High Line Now Opens for Strolling," *NYT,* June 8, 2009.

37. New York City Housing Authority, *Development Data Book 2010,* http://www.nyc.gov/html/nycha/downloads/pdf1/pdb2010.pdf.

38. See NAIS membership requirements: http://www.nais.org/Articles/Pages/School-Membership.aspx (last updated June 17, 2013). Of the sixty-seven private schools in Manhattan, five are run as for-profit operations: Avenues, British International, Dwight, Léman Manhattan Preparatory (formerly Claremont Academy), and York Preparatory.

39. The Web site for Avenues is www.avenues.org. While .org is widely understood as the suffix for nonprofit institutions, there is no rule limiting its usage. As no .com domain name exists for Avenues, the issue was not lack of availability. Incidentally, Edison and EdisonLearning both employed .com domain names.

40. In commenting on Whittle's contention that Avenues can make money from tuition alone, Steve Nelson, the head of the Calhoun School, a traditional nonprofit private school in Manhattan, said, "As far as I know, there's not an

independent school in New York City that covers its expenses from tuition, no matter how many students they have." See Anderson, "The Best School."

41. According to the Web sites of these five schools, tuition and fees for 2013–2014 were as follows: Brearley, $39,000; Collegiate, $41,200; Dalton, $40,220; Nightingale-Bamford, $39,985; and Trinity, $40,628 (in the last case, the cost was a weighted average reflecting different costs for different cohorts). The average for all five was $40,387.

42. According to the 990 forms filed with the IRS for fiscal year 2010, Brearley, Collegiate, Dalton, Nightingale-Bamford, and Trinity together conferred $23,534,826 in aid on approximately 4,144 students, assuming enrollment in 2010 was the same as in 2013. The weighted average of assistance in 2010 was accordingly $5,679 per student; aid averaged by institution was at $5,688 nearly indistinguishable. Using an inflation multiplier of 1.0726 to cover the subsequent three years, the projected allocation for 2013 would be $6,091.

43. The commitment of NAIS to diversity serves as a clear example of the belief of many educators in the importance of a heterogeneous student body. See, for example, the 2012 NAIS statement entitled "Equity and Justice," http://www.nais.org/Series/Pages/Equity-and-Justice.aspx.

44. Gardner Dunnan, interview, New York, February 23, 2012.

45. Whittle, Fourth Annual Avenues New Year Letter, 3, 5–7, 9–12. According to Miron and Gulosino, *Profiles*, November 2013, 5, National Heritage Academies ran sixty-eight schools with 44,338 students in 2011–2012. While Imagine Schools operated more sites, the company had fewer students.

46. Sophia Hollander, "Education Entrepreneur Chris Whittle Resigns from Avenues School," *WSJ*, March 6, 2015.

47. Zoe Alsop, "Wealthy Chinese Love Private Schools but Private Equity Finds Profits Harder," CNBC, November 29, 2015, http://www.cnbc.com/2015/11/29/wealthy-chinese-love-private-schools-but-private-equity-finds-profits-harder.html.

48. "International Schools: The New Local," *The Economist*, December 20, 2014, 88.

49. School counts come from company Web sites: http://www.meritas.net/; http://www.nordangliaeducation.com/; http://www.gemseducation.com/.

50. Nord Anglia, press release, "Nord Anglia Education Completes Acquisition of Six Schools from Meritas," June 25, 2015, http://www.prnewswire.com/news-releases/nord-anglia-education-completes-acquisition-of-six-schools-from-meritas-300104965.html.

51. Jeff Wahl, interview, New York, May 5, 2010.

52. Ibid.

53. Ibid.

54. Jeff Wahl, "From the Office of the President and CEO, EdisonLearning," December 2009, 7, obtained from Wahl.

55. Ibid.

56. Ibid.

57. Wahl, interview, New York, May 5, 2010.

58. Ibid.

59. Jeff Wahl, speech, ELDA, San Diego, July 8, 2010.

60. Karen Grigsby Bates, "Cornel West, a Fighter, Angers Obama Supporters," National Public Radio, October 24, 2011, http://www.npr.org/20117p6.423/10/24 /141598911/cornel-west-a-fighter-angers-obama-supporters; Lisa Miller, "I Want to Be Like Jesus," *New York Magazine,* May 6, 2012, http://nymag.com/news/fea tures/cornel-west-2012-5/.

61. Todd McIntire, telephone interview, July 1, 2014.

62. Cornel West, keynote speech, ELDA, San Diego, July 9, 2010.

63. Melissa Harris-Perry, keynote speech, ELDA, Palm Springs, November 19, 2010; Michael Eric Dyson, keynote speech, ELDA, Palm Springs, November 20, 2010. DVDs obtained from EdisonLearning, January 2011.

64. Dyson, keynote speech, ELDA.

65. Jeffrey R. Henig, *Rethinking School Choice: Limits of the Market Metaphor* (Princeton, NJ: Princeton University Press, 1994), 3–12, 101–148.

66. Jeff Wahl, interview, New York, February 25, 2011.

67. Menash Dean, "Edison to Manage Two More Troubled City Schools," *PDN,* May 26, 2005; Dale Mezzacappa, "Edison in Chester: How Plan Failed," *TPI,* June 16, 2005.

68. Susan Snyder, "Power Struggle Brewing in SRC?," *TPI,* May 23, 2007; Kristen A. Graham, "Philadelphia Taking Back Six Privatized Schools," *TPI,* June 19, 2008.

69. Menash Dean, "SRC: Schools Must Hire More Minority Teachers," *PDN,* June 25, 2009.

70. Todd McIntire, telephone interview, November 26, 2013.

71. Ibid.

72. McIntire, interview, New York, October 23, 2013.

73. Ibid.

74. Wahl, interview, New York, February 25, 2011.

75. Ibid.

76. Todd McIntire, interview, Philadelphia, January 13, 2009.

77. Todd McIntire, interview, New York, July 29, 2009.

78. Charlotte Buonassisi, interview, Philadelphia, February 3, 2009.

79. Visit to Shaw Middle School, February 2, 2009, and to Waring Elementary School, February 9, 2009.

80. Visit to Ludlow Elementary School, February 3, 2009.

81. Ibid.

82. Todd McIntire, interview, Philadelphia, February 5, 2009.

83. Ibid.

84. Visit to Lincoln Charter School, York, Pennsylvania, February 5, 2009.

85. Paul E. Peterson and Matthew M. Chingos, "Impact of For-Profit and Non-Profit School Management on Student Achievement: The Philadelphia Experiment," PEPG 07-07, November 1, 2007, http://www.hks.harvard.edu/pepg/PDF/Papers/PEPG07-07_Peterson_Chingos_Philadelphia.pdf; Peterson and Chingos, "Impact of For-Profit and Non-Profit Management on Student Achievement: The Philadelphia Intervention, 2002–2008," PEPG 09-02, 2009, http://www.hks.harvard.edu/pepg/PDF/Papers/PEPG09-02_Peterson_Chingos.pdf.

86. Karla Scoon Reid, "Analysis Finds Gains in Edison Schools, but Model Is No Quick Fix," *EW*, October 19, 2005, 6.

87. Brian Gill et al., *Inspiration, Perspiration, and Time: Operations and Achievement in Edison Schools* (Santa Monica: RAND, 2005), xxii–xxix, 122–134.

88. Ibid., xxiii, 121–130.

89. See Henry Levin, "Déjà Vu All Over Again," *Education Next* 6 (Spring 2006): 21–24; and Chris Whittle, "Growth Is Possible," *Education Next* 6 (Spring 2006): 15–19. In challenging Levin's conclusion that Edison's schools had not produced statistically significant gains, Whittle quoted from the RAND study, p. xxiii: "From 2002 to 2004, average proficiency rates in currently operating Edison schools increased by 11 percentage points in reading and 17 percentage points in math. Meanwhile, average proficiency rates in a matched set of comparison schools serving similar student populations increased . . . nine percentage points in reading and 13 percentage points in math (although the Edison advantage is statistically significant only in math)."

90. Gill et al., *Inspiration, Perspiration, and Time*, xxiv–xxvii, 131–134.

91. Ibid., xxiv–xxv.

92. Ruth Curran Neild, Elizabeth Useem, and Elizabeth Farley, *The Quest for Quality: Recruiting and Retaining Teachers in Philadelphia* (Philadelphia: Research for Action, 2005), 17–18.

93. Kurt Spiridakis, "Teacher Turnover High at 'Takeover Schools,'" *PPSN*, Summer 2003, http://thenotebook.org/summer-2003/03881/teacher-turnover-high-takeover-schools.

94. Gill et al., *Inspiration, Perspiration, and Time*, xxiii.

95. Reid, "Analysis Finds Gains."

96. Douglas J. MacIver and Martha Abel MacIver, "Effects on Middle Grades' Mathematics Achievement of Educational Management Organizations (EMOs) and New K–8 Schools," paper presented at the Annual Meeting of the American Educational Research Association, San Francisco, April 10, 2006, 11–17, www.csos.jhu.edu/new/AERA_2006.pdf.

97. Brian Gill et al., *State Takeover, School Restructuring, Private Management, and Student Achievement in Philadelphia* (Santa Monica: RAND, 2007).

98. Ibid., 1, 7. Initially, there were seven outside managers: Edison, Victory, and Chancellor Beacon, all for-profit operators; and Foundations, Universal

Companies, Temple University, and University of Pennsylvania. But Chancellor Beacon, as noted in Chapter 6, lasted only one year.

99. Ibid., 9.

100. Ibid., xii–xiv, 18.

101. Peterson and Chingos, "Impact of For-Profit and Non-Profit School Management: The Philadelphia Experiment," 2–3, 11–20.

102. Peterson and Chingos, "Impact of For-Profit and Non-Profit Management on Student Achievement: The Philadelphia Intervention, 2002–2008," 3.

103. Vaughan Byrnes, "Getting a Feel for the Market: The Use of Privatized School Management in Philadelphia," *American Journal of Education* 115 (May 2009): 437–455.

104. Pennsylvania Department of Education, 2005–2006 PSSA and AYP Results and 2010–2011 PSSA and AYP Results, http://www.portal.state.pa.us/portal /server.pt/community/school_assessments/7442/2005–2006_pssa_and_ayp _results/507507 and http://www.portal.state.pa.us/portal/server.pt/community /school_assessments/7442/2010–2011_pssa_and_ayp_results/1014980. To arrive at net numbers for the district, the Edison numbers were subtracted. Of 930 fifth-graders in Edison's schools taking the writing exam, 930 were classified as economically disadvantaged; of 1,211 eighth-graders in Edison's schools taking the writing exam, 1,211 were classified as such. For the district, minus Edison, 9,775 of 11,350 fifth-graders belonged to this category, as did 9,171 of 11,201 eighth-graders. In 2011, when Edison was running only four schools, 167 of 168 fifth-graders and 246 of 248 eighth-graders belonged to this category; for the district, minus Edison, 8,916 of 10,389 fifth-graders and 8,063 of 9,772 eighth-graders belonged to this category.

105. Donald T. Campbell, "Assessing the Impact of Planned Social Change," in *Social Research and Public Policies: The Dartmouth/OECD Conference,* ed. G. M. Lyons (Hanover, NH: Public Affairs Center, Dartmouth College, 1975), 35.

106. Brian A. Jacob, "Accountability, Incentives and Behavior: The Impact of High-Stakes Testing in the Chicago Public Schools," *Journal of Public Economics* 89 (June 2005): 761–796.

107. Gill et al., *State Takeover,* 11.

108. Pennsylvania Department of Education, 2005–2006 through 2010–2011 PSSA and AYP Results, http://www.portal.state.pa.us/portal/server.pt/community /school_assessments/7442. The sample sizes for Edison's fifth-graders for reading/ writing for 2006 to 2011 were 1,003/930, 708/684, 698/713, 593/570, 486/464, and 175/167. For Edison's eighth-graders, the sample sizes were 1,277/1,211, 1,296/1,188, 1,168/1,136, 1,106/971, 809/779, and 249/246. The sample sizes for Victory's fifth-graders for reading/writing for 2006 to 2010 were 287/259, 248/242, 247/246, 234/217, and 210/206. For Victory's eighth-graders, the sample sizes were 410/384, 311/278, 319/321, 277/270, and 266/259. For the district, the sample sizes from 2006 to 2011 ranged from 7,743 to 10,093.

109. Laura Simmons, "Whittle to Build 1,000 Schools: Cost of First 200 to Be $2.5 Billion," *Knoxville News Sentinel,* May 15, 1991; Mark Walsh, "Entrepreneur Whittle Unveils Plans to Create Chain of For-Profit Schools," *EW,* May 22, 1991, 1, 13.

110. Michael T. Moe, Kathleen Bailey, and Rhoda Lau, *The Book of Knowledge: Investing in the Growing Education and Training Industry* (New York: Merrill Lynch, April 9, 1999), 74–75.

111. Miron and Gulosino, *Profiles,* November 2013, 9.

112. Whittle, Fourth Annual Avenues New Year Letter, 9.

113. BMO Capital Markets, M&A Advisory Deals, December 13, 2013, http://www.bmocm.com/industry-expertise/busservices/deals/.

114. Richard Pérez-Peña, "College Group Run for Profit Looks to Close or Sell Schools," *NYT,* July 5, 2014.

115. Business Wire, "Alloy Broadens Media Offerings; Acquires Channel One," April 23, 2007, http://www.businesswire.com/news/home/20070423005476/en.

116. Had Liberty played the tortoise instead of the hare, it could have invested that $91 million in an S&P 500 index fund such as State Street Global Advisors' SPY. On July 11, 2003, when Liberty was finalizing its purchase of Edison, SPY closed at $100.24 a share. On December 13, 2013, when BMO recorded the sale of EdisonLearning to Catapult, SPY closed at $178.11. With annual dividends of 2 percent reinvested and taxed at the qualified dividend rate of 15 percent conferred on corporations, that $91 million would have grown by December 2013 to nearly $200 million.

117. EdisonLearning, "EdisonLearning Names New Leadership Team," January 31, 2014, http://edisonlearning.com/press-releases.

118. Catapult Learning, "Combination Creates Largest Intervention Services and Professional Development Provider," January 6, 2014, https://www.catapultlearning.com/catapult-learning-acquires-newton-alliance/.

119. EdisonLearning, "EdisonLearning Names New Leadership Team."

120. Thomas Fitzgerald, "Pennsylvania Proposal Would Raise Income Tax to Aid Schools," *TPI,* November 14, 2001.

121. The per-pupil expenditure for Philadelphia versus the weighted per-pupil expenditure for these five Main Line school districts constitutes a consistent pattern from 1995–1996 through 2012–2013: 1995–1996 ($6,550/$9,569: 0.68); 1996–1997 ($6,810/$9,559: 0.71); 1997–1998 ($6,720/$9,995: 0.67); 1998–1999 ($7,105/$10,348: 0.69); 1999–2000 ($7,378/$10,763: 0.69); 2000–2001 ($7,944/$11,421: 0.70); 2001–2002 ($8,332/$11,973: 0.70); 2002–2003 ($8,790/$12,301: 0.71); 2003–2004 ($9,768/$13,117: 0.74); 2004–2005 ($10,223/$13,888: 0.74); 2005–2006 ($10,653/$14,398: 0.74); 2006–2007 ($10,662/$14,825: 0.72); 2007–2008 ($10,786/$15,664: 0.69); 2008–2009 ($11,394/$16,320: 0.70); 2009–2010 ($12,223/$16,858:

0.73); 2010–2011 ($13,096/$17,120: 0.76); 2011–2012 ($12,352/$17,015: 0.73); 2012–2013 ($13,206/$18,006: 0.73). All figures come from the Web site of the Pennsylvania Department of Education, http://www.portal.state.pa.us.

122. Benjamin Herold, "Consulting Group Playing Key Role in Philadelphia Plan," *EW,* August 8, 2012, 12–13. The William Penn Foundation provided $1.5 million; the remainder came from other donors.

123. Edison Schools Inc., "Strengthening the Performance of the Philadelphia School District: Report to the Governor of Pennsylvania," October 2001, 4, 14–17, 34, 45, 58–60.

124. Boston Consulting Group Inc., "Transforming Philadelphia's Public Schools: Key Findings and Recommendations," August 2012, 11, 12, 19, 38–40, 73, http://webgui.phila.k12.pa.us/uploads/v_/IF/v_IFJYCOr72CBKDpRrGAAQ /BCG-Summary-Findings-and-Recommendations_August_2012.pdf.

125. Ibid., 55.

8. Market Failure

1. Laws of New York, 2010, Chapter 101, Section 1: "An application to establish a charter school may be submitted by teachers, parents, school administrators, community residents or any combination thereof... *Provided however, for-profit business or corporate entities shall not be eligible.*" (Emphasis in original.) Those EMOs with contracts were grandfathered.

2. Brent Staples, "Editorial Observer: Fighting Poverty in a Worst-Case School," *NYT,* March 4, 2002.

3. Scott E. Carrell and Mark L. Hoekstra, "Externalities in the Classroom: How Children Exposed to Domestic Violence Affect Everyone's Kids," *American Economic Journal: Applied Economics* 2 (January 2010): 211–228. The authors confined their study to the impact on classmates of children from homes documented in court records for domestic violence in one central Florida school district from 1995 to 2003. The study concerned students in grades three through five in the district's twenty-two elementary schools.

4. Hoekstra confirmed this determination by e-mail, August 5, 2015.

5. See Richard Rothstein, *Class and Schools: Using Social, Economic, and Educational Reform to Close the Black-White Achievement Gap* (Washington, DC: Economic Policy Institute, 2004), 13–59; David C. Berliner, "Our Impoverished View of Educational Reform," *Teachers College Record* 108 (2006): 949–995. See also David K. Cohen and Susan L. Moffitt, *The Ordeal of Equality: Did Federal Regulation Fix the Schools?* (Cambridge, MA: Harvard University Press, 2009), 211–213, regarding the difficulty of turning around schools in low-income communities.

6. Tung Le, interview, New York, March 16, 2009.

7. Kenneth J. Arrow, "Uncertainty and the Welfare Economics of Medical Care," *AER* 53 (December 1963): 941–973.

8. Ibid.

9. Ibid.

10. Ibid.

11. Steven Brill, "Bitter Pill: Why Medical Bills Are Killing Us," *Time,* March 4, 2013, 16–55; H. Gilbert Welch, "Diagnosis: Insufficient Rage," *NYT,* July 4, 2013.

12. George A. Akerlof, "The Market for 'Lemons': Quality Uncertainty and the Market Mechanism," *Quarterly Journal of Economics* 84 (August 1970): 488–500.

13. Marc Santora and Michaelle Bond, "Many Bars Misled Drinkers, New Jersey Says," *NYT,* July 31, 2013.

14. U.S. Department of Education, Federal Student Aid, https://studentaid.ed .gov/about/data-center/school/proprietary. See also Alia Wong, "The Downfall of For-Profit Colleges," *The Atlantic,* February 23, 2015, http://www.theatlantic .com/education/archive/2015/02/the-downfall-of-for-profit-colleges/385810/.

15. U.S. Department of Education, "First Official Three-Year Student Loan Default Rates Published," September 28, 2012, http://www.ed.gov/news/press-releases /first-official-three-year-student-loan-default-rates-published. See also Wong, "Downfall of For-Profit Colleges."

16. Wong, "Downfall of For-Profit Colleges."

17. Floyd Norris, "Corinthian Colleges Faltering as Flow of Federal Money Slows," *NYT,* June 26, 2014; Michael Stratford, "Corinthian Closes for Good," *Inside HigherEd,* April 27, 2015, https://www.insidehighered.com/news/2015/04/27 /corinthian-ends-operations-remaining-campuses-affecting-16000-students.

18. Share prices for the five-year span come from the close of trading on April 23, 2010, and May 13, 2015. For Career Education (CECO), the decline was from $34.10 a share to $4.24; ITT (ESI), $111.78 to $2.23; Strayer (STRA), $253.03 to $48.01; and the University of Phoenix (APOL), $63.53 to $16.82.

19. Henry B. Hansmann, "The Role of Nonprofit Enterprise," *Yale Law Journal* 89 (April 1980): 835–901.

20. Ibid.

21. Ibid.

22. Ibid.

23. U.S. Department of Health and Human Services, National Center for Health Statistics, *National Nursing Home Survey, 1973–1974,* DHEW Publication No. (H RA) 77–1779 (Hyattsville, MD: U.S. Department of Health and Human Services, National Center for Health Statistics, July 1979), 2; Lauren Harris-Kojetin et al., "Long-Term Care Services in the United States: 2013 Overview," National Center for Health Statistics, *Vital Health Statistics* 3 (37) (2009): 12.

24. American Hospital Association, Fast Facts on U.S. Hospitals from the 2013 AHA Annual Survey, http://www.aha.org/research/rc/stat-studies/fast-facts .shtml.

25. U.S. Department of Justice, Bureau of Justice Statistics, *Census of State and Federal Correctional Facilities, 1990* (Washington, DC: U.S. Government Printing Office, 1992), 1, 20; U.S. Department of Justice, Bureau of Justice Statistics, *Census of State and Federal Correctional Facilities, 2000,* August 2003, 2, http://www.bjs .gov/content/pub/pdf/csfcf00.pdf; U.S. Department of Justice, Bureau of Justice Statistics, *Census of State and Federal Correctional Facilities, 2005,* October 1, 2008, 1, A1, http://www.bjs.gov/content/pub/pdf/csfcf05.pdf. The proportion of the nation's inmates in privately managed prisons does not correspond to the share of the nation's prisons under private management, as privately run prisons, on average, house fewer inmates. The growth rate has nevertheless been significant. In 1990, 1 percent of the nation's inmates were held in privately run prisons; in 1995, 2 percent; in 2000, 7 percent; and in 2005, 8 percent.

26. For illustrations of breaches of protocol by for-profit hospitals and health-care companies, see, for example, Steffie Woolhandler and David U. Himmelstein, "When Money Is the Mission—The High Costs of Investor-Owned Care," *New England Journal of Medicine* 341 (August 5, 1999): 444–446; Solomon Moore, "Alleged Scheme Involved Homeless," *NYT,* August 10, 2008; Alex Berenson, "Long-Term Care Hospitals Face Little Scrutiny" and "Trail of Disquieting Reports from Hospitals of Select Medical," *NYT,* February 10, 2010; John Carreyrou, "Home-Health Firms Blasted: Senate Panel Alleges Big Providers Abused Medicare by Tailoring Patient Care to Maximize Profits," *WSJ,* October 3, 2011; Julie Creswell and Reed Abelson, "A Giant Hospital Chain Is Blazing a Profit Trail," *NYT,* August 14, 2012; and Eduardo Porter, "Health Care and Profits, a Poor Mix," *NYT,* January 8, 2013. For such breaches by for-profit prison management organizations, see, for example, Eric Schlosser, "The Prison-Industrial Complex," *The Atlantic,* December 1998, 51–77; Margaret Talbot, "The Lost Children: What Do Tougher Detention Policies Mean for Illegal Immigrant Families?," *New Yorker,* March 3, 2008, 58–67; Christopher Hartney and Caroline Glesman, *Prison Bed Profiteers: How Corporations Are Reshaping Criminal Justice in the U.S.* (Oakland, CA: National Council on Crime and Delinquency, 2012); Sam Dolnick, "As Escapees Stream Out, a Penal Business Thrives," *NYT,* June 16, 2012; Dolnick, "At a Halfway House, Bedlam Reigns," *NYT,* June 17, 2012; Holly Kirby et al., "The Dirty Thirty: Nothing to Celebrate about 30 Years of Corrections Corporation of America," Grassroots Leadership, June 2013, http://grass rootsleadership.org/cca-dirty-30; and Margaret Newkirk and William Selway, "Gangs Ruled Prison as For-Profit Model Put Blood on Floor," *BloombergBusiness,* July 12, 2013, http://www.bloomberg.com/news/articles/2013-07-12/gangs-ruled -prison-as-for-profit-model-put-blood-on-floor.

27. See Bruce C. Vladeck, *Unloving Care: The Nursing Home Tragedy* (New York: Basic Books, 1980), 122–127. Vladeck faulted both proprietary and non-profit nursing homes for deficiencies in care. While Vladeck noted that comparative studies had "found no statistically significant differences in the quality of care," he added that it would be incorrect to infer much from these studies given that measurements for differentiation had, so far, been "too primitive." Vladeck wrote that his impression from interviews and observations was that, on average, nonprofit nursing homes were "somewhat better." Sophisticated statistical assessments have since found significant differences in quality of care. This may be the result of improvements in measurement or changes in practice at nursing homes or some combination of the two.

28. See Shin-Yi Chou, "Asymmetric Information, Ownership and Quality of Care: An Empirical Analysis of Nursing Homes," *Journal of Health Economics* 21 (March 2002): 293–311; Jane Banaszak-Holl et al., "Comparing Service and Quality among Chain and Independent U.S. Nursing Homes during the 1990s," Center for the Advancement of Social Entrepreneurship, Fuqua School of Business, Duke University, 2002, https://centers.fuqua.duke.edu/case/knowledge_items /comparing-service-and-quality-among-chain-and-independent-nursing-homes -during-the-1990s/; Will Mitchell et al., "The Commercialization of Nursing Home Care: Does For-Profit Cost-Control Mean Lower Quality or Do Corporations Provide the Best of Both Worlds?," presentation, Strategic Management Society, Baltimore, November 2003, https://faculty.fuqua.duke.edu/seminarscalendar/Aparna _seminar_paper.pdf; Daniel R. Levinson, "Trends in Nursing Home Deficiencies and Complaints," Office of Inspector General, Department of Health and Human Services, Washington, DC, September 18, 2008, http://oig.hhs.gov/oei/reports/oei -02-08-00140.pdf; and Anna A. Amirkhanyan, Hyun Joon Kim, and Kristina T. Lambright, "Does the Public Sector Outperform the Nonprofit and For-Profit Sectors? Evidence from a National Panel Study on Nursing Home Quality and Access," *Journal of Policy Analysis and Management* 27 (Spring 2008): 326–353.

29. Chou, "Asymmetric Information."

30. Steve Schaefer, "Jailhouse Shock," *Forbes,* October 21, 2009, http://www .forbes.com/2009/10/21/ackman-corrections-corp-markets-equities-value.html.

31. Shaila Dewan, "Experts Say Schools Need to Screen for Cheating," *NYT,* February 13, 2010; Brian A. Jacob and Steven D. Levitt, "Rotten Apples: An Investigation of the Prevalence and Predictors of Teacher Cheating," *Quarterly Journal of Economics* 118 (August 2003): 843–877. See also Levitt and Stephen J. Dubner, *Freakonomics: A Rogue Economist Explores the Hidden Side of Everything* (New York: HarperCollins, 2005), 25–37.

32. Barbara Martinez and Tom McGinty, "Students' Regents Test Scores Bulge at 65," *WSJ,* February 2, 2011; Jack Gillum and Marisol Bello, "When Standardized Test Scores Soared in D.C., Were the Gains Real?," *USA Today,* March 28, 2011; Kim Severson, "Systematic Cheating Is Found in Atlanta's School System,"

NYT, July 5, 2011; Benjamin Herold and Dale Mezzacappa, "2009 Report Identified Dozens of PA Schools for Possible Cheating," *PPSN,* July 8, 2011, http://the notebook.org/blog/113871/2009-report-identified-pa-schools-possible-cheating.

33. Ronald Coase, "The Nature of the Firm," *Economica* 4 (November 1937): 386–405.

34. Oliver E. Williamson, "The Vertical Integration of Production: Market Failure Considerations," *AER* 61 (May 1971): 112–123; and Williamson, *The Economic Institutions of Capitalism* (New York: Free Press, 1985).

35. Williamson, "Vertical Integration of Production."

36. John D. Donahue, *The Privatization Decision: Public Ends, Private Means* (New York: Basic Books, 1989), 126.

37. Williamson, *Economic Institutions of Capitalism,* 120–123.

38. Ibid., 114–115.

39. Louis T. Wells and Rafiq Ahmed, *Making Foreign Investment Safe: Property and National Sovereignty* (Oxford: Oxford University Press, 2007), 281.

40. Barbara J. Stevens, "Comparing Public- and Private-Sector Productive Efficiency: An Analysis of Eight Activities," *National Productivity Review* 3 (Autumn 1984): 395–406. The determinations of the cost savings are derived from inverting the additional costs ascribed by Stevens to each function in table 5, p. 401. The savings yielded in this study by municipalities that used contractors are as follows for other services: 29 percent for turf maintenance; 30 percent for trash collection; 30 percent for street cleaning; 36 percent for traffic signal maintenance; and 42 percent for building janitorial service. For opinions of Stevens's article and of outsourcing by municipal governments, see Donahue, *Privatization Decision,* 131–149, and Elliott Sclar, *You Don't Always Get What You Pay For: The Economics of Privatization* (Ithaca, NY: Cornell University Press, 2001), 47–68.

41. See Craig E. Richards, Rima Shore, and Max B. Sawicky, *Risky Business: Private Management of Public Schools* (Washington, DC: Economic Policy Institute, 1996), 144–148.

42. Albert Shanker, American Federation of Teachers advertisement, "Where We Stand: Striking a Good Bargain," *NYT,* June 5, 1994.

43. Wells and Ahmed, *Making Foreign Investment Safe,* 66–73.

44. Raymond Vernon, "Long-Run Trends in Concession Contracts," *Proceedings of the American Society for International Law,* April 1967, 84. See also Raymond Vernon, *Sovereignty at Bay* (New York: Basic Books, 1971).

45. Wells and Ahmed, *Making Foreign Investment Safe,* 9, 34, 47.

46. Ibid., 68.

47. Winston Brooks, interview transcript for *Frontline: Public Schools Inc.,* PBS, July 3, 2003, www.pbs.org/wgbh/pages/frontline/shows/edison.

48. D. C. Denison, "School of Hard Knocks in the Bull Market," *Boston Globe,* May 26, 2002.

49. See George A. Akerlof and Rachel E. Kranton, *Identity Economics: How Our Identities Shape Our Work, Wages, and Well-Being* (Princeton, NJ: Princeton University Press, 2010), 22–25. In contrast to conventional economic theory, whereby workers respond to financial incentives to maximize their "utility" as consumers, workers, according to Akerlof and Kranton, may aim as much to advance a cause to maximize their "utility" as servants of that cause.

50. See Dan Lortie, *Schoolteacher: A Sociological Study* (Chicago: University of Chicago Press, 1975), 28–29, 103–106, 111–116, 121–124.

51. Richard M. Titmuss, *The Gift Relationship: From Human Blood to Social Policy* (1970; reprint, New York: New Press, 1997), 114–116, 289–292.

52. Roland Bénabou and Jean Tirole, "Incentives and Prosocial Behavior," *AER* 96 (December 2006): 1652–1678.

53. Carl Mellström and Magnus Johannesson, "Crowding Out in Blood Donation: Was Titmuss Right?," *Journal of the European Economic Association* 6 (June 2008): 845–863. The authors note, however, that the effect was statistically significant only in the case of female participants in their study, which involved thirty-five men and fifty-four women.

54. To Akerlof and Kranton, workers who identify with the mission of their leaders are "insiders," dedicating themselves selflessly to their work, whereas workers who do not are "outsiders." See Akerolf and Kranton, *Identity Economics,* 41–49.

55. William J. Baumol, *The Cost Disease: Why Computers Get Cheaper and Health Care Doesn't* (New Haven, CT: Yale University Press, 2012), 20–24.

56. While the National Center for Education Statistics (NCES) did publish data on expenditures for K–12 schooling by function and subfunction for fiscal year 2011, it did not identify amounts allocated for salaries and benefits, as it had for 2009 and earlier. See NCES, Revenues and Expenditures for Public Elementary and Secondary Education: School Year 2010–11 (Fiscal Year 2011), Table 2, http://nces.ed.gov/pubs2013/expenditures2/tables/table_02.asp.

57. Interpublic Group of Companies Inc., "Securities and Exchange Commission File No. 1-6686 (Form 10-K)," December 31, 2009, 13; Aon Corporation, "Securities and Exchange Commission File No. 1-7933 (Form 10-K)," December 31, 2009; Accenture PLC, "Securities and Exchange Commission File No. 001-16565 (Form 10-K)," August 31, 2009, F-5; James D. Cotterman, "Compensating Partners and Associates in Trying Economic Times," *Altman Weil Direct: Report to Legal Management,* September 2009, 1, http://www.altmanweil.com/dir_docs/resource /64272ef8-56f0-4b9a-b519-95351ee0310a_document.pdf.

58. Trenton H. Norris, "Law Firm Economics 101," presentation, Berkeley School of Law, March 13, 2012, http://www.law.berkeley.edu/files/careers/Law _Firm_Economics_101_Mar_2012_Berkeley.pdf.

59. See Sclar, *You Don't Always Get What You Pay For,* 23–26. Sclar cites shoes and theater tickets as classic illustrations of private goods. Sclar writes with re-

gard to education: "There are many examples of goods that can be produced privately for a specific group of people but are so valued in terms of their external impacts that they are publicly provided to foster wider use. Primary and secondary education is the most obvious and salient example."

60. See NAIS membership requirements: http://www.nais.org/Articles/Pages /School-Membership.aspx (last updated June 17, 2013).

61. Regarding the power of optics, or appearances, in corporate psychology, see Nick Paumgarten, "The Death of Kings: Notes from a Meltdown," *New Yorker,* May 18, 2009, 43.

62. Regarding fractals, see Jim Holt, "He Conceived the Mathematics of Roughness," *New York Review of Books,* May 23, 2013, http://www.nybooks.com /articles/archives/2013/may/23/mandlebrot-mathematics-of-roughness/.

63. Alan Finder and Kate Zernike, "Embattled President of Harvard to Step Down at End of Semester," *NYT,* February 21, 2006; Marcella Bombardieri, "Leader Forgoes Campus Salary: Harvard's Bok Resists a Trend," *Boston Globe,* November 22, 2006.

64. Henry Rosovsky, *The University: An Owner's Manual* (New York: W. W. Norton, 1990), 54, 257–258.

65. *Scent of a Woman,* directed by Martin Brest (Santa Monica, CA: City Light Films, 1992).

66. Vance H. Trimble, *An Empire Undone: The Wild and Hard Fall of Chris Whittle* (New York: Birch Lane, 1995), 192; anonymous Edison staff lawyer, 2008.

67. Richard Rothstein, "Teacher Shortages Vanish When the Price Is Right," *NYT,* September 25, 2002.

68. For selectivity and retention, see Morgan L. Donaldson and Susan Moore Johnson, "TFA Teachers: How Long Do They Teach? Why Do They Leave?," *Phi Delta Kappan* 93 (October 2011): 47–51; Michael Winerip, "A Chosen Few Are Teaching for America," *NYT,* July 12, 2010; and Andrew Doughman, "Legislative Showdown Brewing over $2 Million for Teach for America," *Las Vegas Sun,* May 20, 2013. For detail regarding the Summer Institutes, see Annie Em, "No Pay from TFA," *Daily Kos,* April 16, 2013, http://www.dailykos.com/story/2013/04/16/1202 244/-No-pay-from-TFA-Teach-for-America.

69. "Schoolhouse Rocked," *Time,* February 23, 2015, 15.

70. See the Web site for TFA summits: http://www.teachforamerica.org/corp s-member-and-alumni-resources/alumni-summits.

71. See the Web site for KIPP summits: http://www.kipp.org/kipp-school -summit. According to Steve Mancini, KIPP's director of public affairs, about half of KIPP School Summit attendees are there on their own time. Mancini, interview, New York, July 18, 2014.

72. NCES, "Characteristics of the 100 Largest Public Elementary and Secondary School Districts in the United States: 2002–03," table 1, http://nces.ed .gov/pubs2005/100_largest/tables/table_1.asp.

73. Karla Scoon Reid, "Former Justice Official to Head NYC Schools," *EW*, August 7, 2002.

74. Edison Schools Inc., "Securities and Exchange Commission File No. 000-27817 (Form 10-K)," September 30, 2003, 59.

75. Megan Zor, interview, Philadelphia, February 10, 2009.

76. Menash Dean, "Edison Schools Loses Top Official," *PDN*, January 17, 2006.

77. Ann Grimes, "School Board Seeks to Revoke Edison Charter," *WSJ*, February 20, 2001.

78. Jay Mathews, *Work Hard. Be Nice.* (Chapel Hill, NC: Algonquin, 2009), 263–268.

79. KIPP School Directory, http://www.kipp.org/schools/school-directory -home.

9. The Fourth Way

1. Jay Mathews, *Work Hard. Be Nice.* (Chapel Hill, NC: Algonquin, 2009), 94–99, 252–253. For Edison data, see Table 6.1.

2. EdisonLearning lost its contract in 2014 to continue running an elementary school in Davenport, Iowa.

3. Data collected from the KIPP Web site on July 20, 2014.

4. Data collected from Web sites of each EMO on July 24, 2014; to guard against double-counting schools for Mosaica that have both elementary and middle divisions, schools with one address and one principal were counted as one school.

5. Gary Miron and Charisse Gulosino, *Profiles of For-Profit and Nonprofit Education Management Organizations: Fourteenth Edition, 2011–2012*, November 2013, 69, 79, http://nepc.colorado.edu/publication/EMO-profiles-11-12.

6. Ibid., 9, 11.

7. This projection is based on the following local polynomial regression: $y = 1915x^2 - 10926x + 28319$, with $R^2 = 0.99$.

8. This projection is based on the following linear regression: $y = 40568x - 95004$, with $R^2 = 0.81$.

9. This projection is based on the following local polynomial regression: $y = 0.5366x^2 - 4.023x + 7.2617$, with $R^2 = 0.99$. The estimate of KIPP enrollment per school comes from Miron and Gulosino, *Profiles*, November 2013, 117.

10. KIPP's Five Pillars, http://www.kipp.org/our-approach/five-pillars.

11. Ibid., 13, 15.

12. Visit to KIPP Foundation headquarters, New York, September 30, 2014. For detail regarding KIPP's initiative for character education, see Paul Tough, "What if the Secret to Success Is Failure?," *NYT*, September 14, 2011. See also the

KIPP Web page on character education, http://www.kipp.org/our-approach /character.

13. Data come from GuideStar, www.guidestar.org. In the case of Peiser, his base pay was $223,984, supplemented by $25,000 in additional compensation, $500 in incentive pay, and $17,912 in nontaxable benefits; in the case of Willcox, his base pay was $211,405, supplemented by $40,000 in incentive pay and $15,182 in nontaxable benefits.

14. Henry B. Hansmann, "The Role of Nonprofit Enterprise," *Yale Law Journal* 89 (April 1980): 838: "A nonprofit organization is, in essence, an organization that is barred from distributing its net earnings, if any, to individuals who exercise control over it, such as members, officers, directors, or trustees. By 'net earnings' I mean here pure profits—that is, earnings in excess of the amount needed to pay for services rendered to the organization."

15. See, for example, Meredith Kolodner and Rachel Monahan, "Charting New Territory in Ed Salaries," *NYDN*, December 13, 2009; Kolodner, "Top 16 NYC Charter School Executives Earn More Than Chancellor Dennis Walcott," *NYDN*, October 26, 2013; and Kate Taylor, "New York City Comptroller to Audit Success Academy Charter Network," *NYT*, October 30, 2014.

16. Kyle Spencer, "Charter Schools Prepare for a New Regime at City Hall," WNYC, June 7, 2012, http://www.wnyc.org/story/301567-charter-schools-prepar e-for-a-new-regime-at-city-hall/; Ben Chapman, "Charter School Rally Sends Message to Bill de Blasio, Joe Lhota," *NYDN*, October 8, 2013; Al Baker and Javier C. Hernández, "De Blasio and Operator of Charter School Empire Do Battle," *NYT*, March 4, 2014; Elizabeth A. Harris, "Charter School Backers Rally, Hoping to Influence de Blasio's Policies," *NYT*, October 2, 2014.

17. Richard Barth, telephone interview, July 19, 2006.

18. Ibid.

19. Dave Levin, interview, New York, November 16, 2008.

20. Susan Snyder and Martha Woodall, "Schools to Make Modest Changes," *TPI*, April 17, 2003.

21. School counts come from Mastery's Web site, http://www.masterycharter .org/schools.html.

22. The one exception to this rule for Mastery was its Lenfest Campus, according to Sharif El-Mekki, interview, Philadelphia, May 5, 2014.

23. Bill Hangley Jr., "Mastery Drops Out; Steel to Stay in District," *PPSN*, May 8, 2014, http://thenotebook.org/blog/147222/steel-stay-district-hands-mastery -drops-out.

24. El-Mekki, interview, Philadelphia, May 5, 2014.

25. Ibid. See also Lea Sitton, "Ball Game Ends with Two Men Shot," *TPI*, October 5, 1992.

26. Ibid.

27. Ibid.

28. Ibid.

29. Ibid.

30. Sharif El-Mekki, interview, Philadelphia, February 10, 2009.

31. Robert Moran and Daniel Rubin, "Two Arrested in Philadelphia Protest," *TPI,* December 13, 2005. Charges against El-Mekki were soon after dropped for lack of evidence. See Robert Moran, "Assault Charges against Principal Are Dropped," *TPI,* December 17, 2005.

32. El-Mekki, interview, Philadelphia, May 5, 2014.

33. Ibid.

34. Joseph Ferguson, telephone interview, May 6, 2014.

35. Simon Gratz High School, Mastery Charter Schools, visit, May 7, 2014. See Chapter 7 regarding Prifti's battle at Shaw in 2009.

36. Based on visits to Shaw Middle School under Edison, February 2, 2009, and to Shaw as Mastery Hardy Williams High, May 6, 2014.

37. Martha Woodall, "Hardy Williams Academy Joins Mastery Charter Schools Network," *TPI,* March 11, 2011; Menash Dean and Solomon Leach, "Candidate Williams' Grade as School Founder: Incomplete," *PDN,* March 19, 2015.

38. Dean and Leach, "Candidate Williams' Grade." See also Steven F. Wilson, *Learning on the Job: When Business Takes on Public Schools* (Cambridge, MA: Harvard University Press, 2006), 66.

39. Much as George A. Akerlof and Rachel E. Kranton described enfranchised, committed workers as "insiders" and their opposites as "outsiders," these respondents defined their experiences at Mastery and Edison, respectively, in similar terms. See Akerlof and Kranton, *Identity Economics: How Our Identities Shape Our Work, Wages, and Well-Being* (Princeton, NJ: Princeton University Press, 2010), 41–49.

40. These figures derive from numbers of eighth-graders taking the PSSA math exam in 2009, as reported by the Pennsylvania Department of Education, http://www.portal.state.pa.us/portal/server.pt/community/school_assessments /7442: for the Philadelphia School District (minus students enrolled in schools run by Edison, KIPP, and Mastery), 8,233 of 10,064 were classified as economically disadvantaged; for the fourteen schools with eighth-graders run by Edison, 983 of 996 belonged to this category; for the one school with eighth-graders run by KIPP, 59 of 75 students; and for the three schools with eighth-graders run by Mastery, 217 of 273.

41. Pennsylvania Department of Education, 2007–2008 through 2010–2011 PSSA and AYP Results, http://www.portal.state.pa.us/portal/server.pt/community /school_assessments/7442. The sample sizes for Edison are provided in note 108 in Chapter 7. The sample sizes for KIPP's fifth-graders for reading/writing for 2008 to 2012 were 67/65, 63/64, 122/123, 137/144, and 132/141. For KIPP's eighth-graders,

the sample sizes from 2008 to 2012 were 42/43, 58/58, 55/55, 60/64, and 51/54. The sample sizes for Mastery's fifth-graders for reading/writing for 2011 and 2012 were 193/203 and 252/263. For Mastery's eighth-graders, the sample sizes from 2008 to 2012 were 227/225, 217/217, 284/284, 367/376, and 431/439. The years 2006–2007 are not covered in this table because the sample sizes for KIPP and Mastery were quite small. For the district, the sample sizes from 2008 to 2012 all exceeded 7,700.

42. According to the Web site of the Pennsylvania Department of Education, cited in note 41 above, of the 2,071 eighth-graders in the Main Line school districts who took the PSSA math exam in 2008–2009, 122 were classified as economically disadvantaged.

43. Pennsylvania Department of Education, 2007–2008 through 2010–2011 PSSA and AYP Results, http://www.portal.state.pa.us/portal/server.pt/community /school_assessments/7442. The sample sizes for math/science were as follows: for Edison, 973/944, 942/918, 809/783, and 247/245; for Philadelphia, 8,958/8,649, 8,550/8,340, 7,855/7,798, 8,126/8,066, and 8,089/7,930; for KIPP, 42/41, 59/59, 58/56, 60/60, and 50/51; for Mastery, 226/208, 217/213, 274/286, 371/361, and 429/415; and for the Main Line, 68/65 (with Radnor and Tredyffrin-Easttown not reporting), 121/122, 130/145, 131/135, and 162/167.

44. Pennsylvania Department of Education, Expenditure Data for All LEAs, http://www.portal.state.pa.us.

45. Barth, telephone interview, July 19, 2006.

46. CBS, *60 Minutes,* September 19, 1999, and August 6, 2000. See also David Grann, "A Public School That Works: Back to Basics in the Bronx," *New Republic,* October 4, 1999, 24–26.

47. Survey of Nexis articles done on July 19, 2006, via www.web.lexis-nexis .com.

48. ABC, *ABC World News,* October 15, 2007, and February 27, 2010; CBS, *CBS Evening News,* March 7, 2010, and February 27, 2014; CBS, *The Oprah Winfrey Show,* April 12, 2006; Comedy Central, *The Colbert Report,* October 1, 2008; National Public Radio, *All Things Considered,* May 28, 2005, *News and Notes,* September 6, 2007, *Weekend Edition Saturday,* October 7, 2006, and *Morning Edition,* January 18, 2010; NBC, *NBC Nightly News,* October 5, 2009; PBS, *Frontline,* October 5, 2005.

49. Bob Herbert, "A Chance to Learn," *NYT,* December 16, 2002; Herbert, "48 of 48," *NYT,* June 5, 2009; Thomas Friedman, "Steal This Movie, Too," *NYT,* August 24, 2010; Stanley Crouch, "Teachers Deserve More; So Do We," *NYDN,* September 9, 2000; Crouch, "Mayor Can Look in City for Schools That Work," *NYDN,* June 27, 2002; Leonard Pitts Jr., "Schools Where Students Learn," *Miami Herald,* November 25, 2007; Pitts, "Leave Education to the Principals, Teachers, Parents," *Miami Herald,* November 28, 2007; Mathews, *Work Hard. Be Nice.*

50. Abigail and Stephan Thernstrom, *No Excuses: Closing the Racial Gap in Learning* (New York: Simon and Schuster, 2003), 43–60, 66–80, 272–273; Malcolm Gladwell, *Outliers: The Story of Success* (New York: Little, Brown, 2008), 250–269; Paul Tough, *How Children Succeed: Grit, Curiosity, and the Hidden Power of Character* (New York: Houghton Mifflin, 2012), 44–54, 86–104.

51. Steve Mancini, director of public affairs, KIPP Foundation, interview, New York, September 30, 2014.

52. Motoko Rich, "A Walmart Fortune, Spreading Charter Schools," *NYT,* April 25, 2014.

53. According to the Web site of the Bill and Melinda Gates Foundation, the total given to KIPP through 2014 was $25,429,087: http://www.gatesfoundation .org/How-We-Work/Quick-Links/Grants-Database#q/k=kipp.

54. Audited financial reports for 1997 to 2013 acquired by e-mail from the Robin Hood Foundation.

55. Based on correspondence with Liz Nellis, program associate, Tiger Foundation, September 18, 2014.

56. According to the Web site of Atlantic Philanthropies, the purpose of this one-time contribution was core support along with evaluation: http://www.atlan ticphilanthropies.org/grant/core-support-and-evaluation.

57. Michele McNeil, "49 Applicants Win i3 Grants," *EW,* August 11, 2010, 1, 28–29.

58. Gary Miron, Jessica L. Urschel, and Nicholas Saxton, "What Makes KIPP Work? A Study of Student Characteristics, Attrition, and School Finance," March 2011, 21, published jointly by the National Center for the Study of Privatization in Education, Teachers College, Columbia University, and the Study Group on Educational Management Organizations, Western Michigan University, March 2011, http://www.ncspe.org/publications_files/OP195_3.pdf. For detail regarding philanthropic funding, see 21; appendix C, 17–29; appendix D, 30. The number of schools in this sample (twenty-eight) was derived from appendix D.

59. Ibid., 32, citing *KIPP: 2009 Report Card,* 105, http://www.kipp.org/report card/2009.

60. KIPP press release, March 30, 2011, http://www.kipp.org/news/state ment-by-kipp-regarding-report-what-makes-kipp-work-by-dr-gary-miron-and-colleagues-at-western-michigan-university.

61. Sam Dillon, "Study Says Charter Network Has Financial Advantages over Public Schools," *NYT,* March 31, 2011.

62. See Department of the Treasury, Internal Revenue Service, Form 990, for separate KIPP regions as well as the KIPP Foundation, available online via GuideStar at www.guidestar.org. Enrollment data come from summing student counts for each region from KIPP's annual report cards, available at www .kipp.org.

63. The bulk of this money was raised by the board of KIPP NYC. The board of KIPP AMP independently raised $15,875 in 2010–2011 and $16,615 in 2011–2012; that of KIPP Academy (or Bronx), $254,004 in 2010–2011 and $61,950 in 2011–2012; that of KIPP Infinity, $46,222 in 2011–2012; and that of KIPP STAR, $19,134 in 2010–2011 and $18,035 in 2011–2012.

64. *KIPP: 2011 Report Card,* http://www.kipp.org/results/annual-report-card /2011-report-card. For free co-location for New York and Tulsa, see 90–96, 103. For leases from local archdioceses, see 43, 50–51, 82–83, 85, 133, 135.

65. Occupancy costs are listed on page 10 of Form 990 filings.

66. Jack Chorowsky, COO, KIPP Foundation, interview, New York, September 30, 2014.

67. Ken Paul, vice president for development, Achievement First, interview, New Haven, CT, March 26, 2015.

68. Matthew Kaminski, "A South Bronx Success Worried about the Next Mayor," *WSJ,* November 4, 2013. Researchers at the University of Arkansas soon after published a detailed study documenting significant underfunding of charter schools in states and specific districts across the country. The researchers concluded that in New York City, in particular, in fiscal year 2011 district schools received $24,044 per pupil, while charter schools received $16,420 per pupil, or 31.7 percent less. See Patrick J. Wolf et al., "Charter School Funding: Inequity Expands," April 2014, http://www.uaedreform.org/charter-funding-inequity -expands/. This study did not cite the IBO analysis of 2010 or 2011.

69. New York City Charter School Center, press release, "NYC Charter School Center Statement and Background Advisory Regarding New Report from Save Our States," October 4, 2013, http://www.nyccharterschools.org/re sources/statement-report-save-our-states. See also Harry J. Wilson and Jonathan Trichter, "A Full Analysis of the All-In Funding Costs for District Public Schools and Charter Schools: The IBO February 2010 Fiscal Brief Revisited," https:// www.scribd.com/doc/173211810/NYC-School-Funding-White-Paper-FINAL, October 16, 2014.

70. Doug Turetsky, "Answering Back: SOS Report on IBO's Comparison of Public Funding for Charter and Traditional Schools Doesn't Make the Grade," *IBO Web Blog,* October 10, 2013, http://ibo.nyc.ny.us/cgi-park/.

71. New York City Independent Budget Office (hereafter IBO), Fiscal Brief: "Comparing the Level of Public Support: Charter Schools versus Traditional Public Schools," February 2010, 3, http://www.ibo.nyc.ny.us/iboreports/charter schoolsfeb2010.pdf. For qualifications the following year to update data, see Ray Domanico and Yolanda Smith, "Charter Schools Housed in the City's School Buildings Get More Public Funding per Student Than Traditional Public Schools," *IBO Web Blog,* February 15, 2011, http://ibo.nyc.ny.us/cgi-park/.

72. IBO, Fiscal Brief: "Comparing the Level of Public Support," 2010, 3, 7; Domanico and Smith, "Charter Schools Housed in the City's School Buildings,"

2011, along with a supplement on change in methodology, http://www.ibo.nyc.ny .us/iboreports/chartersupplement2.pdf.

73. IBO, Fiscal Brief: "Comparing the Level of Public Support," 2010, 7.

74. Domanico and Smith, "Charter Schools Housed in the City's School Buildings," 2011.

75. Ola Duru, director of operations for charter school accountability and support, interview, New York City Department of Education, New York, July 29, 2014.

76. Javier Hernández, "State Protections for Charter Schools Threaten de Blasio's Education Goals," *NYT,* March 30, 2014.

77. New York City Independent Budget Office, "Schools Brief: Charter Schools versus Traditional Public Schools," July 2015, http://www.ibo.nyc.ny.us /iboreports/charter_schools_versus_traditional_public_schools_comparing_the _level_of_public_support_in_school_year_2014_2015_july_23_2015.pdf.

78. Mancini, interview, New York, September 30, 2014.

79. Ibid.

10. Limits

1. For detail on the challenge of recruiting the necessary human capital to scale up "no excuses" CMOs, see Steven F. Wilson, "Success at Scale in Charter Schooling," American Enterprise Institute, March 19, 2009, https://www.aei.org /publication/success-at-scale-in-charter-schooling/.

2. Enrollment for 2013–2014 reported by Steve Mancini, August 12, 2014. Demographic data comes from *KIPP: 2013 Report Card,* 14, http://www.kipp .org/reportcard.

3. Katrina Woodworth et al., *San Francisco Bay Area KIPP Schools: A Study of Early Implementation and Achievement* (Menlo Park, CA: SRI International, 2008), x, 32–33. SRI did not provide the number of teachers on staff in 2004–2004 or 2006–2007.

4. Ashley Keigher, *Teacher Attrition and Mobility: Results from the 2008–09 Teacher Follow-Up Survey* (Washington, DC: National Center for Education Statistics, 2010), 7–8, http://nces.edu.gov/pubsearch.

5. Woodworth et al., *San Francisco Bay Area KIPP Schools,* 32–34.

6. *KIPP: 2009 Report Card,* http://www.kipp.org/reportcard/2009, 14.

7. Matthew Ronfeldt, Susanna Loeb, and James Wyckoff, "How Teacher Turnover Harms Student Achievement," *American Educational Research Journal* 50 (February 2013): 4–36. For additional analysis of the institutional costs of high teacher turnover, see Michael A. Abelson and Barry D. Baysinger, "Optimal and Dysfunctional Turnover: Toward an Organizational Level Model," *Academy of Management Review* 9 (April 1984): 331–341; Anthony S. Bryk and Barbara Schneider, *Trust in Schools: A Core Resource for Improvement* (New York: Russell

Sage Foundation, 2002); Kacey Guin, "Chronic Teacher Turnover in Urban Elementary Schools," *Education Policy Analysis Archives* 12 (August 2004): 1–25; Judith Warren Little, "Norms of Collegiality and Experimentation: Workplace Conditions of School Success," *American Educational Research Journal* 19 (Autumn 1982): 325–340; and Fred M. Newmann et al., *School Instructional Program Coherence: Benefits and Challenges* (Chicago: Consortium on Chicago Research, 2001).

8. *KIPP: 2009 Report Card.*

9. All data were derived from KIPP's annual report cards, http://www.kipp .org/reportcard. Raw numbers come from the report cards. Weighted averages were computed by the author. Mathematica Policy Research reported a weighted retention rate of 78.9 percent for 2010–2011, but this rate was based on a survey of principals at fifty-three middle-schools out of a total of ninety-six schools in the network; the response rate from those principals was, in turn, 93 percent. Regarding the retention rate reported by Mathematica Policy Research, described earlier as the inverse of the reported attrition rate, see Christina Clark Tuttle et al., "KIPP Middle Schools: Impacts on Achievement and Other Outcomes," Mathematica Policy Research, February 27, 2013, 14, 29, 103, http://www.mathematica -mpr.com/~/media/publications/PDFs/education/KIPP_middle.pdf. Interpretation of the data was confirmed by Tuttle by email on September 15, 2014.

10. IDEA Public Schools has shared teacher retention data in reports issued every two years since 2008, available at http://www.ideapublicschools.org, accessed September 21, 2014: in 2008 teacher retention was 80 percent; in 2010, 87 percent; and in 2012, 77 percent. Rocketship posted on its Web site that teacher retention has been 70 percent year after year. See http://www.rsed.org/faq.cfm, accessed September 19, 2014.

11. New York City Charter School Center, *The State of the NYC Charter School Sector, 2012*, 39, http://www.nyccharterschools.org/data.

12. Rebecca Goldring, Soheyla Taie, and Minsun Riddles, *Teacher Attrition and Mobility: Results from the 2012–13 Teacher Follow-Up Survey* (Washington, DC: National Center for Education Statistics, 2014), 7–8, http://nces.edu.gov/pubsearch.

13. These determinations are based simply on compounding the retention rates over four years (i.e., $0.754^4 = 0.323$).

14. Blanca Ruiz, principal, KIPP Academy, interview, New York, October 20, 2008.

15. Marya Murray-Diaz, school operations manager, KIPP Infinity, interview, New York, October 22, 2008.

16. Amber Williams, principal, KIPP STAR, interview, New York, October 16, 2008.

17. Nicole Lavonne Smith, dance instructor, KIPP AMP, interview, New York, July 29, 2011.

18. Ashley Toussaint, KIPP AMP social studies teacher since 2009, telephone interview, October 28, 2014; Anastasia Michals, KIPP AMP math teacher from 2009 to 2013, telephone interview, November 8, 2014; and Nicole Lavonne Smith, telephone interview, November 14, 2014.

19. Michals, telephone interview, November 8, 2014.

20. Matthew Nestel and John Lauinger, "Brooklyn Teen Shot to Death Just Blocks from His Home while Walking with His Friends," *NYDN*, June 3, 2011.

21. Ky Adderley, principal, KIPP AMP, interview, New York, June 6, 2011.

22. When asked about Lewis's departure, Steven Mancini said on August 8, 2014, only that the appointment did not work out. Toussaint said in a telephone interview on October 28, 2014, that the staff was left in the dark. Subsequent efforts to reach Lewis by e-mail and telephone for comment proved unsuccessful.

23. Adderley, interview, June 6, 2011.

24. Ky Adderley, interview, New York, October 15, 2008.

25. Ibid.

26. Ibid.

27. Yabome Kabia, telephone interview, October 24, 2014.

28. Adderley, interview, October 15, 2008; Jennifer Medina, "Charter School's Deadline to Recognize Union Passes," *NYT*, February 13, 2009.

29. Meredith Kolodner, "Charter School Teachers Push to Join UFT," *NYDN*, January 14, 2009.

30. Steven Greenhouse and Jennifer Medina, "Teachers at 2 Charter Schools Plan to Join Union, despite Notion of Incompatibility," *NYT*, January 14, 2009.

31. Smith, interview, July 29, 2011; see also Kolodner, "Charter School Teachers Push to Join UFT."

32. Greenhouse and Medina, "Teachers at 2 Charter Schools."

33. United Federation of Teachers, press release, April 23, 2009, http://www.uft .org/press-releases/kipp-s-amp-academy-teachers-are-certified-union-bargainin g-unit.

34. Elizabeth Green, "After Opting In, KIPP Staff Vote Themselves Out of Teachers Union," *Chalkbeat*, April 23, 2010, http://ny.chalkbeat.org/2010/04/23/after -opting-in-kipp-staff-vote-themselves-out-of-teachers-union/#.VEfTjovF-8w.

35. United Federation of Teachers, press release, April 23, 2009.

36. Ibid.

37. Yabome Kabia, interview, New York, October 15, 2008.

38. Kabia, telephone interview, October 24, 2014.

39. Ibid.

40. Tuttle et al., "KIPP Middle Schools: Impacts on Achievement," 7–9. According to a KIPP memo entitled "Schools Opened by KIPP That Are No Longer Part of the KIPP Network," obtained from Steven Mancini on July 5, 2006, the two schools that broke away because of philosophical differences were KIPP PATH Academy in Dekalb County, Georgia, which became PATH Academy, and

KIPP SAC Prep in Sacramento, which became SAC Prep. In the case of the KIPP school in Annapolis, the problem was inadequate resources. The school had outgrown its space, the district had no space available, and the local KIPP board did not have the funds to rent sufficient space. See Jay Mathews, "KIPP's Mysterious Tale of Three Cities," *WP*, June 26, 2007.

41. Michals, telephone interview, November 8, 2014.

42. Ashley Toussaint, interview, New York, July 28, 2011.

43. Emily Carroll, interview, New York, June 16, 2011.

44. Antonia Phillip, interview, New York, June 6, 2011.

45. Ibid.

46. Jay Mathews, *Work Hard. Be Nice.* (Chapel Hill, NC: Algonquin, 2009), 179.

47. Ibid.

48. Based on visits to Mastery Simon Gratz, Shoemaker, and Hardy Williams, May 6–7, 2014.

49. Based on visits to the five Achievement First schools in New Haven, March 26, 2015.

50. Mathews, *Work Hard. Be Nice.*, 31–42, 52–55.

51. Emphasis in all posters in original.

52. Lyndon B. Johnson, State of the Union Address, January 8, 1964.

53. Visit to Simon Gratz High School, May 7, 2014.

54. James S. Coleman et al., *Equality of Educational Opportunity* (Washington, DC: U.S. Office of Education, 1966).

55. LuQuan Graham, guidance counselor, KIPP Infinity, interview, New York, October 22, 2008.

56. Mathews, *Work Hard. Be Nice.*, 188–191; *The Oprah Winfrey Show*, "American Schools in Crisis," CBS, April 12, 2006.

57. Visit to KIPP STAR, October 16, 2008.

58. Visit to KIPP Academy, October 20, 2008.

59. Mathews, *Work Hard. Be Nice.*, 208–209.

60. Frank Corcoran, math teacher, KIPP Academy, interview, New York, October 20, 2008.

61. Ibid.

62. Malcolm Gladwell, *Outliers: The Story of Success* (New York: Little, Brown, 2008), 262–263.

63. Frank Corcoran, e-mail, October 28, 2014.

64. Joseph Negron, principal, KIPP Infinity, interview, New York, November 16, 2008.

65. Sharif El-Mekki, telephone interview, December 4, 2013.

66. Scott Gordon, CEO, Mastery Schools, telephone interview, February 23, 2009.

67. Joseph Ferguson, COO, Mastery Schools, telephone interview, May 6, 2014.

68. This survey was conducted in May 2014.

69. Ibid.

70. Ibid.

71. Visit to Shoemaker, May 5, 2014.

72. Paul Tough, *How Children Succeed: Grit, Curiosity, and the Hidden Power of Character* (Boston: Houghton Mifflin, 2012).

73. KIPP, "The Promise of College Completion: KIPP's Early Successes and Challenges," 2011, http://www.kipp.org/files/dmfile/CollegeCompletionReport.pdf.

74. Ibid.

75. Tough, *How Children Succeed*, 49–54, 75–81; Sarah D. Sparks, "Students Rated on 'Grit' with New Report Cards," *EW*, June 5, 2014, 23.

76. KIPP Character Report Card and Supporting Materials, http://www.sas.upenn.edu/~duckwort/images/KIPP%20NYC%20Character%20Report%20Card%20and%20Supporting%20Materials.pdf.

77. Tough, *How Children Succeed*.

78. Sarah D. Sparks, "'Grit' May Not Spur Creative Success, Say Researchers," *EW*, August 19, 2014, 9.

79. Jeffrey Aaron Snyder, "Teaching Kids 'Grit' Is All the Rage. Here's What's Wrong with It," *New Republic*, May 6, 2014, http://www.newrepublic.com/article/117615/problem-grit-kipp-and-character-based-education.

80. Benjamin Herold, "Is 'Grit' Racist?," *EW*, January 24, 2015, http://blogs.edweek.org/edweek/DigitalEducation/2015/01/is_grit_racist.html.

81. Steven Mancini, interview, New York, September 30, 2014.

82. Dave Levin, interview, New York, November 16, 2008.

83. Joshua D. Angrist et al., "Inputs and Impacts in Charter Schools: KIPP Lynn," *AER* 100 (May 2010): 239–243; Albert Cheng et al., "What Effect Do 'No Excuses' Charter Schools Have on Academic Achievement?," September 2015, National Center for the Study of Privatization in Education, Occasional Paper 226, http://www.ncspe.org/publications_files/OP226.pdf.

84. Martin Carnoy et al., *The Charter School Dust-Up: Examining the Evidence on Enrollment and Achievement* (New York: Teachers College Press, 2005), 51–65. Regarding students with special needs as well as students in all other mentioned categories, see Gary Miron, Jessica L. Urschel, and Nicholas Saxton, "What Makes KIPP Work? A Study of Student Characteristics, Attrition, and School Finance," March 2011, 21, published jointly by the National Center for the Study of Privatization in Education, Teachers College, Columbia University, and the Study Group on Educational Management Organizations, Western Michigan University, http://www.ncspe.org/publications_files/OP195_3.pdf, 7–9; Christina Clark Tuttle et al., "Student Characteristics and Achievement in 22 KIPP Middle Schools," Mathematica Policy Research, June 2010, 17–18, http://www.mathematica-mpr.com/~/media/publications/PDFs/education/KIPP_fnlrpt.pdf; and Sean P. Corcoran and Jennifer L. Jennings, "The Gender Gap in Charter School

Enrollment," March 2015, National Center for the Study of Privatization in Education, Occasional Paper 223, http://ncspe.org/publications_files/OP223.pdf.

85. Carnoy et al., *Charter School Dust-Up,* 56–57.

86. Miron, Urschel, and Saxton, "What Makes KIPP Work?," 13–14.

87. This finding calls for qualification in light of the conclusion by Mathematica researchers in their 2012 report on KIPP that attrition rates in district schools were indistinguishable from KIPP's attrition rates. See ibid., 10–13, in comparison to Ira Nichols-Barrer et al., "Student Selection, Attrition, and Replacement in KIPP Middle Schools," Mathematica Policy Research, September 2012, 6–7, http://www.mathematica-mpr.com/our-publications-and-findings /publications/student-selection-attrition-and-replacement-in-kipp-middle schools. Miron, Urschel, and Saxton compared enrollment rates from sixth to eighth grade for KIPP and host district schools, whereas Nichols-Barrer et al. compared transfer rates. The ultimate differences in enrollment can be explained by the differences in late entry. As Nichols-Barrer et al. concede, KIPP schools admit fewer students into seventh and eighth grades than do district schools. District schools thus do significant "backfilling," while KIPP schools after sixth grade do not.

88. Miron, Urschel, and Saxton, "What Makes KIPP Work?," 10–15.

89. Nichols-Barrer et al., "Student Selection," 17–22.

90. Ibid., 18.

91. Tuttle et al., "Student Characteristics and Achievement," 17–18. The averages were derived from table II.2.

92. Tuttle et al., "KIPP Middle School: Impacts on Achievement," 21. For an assessment of five additional studies of KIPP, published between 2002 and 2008, see Jeffrey R. Henig, "What Do We Know about the Outcomes of KIPP Schools?," Education and the Public Interest Center & Education Policy Research Unit, November 2008, http://epicpolicy.org/publication/outcomes -of-kipp-schools.

93. Tuttle et al., "Student Characteristics and Achievement," 2–3.

94. Ibid., 2.

95. Ibid., 22–23.

96. Scott E. Carrell and Mark L. Hoekstra, "Externalities in the Classroom: How Children Exposed to Domestic Violence Affect Everyone's Kids," *American Economic Journal: Applied Economics* 2 (January 2010): 211–228.

97. Roland G. Fryer Jr., "Injecting Charter School Best Practices into Traditional Public Schools: Evidence from Field Experiments," *Quarterly Journal of Economics* 129 (August 2014): 1355–1407.

98. Ibid., 1364.

99. Ibid., 1404.

100. Ibid., 1357, 1371. Fryer maintained that such contracts were only meant to send a message, not be enforced. Fryer wrote that this was consistent with

policy at CMOs like KIPP. However, this conflicts with much of what I observed in visits to KIPP schools in Baltimore, Los Angeles, New York, and San Diego. See also Mathews, *Work Hard. Be Nice.*, 88–91, 100–101, 180–181, 217–218. Consequences at KIPP may not mean expulsion, but they can mean stern parent-teacher-student conferences and home visits as well as suspension of everyday privileges.

101. Anthony Bryk, Valerie E. Lee, and Peter B. Holland, *Catholic Schools and the Common Good* (Cambridge, MA: Harvard University Press, 1993); William N. Evans and Robert M. Schwab, "Finishing High School and Starting College: Do Catholic Schools Make a Difference?," *Quarterly Journal of Economics* 110 (November 1995): 941–974; Derek Neal, "The Effect of Catholic Secondary Schooling on Educational Attainment," *Journal of Labor Economics* 15 (January 1997): 98–123.

102. Anonymous Achievement First executive, April 30, 2015.

103. Forum at Teachers College, Columbia University: "Taking the First Step," cosponsored by EdLab and the Society for Entrepreneurship and Education, April 19, 2010.

104. John Rawls, *A Theory of Justice* (Cambridge, MA: Harvard University Press, 1971), 12, 140.

105. Jeffrey R. Henig, *Rethinking School Choice: Limits of the Market Metaphor* (Princeton, NJ: Princeton University Press, 1994), 3–12, 101–148.

106. Elizabeth A. Harris, "Charter School Backers Rally, Hoping to Influence de Blasio's Policies," *NYT,* October 3, 2013.

107. John Paul Stevens, dissent, *Zelman v. Simmons-Harris,* 536 U.S. 639 (2002).

108. Motoko Rich, "A Walmart Fortune, Spreading Charter Schools," *NYT,* April 25, 2014.

11. A Distant Mirror

1. For an overview of Nordic equity, see Mary Hilson, *The Nordic Model: Scandinavia since 1945* (London: Reaktion, 2008), 87–115, and Francis Sejersted, *The Age of Social Democracy: Norway and Sweden in the Twentieth Century* (Princeton, NJ: Princeton University Press, 2011), 99–114. In addition, regarding equity in funding of schools, see Svein Lie, Pirjo Linnakylä, and Astrid Roe, eds., *Northern Lights on PISA: Unity and Diversity in the Nordic Countries in PISA 2000* (Oslo: Department of Teacher Education and School Development, University of Oslo, 2003), 8. Regarding paid parental leave and child-care subsidies, see Nabanita Datta Gupta, Nina Smith, and Mette Verner, "Child Care and Parental Leave in the Nordic Countries: A Model to Aspire To?," Institute for the Study of Labor (IZA), Discussion Paper No. 2014, March 2006, 8–10, http://ftp.iza.org

/dp2014.pdf. Regarding income distribution, see the OECD Income Distribution Database, http://www.oecd.org/social/income-distribution-database.htm. Regarding income taxes, the top marginal rate in 2014 in Denmark was 56 percent; in Finland, 52 percent; in Iceland, 46 percent; in Norway, 39 percent; and in Sweden, 57 percent. In addition, the sales tax in these countries is about 25 percent. See http://www.tradingeconomics.com/country-list/personal-income-tax-rate.

2. Hilson, *The Nordic Model,* 105–106.

3. Ibid., 106.

4. Aksel Sandemose, *A Fugitive Crosses His Tracks (En flyktning krysser sitt spor,* 1933; translated from the Norwegian by Eugene Gay-Tifft, New York: Knopf, 1936), 77–78.

5. Laws of Minnesota 1991, Chapter 265.9.3, www.revisor.mn.gov/laws/?id=265&year=1991.

6. Gary Miron, *Choice and the Use of Market Forces in Schooling: Swedish Education Reforms for the 1900s* (Stockholm: Institute of International Education, Stockholm University, 1993), 60.

7. Political Platform for a Government Formed by the Conservative Party and the Progress Party, October 7, 2013, 55, http://www.hoyre.no/filestore/Filer/Politikkdokumenter/politisk_platform_eng.pdf. While the platform stipulated that such schools "will be prohibited from paying dividends to the owners," there was no language restricting schools from being treated as long-term investments that could be sold for profit.

8. Hilson, *The Nordic Model,* 180–181.

9. Data on the Web site of Skolverket, the Swedish School Agency, go back only to the academic year of 1992–1993. Other sources were accordingly used. The total number of students in Sweden at the primary and secondary levels in 1991–1992 was 1,166,833, according to the UNESCO database, http://www.uis.unesco.org/Education/Pages/default.aspx. At the compulsory level (for grades one through nine), there were 8,337 students attending independent schools; at the upper-secondary level (for the equivalent of grades ten through twelve), there were 4,950 students attending independent schools. The Swedish numbers come from Gary Miron, ed., *Restructuring Education in Europe: Country Reports from the Czech Republic, Denmark, Germany and Sweden* (Stockholm: Institute of International Education, Stockholm University, 1997), 140–141.

10. Miron, *Choice and the Use of Market Forces,* 46–47, 162–170.

11. See Anders Böhlmark and Mikael Lindahl, "Does School Privatization Improve Educational Achievement? Evidence from Sweden's Voucher Reform," IZA Discussion Paper No. 3691, September 2008, 5, http://ftp.iza.org/dp3691.pdf. The authors note that once vouchers were introduced in 1992, they covered all schools but these three.

12. Sejersted, *Age of Social Democracy*, 267–272.

13. Susanne Wiborg, "Swedish Free Schools: Do They Work?," LLAKES Research Paper 18, Centre for Learning and Life Chances in Knowledge Economies and Societies, London, 2010, 7–8, http://www.llakes.org/wp-content/uploads/2010/09/Wiborg-online.pdf.

14. Sejersted, *Age of Social Democracy*, 271.

15. Ibid., 419.

16. Ibid., 421.

17. See E. D. Hirsch, *Cultural Literacy: What Every American Needs to Know* (Boston: Houghton Mifflin, 1987).

18. Sejersted, *Age of Social Democracy*, 421.

19. Michael Baggesen Klitgaard, "School Vouchers and Political Institutions: A Comparative Analysis of the United States and Sweden," December 2007, Occasional Paper 153, 15, http://www.ncspe.org/publications_files/OP153.pdf.

20. Swedish Ministry of Education, "Internationella skolor," September 2, 2014, and "Riksinternatskolor," March 13, 2014, http://www.regeringen.se.

21. The numbers of students and schools were obtained from Skolverket, the Swedish School Agency, http://www.skolverket.se/statistik-och-utvardering/statistik-i-tabeller. The number of schools run by *aktiebolag* is an estimate derived from the percentages provided for 2013–2014 by Friskolornas riksförbund, the Swedish Association of Independent Schools, in a report entitled "Fakta om friskolor," April 2015, 2, http://www.friskola.se/fakta-om-friskolor. According to this report, *aktiebolag* ran 69 percent of *grundskolor* and 86 percent of *gymnasieskolor*. Given those same percentages for 2010–2011, when 741 *grundskolor* and 489 *gymnasieskolor* were independent schools *(friskolor)*, the total number of schools run by *aktiebolag* comes to 932. See also "Making Them Happen," *The Economist*, September 26, 2009, 69–70.

22. Michael T. Moe, Kathleen Bailey, and Rhoda Lau, *The Book of Knowledge: Investing in the Growing Education and Training Industry* (New York: Merrill Lynch, April 9, 1999), 74–75.

23. Gary Miron and Charisse Gulosino, *Profiles of For-Profit and Nonprofit Education Management Organizations: Fourteenth Edition, 2011–2012*, November 2013, 9, http://nepc.colorado.edu/publication/EMO-profiles-11-12.

24. New York City Independent Budget Office, Fiscal Brief: "Comparing the Level of Public Support: Charter Schools versus Traditional Public Schools," February 2010, http://www.ibo.nyc.ny.us/iboreports/charterschoolsfeb2010.pdf.

25. Peje Emilsson, chairman, Kunskapsskolan, interview, Stockholm, May 11, 2009; and the Web site of Magnora AB, http://www.magnora.com/start.html.

26. Emilsson, interview, May 11, 2009.

27. Ibid.

28. Per Ledin, CEO, Kunskapsskolan, interview, Stockholm, May 4, 2009.

29. Emilsson, interview, May 11, 2009.

30. Klas Hillström, partner, 3i, interview, Stockholm, May 11, 2009. See also Investor, Annual Reports, 1997–2002, http://www.investorab.com/investors -media/reports/.

31. All stock prices come from Wharton Research Data Services, Center for Research in Security Prices (CRISP), https://wrds-web.wharton.upenn.edu/wrds/, subscription required.

32. Hillström, interview, May 11, 2009.

33. Per Ledin, e-mail correspondence, August 4, 2015.

34. Birgitta Ericson, interview, Stockholm, May 5, 2009. This number calls for qualification. Ericson explained that at the schools, the ratio was 5.4 teachers per 100 students. However, Cecilia Carnefeldt subsequently explained in a telephone interview on August 20, 2015, that once the teachers at the craft centers and in lower grades added in 2012 were counted, the ratio climbed to 6.2 teachers per 100 students.

35. Per Ledin, interview, Stockholm, May 4, 2009.

36. Ibid. All details confirmed by visits in May 2009 to Kunskapsskolan sites in Nacka, Uppsala, and the Enskede, Kista, and Liljeholmen districts of Stockholm.

37. Ibid.

38. Ericson, interview, May 5, 2009.

39. Tord Hallberg, interview, Uppsala, May 8, 2009.

40. School visit, Kunskapsskolan, Enskede, May 5, 2009.

41. School visit, Kunskapsskolan, Nacka, May 7, 2009. The discussion took place in Swedish. Brorsson explained the dialogue over lunch later in the day.

42. Ledin explained the method for evaluation and compensation; interview, Stockholm, May 4, 2009. Teacher interviews were done in May 2009 during and after visits to the six Kunskapsskolan sites listed earlier.

43. Deborah Nusche et al., *OECD Reviews of Evaluation and Assessment in Education: Sweden* (Paris: OECD, 2011), 46. See also the Swedish National Agency for Education, http://www.skolverket.se/bedomning/nationella-prov/alla-nationella -prov-i-skolan/gymnasieskolan.

44. Magnus Henrekson and Jonas Vlachos, "Konkurrens om elever ger orätt-visa gymnasiebetyg," *Dagens Nyheter,* August 17, 2009.

45. Skolinspektionen, "Lika eller olika? Omrättning av nationella prov i grundskolan och gymnasieskolan," May 16, 2011; "Lika för alla? Omrättning av nationella prov i grundskolan och gymansieskolan under tre år," August 31, 2012; "Olikheterna är för stora. Omrättning av nationella prov i grundskolan och gymnasieskolan," September 2, 2013; and "Uppenbar risk för felaktiga betyg," 2014, http://www.skolinspektionen.se.

46. Patrik Levin, director of education, Skolinspektionen, telephone interview, August 18, 2015.

47. Ledin, "Introduction to Kunskapsskolan," presentation, Stockholm, May 4, 2009; Kunskapsskolan Education Sweden AB, "Årsredovisning och

koncernredovisning för räkenskapsåret 2014," March 20, 2015, accessed via Bolagsverket at http://www.bolagsverket.se, with financial data reset from calendar year to academic year (July 1 to June 30) by Fredrik Lindgren, CEO, Kunskapsskolan i Sverige AB, August 20, 2015.

48. Emilsson, interview, Stockholm, May 11, 2009.

49. Ibid.

50. See Web site for Kunskapsskolan Gurgaon: http://kunskapsskolan.edu.in /gurgaon/.

51. Per Ledin, interview, New York, March 8, 2011.

52. Cecilia Carnefeldt, CEO, Kunskapsskolan Sweden Education AB, e-mail correspondence, August 21, 2015.

53. Ledin, interview, New York, March 8, 2011.

54. Ian Quillen, "Ed-Tech Advocates Eye Rupert Murdoch's Move into K–12 Market," *EW,* December 8, 2010, 16; Benjamin Herold, "Big Hype, Hard Fall for News Corp.'s \$1 Billion Ed Tech Venture," *EW,* August 26, 2015, 1, 12–13.

55. See the following articles in *The Economist:* "Free to Choose, and Learn," May 5, 2007, 65; "Our Friends in the North," June 6, 2008, http://www.economist .com/node/11477890; "Private Education: The Swedish Model," June 14, 2008, 83; "Making Them Happen," September 26, 2009, 69–70; "A Classroom Revolution," April 24, 2010, 22; and "Britain: Cutting the Knot," May 29, 2010, 34.

56. Information on these companies comes from the Web sites of EQT, Polaris, and TA Associates.

57. Information on these companies comes from the Web sites of Axcel and FSN.

58. Information on these companies comes from the Web sites of Bure Equity, EQT, and Polaris.

59. Investor AB, Annual Report, 2014, http://ir.investorab.com/files/press / investor/201504017999–1.pdf.

60. Helen Warrell, "Free Schools: Lessons in Store," *Financial Times,* August 27, 2014.

61. Ibid.

62. Bengt Westerberg, interview, Stockholm, May 15, 2012.

63. Ibid.

64. Ibid.

65. Sejersted, *Age of Social Democracy,* 218–221. Regarding the Wallenbergs, Sejersted referenced Stockholms Enskilda Bank, the family's private bank, which merged with Skandinaviska Banken in 1972 to become SE-Banken and then SEB, which is controlled by Investor, the Wallenberg's publicly traded holding company.

66. "Seemly Success," *Time,* June 7, 1963, 120.

67. Information about Transparency International and its system for measuring perceptions of corruption may be found on its Web site, http://www.trans

parency.org/. For data on relative childhood poverty, see UNICEF Innocenti Research Center, "Report Card 10: Measuring Child Poverty," May 2012, http://www.unicef-irc.org/publications/pdf/rc10_eng.pdf.

68. Transparency International, Corruptions Perception Index, http://www.transparency.org/research/cpi/overview. The precise averages were as follows: Sweden, 4.2; the United States, 17.9; Denmark, 1.9; Finland, 2.4; and Norway, 8.4. The number of nations surveyed in 1995 was 45; in 2014, 174.

69. Anna Jändel-Holst, interview, Stockholm, May 15, 2009.

70. Ibid.

71. OECD, *Education at a Glance 2011* (Paris: OECD, 2011), table D3.4, 419. For Norway, the change at each level was from 1.05 to 1, 1.05 to 1, and 1.05 to 1.06; for Denmark, 1.21 to 1.41, 1.21 to 1.41, and 1.42 to 1.61; and for Finland, 1.08 to 1.13, 1.23 to 1.21 (representing the only decline), and 1.29 to 1.35.

72. Jändel-Holst, interview, Stockholm, May 15, 2015; Olof Lundberg, telephone interview, May 13, 2015.

73. Ledin, interview, Stockholm, May 4, 2009. Regarding profit forecasts made by John Golle and Chris Whittle, see Chapter 2 and Chapter 6, respectively.

74. Based on visits to Kunskapsskolan headquarters on May 5, 2009, and May 11, 2012.

75. Ledin, interview, Stockholm, May 4, 2009.

76. Fredrik Lindgren, CEO, Kunskapsskolan i Sverige AB, telephone interview, August 18, 2015.

77. Ibid.

78. According to Statistics Sweden, in 2007, the latest year for which data are available, Borlänge ranked 231st out of 298 municipalities in assets per capita; Enköping, 150th; Katrineholm, 206th; Norrköping, 212th; Örebro, 134th; and Trelleborg, 132nd. Data from http://www.scb.se/en_/.

79. UNICEF, "Report Card 10: Measuring Child Poverty," 2.

80. Ibid., 3.

81. Swedish National Council for Crime Prevention, Crime and Statistics, http://www.bra.se/bra/bra-in-english/home/crime-and-statistics/murder-and-manslaughter.html. For county data, see Brottsförebyggande rådet, "Konstaterade fall av dödligt våld: Statistik för 2014," http://www.bra.se/bra/publikationer/arkiv/publikationer/2015-04-01-konstaterade-fall-av-dodligt-vald.html.

82. U.S. Department of Justice, Federal Bureau of Investigation, Uniform Crime Reporting Statistics, http://www.ucrdatatool.gov/index.cfm.

83. Niklas Magnusson and Johan Carlstrom, "Sweden Riots Put Faces to Statistics as Stockholm Burns," *BloombergBusiness*, May 27, 2013, http://www.bloomberg.com/news/articles/2013-05-26/sweden-riots-put-faces-to-statistics-as-stockholm-burns.

84. See Harvey Morris, "Riots Dent Image of Sweden's Classless Social Model," *NYT,* May 24, 2013.

85. Observations based on visits in May 2009.

86. Ibid.

87. See Hilson, *The Nordic Model,* 87–115; and Sejersted, *Age of Social Democracy,* 99–114.

88. Patrik Levin, interview, Stockholm, May 22, 2012. See also Skolverket, *Gymnasieskola 2011* (Stockholm: Skolverket, 2011), http://www.skolverket.se /om-skolverket/publikationer.

89. Levin, interview, Stockholm, May 22, 2012.

90. Axcel, "Berättelsen om JB Education: Om Axcels investering i John Bauer Organization och avvecklingen av JB Education," October 24, 2013, obtained by e-mail from Vilhelm Sundström, Partner, Axcel, January 22, 2014.

91. Laura Hartman, ed., *Konkurrensens konsekvenser: Vad händer med svensk välfärd?* (Stockholm: SNS Förlag, 2011).

92. Laura Hartman, "Privatiskeringar i välfärden har inte ökat effektiviten," *Dagens Nyheter,* September 7, 2011.

93. Jonas Vlachos, "Friskolor i förändring," in Hartman, *Konkurrensens konsekvenser,* 66–67, 70–73.

94. Ibid., 66, 96–99.

95. Per Ledin, interview, Stockholm, May 11, 2012. See also Richard Orange, "Doubts Grow over the Success of Sweden's Free Schools Experiment," *The Guardian,* September 10, 2011.

96. Johan Anderberg, "SNS förlorade heder," *Fokus,* September 30, 2011, http://www.fokus.se/2011/09/sns-forlorade-heder/.

97. Laura Hartman, interview, Stockholm, May 18, 2012.

98. Einar Fransson, interview, Nacka, May 16, 2012.

99. Ibid.

100. Ibid.

101. For early coverage in *Dagens Nyheter,* see Josefine Hökerberg, "Carema försökte köpa min tystnad," October 13, 2011; Mia Tottmar, " 'Oacceptabla förhållanden' på äldreboende i Välingby," October 13, 2011; and Tottmar, "Sköterskans larmrapport stoppades," October, 19, 2011.

102. Martin Arnold, "KKR to Partner with Triton in Ambea Acquisition," *Financial Times,* March 26, 2010.

103. Erik Palm, *Caremaskandalen: Tiskkapitalets fantastiska resa i äldrevården* (Stockholm: Carlsson, 2013).

104. Cecilia Stenshamn, *Lögnen om Koppargården: Skandalen bakom Caremaskandalen* (Stockholm: Timbro, 2013).

105. Ambea, "Carema Is Changing Its Name," August 27, 2013, http://news.cision .com/ambea/r/carema-is-changing-its-name,c9456926.

106. Ledin, interview, Stockholm, May 11, 2012.

107. Though singular in form, the title in translation into English is better conveyed in the plural. The title literally means "The World's Best Shit School."

108. Lili Loofbourow, "No to Profit: Fighting Privatization in Chile," *Boston Review*, May/June 2013, 30–35.

109. Anthony Esposito, "Chile's Bachelet Prepares Next Phase of Education Reform," Reuters, January 27, 2015, http://www.reuters.com/article/2015/01/27/us-chile-education-reform-idUSKBN0L01W620150127.

110. For evidence of "PISA shock," see OECD, *Improving Schools in Sweden: An OECD Perspective* (Paris: OECD, 2015), http://www.oecd.org/edu/school/improving-schools-in-sweden-an-oecd-perspective.htm.

111. Sveriges Utbildningsradio AB, *Världens bästa skitskola: Vinstmaskinerna*, December 11, 2011, http://www.ur.se/Produkter/165325-Varldens-basta-skitskola-Vinstmaskinerna.

112. Ibid. Dollar approximations are based on exchange rates at the time of transactions.

113. Ibid.

114. Vilhelm Sundström, interview, Copenhagen, January 13, 2014; Per Ledin, telephone interview, August 12, 2015; Joachim Sperling, head of corporate affairs, Axcel, telephone interview, August 12, 2015.

115. Ledin, interview, Stockholm, May 11, 2012.

116. Per Ledin, e-mail, June 19, 2012. Ledin reported that he was asked to step down on May 28.

117. Sundström, interview, Copenhagen, January 13, 2014.

118. Axcel, "Berättelsen om JB Education"; Axcel, press release, "JB Education avyttrar vuxenutbildningen," June 11, 2013, http://www.axcel.se/media/135670/pressmeddelande_jb_education_130611_slutlig_1_.pdf.

119. Sundström, interview, Copenhagen, January 13, 2014.

120. Axcel, "Berättelsen om JB Education"; Sundström, interview, Copenhagen, January 13, 2014. Dollar approximations are based on exchange rates at the time of transactions.

121. Joachim Sperling, telephone interview, August 12, 2015.

122. Sundström, interview, Copenhagen, January 13, 2014.

123. Ibid.

124. Carnefeldt, telephone interview, August 20, 2015. Enrollment numbers come from Kunskapsskolan Education Sweden AB, "Årsredovisning och koncernredovisning för räkenskapsåret 2014," March 20, 2015.

125. Sarah Darville, "Recruitment, Finance Troubles Force Closure of Charter School That Opened in Tweed," *Chalkbeat*, March 4, 2015, http://ny.chalkbeat.org/2015/03/04/recruitment-finance-troubles-force-closure-of-charter-school-that-opened-in-tweed/.

126. New York City Department of Education, Middle School Quality Snapshot 2013–2014, http://schools.nyc.gov/SchoolPortals/01/M524/AboutUs /Statistics/default.htm.

127. See New York State Department of Education, District Data, 2013–2014, http://data.nysed.gov/. For data regarding Innovate Manhattan Charter, see New York School Quality Guide 2013–2014, http://schools.nyc.gov/SchoolPortals/01 /M524/AboutUs/Statistics/default.htm.

128. Carnefeldt, telephone interview, August 20, 2015.

12. Across the Gulf

1. Francis Sejersted, *The Age of Social Democracy: Norway and Sweden in the Twentieth Century* (Princeton, NJ: Princeton University Press, 2011), 267–272.

2. Erkki Aho, Kari Pitkänen, and Pasi Sahlberg, *Policy Development and Reform Principles of Basic and Secondary Education in Finland since 1968* (Washington, DC: World Bank, 2006), 6, 21–25, 78–86; Pasi Sahlberg, *Finnish Lessons: What Can the World Learn from Educational Change in Finland?* (New York: Teachers College Press, 2010), 21–25, 78–86. Regarding the postponement of tracking in Sweden, see Susanne Wiborg, "Swedish Free Schools: Do They Work?," LLAKES Research Paper 18, Centre for Learning and Life Chances in Knowledge Economies and Societies, London, 2010, 7–8, http://www.llakes.org/wp-content /uploads/2010/09/Wiborg-online.pdf.

3. Aho, Pitkänen, and Sahlberg, *Policy Development and Reform Principles*, 50, 58–59. Regarding pay in particular, the authors wrote: "A teacher's status should not be determined by the grade level they teach, by their pupils' age or by the subjects taught. Wages must not be tied to their office but to their degree." In practice, this meant primary school teachers in particular saw a significant increase in pay, as they had to have a master's degree from 1979 forward. A major boost also resulted from a teachers' strike in April 1984. When authorities called for the elimination of tracking in grades seven through nine, teachers protested that as their jobs at that level would be that much more challenging, their pay should increase and class sizes should decrease. Authorities conceded. Erkki Aho, director general, Finnish National Board of General Education, 1972–1991, interview, Helsinki, December 7, 2010.

4. Matti Saarinen, Finnish MP, interview, Helsinki, December 7, 2010.

5. Mary Hilson, *The Nordic Model: Scandinavia since 1945* (London: Reaktion, 2008), 100; David Kirby, *A Concise History of Finland* (Cambridge: Cambridge University Press, 2006), 173.

6. Hilson, *The Nordic Model*, 91–99.

7. Kirby, *Concise History*, 214–216, 232, 240, 287; William R. Trotter, *A Frozen Hell: The Russo-Finnish Winter War, 1939–1940* (New York: Algonquin, 2000), 263–270; Hildi Hawkins and Päivi Vallisaari, *Finland: A Cultural Encyclo-*

pedia (Helsinki: Finnish Literature Society, 1999), 173, 327; Jari Leskinen and Antti Juutilainen, eds., *Jatkosodan pikkujättiläinen* (Helsinki: Werner Söderström Osakeyhtiö, 2005), 1150–1162.

8. For a good depiction of the contrast between Finnish and Korean practice, see Amanda Ripley, *The Smartest Kids in the World: And How They Got That Way* (New York: Simon and Schuster, 2013).

9. Kallahden peruskoulu, visit, December 3, 2010. Timo Heikkinen summarized in translation the talks by the veterans later in the day.

10. Based on visits to the Ministry of Education and Culture, April 23, 2009, December 8, 2010, January 30, 2014; the FNBE, April 24, 2009, December 13, 2010, May 3–4, 2012; FINEEC, offices in Jyväskylä, April 28, 2009; Helsinki Department of Education, April 20, 2009, February 3, 2014; and the OAJ, December 6, 2010, January 28, 2014.

11. Based on visits from 2009 to 2014 to fifteen schools spread across the following six municipalities: Espoo, Helsinki, Jyväskylä, Lohja, Raisio, and Turku. See also Caroline Brizard, "École: la leçon finlandaise," *Le Nouvel Observateur*, February 17, 2005, 62–64.

12. Finnish National Board of Education, *School Meals in Finland: Investment in Learning*, 2008, http://www.oph.fi/download/47657_school_meals_in_finland .pdf. See also Eduardo Andere, *Teachers' Perspectives on Finnish School Education: Creating Learning Environments* (New York: Springer, 2014), 40–41.

13. Based on visits from 2009 to 2014 to fifteen schools spread across the following six municipalities: Espoo, Helsinki, Jyväskylä, Lohja, Raisio, and Turku.

14. Based on school visits in Norway in November 2010 and in Denmark in January 2014.

15. Skollag (School Law) 1997:1212, December 29, 1997. In the United States, school lunch is free only for "children from families with incomes at or below 130 percent of the poverty level." See Food and Nutrition Service, National School Lunch Program Fact Sheet, September 2013, http://www.fns.usda.gov/sites /default/files/NSLPFactSheet.pdf.

16. Maddison Project, http://www.ggdc.net/maddison/maddison-project/home .htm, 2013 version.

17. UNICEF Innocenti Research Center, "Report Card 10: Measuring Child Poverty," May 2012, http://www.unicef-irc.org/publications/pdf/rc10_eng.pdf., 2.

18. Ibid., 3.

19. See, for example, "Our Friends in the North," *The Economist*, June 6, 2008, http://www.economist.com/node/11477890.

20. Päivi Juntti, director, special education, Friisilän koulu, Raisio, interview, Helsinki, April 27, 2012.

21. Alan Klaebel Weisdorf, special adviser, Danish Ministry of Science, Innovation, and Higher Education, interview, Copenhagen, January 7, 2014; Morten Rosenqvist, senior policy adviser, Norwegian Ministry of Education, interview,

Oslo, November 24, 2010; Christer Blomkvist, director, School Inspectorate, Stockholm Department of Education, interview, Stockholm, May 15, 2012.

22. Weisdorf, interview, Copenhagen, January 7, 2014.

23. Rosenqvist, interview, Oslo, November 24, 2010.

24. Blomkvist, interview, Stockholm, May 15, 2012.

25. Jaana Inki, Eila Lindfors, and Jaakko Sohlo, eds., *Käsityön työturvallisuus-opas* (Helsinki: Finnish National Board of Education, 2011), 38–39. This rule for courses in crafts was confirmed by many principals in schools across Finland during visits from 2009 to 2014 as applicable to science courses too.

26. Rosenqvist, interview, Oslo, November 24, 2010; Blomkvist, interview, Stockholm, May 15, 2012; Weisdorf, interview, Copenhagen, January 7, 2014. In addition, in the course of making visits to five schools in Denmark, six in Norway, and nine in Sweden as well as fifteen in Finland, I inquired about science instruction.

27. Kristine Stangeland, Teach First Norway science teacher, Gran skole, Oslo, interview, November 30, 2010.

28. Rosenqvist, interview, Oslo, November 24, 2010; Blomkvist, interview, Stockholm, May 15, 2012; Weisdorf, interview, Copenhagen, January 7, 2014.

29. Aho, interview, Helsinki, December 7, 2010.

30. See Daniel M. G. Raff and Lawrence H. Summers, "Did Henry Ford Pay Efficiency Wages?," *Journal of Labor Economics* 5 (October 1987): S57–S86; Jeff Nilsson, "Why Did Henry Ford Double His Minimum Wage?," *Saturday Evening Post,* January 3, 2014, http://www.saturdayeveningpost.com/2014/01/03/history /post-perspective/ford-doubles-minimum-wage.html.

31. Because the U.S. National Center for Education Statistics long overstated teaching time on account of an error in data collection and because the OECD repeated this misinformation in *Education at a Glance,* its annual volume of educational statistics and analysis, from 1998 to 2014, the common perception among scholars and journalists has been that U.S. teachers spend nearly twice as much time leading classes as their counterparts in Finland and many other OECD nations. I addressed this matter in a 2015 study, "The Mismeasure of Teaching Time," Working Paper, Center for Benefit-Cost Studies of Education, Teachers College, Columbia University, January 2015, http://cbcse.org/publications/#reform.

32. W. Edwards Deming, *Out of the Crisis* (1982; reprint, Cambridge, MA: MIT Press, 2000), 101–109.

33. Alfred D. Chandler, *The Visible Hand: The Managerial Revolution in American Business* (Cambridge, MA: Harvard University Press, 1977), 381–382, 390, 416–417, 452, 491. See also Kevin Clark, "Why the Green Bay Packers Promote from Within," *WSJ,* January 16–17, 2016.

34. Aho, Pitkänen, and Sahlberg, *Policy Development and Reform Principles.*

35. This determination is based on interviews in Copenhagen, Oslo, and Stockholm as well as several cities across the United States. Prominent examples

of U.S. educational leaders without any classroom experience include Alan Bersin, Arne Duncan, Harold Levy, Roy Romer, and Paul Vallas. Effective or not, these U.S. leaders have no counterparts in Finland (with the exception of the minister of education and culture, who is a member of Parliament rather than an appointee designated to steer policy) and reflect a decidedly different approach to educational management.

36. Deming, *Out of the Crisis,* 28–31, 54–62.

37. Ibid., 23.

38. Ibid., 29–30.

39. Pasi Sahlberg, interview, Helsinki, December 1, 2010.

40. Transparency International, Corruptions Perception Index, http://www.transparency.org/research/cpi/overview. The precise average for Finland was 2.4. The number of nations surveyed in 1995 was 45; in 2014, 174.

41. Eeva Penttilä, director of international relations, Helsinki Department of Education, interview, Helsinki, April 20, 2009.

42. No Child Left Behind Act of 2001, Pub. L. 107-110, January 8, 2002, Section 1001(3) and Section 1111(b)(3)(C)(v).

43. Claire Shewbridge et al., *OECD Reviews of Evaluation and Assessment in Education: Denmark* (Paris: OECD, 2011), 47.

44. Deborah Nusche et al., *OECD Reviews of Evaluation and Assessment in Education: Norway* (Paris: OECD, 2011), 25.

45. Deborah Nusche et al., *OECD Reviews of Evaluation and Assessment in Education: Sweden* (Paris: OECD, 2011), 46. See also the Swedish National Agency for Education, http://www.skolverket.se/bedomning/nationella-prov/alla-nation ella-prov-i-skolan/gymnasieskolan.

46. Jari Metsämuuronen, senior researcher, Finnish Education Evaluation Center, e-mail correspondence, June 9–12, 2015.

47. Pasi Sahlberg, symposium on Finnish education, hosted by Bill Doyle and Maarit Glocer, New York, November 13, 2014.

48. Sahlberg, *Finnish Lessons,* 31–32.

49. Observations at the University of Helsinki, April 23–27, 2012, and January 30 and February 3 and 5, 2014; and at the University of Jyväskylä, April 28, 2009.

50. See, for example, McKinsey & Company, *How the World's Best-Performing School Systems Come Out on Top,* September 2007, 19, http://mckinseyonsociety.com/how-the-worlds-best-performing-schools-come-out-on-top/; McKinsey & Company, *Closing the Talent Gap: Attracting and Retaining the Top-Third Graduates to Careers in Teaching,* September 2010, 17, http://www.mckinseyonsociety.com/downloads/reports/Education/Closing_the_talent_gap.pdf; Sahlberg, *Finnish Lessons,* 73–76; Ripley, *The Smartest Kids,* 85–91; and Hannu Simola, *Historical and Sociological Essays on Schooling in Finland* (New York: Routledge, 2015), 262–264.

51. Tuuli Asunmaa, admission coordinator, Teacher Education, University of Helsinki, interview, Helsinki, January 27, 2014, on successful applicants representing a cross section of upper-secondary graduates. Asunmaa said there are no data to support the contention that successful applicants come from the top decile or quintile of their upper-secondary schools. Anu Laine, a senior professor of math education at the University of Helsinki who has worked with Asunmaa on admission matters, confirmed in a February 5, 2014, interview that students in teacher education programs represent a cross section of upper-secondary graduates. The breakdown of paths taken by lower-secondary graduates comes from Official Statistics of Finland, *Entrance to Education*, 2013, Appendix table 1: Direct Transition to Further Studies of Completers of the 9th Grade of Comprehensive School, 2005–2013, http://www.stat.fi/til/khak/2013/khak_2013_2015-02-12_tau_001_en.html.

52. Asunmaa, interview, Helsinki, January 27, 2014.

53. If the program at Vaasa, which is strictly for Swedish-speaking Finns and less selective than most of Finland's other teacher education programs, is excluded, the rate of acceptance over this time period averaged 15 percent and ranged from 14 percent to 18 percent. Data on admissions to teacher education programs for 2001 to 2013 come from the University Application Registry, Yliopistojen hakija-ja opinto-oikeusrekisteri (HAREK), obtained by e-mail from the Finnish National Board of Education, January 23, 2014. Additional information for 2007 to 2013 for all universities but Vaasa comes from the National Selection Cooperation Network in the Field of Education, Valtakunnallinen kasvatusalan valintayhteistyöverkosto (VAKAVA), provided by Asunmaa on January 20, 2014. All numbers were reviewed and explained by Asunmaa in the course of meetings on January 20, 2014, and January 27, 2014.

54. Olli Luukkainen, president, Finnish teachers' union, Opetusalan Ammattijärjestö (OAJ), interview, Helsinki, January 28, 2014. See also European Commission, Economic Policy Committee and the Directorate-General for Economic and Financial Affairs, "Efficiency and Effectiveness of Public Expenditure on Tertiary Education in the EU," Annex: Country Fiche Finland, October 2010, 15, http://ec.europa.eu/economy_finance/publications/occasional_paper/pdf/country_fiches/finland.pdf.

55. Weisdorf, interview, Copenhagen, January 7, 2014. See also European Commission, Economic Policy Committee and the Directorate-General for Economic and Financial Affairs, Annex: Country Fiche, Denmark, October 2010, 13, http://ec.europa.eu/economy_finance/publications/occasional_paper/pdf/country_fiches/denmark.pdf.

56. Samordna opptak [Norwegian Universities and Colleges Admission Service], http://www.samordnaopptak.no/info/om/sokertall/sokertall-2012/index.html; European Commission, Economic Policy Committee and the Directorate-General for Economic and Financial Affairs, Annex: Country Fiche, Sweden,

October 2010, 12–13, http://ec.europa.eu/economy_finance/publications/occasional
_paper/pdf/country_fiches/sweden.pdf; Universitets Kanslers Ämbetet, http://www
.uk-ambetet.se/statistikuppfoljning.

57. Anonymous, interview, January 2014.

58. Luukkainen, interview, Helsinki, January 28, 2014.

59. Asunmaa, interview, Helsinki, January 27, 2014.

60. Based on interviews with university students in April 2009, December 2010, April 2012, and January 2014.

61. Krista Kiuru, Finnish minister of education and culture, Helsinki, interview, February 6, 2014.

62. Danish, Norwegian, and Swedish schools place admirable emphasis on educating the whole child. However, schools in all three countries exercise much more autonomy in designing basic curricula. In Finland, by contrast, expectations regarding arts, music, crafts, and play are formally expressed.

63. I observed this practice in fifteen schools across Finland in visits from 2009 to 2014 and confirmed it as official practice by Luukkainen, interview, Helsinki, January 28, 2014. The practice is grounded in Section 23 of the School Law of October 12, 1984, which stipulates that classes should run forty-five minutes, with at least ten minutes as a break between classes. Details about this provision in Finnish school law may be accessed at http://www.finlex.fi/fi/laki/alkup/1984/19840718.

64. Finnish National Board of Education, http://www.oph.fi/english/curricula_and_qualifications/basic_education. The table of lesson periods stipulates a minimum of four periods a week of music, art, and crafts. Timo Heikkinen, principal of the Kallahti Comprehensive School, explained in a December 3, 2010, interview that students in lower-secondary school may take up to eleven periods a week of such electives.

65. Steve Lohr, "At a Software Powerhouse, the Good Life Is under Siege," *NYT,* November 21, 2009; James B. Stewart, "Looking for a Lesson in Google's Perks," *NYT,* March 15, 2013; David Gelles, "At Aetna, a C.E.O.'s Management by Mantra," *NYT,* February 27, 2015.

66. Kallahden peruskoulu, visit, April 20, 2009.

67. Center on Education Policy, "NCLB Year 5: Choices, Changes, and Challenges: Curriculum and Instruction in the NCLB Era," July 24, 2007, 5–10, http://www.cep-dc.org/publications/; Basmat Parsad and Maura Spiegelman, *Arts Education in Public Elementary and Secondary Schools: 1999–2000 and 2009–10,* National Center for Education Statistics, Institute of Education Sciences, U.S. Department of Education, Washington, DC, 2012, http://nces.ed.gov/pubs2012/2012014rev.pdf.

68. Juvenal, *Satires,* x.356 (ca.130): "Mens sana in corpore sano."

69. Johan Huizinga, *Homo Ludens: A Study of the Play-Element in Culture* (1938; reprint, Boston: Beacon Press, 1955).

70. William Harrison Woodward, *Vittorino da Feltre and Other Humanist Educators* (1897; reprint, Toronto: University of Toronto Press, 1996), 32, 35.

Epilogue

1. See, in particular, Richard Rothstein, *Class and Schools: Using Social, Economic, and Educational Reform to Close the Black-White Achievement Gap* (Washington, DC: Economic Policy Institute, 2004), 13–59; and David C. Berliner, "Our Impoverished View of Educational Reform," *Teachers College Record* 108 (2006): 949–995.

2. UNICEF Innocenti Research Center, "Report Card 10: Measuring Child Poverty," May 2012, http://www.unicef-irc.org/publications/pdf/rc10_eng.pdf, 3; Swedish National Council for Crime Prevention, Crime and Statistics, http://www.bra.se/bra/bra-in-english/home/crime-and-statistics/murder-and-manslaughter.html. For county data, see Brottsförebyggande rådet, Konstaterade fall av dödligt våld: Statistik för 2014, http://www.bra.se/bra/publikationer/arkiv/publikationer/2015-04-01-konstaterade-fall-av-dodligt-vald.html; and U.S. Department of Justice, Federal Bureau of Investigation, Uniform Crime Reporting Statistics, http://www.ucrdatatool.gov/index.cfm.

3. Michael J. Petrilli and Brandon L. Wright, "America's Mediocre Test Scores," *Education Next* 16 (Winter 2016): 47–52.

4. W. Edwards Deming, *Out of the Crisis* (1982; reprint, Cambridge, MA: MIT Press, 2000), 5.

5. The advertorials ran on page 2 of *Education Week* in the following issues: September 28 and December 7, 2005; and February 15 and 22 and May 3, 2006.

6. "Course Correction for School Testing," *NYT*, December 7, 2015.

7. No Child Left Behind Act of 2001, Pub. L. 107-110, January 8, 2002, Section 1111(b)(2)(C)(v).

8. Michael Hout and Stuart W. Elliott, eds., *Incentives and Test-Based Accountability in Education* (Washington, DC: National Academies Press, 2011). See also Sarah D. Sparks, "Panel Finds Few Learning Benefits in High-Stakes Exams," *EW*, June 8, 2011, 1, 14.

9. Michael Jonas, *Commonwealth Magazine,* June 5, 2008, http://commonwealthmagazine.org/education/held-back/. For more detail, see also David K. Cohen and Susan L. Moffitt, *The Ordeal of Equality: Did Federal Regulation Fix the Schools?* (Cambridge, MA: Harvard University Press, 2009), 211–213.

10. Associated Press, "N.Y.C. Chancellor Forms Anti-Cheating Task Force," *EW*, August 19, 2015, 4; Elizabeth A. Harris, "New York City Task Force Targets Cheating by Teachers and Principals," *NYT*, August 4, 2015.

11. Kari Louhivuori, principal, Kirkkojärven koulu, Espoo, interview, Helsinki, December 11, 2010.

12. National Center for Education Statistics, NAEP Overview, http://nces.ed
.gov/nationsreportcard/about/.

13. Motoko Rich, "Teacher Shortages Spur a Nationwide Hiring Scramble
(Credentials Optional)," *NYT*, August 10, 2015; letters to the editor, "The Teacher
Shortage," *NYT*, August 15, 2015.

ACKNOWLEDGMENTS

In writing this book, I've accumulated many debts. Those debts begin with Henry Levin. As I explained in the prologue, this book started as a research paper for a course on privatization I took with Levin at Teachers College in 2002. At Levin's recommendation, I developed that research paper into a master's thesis, which Levin recommended I flesh out into a book. After I obtained the contract for this book, Levin got me an appointment as a visiting scholar at Teachers College to work on it. But for Levin's encouragement, advice, and support, this study would have amounted to no more than a research paper.

For the contract for this book and more, I am indebted to Michael Aronson. As an editor, Aronson gambled that a master's thesis constituted the foundation of a book. For his confidence in my book proposal, for his patience, and for his close reading of the final product, I am grateful. I am likewise grateful to Andrew Kinney, who took over as editor of this book upon Aronson's retirement and provided additional insight. For their expertise in preparing the manuscript for publication, I owe a great deal to Kathleen Drummy, Aronson's editorial assistant, and to Mikala Guyton and Barbara Goodhouse, production editor and copyeditor, respectively, at Westchester Publishing Services.

Funding for my research came from the Smith Richardson Foundation and the Anthony E. Meyer Family Foundation. I am especially indebted to Mark Steinmeyer, my grant officer at Smith Richardson, and to Anthony E. Meyer for their insight into the subject matter of this book as well as their support.

For detailed discussions about market theory when I started working on this book, I am grateful to David Moss, Henry Rosovsky, and Arthur Small. Those discussions proved fundamental to the formation of my analysis. For research assistance as well as candid assessment of much of the manuscript, I am indebted to two former Beacon students who went on to do graduate work at Columbia: Goran Murgoski and Justine Rogoff. Their attention to detail and their probing questions made work on this book both more manageable and rewarding. I am also indebted to two librarians for their gracious help: Jim Coen of Columbia's Watson Library of Business and Economics for assistance with several financial databases; and Holly Peele of *Education Week* for access to the publication's bound volumes, which proved critical for studying the advertising patterns of education companies, as ads do not appear in online archives and as turning pages in bound volumes was far easier than scrolling through decades of microfiche. For assistance at crucial stages of my research, I am moreover grateful to Annah Abrams, Karen Hübert, Jonah Liebert, and Ina Seok.

For comments on the manuscript, I owe much to the two anonymous external reviewers selected by Harvard University Press. Their critiques forced me to fortify central aspects of my analysis. I am also grateful to the following readers for comments on portions of the manuscript: Frances and Robert Abrams, Julian Cohen, Sam DeWind, Michelle Hodara, Mike Johanek, Alli Klapp, Jordan Kravitz, Brian Letiecq, Henry Levin, Abby Lublin, Jonathan Margolis, Richard Miller, Martha Olson, Diane Ravitch, Abby Rischin, Sam Roberts, David Rogers, Pasi Sahlberg, Ben Siegel, Joan Steiger, and Mary Whittemore.

As this book depended as much on school visits and interviews as it did on published research, I am obligated to acknowledge numerous personal sources. In writing about Edison, I benefited from the openness of many people at both company headquarters and schools: in particular, Camille Bell, Charlotte Buonassisi, Ken Cherry, the late John Chubb, Brianna Dunn, David Graff, Marge Hendricks, Ledonnis Hernandez, Erin Holman, Jim Howland, Kwand Lang, Tung Le, Paul Lincoln, Todd McIntire, Babette Moreno, Marlaina Palmeri, Paul Perry, Audie Rubin, Benno Schmidt, Gwen Stephens, Robin Vigderman, Jeff Wahl, Chris Whittle, and David Zeiler. I also learned much from anonymous sources on Wall Street and the following people outside Edison who either studied the company or worked with or against it: Nijmie Dzurinko, Robert Embry, Eva Gold, Helen Gym, Len Rieser, Paul Socolar, John Tulenko, and Laura Weeldreyer. In addition, I could not have written about Edison without the detailed coverage of the company by reporters for the *Baltimore Sun*, *Education Week*, the *New York Times*, the *Philadelphia Daily News*, the *Philadelphia Public School Notebook*, and the *Philadelphia Inquirer*.

For my analysis of KIPP, Steve Mancini, the organization's director of public affairs, played a pivotal role, clarifying key matters in several meetings and making many introductions. Of the many administrators, teachers, and support staff I interviewed, I am indebted to the following: Ky Adderley, Richard Barth, Jason Botel, Jack Chorowsky, Kim Conroy, Frank Corcoran, Barbara De Pesa, LuQuan Graham, Yabome Kabia, Dave Levin, Angella Martinez, Anastasia Michals,

Joseph Negron, Charlie Randall, Asiya Razvi, Sue Rodriguez, Blanca Ruiz, Nicole Lavonne Smith, Stacey Staples, Jasper Steenhuis, Hilarie Szczygiel, Ashley Toussaint, Michael Vea, Auriel Watson, Natalie Webb, and Amber Williams.

For my analysis of Mastery, I am indebted, in particular, to Sharif El-Mekki for many introductions and discussions; for their time and insight, I am also grateful to Carrie Brownell, Neil Dwyer, Joseph Ferguson, Scott Gordon, George Prifti, Heather Scheg, Jen Slavick, Erica Smith, Erin Swan, and Megan Zor. For my analysis of Achievement First, I am indebted, in particular, to Ken Paul for many introductions and discussions; for their time and insight, I am also grateful to Lauren Cohen, Robert Hawke, Becca Howlett, Michael Kerin, Doug McCurry, Matt Taylor, and Dacia Toll.

My analysis of Nordic education would not have been possible but for the advice and cooperation of many people. For my understanding of Danish education, Jørgen Balling Rasmussen of the Danish Education Ministry could not have been more helpful, coordinating school visits and interviews and meeting several times to discuss policy. For their time and insight, I am indebted, as well, to the following administrators, government officials, and teachers: Henrik Andersen, Thomas Bredahl, René Bühlmann, Henrik Carlson, Michael Dyrby, Ajmal Faizi, Susanne Gottlieb, Lotte Højensgård Kanstrup, Thilde Nordly, Jørn Skovsgaard, Alan Klaebel Weisdorf, Jean Wellings, and Benny Wielandt.

For my chapter on Finnish education, I am indebted to Laura Kamras of the Finnish Foreign Ministry for assistance in planning the first of four research trips and to Aili Flint, Riitta Gerlander, Ritva Jolkkonen, Kari Louhivuori, Matti Saarinen, and Pasi Sahlberg for many introductions and discussions. For their time and insight, I am also grateful to the following administrators, government officials, scholars, and teachers: Erkki Aho, Ville Asikainen, Tuuli Asunmaa, Anna Carpelan, Maria Dean, Riitta Erkinjuntti, Ulrica Gabrielsson, Liisa Hakala, Irmeli Halenin, Veli-Matti Harjula, Timo Heikkinen, Pirjo Hellemaa, Antti Hilmola, Jukka Husu, Hannu Isolauri, Petri Järvinen, Päivi Juntti, Markku Kaikkonen, Dan Kantor, Pirjo Karhu, Esa Karvinen, Krista Kiuru, Heidi Krywacki, Pekka Kupari, Sirkku Kupiainen, Anu Laine, Hanna Lehtonen, Harri Lehtonen, Jorma Lempinen, Ritva Lempinen, Eija Lipponen, Nelli Louhivuori, Olli Luukkainen, Heikki Lyytinen, Jari Metsämuuronen, Teija Naskali, Tom Nevanpää, Lars Nyberg, Päivi Paakkanen, Kimmo Paavola, Eeva Penttilä, Jukka Pietikäinen, Mirja Pietikäinen, Jari Rajanen, Virpi Ravolainen, Inkeri Ruokonen, Seppo Ryösä, Eero Sahlberg, Beata Segercrantz, Lasse Suominen, Auli Toom, Mika Väisänen, Jouni Välijärvi, and Mervi Willman.

For my understanding of Norwegian education, I am indebted, in particular, to Geir Knudson of the University of Oslo for several discussions and for help coordinating a research trip. For their time and insight, I am also grateful to the following administrators, government officials, scholars, and teachers: Bjørn

Croff, Courtney Dern, Renate Evjenth, Karen Hammerness, Kirsti Klette, Hallgeir Muren, Anna Nyholm, Pål Riis, Morten Rosenkvist, Mikael Skovlie, Kristine Stangeland, and Per Tronsmo.

For my chapter on Swedish education, Cecilia Göransson of the Stockholm Department of Education was instrumental in coordinating the first of two research trips, as were Gary Miron, Per Ledin, Patrik Levin, and Carl Wennerlind in providing background. I am also indebted for their time and insight to the following administrators, businessmen, financiers, government officials, scholars, and teachers: Marika Lindgren Åsbrink, Daniel Bäckman, Christer Blomkvist, Pernilla Brorsson, Emil Burman, Cecilia Carnefeldt, Peje Emilsson, Birgitta Ericson, Einar Fransson, Elisabeth Gejrot, Tord Hallborg, Laura Hartman, Klas Hillström, Anna Jändel-Holst, Fredrik Lindgren, Olof Lundberg, Robert Lundh, Charlotte Mörck, Fredrik Nysten, Rolf Öden, Sofia Paulsson, Owe Sandström, Anna Söderberg, Teddy Söderberg, Joachim Sperling, Stefan Stern, Vilhelm Sundström, Jonas Vlachos, Ninni Wahlström, André Wallin, Peter Weiderman, and Bengt Westerberg.

Beyond learning from these sources and from my students in the course of twenty years of teaching (eighteen and two at the secondary and graduate levels, respectively), I have benefited from discussions with a range of administrators, advocates, researchers, and teachers in addition to those already listed as readers of portions of the manuscript. These discussions considerably shaped my understanding of pedagogy and policy. I must thank, in particular, my former colleagues at Beacon, especially Nicole Cherry, Tom Covotsos, Bob DiLullo, Bayard Faithfull, the late Jon Goldman, Maura Gouck, Kevin Jacobs, Ruth Lacey, Chris Lehmann, Mike Lupinacci, Daniel Markovic, Shelly Matthews, Judy Moore, Jess Radin, Lewis Rosenbluth, Steve Stoll, Harry Streep, Mike Thayer, and Tony Yick; my colleagues at Teachers College, especially Randall Allsup, Clive Belfield, Magdalena Bennett-Colomer, Brooks Bowden, Ilja Cornelisz, Emma Garcia, Tom Hatch, Jeffrey Henig, Fiona Hollands, Luis Huerta, Yilin Pan, Douglas Ready, Amra Sabic-El-Rayess, and Rob Shand; and my fellow coaches in the Ice Hockey in Harlem program, who take pedagogy to another level in making tough practices fun for children and teenagers. Outside these realms, I am indebted to the late Karen Blank, Carol Comeau, Jean-Claude Couture, David Denby, John Dreger, the late Roger Erikson, Sarah Rischin Gadye, Louisa Garry, Jonathan Harber, the late Thomas Hornish, Julie Kohler, Michelle Neuman, Mike Rosovsky, Dale Smith, Karen Solimando, Burton Staniar, Rick Sullivan, Geoff Wagg, and Jean Yip.

Starting this book was hard, finishing it was harder, as the material to cover grew more complex than I had expected and the volume of data to analyze more abundant. For the support of my wife, Laura, through this journey, I am grateful. In addition to tolerating my nights and weekends at my desk, Laura provided invaluable help in proofreading much of the manuscript and translating Finnish and Swedish documents. My gratitude extends to her parents, Risto and Ritva Toivonen, for their hospitality in Finland during extended stays spent writing. To my parents, Frances and Robert Abrams, I am indebted for their comments on portions of the manuscript, as noted, and, more fundamentally, for their example of intellectual and civic engagement. Their love of learning and their involvement in community affairs long ago put me on the path to social science research.

Finally, as stated at the outset, this book is dedicated to the memory of Dorothy Bach and Walter Clarkson, model teachers. Bach taught English in the public schools of her native Holyoke, Massachusetts, from 1955 to 1984, first at Lynch Junior High and then Holyoke High. I was fortunate to have Bach as my teacher sophomore year. Clarkson taught English at Westfield High in his native Westfield, New Jersey, from 1959 to 1990. I was fortunate to have Clarkson as a senior colleague my first year of teaching, which was his last. Kind, learned, exacting, and devoted, both inspired countless students to read critically and write with feeling and precision.

INDEX